nd

he

Iranian Revolution

Class, Politics, and Ideology in the Iranian Revolution

Mansoor Moaddel

Columbia University Press
New York

Columbia University Press
New York   Chichester, West Sussex

Copyright © 1993 Columbia University Press
All rights reserved

Library of Congress Cataloging-in-Publication Data
Moaddel, Mansoor.
    Class, politics, and ideology in the Iranian revolution/Mansoor
Moaddel.
        p.   cm.
    Includes bibliographical references and index.
    ISBN 0-231-07866-8
    ISBN 0-231-07867-6 (pbk.)
    1. Iran—Politics and government—1979–   2. Iran—Politics and
government—1941–1979.   3. Islam and politics—Middle East.
4. Social classes—Iran.   I. Title.
DS318.81.M64   1992
955.05—dc20   92-21912
                                                            CIP

Printed in the United States of America
C 10 9 8 7 6 5 4 3 2 1
P 10 9 8 7 6 5 4 3 2 1

*Dedicated to
the Iranian political prisoners
and their families*

Contents

Preface

This book analyzes the Iranian Revolution from a sociological perspective. Its central purpose is to contribute to the social scientific understanding of revolution. Although the historical narrative presented in the book may contain political implications, it is not designed to make a conscious value judgment about any of the actors involved in Iran's politics.

Yet I must indicate that I was greatly disappointed with the outcome of the Iranian Revolution. Like many Iranians, I believed that revolution was the key to solving many of Iran's problems, the imaginary as well as the real. As it turned out, however, the Iranian Revolution did not lead to a political democracy. The leaders of the Islamic Republic have behaved in an arbitrary manner. I hope that the current rulers of the Islamic Republic will realize that the wave of democratic movements that have swept various parts of the globe will sooner or later engulf Iran, and will begin to respect the rule of law and democratic process.

In their struggle for a democratic Iran, many Iranians have lost their lives in the postrevolutionary period, and many others are currently held prisoner by the leaders of the Islamic Republic. It is to their selfless efforts for the realization of democratic ideals and to their families who are suffering with them that I dedicate this book.

A number of prominent scholars have made valuable comments on this book at various stages. I wish to express my gratitude to professors Joseph Elder, Richard Lachmann, Erik Wright, and Ivan Szelenyi for their comments on this work when it was at a dissertation stage; to Professor Guillermo O'Donnell for his comments on the early version of chapters 1 and 2; to Professor Afaf Marsot for her detailed comments and suggestions on chapter 6; and to anonymous readers for Columbia University Press. Professor Charles Tilly read an earlier draft of the manuscript and made useful suggestions, for which I am very grateful. Jay Weinstein, the former head of the Department of Sociology, and Ronald Goldenberg, the dean of the Graduate School at Eastern Michigan University, awarded me a grant to collect relevant information on postrevolutionary Iran. The staff of the libraries of the University of Chicago, University of Michigan, and University of Wisconsin obtained and made available various documents related to the Iranian Revolution. Thanks also to John Downey at the Graduate Library, University of Michigan, and Laurie Senteney at University Computing, Eastern Michigan University. I owe a great debt of appreciation to Robert L. Ferrett, director of the Center for Instructional Computing, for his generously helping me to use the computer facilities of the center and for his invaluable editorial assistance, and to the center's staff whose support made work at the center an exceptionally pleasant experience.

Many thanks also to Kate Wittenberg, editor in chief, Anne McCoy, managing editor, and Roy Thomas, copyeditor, and other staff of Columbia University Press for their assistance in preparing the manuscript.

This work is partially supported by fellowships from the National Endowment for the Humanities and Eastern Michigan University.

Class, Politics, and
Ideology in the
Iranian Revolution

Introduction: Theories of Revolution

In the mid-1970s, Iran, a country once characterized as an island of peace and tranquility in the stormy waters of the world's politics, began to experience economic difficulties that soon developed into a major revolutionary crisis, one that toppled what had been up until that time one of the world's oldest institutions of monarchy. In a very short span —from 1977 to 1979—the Iranian Revolution proceeded so quickly that it took by surprise not only foreign observers but, ironically, the revolutionaries as well.

The outbreak of the Iranian Revolution surprised social scientists also. The rapidity with which the revolutionary movement proceeded, the unanimity of the public in demanding the overthrow of the Shah in mass demonstrations that crippled one of the strongest repressive regimes in the Third World, the decline of laicized politics and the increasing importance of religious ideology in the revolutionary movement— all become particularly intriguing when viewed against the fact that prerevolutionary Iran had not been experiencing a major economic or political crisis. How does a revolution happen in this way? The variety of structural and organizational models advanced by such eminent scholars as Moore, Wolf, Paige, Tilly, and Skocpol provide inadequate guidelines for an analysis of the Iranian Revolution. Moore, Wolf, and Paige deal with the specific landlord-peasant conflict that produces a revolutionary outcome. But to say that Iran shows a marked contrast with many existing revolutionary experiences because peasants were not particularly significant is to point only to a minor aspect of the distinctiveness of the Iranian Revolution. Moreover, Tilly's organizational model on revolution overemphasizes the causes emanating from the rational dictate of contention for power and does not capture the revolutionary phenomenon in its entirety—as a mode of action and not simply as an outcome of the contention for power or class conflict. Finally, in addition to the difficulties Skocpol avowedly exposes as challenging her theory of revolution,[1] the Iranian Revolution brings to the center of the problem the factor of ideology, a variable ignored in structural theories of revolution.

The significant role ideology played in making and sustaining the Iranian Revolution points to a need for a serious reexamination of the existing theories of revolution. These theories have either ignored ideology or used a reductionist conception of ideology in their explanations of the causes and processes of revolution. This work, however, argues that ideology is not simply another factor that adds an increment to the causes of revolution. *Ideology is the constitutive feature of revolution.* Ideology makes revolution a phenomenon distinct from the routine contention for power or class conflict.

This chapter first presents a brief summary of the existing theories of revolution and examines the conception of ideology used in these theories. It then argues that these theories fail to explain all aspects of the Iranian Revolution. Next, following Furet,[2] it makes a distinction between revolution as content and revolution as mode. Fourth, it advances a nonreductionist conception of ideology to specify the way ideology shapes the action of the people involved and affects the content of revolutionary change. Finally, this chapter reexamines the concepts of class and state in conjunction with the conception of ideology advanced here in order to formulate a consistent conceptual framework for the analysis of the Iranian Revolution.

Agency and Theories of Revolution

Theories of revolution are classified into overlapping categories such as social-psychological theories, structural functional theories, political conflict theories, and so forth.[3] Such classifications are often informed by the specific explanatory logic of the theories themselves. However, the major dimension of variations among all the existing theories of revolution revolves around the question of agent, namely, individuals, organizations, and classes. Except for Skocpol's departure from agent-centered theories of revolution, virtually all the existing theories in one way or another have given a central role to either individuals, organizations, or classes—hence individualistic, organizational, and class-centered theories of revolution. The central task of each of the theories is then to delineate the conditions under which these individuals, organizations, or classes resort to revolutionary actions.

Individualistic Theories of Revolution

The major assumption of this perspective, as aptly described by Tilly, is that revolution "is an individual act intimately dependent on a certain attitude toward some or all authorities."[4] In this perspective, revolutions arise because excessively rapid structural change builds up unresolved tensions which burst into disorder when and where restraints are weak. Tensions are produced in several ways: (1) through a disequilibrated system producing disoriented individuals (i.e., feeling panic, anxiety, shame, and guilt) whose social ties are broken down,[5] (2) through the breakdown of the intermediate social and political organizations that link individuals to the political system, and the subsequent social isolation and marginality of individuals and groups,[6] (3) through frustrations caused by rising expectations that outpace achievements,[7] and (4) through the disjunction produced by rapid modernization that outpaces institutionalization.[8] Tensions are primarily built up in individuals, but with the failure of the authorities to maintain social order they are eventually manifested in collective revolutionary behavior. There is thus a discontinuity between revolutionary movements and nonrevolutionary contention for power.[9]

Disorientation and discontent alone are not enough to cause individual revolutionary action. They are aspects of "critical situations" furnishing the psychological predispositions "that make individuals suggestible"[10] and "vulnerable to the appeal of mass movement."[11] Individuals begin to act when an ideology is present that, through its alternative value system, relieves their tensions,[12] explains the loss of community, politicizes some of their most basic needs ("identity, belonging, worthiness, efficacy"),[13] and presents "a 'cafeteria' of appeals, catering to a diversity of needs."[14] Ideology is portrayed as a hierarchy of values and beliefs whose effectiveness in guiding human action is contingent upon the degree to which they are internalized by the individuals. Concepts such as "generalized beliefs,"[15] "framework of consciousness," and "cultural and mental complex" are suggested to explain the specific manner in which ideology functions to bind community together, define ultimate purpose, and ensure social consensus.[16]

The connecting link between ideology and human action is therefore excessively subjectivist and psychological. This poses a serious problem for testing its validity because the subjectivist link is difficult to operationalize using historical materials.[17] In fact, the proponents of this perspective never directly measure individual psychological conditions. Nor do they demonstrate how ideology shapes individuals' mental conditions except by recourse to the actual occurrence of social movement or revolution. Their methodological procedure involves demonstrating the presence of certain proxy measures of independent variables (e.g., systemic disequilibrium, relative deprivation, critical situations) preceding the occurrence of protest movement or revolution. For example, Johnson uses rising suicide rates, heightened ideological activity, rising military participation ratios, and increases in rates of crime, especially political crime, as indicators of the normative disturbances produced by social change.[18] Davies looks at the sudden drop in economic activitity preceding some great rebellions and revolutions as an indicator of the frustration produced by the gap between achievement and need gratification.[19] Kornhauser implicitly considers social isolation and marginality as indicators of a psychological predisposition favoring the mass appeal of totalitarian ideologies.[20] In Toch, the kind of mental conditions that predispose people toward accepting certain beliefs becomes coterminous with social structural variables. For example, Toch claims that belief in miracles is accepted by people living in unbearable and dead-end situations.[21] Cantril also follows a similar methodological procedure. Economic and political crises in Germany in the 1930s and 1940s are presumed to have produced the kind of mental state in people that made them highly suggestible to the Nazi appeal.[22]

Despite the difficulties of doing so, it may still be possible to evaluate the explanatory power of the individualistic theories. One way is to seek the roots of the Iranian Revolution in the incompatibility of the political theory of early Shi'ism with the ideology of the monarchy. This interpretation is consistent with the individualistic model because it considers ideology as a hierarchy of values that guide the revolutionary actors. For example, Algar, following Watt,[23] derives the oppositional role of Shi'ism from its political theory and primordial political values. Since Shi'i Islam believes in the Imamate, a succession of charismatic figures believed to be the dispensers of true guidance after the death of the prophet Muhammad, and since the twelfth Imam is in occultation, no worldly legitimate authority has been left on earth.[24] Similarly, Savory claims that "there is no theological basis in Twelver Shi'i state for an accommodation between the *mujtahids* and any form of polity."[25] This ideological precedent, which seemingly renders all temporal rulers illegitimate, is thought to be the underlying cause of the oppositional role of the Shi'i Islam in Iran's politics.

This interpretation, however, is not supported by historical facts. This is because, first, the Shi'i religious movement in Iran has always been diverse and the ulama (scholars of religion) a politically heterogeneous category. Over many historically significant issues that appeared in Iran's political scene in the nineteenth and twentieth centuries, one group of the ulama tended to support the monarchy, while another favored the opposition movement. It is therefore difficult to explain a politically diverse movement by recourse to the constancy of Shi'i political theory. As will be explained in detail in the following chapters, the ulama's political unity against the state was a post-1963 phenomenon. Second, even then, ulama unity against the late Shah by itself does not adequately explain the cause of the popularization and politicization of religion in the postcoup (1953) period. Lay intellectuals played a crucial role in advancing the Islamic alternative to the Pahlavi monarchy.

Another way of framing the problem of individualistic perspective is to argue that the rapid economic growth of the 1960s and 1970s was followed by an economic crisis intensive enough to produce the mental state that made people highly suggestible to Khomeini's fundamentalist appeal. This argument also is problematic because while Iran's prerevolutionary economic growth was unprecedented, the problem of the late seventies can hardly be labeled as a crisis. True, there existed some economic difficulties that contributed to the general discontent in society, but they were not of the nature to produce an intolerable gap between expectation and achievement, thereby causing individual disorientation and confusion. A third line of defense of the individualistic perspective is advanced in Arjomand's *The Turban for the Crown* (1988). Arjomand argues that Iran's rapid social change resulted in social dislocation and normative disturbance. With the state's failure to reintegrate the dislocated groups and individuals, Shi'i Islam as the rival integrative social and political movement arose to perform this function.[26] Arjomand, however, does not bring much empirical data in support of his thesis. Only in one instance does Arjomand begin to provide an example of how a particular dislocated group—recent emigrants to towns—

turns to religion, because "the Shah did not integrate this group into his political system."[27] Even then, Arjomand cannot claim that these people were the major participants in the revolution. As even he acknowledges, "The extent of participation of recent migrants in the revolutionary movement is not clear."[28] As for the urban poor living in the shanty towns, a study has concluded that this group did not participate in the revolution to any significant degree.[29] The available evidence strongly suggests that the marginal and isolated individuals and groups played a minor role in the revolutionary movement. Even some of Arjomand's assertions run contrary to his theoretical claim. For example, more than once he emphasizes the alliance of the ulama and the *bazaaris* (classes tied to traditional industry and trade) against the state and foreign penetration.[30] None of these people could be treated as the marginal and isolated groups produced by social change.

Finally, Abrahamian's *Iran Between Two Revolution* (1982) refers to Huntington's theory of uneven development in his explanation of the causes of the Iranian Revolution. At the outset, Abrahamian proposes to examine the politics of modern Iran by analyzing the interaction between political organization and social forces, the latter consisting of ethnic groups and social classes. The concept of ethnic group is defined as the vertical groupings of individuals with common ties of language, tribal lineage, religion, or regional affiliation. The concept of social class is applied to the broad horizontal layers composed of individuals with common relationships to the means of production, common interactions with the mode of administration, and, in a developing environment, common attitudes toward economic, social, and political modernization. Following Thompson, Abrahamian treats class not simply as a structure but as a historical concept that is to be understood "in the context of historical time and of social friction with other contemporary classes."[31] Abrahamian then begins his social history by analyzing the social structure, communal organization, classes, and the political order in nineteenth-century Iran. Then he explains how these domestic social and political forces were affected by the impact of the West. The interaction between European economic infiltration, class conflict, and the growth of new intelligentsia produced the Constitutional Revolution of 1905–11. In characteristic detail, Abrahamian presents the historical factors leading to the rise of Reza Shah to power and the establishment of the Pahlavi dynasty in the early 1920s. His conceptual scheme is then effectively applied to the era of political conflict that ensued following the forced abdication of Reza Shah by the Allies in 1941 until the coup of 1953. Abrahamian's distinctive contribution is his examination of the social bases of Iranian politics, a crucial topic commonly ignored by past and contemporary writers on Iran.

Unfortunately, toward the end of his book, Abrahamian does not remain faithful to the conceptual scheme he initially proposes. Instead, Abrahamian follows Huntington's model of revolution to suggest that the Iranian Revolution was produced by rapid economic development, creating a vast discrepancy with the existing political institution:

> Although the shah helped modernize the socioeconomic structure, he did little to develop the political system—to permit the formation of pressure groups, open the political arena for various social forces, forge links between the regime and the new classes, preserve the existing links between the regime and the old classes, and broaden the social base of the monarchy that, after all, had survived mainly because of the 1953 military coup d'etat. Instead of modernizing the political system, the shah, like his father, based his power on the three Pahlavi pillars: the armed forces, the court patronage network, and the vast state bureaucracy.[32]

Huntington's theoretical model is too weak to carry the weight of the extensive historical materials Abrahamian meticulously presents in his work. Crucial in Huntington's model is the state's capacity to handle the problems generated by economic development. It was not so much a disjunction between institutionalization and modernization that produced the Iranian Revolution, but rather, among other things, the conflict of interests generated by the very process of economic development. True, the state's economic policies and bureaucratic expansion destroyed the intermediate organizations that historically had connected the state to civil society. Nevertheless, one cannot conclude that the gap between the state and civil society was the major cause of the revolution.

Thus it appears that Shi'i primordial values do not explain the diversity of Shi'i movements in contemporary Iran. Furthermore, the kind of variables such as war and intense social and economic crises often presented in the literature as proximate measures of individual disorientation were absent in prerevolutionary Iran. Third, Iran provides little support for the integrative/value-consensus argument because the marginal and isolated groups played a minor role in the revolution. Finally, the historical processes that culminated in the Iranian Revolution are too complex to be captured entirely by Huntington's notion on the disjunction between political institutionalization and economic development.

Organizational Theories of Revolution

What is taken for granted in the individualistic theories becomes problematic in the organizational theories of revolution: how dissatisfied individuals accept revolutionary ideology and are organized into collective action against the state. Revolutionary ideology must first be brought into contact with interested audiences. Books and articles are to be written, pamphlets and newspapers published, audiences brought to the appropriate sites, speeches to be prepared and effectively delivered—in short, ideas are to be produced and disseminated. All are contingent upon the availability of resources. Resource mobilization is a collective endeavor; without the presence of an organization capable of mobilizing resources and coordinating individual dissatisfactions, no revolutionary movement is forthcoming. Revolution is thus a form of collective action whereby people act together and mobilize their resources in pursuit of common goals. Parallel with the methodological shift from individualism to collectivism is a substantive shift from social-psychological analysis to political conflict analysis. While individualistic theorists tend to overlook the importance of the state, organizational theorists conceptualize revolutionary processes in terms of political conflict.

The basic idea is resource: "This could be anything from material resources—jobs, income, savings, and the right to material goods and services, to nonmaterial resources—authority, moral commitment, trust, friendship, skills, habits of industry, and so on."[33] Oberschall conceptualizes group conflict from the point of resource management: "Mobilization refers to the processes by which a discontented group assembles and invests resources for the pursuit of group goals. Social control refers to the same processes, but from the point of view of the incumbents or the group that is being challenged."[34] Therefore, "social conflict arises from the structured arrangement of individuals and groups in a social system—from the very fact of social organization."[35]

Tilly's pathbreaking works on revolution also rest on the simple idea of resource mobilization. He suggests two models on collective actions.

The first is the "mobilization model," which refers to the process by which contenders for power gain collective control over resources. The parameters of the model are interests, organization, mobilization, collective action, and opportunity. The second is the "polity model," which "relates contenders to a government and to other contenders—both challengers and members of the polity—via coalitions and struggles for power."[36] The polity model consists of the government and contenders for power, which includes those who have routine access to government resources (members of the polity) and those who do not (challengers or nonmembers of the polity).

Revolution is a form of collective action involving the process of mobilization, the structure of power, and the relations between the two. Revolution emerges out of the condition of a multiple sovereignty (i.e., a revolutionary situation) in which "a government previously under the control of a single, sovereign polity becomes the object of effective, competing, mutually exclusive claims on the part of two or more distinct polities."[37] A revolutionary situation is produced when contenders emerge who advance exclusive alternative claims to the control over the government, a significant segment of the population makes commitment to these claims, coalitions are formed between the contenders and polity members, and the government is unable or unwilling to repress the alternative claim. A revolution succeeds when one set of power holders displaces another set.

In the individualistic perspective, the individual mental state is considered the context for the growth of a revolutionary ideology. In the organizational model, ideological change—that is, the growth of alternative claims—is analyzed in terms of the specific contexts in which "ideological producers respond to the problem of contested authority."[38] Political groups develop or use a revolutionary ideology when they "lose their position in the polity and . . . are refused access to power."[39] The contexts vary from situation to situation. For example, in Fulbrook, varying political responses of Puritanism and Pietism to absolutist rule in England, Wurttemberg, and Prussia are analyzed in terms of the kind of obstacles these movements faced "in pursuit of their specifically religious goals."[40] Similarly, Zaret explains the significance of the idea of the heavenly contract in Puritan divinity in sixteenth- and seventeenth-century England in terms of "the organizational *pressures* the Puritan clerics faced in their dual role as ordained ministers and as pastoral leaders of a popular social movement."[41] Wuthnow relates ideological outcomes to variations in state structure.[42]. Stepan's analysis of state power in the southern cone of Latin America leads him to conclude that "the character of the state affects the evolution of opposition politics."[43] Finally, Neuhouser relates the radicalization of the Brazilian Catholic church to the organizational crisis produced by a decline in popular support.[44] In each case, the organizational interests and goals interact with broader environmental conditions to affect the likelihood of ideological change, including the rise of revolutionary ideologies.

Therefore, to support the organizational model, the rise of revolutionary Shi'ism must be adequately explained in terms of the interaction between the organization of Shi'i religion and Iran's prerevolutionary social conditions. Considering the first variable, some analysts have emphasized ulama institutional autonomy. As a leading proponent of this interpretation, Keddie relates the change in Shi'i institutional doctrine in the late eighteenth century—the rise of the *Usuli* school and the decline of the *Akhbari*—to the growth in ulama power in society. The Usuli assigned the ulama the key role in the interpretation of law and demanded all believers to pick a living *mujtahid* to follow and abide by his judgments. The Akhbaris, on the other hand, rejected the permissibility for the religious scholars to use their reasons to enact certain judgments. Thus the Usuli doctrine, says Keddie, "gave the living mujtahids a power beyond anything claimed by the Sunni ulama, and gave to their rulings a sanction beyond anything merely decreed by the state."[45] The Usuli doctrine thus eliminated confusion among the ulama regarding the nature of their role in society, and provided a strong organizational ideology justifying their intervention in politics. The ulama's independent sources of income, from religious endowments and religious taxes, further expanded their institutional autonomy and political power, for they did not have to rely on the state for financial support.

The growth of the Islamic alternative to the Shah's rule is then explained within the context of ulama-state interaction. The state's modernization policies in the sixties and seventies stripped the ulama of their traditional socioeconomic and political privileges. The rise of Khomeini's political ideology is thus understood within this context, for it sought to resolve the problem of contested authority generated by the state, justifying ulama participation in the revolution. In short, ulama institutional autonomy (as the organizational context) and the

state's modernization policies (as the environmental condition) interacted in such a fashion to set in motion the production and growth of an
Islamic alternative to the ideology of the monarchy.

The argument, although interesting and plausible, is not without serious problems, however. First, the state's anticlerical policies started
under Reza Shah, the first shah of Pahlavi (1925–41). In fact, from virtually every angle—economic, political, and cultural—the whole ecclesiastical establishment came under Reza Shah's bold attack. Under
his rule, the ulama gradually lost control of the educational and judicial
institutions as well as their seats in the parliament. Religious endowments came under the government's control. Considerable changes
were initiated and enforced in the way people dressed, including sanctioning women not to wear the veil. The importance of Islam was downplayed, while the Shah's ideologues glorified the pre-Islamic Iranian
kingship and culture. Apparently, the ulama did not like these policies.
Nevertheless, they did not form a united opposition against him. What
is even harder to explain in terms of the organizational model is that the
grand ayatollah of the time, Burujirdi, maintained a friendly relationship with the Pahlavis during his entire career. Even after the forced abdication of the Shah by the Allies in 1941 and the emergence of a strong
democratic nationalist movement in the country, ulama orientation toward the state was not predominantly oppositional. On the contrary,
some sort of ulama-state alignment was forged which lasted until 1959.
And in a large conference he organized in Qum in 1949, Ayatollah Burujirdi went as far as prohibiting the ulama from joining parties and traf-
ficking in politics.

Apparently, as his Muslim apologists have argued, the Ayatollah was
attempting to protect the religious establishment by depoliticizing it.
However, the politics of the ulama in this period runs against Tilly's assertion, for it shows that when powerholders lose their positions in the
polity they do not necessarily join the opposition. The organizational
structure and environmental change, while important, by themselves
were not enough to transform the Shi'i ulama into full-time revolutionaries. The second problem pertains to the question of the availability of
audiences. A strict organizational analysis cannot explain the conditions that prompt a significant number of people to participate in an
ulama-led opposition movement. For it is evidently true that without
devout followers any attempt on the part of the ulama to oppose the
state is doomed at the very outset (as was the case when a small faction

of the ulama attempted to resist Reza Shah's modernization policies). It is one thing to have the ulama demanding to be followed, and quite another for the laity to actually follow their lead.

Class Theories of Revolution

The status of the kind of people most likely to participate in a revolutionary movement remains vague in the organizational theories. In fact, the commitment of a significant number of people to the alternative claims advanced by contenders for power is most enigmatic among Tilly's proximate causes of revolution. In class theories, in contrast, audiences become central. According to Marx, changes in the economy and the emergence of new class positions are the key historical processes that produce revolutionary actors. The development of productive forces and their increasing contradiction with the social relations of production underlie the structural cause of revolution and, at the same time, determine the nature of the revolutionary and counterrevolutionary classes. In a revolutionary situation, class struggle is intensified, the repressive apparatus of the ruling class collapses, the ideological superstructure loses its validity, and the revolutionary consciousness associated with the ascending mode of production negates the existing social order and provides an alternative vision of society.[46]

Does Marx's theory explain the Iranian Revolution? Yes, says Keddie, in her comparative analysis of the Constitutional Revolution of 1905–11 and the Revolution of 1977–79:

> The closest socioeconomic revolutionary model for Iran's experience appears to be the Marxist formula, without any of the elaborations or modifications added recently. This formula, in essence, postulates that revolution occurs whenever the relations of production— particularly the control and ownership of the society's basic means of production—have changed beyond the ability of the old forms of political power and state organization to subsume the new economic order. This situation essentially obtained prior to both Iranian revolutions.[47]

Despite Keddie's assertion, however, the economy and the state remained quite compatible in the prerevolutionary period. Capitalism was the dominant mode of production in prerevolutionary Iran, and the state was deeply committed to the protection and reproduction of the institution of private property. More crucially, however, Keddie's own historical narrative, as masterfully presented in her *Roots of Revolution*, tells a different story. What is central in this work is not changes in the relations of production or the development of productive forces. It is rather Iran's interactions with the West which constitute a major thread tying together many aspects of nineteenth- and twentieth-century Iranian history.[48] To demonstrate this, Keddie skillfully and clearly explains how Western economic infiltration and political domination have systematically produced native reactions which were manifested in a sequence of such historical events as the tobacco movement of 1890–92, the Constitutional Revolution of 1905–11, the oil nationalization movement under Mosaddeq in the mid-twentieth century, and the Revolution of 1977–79. Keddie seeks the roots of the last revolution in the overall state agricultural and industrial policies which from the late 1960s on supported large establishments in these sectors. These policies benefited large domestic and foreign companies, while small and middle peasants (to say nothing of the impoverished agricultural laborers in the rural areas) and those on the bottom rungs of the economic scale in the urban areas starved from lack of government financial support.[49] In Keddie's historiography, international structure and state policies play a central role, factors that go beyond the contradiction between the forces and relations of production.

A more powerful explanation of the Iranian Revolution that incorporates both class analysis and organizational theories of revolution is presented in Parsa's *Social Origins of the Iranian Revolution* (1989). Parsa argues that the Iranian Revolution is an instance of the twentieth-century revolutions produced by the interaction between high state intervention in the economy and a high level of social cohesion among disadvantaged groups within the third world context of economic dependency and vulnerability. In Iran, the state's intervention in capital allocation and accumulation favored large and modern enterprises to the disadvantage of small, traditional businesses and industries in the bazaar as well as the working class. These policies undermined the state's legitimacy as they revealed that it served particular, rather than societal, interests. The oil sector's uneven development led to a crisis of revenues absorption, which in turn resulted in a high rate of inflation. The state's management of the crisis adversely affected the bazaaris. Legislative changes in 1977 reduced the cost of repression and provided an opportunity for bazaaris to take collective action against the state.

The struggles of bazaaris were soon channeled through the mosque because government repression left no other option for mobilization. The proclamation of reforms provided an opportunity for other collectivities that lacked autonomous resources (such as workers and white-collar employees) to engage in collective action against the state. Toward the end of 1978, all major opposition social classes formed a coalition and recognized the leadership of Ayatollah Khomeini. Eventually, a combination of social disruption, defections in the military, and assaults on the armed forces paralyzed the government and led to the rise of dual sovereignty and the overthrow of the monarchy in February 1979.[50]

Parsa, however, does not present a complete picture of Iran's revolutionary development. It is one thing to argue that the bazaaris were antagonized by the state's policies and therefore supported the Islamic alternative to the Shah's rule. It is quite another to explain the emergence of coordinated actions by the members of diverse classes in the revolution and their fascinating harmony in demanding the overthrow of the monarchy and the establishment of an Islamic government. Parsa is not interested in the highly interesting questions of why Shi'ism became the dominant all-encompassing ideology of the Iranian Revolution after the country had experienced several decades of extensive secularization, or why other ideologies such as Marxism, nationalism, and liberalism failed to arouse more than a minimal interest among the various classes and groups involved in the revolution. After all, not all the participating classes and groups had in the past adhered to Islam in their political struggles. Most puzzling is the question of why many secular intellectuals began to espouse recourse to Islam in their critique of the existing order in the postcoup (1953) period. In fact, these intellectuals played a crucial role in the popularization of Islam in society. Without their efforts, Khomeini's political theory was too narrow to attract the educated masses to Islam in this period. Parsa reduces the whole question of the role of religion in the Iranian Revolution to a tactical decision by the opposition and bazaaris: "Repression made it very difficult to mobilize . . . and bazaaris increasingly turned to the mosque for mobilization."[51] But why did not repression under Reza Shah produce the rise of religious opposition to him, and why did the ideologies of the opposition remain secular? Parsa had overlooked the significant changes that had occurred in the attitude of many intellectuals and activists toward religion years before the economic difficulties of the

1970s. State repression was only one of many factors for the growth of the religious alternative to the monarchy.

It is noteworthy that Parsa's analytical model is informed by some sort of diffused conception of ideology in the guise of such phrases as, "It is essential that disadvantaged groups first identify a concrete target of collective action,"[52] or that high state intervention makes the state appear "non-autonomous," and "the narrow alliance between the state and the upper class precluded any claim of state autonomy."[53] These statements imply that, albeit in an obfuscated form, one essential connection between state intervention and politicization of class conflict is the erosion of state legitimacy vis-à-vis disadvantaged classes. In other words, the state's own ideological crisis is a crucial factor for the development of a revolutionary movement. How a state's ideological crisis transpires and how disadvantaged groups identify a concrete target of attack are complex questions for which Parsa's model provides little guidelines. All in all, Parsa has presented a strong defense of collective action/organizational perspective on social movements and revolution. In fact, the limitation of his work reflects the limitation of the paradigm itself.

The central problem in all these theories of revolution is their failure to take ideology seriously in their explanations of the causes and processes of revolution. This work argues that ideology is the constitutive feature of revolution. It defines and makes revolution a phenomenon distinct from routine contention for power. Revolution is a particular form of historical action shaped by ideology. Revolution has also a content, which is produced by the interaction between class, politics, and ideology. Ideology is conceptualized as *episodic discourse*. Class is treated as a historical-structural concept that is constituted by the nature of the existing political and ideological factors. Finally, while the state is considered an organization with a certain repressive and bureaucratic apparatus, ideology plays an important role in shaping the actions and policies of the state. This work argues that ideology mediates class relations as well as the relations between the state and civil society.

Ideology as Episodic Discourse

The conception of ideology used in all the aforementioned theories of revolution tend toward reductionism. Because the dynamics of ideology is explained in terms of its psychological functions for disoriented and discontented individuals, or in terms of the dynamics of organized contention for power or class conflict, these theories tend to overlook the autonomy of ideology in the revolutionary process. Outside the parameters individual psychology, the organization of the power contenders, and social classes, ideology does not seem to have any significant presence. The reductionistic tendencies dominant in many analyses of the Iranian Revolution underlie their inability to account for the historical processes that caused the production and rise of Shi'i revolutionary ideology, produced harmony and coordination among the masses, established some channels of effective communication between the masses and their leaders in the absence of a strong nationwide organization, caused the collapse of the Shah's repressive machine in a nonmilitary confrontation, and generated many salient features of the postrevolutionary accomplishments.

A second major problem in these theories involves their excessive emphasis on the notion that people act piece by piece according to their interests or values. But action is necessarily integrated into larger assemblages called strategies of action, and ideology plays an independent causal role because it "shapes the capacity from which such strategies of action are constructed."[54] Ideology is not simply a set of ideas in people's minds or in an accomplished text; it can be observed in people's attempts to formulate their strategies of action, in the activities and artifacts of its producers.[55] In other words, ideology operates through discursive practices inscribed in matrices of nondiscursive practices.[56] Ideology is therefore conceptualized as a discourse, consisting of a set of general principles and concepts, symbols and rituals, that human actors use in addressing the problems they face in a particular historical episode.

Discourse is a method according to which people construct their strategies of action and express interests. Discourse permits certain questions to be raised and ignores others. It plays a role in determining what kind of coalition is permissible and what kind is not, and it structures the kind of opportunities available to diverse actors in building intellectual justifications for their actions. Discourse also includes symbolic systems, style of behavior, ritual performances, and metaphor. The autonomous process of symbolic formulation provides a link between social structure and human action.[57] Performances of rituals are phases in broad social processes. They transform the obligatory and constraining into something desirable. "The irksomeness of moral constraint," says Turner, "is transformed into the 'love of virtue.' "[58] Rituals do not always perform an integrative political function in society. "Ritual's primary purpose," says one commentator on Turner, "is social change in the direction of communitarian relations. . . . The primary motivation behind ritual is the desire to break free temporarily of social structure in order to transcend its existential limitations and reconfigure it along communitarian lines."[59] Finally, a metaphor can serve a social movement by facilitating the communication and interaction among the actors involved. The communicative power of a metaphor lies in the fact that even with a small vocabulary, it "manages to embrace a multimillion things."[60]

The construction, maintenance, and domination of a particular ideology should be understood within its specific historical context. For this purpose, macrostructural changes are treated as a succession of episodes. An episode is a sequence of historically significant events that stand out as constituting an era in the history of the society in question. The broad socioeconomic, political, and cultural conditions characterizing an episode can cause changes in the view of ideological producers about the social world and determine the domination of a particular discourse in society. Hence, ideology is conceptualized as episodic discourse. The relationship between ideology and its episodic context is quite complex and does not necessarily warrant the correspondence theory of ideology.[61] However, when an ideology becomes the dominant discourse in society, it tends to impose its own *Weltanschauung* on the rest of the society.

Finally, the existing theories of revolution have failed to distinguish between two principal aspects of the revolutionary processes. One is revolution as content, and the other is revolution as mode.[62] Emphasis on the content of revolutionary change is the feature of virtually all conceptions of revolution. In Marxism, revolution resolves the contradiction between the forces and relations of production, destroys the bureaucratic and military institutions of the old regime, overthrows the rule of the exploiting classes, and removes all the social and cultural obstacles to the objective process of historical development. Similarly, in the organizational theories, revolutionary change begins with a multiple sovereignty and ends with the replacement of one set of powerholders with another. Finally, Huntington defines revolution as "the rapid and violent destruction of existing political institutions, the mobilization of new groups into politics, and the creation of new political institutions."[63] Revolutionary change is then explained in terms of the interaction between a set of variables in a particular historical juncture. In Skocpol's model, for instance, the emergence of a revolutionary situation, the breakdown of state power, and what the revolutionary leaderships end up accomplishing are analyzed in terms of the existing international structure, the exigencies of world historical development, and class conflict. Revolution as a distinct historical phenomenon above and beyond a series of rapid changes in a relatively short period of time is not considered the object of explanation.

The problem with this model is not that Skocpol overlooks ideology in her multiple determination of the causes of revolution as Sewell objects.[64] Even if Skocpol had considered ideology as adding another increment to the genesis of revolution, it would have made little difference to the basic contention of her work that, after all, postrevolutionary France, for example, produced a political structure similar to its neighboring states, which did not experience a revolution. The explanation of the content of revolutionary change is quite important, however; what makes revolution a historically distinctive phenomenon is that it "is a specific mode of historical action; it is a dynamic that one may call political, ideological or cultural, for its enhanced power to activate men and to shape events arose from the fact that it meant many things to many people."[65] The actors behave differently in a revolution, despite the content of revolutionary change. Revolutionary discourse differs from ordinary political discourse advanced, for example, in a democratic election principally because the former negates both the power-holders as well as the routine means of negation. Revolution therefore denotes "the appearance on the stage of history of a practical and ideological mode of social action totally unrelated to anything that came before."[66] The belief that there is a discontinuity between a revolutionary and routine contention for power advanced in the individualistic theories of revolution is quite insightful.

A revolutionary situation is shaped by revolutionary discourse. It is not simply a condition of dual sovereignty. It is a dual sovereignty constituted by and through two mutually negating ideological universes[67]—the state's ideology and the ideology of the opposition. Revolutionary discourse contradicts the discourse of the state and advances an alternative way of viewing—and seeking solutions to—the problem of social life through direct, unmediated revolutionary action of the masses. The idea of discourse is highly useful here because it implies a back-and-forth argument between two parties. Revolutionary discourse is generated within the context of the interaction and propaganda warfare between the state and its opposition as each side of the conflict structures the kind of argument its opponents are likely to advance against it and vice versa. Ideological mobilization does not occur simply through the internalization of the alternative value system by the individuals, or through the organizational effectiveness of the revolutionary movement. It occurs through the discursive field generated by the ideology, that is, "a symbolic space or structure within the ideology itself."[68] In Marxist-Leninist jargon, it is a "breathing space" that structures discourse by determining what kind of argument makes sense, who may speak, and what is relevant and significant. A revolutionary discursive field systematically causes the contraction of the discursive field of the state and narrows down its breathing space.

Revolutionary ideology tends to transcend all the class, ethnic, and even sex differences among the participants (those "locked" within its discursive field), as if they have formed an undifferentiated mass tied together within the imageries and symbolic systems generated by the ideology itself. The Marxist critique that ideology distorts the reality of social inequality and exploitation between classes implicitly acknowledges such a transcendental role of ideology. In a revolutionary situation, this function reaches its peak by transcending social structure in a communitarian direction.[69] It is ideology that is in charge, subjecting human action to its own special internal logic and dynamics. Ideology transforms the individual subjectivity of those committed to it, subordinating their suffering and even possible death to a meaning-of-life defined by the ideology.[70]

Class as a Historical Structural Concept

This work is informed by Marxist conception of class and class conflict.[71] However, it finds little value in analyzing the Iranian Revolution in terms of the contradiction between the forces and relations of production. For one thing, this type of contradiction is not central in all revolutionary movements.[72] For another, while the contradiction may be a permanent feature of the mode of production, class struggle is a variable manifestation that possesses different degrees of intensity and generality, and that may be periodic, sporadic, or latent for a long period.[73] Third, not all class struggles are contradictory.[74] Therefore, the intensity and form of class struggle are not always and totally determined by the contradiction between forces and relations of production or by the "contradictions" between modes of production.

Class is considered here as a historical-structural concept. A historicist definition of the concept considers class as an event that, as Thompson suggests, "happens when some men, as a result of common experience (inherited or shared), feel and articulate the identity of their interests as between themselves, and as against other men whose interests are different from (and usually opposed to) theirs."[75] This definition, however, does not exclude other forms of social groupings (such as religious and ethnic minorities and women) from class. A knowledge of structure, or some assumption about structure, is thus needed to bring to the study from the outside. Otherwise, the empirical reality would appear as a confusing combination of complex relationships among diverse actors, issues, and historically significant and insignificant events.

From a structural point of view, classes are objective positions defined by the social relations of production. These positions broadly determine, among other things, the occupants' political and ideological orientations, and their potentiality for participating in revolutionary movements. The contradictory nature of these positions is the underlying mechanism for the potential generation and reproduction of class struggle. However, a purely structural analysis that relies heavily upon logical or descriptive relationships between concepts has a tendency toward structural abstractionism and formalism, and is often unable to explain the nature of historical specificities.[76] Moreover, the structural theory of class cannot provide enough clues for explaining the actual behavior of the members of a class in their particular historical settings. To be sure, structuralists relegate the problem of class action to the level of class formation—that is, the capacity of the members of a class to realize their interests. This is not, however, a satisfactory solution because on the same structural position, different classes can be formed with somewhat diverse political and ideological orientations, and it does not make much sense to consider such formations as fractions of the same class.

This work suggests that classes are simultaneously determined by structural and historical factors. Classes are not static entities fixed once and for all in time. Nor are they completely determined by objective economic facts such as the social relation of production.[77] Rather than deriving automatically from the structural positions, class capacity is "rooted in traditional culture and communities."[78] Class boundaries, interests, and mobilization are always shifting; interests change, coalitions are formed and break up, positions in the economy are created or destroyed, demobilization occurs.[79] This work agrees with Poulantzas that classes are defined not only by their relations to economic but also by their relations to the political and ideological levels, and that "the economic place of the social agents has a principal role in determining social classes."[80] Contrary to Poulantzas, however, the political and ideological determination of a class is not primarily rooted in the social and technical division of labor at the level of the mode of production. Rather, this determination is rooted in the concrete political and ideological configurations. The kind of ideological discourse that informs economic actors and the nature of their relationship with the state are important factors in their constitution as a class.

A historical-structural conception of class goes beyond the simple assertion that class action should be analyzed within its specific historical context. While class actors are economic agents, they are also, in Coward and Ellis's words, "the language-using subject."[81] And "both aspects of the subject—political actor and social speaker—take form in the context of ideology."[82] Class actors use discourse, specific rituals, and metaphor in *talking-out* their interests. Discourse is not generally class specific, and it often transcends class relations. The form of the action of a class and its relationship with other classes and the state is determined by its discourse, the discourse of other classes, and the discourse of the state. Class is in fact constituted by and through discourse. It is within the discursive context that changes in the resources of the state or disadvantaged classes will determine revolutionary or nonrevolutionary forms of action.

The State and Revolutionary Crisis

Revolutionary movements have been invariably directed toward the seizure or transformation of state power. The analysis of the state and how political crisis transpires, therefore, feature prominently in virtually all the currently dominant theories of revolution. However, less attention is paid to the cause of revolutionary crisis. In Marxism, revolution is produced by class struggle, but since the state protects the social relations of production and the interests of the exploiting classes, class struggle is ultimately resolved in the political rather than economic or ideological arena. "The liberation of the oppressed class," says Lenin, "is impossible not only without a violent revolution, but also without the destruction of the apparatus of state power which was created by the ruling class."[83] Nevertheless, if one questions the class character of the state, the cause of political crisis becomes more complex than a simple intensification of class struggle.

To be sure, contemporary dependency and world systems theorists have gone beyond class analysis on the nation-state level. They argue that state structure, form, autonomy, and probability of facing a revolutionary crisis are broadly determined by its location within the hierarchically organized zones of the world capitalist economy.[84] Even within the post–World War II peripheral context—which has been the scene of contemporary revolutionary movements—there are considerable variations in the structure and form of the state. These variations are functions of the changes and reorganization of the world economy;[85] changes in the international division of labor and the global policies of the imperialist countries;[86] past colonial experiences;[87] the specific combination of late industrialization, the infiltration of international capital and dependent development, and sociopolitical crisis;[88] and the intensification of interimperialist rivalries coupled with the rising of anti-imperialist struggles in the periphery.[89] These factors also condition the capacity of diversely situated classes to affect state structure and policy. The specific combinations of internal and external factors determine state strategy for economic development, the generation of new classes, the distribution of income and wealth, and new forms and intensity of social and political conflict.[90]

In Skocpol's model, on the other hand, political crisis is the outcome of the state's dynamics as an autonomous institution. Inter-state military competition, defeat in war, and the occurrence of contradictory conflict between the state and the dominant classes are conditions for the outbreak of the political crisis. Revolution occurs, in this model, when political crisis is combined with the presence of semiautonomous and potentially rebellious dominated classes. In other words, the breakdown of the state provides the opportunity for the dominated classes and revolutionary leaders to overthrow the existing order. One cannot, however, conclude revolutionary crisis from the condition of economic dependency and vulnerability or political crisis, even though the dominated classes may enjoy considerable organizational resources. Revolution is a particular mode of historical action shaped by revolutionary ideology. Revolutionary crisis occurs when the action of the dominated classes and groups are constituted by a revolutionary discourse. It occurs when the discourse of the state and of the opposition belongs to two mutually negating ideological universes. The growth of revolutionary ideology must be sought within the context of the state-opposition dialectic. State interests in maintaining a monopoly over the means of violence, in implementing socioeconomic programs, and in mobilizing support for its actions vis-à-vis other states in the international scene always require ideological justifications. Since the state operates under varying historical conditions, its interests change, resources fluctuate, and its social bases contract or expand. Hence the need for a new ideology. It may utilize the existing ideology or, in Skocpol's words, "develop new ideological argument in response to the exigencies of unfolding political struggle itself."[91] The discourse of the state then broadly sets the agenda for the opposition and defines its identity. The state's discourse may transcend its relations with the civil society in a communal direction. In such a case, both the state and civil society may appear as parts of the same ideological universe. Or, alternatively, the state discourse may exclude the discourse of the civil society and thus enhance its asymmetrical relationship with the civil society. In such a situation, there is a higher likelihood for ideological production in civil society to become politicized and for oppositional activities to take a revolutionary orientation.

Class, Politics, and Ideology in the Iranian Revolution

This book analyzes the causes and processes of the Iranian Revolution and its outcomes in terms of the interaction between class, politics, and ideology in the postcoup (1953) period. The coup effectively ended the national-liberal episode that began with the Allied invasion of Iran in 1941. The structure of the state and its economic policies in this period were consequential in determining the content of the revolutionary movement of 1977–79. The expansion of the repressive and bureaucratic apparatus of the state systematically undermined the role of intermediate organizations that provided the link between the state and civil society. The state's economic policies in favor of international capital and dependent bourgeoisie antagonized the property-owning classes such as the merchants, the petty bourgeoisie, and the landowners. As a result, these classes began to engage in opposition activities. Moreover, the industrial development of the 1960s and 1970s brought about a growth in the number of industrial workers. In terms of content, the Iranian Revolution was produced by an overlap of two sets of conflict. The first was the conflict of the merchants and the petty bourgeoisie with international capital and the dependent bourgeoisie. This conflict was over the control of the market. The second was the conflict between workers and capitalists that was intensified as a result of the economic difficulties of the seventies. These difficulties were partly the result of Iran's vulnerability to fluctuations in the world economy and externally induced inflation.

However, neither the economic difficulties nor the social discontents explain the emergence of the revolutionary crisis of the late seventies. Revolutionary crisis occurred when the actions of the discontented groups were shaped by Shi'i revolutionary discourse. Therefore, an explanation of the historical processes that led to the growth of Shi'i discourse as the dominant ideology of the opposition is an important aspect of the explanation of the causes of the Iranian Revolution advanced in this book. At the outset it is argued that Shi'i revolutionary discourse is neither rooted in the political theory of pristine Shi'ism nor in the institutional development of Shi'i ulama that began in the nineteenth century. Nor is it correct to argue that Shi'i ideology and religious institutions constituted *preexisting* organizations that were utilized by the revolutionary actors. This work argues that the ideology of Islamic opposition was *produced* by diverse intellectuals. The broad environmental conditions that led to production and growth of Shi'i ideology as the dominant discourse within the opposition were characterized by, first, the unity of the classes constituting the historical bases of the ulama, such as the merchants, petty bourgeoisie, and the landowners, against the state. As a result, ulama became united in their opposition to the Shah. Second, the state ideology that glorified pre-Islamic kingship and culture helped define the identity of the opposition. Finally, the decline of competing oppositional ideologies, such as liberalism and Communism, helped the growth of Shi'i oppositional discourse.

Shi'i revolutionary discourse, in turn, transformed the economic difficulties and social discontents of the 1970s into a revolutionary crisis. Its symbolic structures and ritualism contributed to the revolutionary mobilization of the people against the state and provided an effective channel of communication among the participants in the revolution. Shi'i revolutionary discourse also conditioned contentions for power and class conflict in the postrevolutionary period.

To highlight the causal mechanism suggested in this work, Iran is contrasted with Egypt and Syria. Both of these countries have experienced major religious revolutionary movements in the twentieth century. Egypt was the first to experience the upsurge of Islamic movement under the leadership of the Muslim Brothers. But the overall political role of Islam in Egypt display two diverse tendencies. In contrast with the Muslim Brothers, the ulama associated with al-Azhar University have been either apolitical or strongly in favor of the status quo. As in Iran, Islamic movement in Syria has been predominantly revolutionary but strongly sectarian. It has been a movement within the Sunni community (constituting about 70 percent of the country's total population), and directed against the predominantly non-Sunni Syrian leaders. It is argued that the division in the Egyptian Islamic movement broadly parallels its class politics. The lack of a coalition between the indigenous dominant classes and the petty bourgeoisie, and the former's access to political power, seems to have underlain the emergence of diverse political tendencies in Egypt's religious movement. Syria's religious revolutionary movement between the 1960s and the 1980s converges with the Iranian situation in 1963. Like Iran, the Syrian state was at the center of a class struggle and class coalitions from the 1960s on. The state's intervention in the economy, its nationalization policies, the land reform, and emphasis on socialist ideology provoked a strong reaction among the traditional social classes—the merchants, the petty bourgeoisie, and the landowners—and the ulama. But Syria's religious diversity and the state's stronger basis of support among workers and peasants, in contrast with Iran, hindered the emergence of a revolutionary conjuncture.

PART
ONE
Causes of the
Iranian Revolution

1

Episode and Discourse: The Rise and Decline of Nationalist-Liberal Ideology

It is now a commonplace among political sociologists and social historians investigating various forms of political conflict, protest movements, and revolutionary change to consider the resources and opportunity available to various actors within the context of the changing world economy, interimperialist rivalry and military competition, and the world time (that is, the historical context in general). To say that twentieth-century revolutionary movements in the third world have often taken place within the context of economic dependency and imperialist intervention is simply to reiterate the contemporary historical wisdom that, as Bertolt Brecht aptly stated, "It is not communism that is radical, it is capitalism."[1] In fact, many crucial aspects of protest and revolutionary movements in contemporary Iran such as the Tobacco Movement of 1890–92, the Constitutional Revolution of 1905–11, the nationalist-democratic movement of the early 1950s, and the recent revolution of 1977-79 can be attributed to the interaction between imperialist intervention and native interests. However, what is missing in virtually all the existing analyses of Third World politics is the relevance of the discourses that were dominant in different episodes of the third world's contemporary history to the explanation of the behavior of the actors involved.

Protest and revolutionary movements in the contemporary Middle East, for example, despite their similarities in content, were shaped by diverse political discourses. Three such discourses seemed to have played crucial roles in the political and social events characterizing different episodes. The first is Islamic modernism, which became the dominant political tendency within Islam in the late nineteenth and early twentieth centuries. The second is the ebb of Islam and the rise of various secular ideologies such as nationalism, liberalism, and socialism in the early to mid-twentieth century. The third is the rise of radical Islam as the dominant tendency within the opposition movement in many Middle Eastern countries.

In the first episode, a close affinity existed between Islam and modern (i.e., liberal, constitutional, democratic) ideas. The central theological problem that involved both traditionalist and modernist Islamic thinkers revolved around the question of whether Islamic law should continue to reject all external sources of jurisprudence and confine itself to the four traditional orthodox sources—the Quran, *hadis* (or the dicta attributed to the Prophet), the *ijma* (consensus of the ulama, that is, the theologians), and *qiyas* (juristic reasoning by analogy)—or whether it should reinterpret the first two sources and transform the last two to become the vehicle of modern legal and political notions. In the course of the second half of the nineteenth century, a group of leading Islamic thinkers in various parts of the Islamic world began to adopt the second alternative, forcefully challenging traditionalism. Prominent Islamic intellectuals and theologians such as Sayyid Jamal ud-Din al-Afghani, Sayyid Ahmad Khan, Muhammad 'Abduh, Amir Ali, and Muhammad Iqbal argue that Islam as a world religion is thoroughly capable, by reason of its inner spiritual force, of adapting to the changing conditions of every age.[2] 'Abduh even argues that the real rejection of Islam is the refusal to accept the proof of rational argument, the hallmark of the perfect Muslim community being both law and reason. Muslim can accept the result of science and rational inquiry.[3] They also reject the claim that the only truth that could interest the community of believers is that which comes from Islamic sources. These thinkers consider it appropriate to conduct their investigations by using the best available tools even if to do so obliges them to have recourse to books written by authors not aware of the Islamic revelation.[4] The Protestant Ethic theme in modern Islam was partly a response to an external threat that used European concepts to reinterpret traditional Islam in such a way as to reconcile two different cultural traditions. Islamic society acquired a vocabulary of ascetic motives which both legitimated social change and provided the motivation whereby change could be fostered.[5] Its rise can be partially explained by the growth and formation of the new Muslim dominant classes—landowners and a bourgeoisie.

Although the ideas of Islamic modernism traversed throughout the Middle East and the Indian subcontinent and found many interested audiences, it was in late nineteenth- and early twentieth-century Egypt that Islamic modernism took the form of a definite movement under the leadership of the late Grand Mufti of Egypt, Shaykh Muhammad 'Abduh. The rise of Islamic modernism in Egypt is hardly surprising because this is the era of nationalist struggle against British domination. The growth of the bourgeois-landowning class, the fiscal crisis of the state under Ismail Pasha and his successor Tawfiq Pasha, the promotion of Arabic as the official language of the country, and the emergence of educated elites all constituted the underlying economic, political, and cultural factors for the emergence and growth of nationalist movements in Egypt.[6] Struggles for political independence in 1919–22 eventually culminated, in 1924, in the formation of a constitutional government, when Egypt was officially recognized by Britain as an independent sovereign state having a hereditary form of monarchy. Under the impact of the nationalist revolution of 1919–22, Egypt's first modern mass party, the Wafd, emerged, and the country experienced more than two decades of liberal politics.

Islamic modernism was not as strong in Iran. To be sure, during the course of the Constitutional Revolution, a progressive faction among the ulama (including Sayyid Mohammad Tabataba-i, Mirza Hosein Na'ini, and Molla 'Abdul Rasoul Kashani) were deeply influenced by modern liberal thought and constitutional ideas. These ulama began to reconcile Shi'i political theory with a constitutional government.[7] The failure of the constitutional movement, however, was accompanied by the decline of modernist ideas as the dominant tendency among Islamic groups. After a decade of turmoil, the constitutional movement ended up in Reza Shah's despotism. Iran's first liberal nationalist experience began with the breakdown of Reza Shah's rule and was abruptly ended by the 1953 coup.

The liberal interpretation of Islam was also a dominant trend among the Muslim activists of India before and during the formative periods of the state of Pakistan. The first forceful challenge to traditionalism in India came in the wake of the devastating consequences of the "Mutiny" of 1857–58, or the "War of Independence" as it is called by modern Hindu and Muslim historians. It is epitomized in the thought, analysis, and apologetics of Sayyid Ahmad Khan at Aligarh, and in the modernist trends of his associates, Chiragh 'Ali and Mahdi 'Ali Khan Muhsin al-Mulk. In 1864, Sayyid Ahmad Khan founded a Scientific

Society for the introduction of Western sciences primarily among Muslims in India. In 1874 the scheme of his Anglo-Muhammadan Oriental College at Aligarh assumed a concrete shape: the school classes were opened in 1875, and college classes in 1878. He also began the publication of a journal, *Tahzib al-akhlaq*, apparently modeled on Addison and Steele's *Spectator* and *Tatler*. It covered articles on a wide range of subjects from public hygiene to rationalist speculation on religious dogma. It raised storms of bitter controversy. In its pages modernism emerged as a potent force and considerably changed the course and direction of Islam in India.[8]

As a key figure in twentieth-century modernism, the poet and thinker Muhammad Iqbal equated the Islamic notion of *ijma* (consensus) with parliamentary democracy and worked out a new theory of Muslim nationalism, which marked the theoretical beginning of the Pakistan movement. The lawyers and intellectuals involved in the movement for Pakistan were all inspired by the writings of Amir Ali and Muhammad Iqbal.[9] Both of these writers argue that Islam is a dynamic religion and that all that is best in modern science and democracy is reflected in the principles of Islam. Practices like polygamy, the right of divorce being available only to men, and the so-called inferiority of women to men in Islam are distortions or misguided interpretations of the original principles.[10]

Syria did not experience a strong Islamic modernist movement. It did, however, enjoy a short period of liberal politics. Nationalist movement in this country began first against the Ottoman rules, then against the French mandate between the two world wars. The complete evacuation of French troops by April 1946 brought Syrians a sequence of parliamentary democracy (1946–49), military dictatorship (1949–54), and again parliamentary democracy (1954–58). After the failure of its unification with Egypt (1958–61), the Syrian government gradually drifted to the left and developed a centralized dictatorship.[11]

Parallel with the decline of liberalism/nationalism was the growth of radical Islam in virtually all these countries. Prominent among the producers of radical ideas have been Hasan al-Banna and Sayyid Qutb from Egypt, Mustafa as-Siba'i from Syria, Abul Ala Maududi from Pakistan, and Ayatollah Ruhollah Khomeini from Iran. This group insisted on unconditional fealty to Islam and sought to undermine the validity of any learning that did not have its roots in the Divine Law.[12] The first organized movement of radical Islam was the Society of the

Muslim Brothers, founded by Hasan al-Banna in March 1928. By the late 1930s it had grown to become one of the most important politicoreligious organizations in the country. Although the Society was courted by the British as well as by the Egyptian king and certain conservative groups to curb the influence of the Nationalists and the Communists, its involvement in violence and the assassination of several prominent figures alerted the government that the Society was planning an imminent revolution. Thus in 1948 the government issued an order dissolving the Society. The history of the Muslim Brothers changed in the late 1940s when al-Banna, who had inspired the assassinations of the premier Nuqrashi Pasha and chief of police Salim Zaki, was in turn assassinated by government agents in February 1949.[13]

A branch of the Muslim Brothers was established in Syria. It was organized into the Islamic Socialist Front in November 1949. Mustafa asSiba'i, the leader of the Front, declared that he would work for the realization of Islamic socialism as had been advocated by the prophet. However, this flirtation with the idea of Islamic socialism was shortlived, and by 1961 the group had excised the term altogether from its political vocabulary.[14] Since the mid-1960s the Syrian Muslim Brothers have come into several bloody confrontations with the Baath regime, but none has resulted either in a revolution or political change.[15] In Pakistan the Jamma'at-i Islami was founded in August 1941. The period of its greatest influence, however, followed the decline of Bhutto's secular government and the coup of General Zia al-Haq in 1977.[16] It was in Iran, however, that Islam constituted the dominant ideology in a major revolution.

How these ideologies affected the course of economic development and political processes in different Middle Eastern countries is an important question that cannot be addressed here. However, in the case of Iran it will be attempted to demonstrate that political conflict and class struggle in different periods have taken place within the context of the discourse that was dominant in society.

The National Front

The Iranian Revolution is a product of the recent history that spanned several decades. The episodic context that produced the revolution began with the 1953 coup that overthrew the nationalist-liberal government of Premier Mosaddeq and reinstalled the Shah. The sequence of events that constituted the 1953–1977 episode was quite distinctive in terms of state structure, policy, and ideology as well as the constellation of interests underlying the Shah's rule and that of the opposition. To establish the distinctive character of this episode, it is necessary to gain a basic comprehension of the nationalist-liberal episode that began with the Allied invasion of Iran in 1941 and the decline of nationalist-liberalism in the postcoup period. The contrast between these successive periods also helps to demonstrate the connection between the dominant discourse and its underlying episodic context.

Following World War II, the nationalist-liberal ideology was organized in the National Front and led by a Swiss-educated lawyer, Mohammad Mosaddeq. The main objectives of the nationalist groups were democracy and independence for Iran within the framework of the existing semiconstitutional monarchy. The Front's democratic objective was to check the arbitrary power of the monarch by demanding that he reign, not rule. Its nationalist objective was to eliminate British control of the Iranian oil industry. Both objectives were achieved when Mosaddeq was elected prime minister in the early 1950s. Mosaddeq, however, was overthrown by a British/American-engineered coup in 1953. The coup was a political solution to an economic dispute revolving around the issue of Iranian oil. On one side of the dispute stood the international petroleum cartel that had a monopoly control of the oil reserves and distribution in the capitalist world. On the other side stood a coalition of the indigenous social classes represented by the National Front, which attempted to bring the oil under government control by nationalizing the British-run oil industry. Hence there was a possibility of disturbing the cartelized pattern of production, distribution, and pricing of oil in the world capitalist market. The convergence of U.S. and British oil interests was the factor underpinning their participation in the coup against the nationalist government of Premier Mosaddeq in 1953.

The broad environmental conditions that accounted for the rise of national-liberalism in the 1941–53 period included the breakdown of Reza Shah's despotic rule, the decline of peasant and worker movements and the defeat of the ethnic minorities for autonomy, and the post–World War II growth of U.S. power and its competition with the British in the region. The national-liberal discourse constituted the language and method that the nationalist leaders used to address Iran's economic and political problems.

At the outbreak of the war in September 1939, German influence in Iran was paramount. German agents were active, and the Reza Shah's sympathy for the Germans was no secret. This sympathy caused concern once the Nazis invaded the Soviet Union in June 1941. With the objectives of securing the oil industry vital to the British war effort, preventing the Germans from using Iran as a base against the Soviets, and providing the Soviets with military support, the Allies invaded Iran and forced Reza Shah to abdicate. His son Mohammad Reza became Iran's new shah in September 1941. The collapse of Reza Shah's despotic regime left the dominant classes vulnerable to attacks from below. At he same time, the difficulties caused by the war resulted in an upsurge of peasant and worker movements and of the ethnic demands for autonomy.[17]

In Azarbayjan, the Democratic Party of Azarbayjan was formed with a total membership of 75,000. In December 1945, an autonomous government was established in Azarbayjan. A similar autonomous government was also formed in Kurdistan in the following year.[18] In the rural areas, the conflict between peasants and landowners also intensified. Peasant movements culminated in the formation of peasant associations in various parts of the country such as Gilan, Mazanderan, Khorasan, Yazd, Isfahan, Kerman, Fars, and Khuzistan. With the central government's repressive capacity highly undermined, peasants were able to win concessions from landowners.[19] Similarly, the workers' movement gained considerable strength. In 1944 the Central Council of the Unified Trade Unions of Iranian Workers was formed. By 1945 it claimed a membership of 200,000 workers and, by 1946, a membership of 400,000 with 186 affiliates.[20]

The increasing radicalization of the ethnic minorities, and the peasants' and workers' movements, frightened the dominant classes (i.e., the landowners and capitalists) as well as foreign interests, particularly the British. The common fear of a possible social revolution among these groups underlay the de facto unity in suppressing these movements. Even many of the liberal-minded politicians who later became leaders of the National Front in one way or another participated in suppressing the dominated classes and ethnic minorities.[21] In 1946 a British-instigated attack was launched on a workers' strike in the Khuzistan oil establishments. During the attack many people were wounded or killed. Subsequently, the government pronounced the strike illegal, and the leaders of labor unions in Khuzistan were arrested. The sites of workers' organizations were occupied by the military.[22] In late 1946 and early 1947, the military launched a brutal attack on the Azarbayjan's autonomous government, and then on the Kurdish Democratic Republic, during which thousands of people were wounded or killed. In the cities, labor unions and the clubs of the Tudeh party (Iran's Communist party) were also attacked by the army and right-wing paramilitary bands. In mid-1947 the peasant movement was also suppressed. The military forces occupied the centers of peasants' councils. Many active peasants were either arrested and imprisoned, or killed. All the gains of the peasants were destroyed, and once again the medieval relationships were consolidated in the rural areas.[23] Thus by the end of 1949, "The monarchy appeared to have almost as much power as in the era before August 1941."[24]

The relative ease with which the movements of the dominated classes and ethnic minorities were repressed, despite the collapse of the Reza Shah's military in 1941, cannot be attributed to the organizational strength of the dominant classes. The Shah had dissolved all their formal organizations and political parties including the Reformers' party and the Revival party. Moreover, given that there were considerable internal feuds and dissension among the political leaders of the 1940s, the defeats of these movements cannot be attributed to the combat readiness of these leaders. One indication of such interelite rivalries is that Iran experienced the inauguration of thirteen premiers and seventeen cabinets in the 1941–53 period.[25] These movements were crushed because of the absence of a revolutionary discourse. No overarching ideology existed to connect Iran's independence and development to the idea of regional and ethnic autonomy, the workers' right to unionize, and land reform. They simply aimed at taking advantage of the political vacuum generated by the decline in the power of the central government. More crucially, the demands of these movements were running against the general principles of the nationalist-secular discourse—that is, the themes of national unity and territorial integrity.

These themes were rooted in the secular cultural trend unleashed by the Constitutional Revolution of 1905–11, which had remained unabated under Reza Shah. The country's leading intellectuals and social critics continued to attack Iran's traditional culture, at the center of which were various forms of religious practices, tribalism and ethnic divisions, and communal sectarianism. The solution was sought in the formation of a centralized state with an emphasis on pre-Islamic king-ship and culture, the expansion of secular education, the spread of the Persian language among non-Persians, the adoption of Western phi-losophy and technology, and the destruction of the clerical influence. Modern secular ideas were often expressed in major periodicals of the 1920s such as *Iranshahr, Farangistan,* and *Ayandeh.* Abrahamian's content analysis of these periodicals reveals their socioeconomic and political orientation. Of the 236 articles published in *Iranshahr,* seventy-three stressed the importance of public and secular education, forty-five emphasized the need to improve the status of women, thirty eulogized pre-Islamic Iran, and forty discussed aspects of modern tech-nology and Western philosophy. Similarly, of some seventy articles pub-lished in *Farangistan,* fifteen dealt with modern education, eight with the status of women, ten with industrial technology, nine with Western political philosophy, three with pre-Islamic Iran, three with Azarbay-jan, two with the secular movement in Turkey, four with international relations, and sixteen with Persian literature. Finally, the contents of the monthly *Ayandeh* were similar, but they focused mainly on the need to form a centralized state and a unified national identity.[26]

One of the most effective spokespersons of modern secular discourse was Ahmad Kasravi, Iran's famous social critic and iconoclastic histo-rian. Kasravi began his career first as a student of religion. His dislike of the clergy soon prompted him to leave the traditional school and enter the American Memorial School in Tabriz to study the English language and modern sciences. Kasravi was a prolific writer. He founded the monthly *Payman* in 1933 and the newspaper *Parcham* in 1941. In addi-tion, he published over fifty books and theses with critical and histor-ical perspectives on various aspects of Iranian society.[27] In all likeli-hood his views had a considerable impact on the political and social thinking of the period. Kasravi considers tribal, linguistic, and sec-tarian divisions as the major causes of Iran's backwardness. He is par-ticularly critical of various forms of religious rituals commemorating the martyrdom of Imam Hosein on the grounds that these practices re-flect superstitions and are incompatible with the modern lifestyle.

Kasravi is highly critical of the Islamic establishment. He argues that there are two kinds of Islam. One is the kind of Islam founded by Muhammad over 1,300 years ago, and the other is the currently exist-ing Islam which is divided into diverse sects such as Sunni, Shi'i, Ismaili,

Ali-allahi, Sheikhi, Karim-khani, and so forth.[28] Today Islam is controlled by the clergy. In Kasravi's view, the Shi'i clerical institution not only fails to benefit the people but is also the source of many problems and misfortunes. In his view it represents a major source of Iran's misery, ignorance, underdevelopment, and inferiority vis-à-vis the Europeans. Kasravi believes that the ignorance propagated by the clergy is so extensive that it made the Muslims arrogant. Being so convinced of the rightfulness of their religion, they even wish the Europeans to convert to Islam. Moreover, the clergy block innovation and progress. Foreign states have used the clerical establishment to pursue their policies and to realize their political objectives. Finally, he writes, this kind of Islam has even belittled the name of God.[29]

Of course, the Muslims also have their own excuses, says Kasravi. Whenever one raises the problems facing the Muslim nations (the people's ignorance or sectarianism, for example), they quickly respond: "If people are bad, it is not the fault of Islam." When this argument loses its validity, then they say: "People do not act according to the principles of religion. If they do so, everything is going to be all right." They also claim that the existing divisions and sectarianisms are not caused by religion. Islam is in essence clean and pure. Therefore, they say: "We should return to the fundamentals of religion," or "We should reform religion." Finally, they say that "the book of Islam is the Quran, and as long as it exists, Islam also exists."[30]

Such was the core of the arguments that characterized the dominant discourse under the first shah of Pahlavi. In fact, Reza Shah's success in repressing the autonomous and reformist movements during the turbulent years following the Constitutional Revolution was not a conspiracy dictated by the British to curb the social revolutionary movement that was inspired by the Russian Revolution of 1917. To be sure, the revolution in Russia, the economic crises caused by the war, and the weakness of the central government all created favorable conditions for the upsurge of class conflict and reformist movements. In 1918 trade unions were formed among postal, printing, and other workers in Tehran and Tabriz. Reform movements were especially strong in Tehran and in the northern provinces of Gilan, Mazanderan, and Azarbayjan. Between 1919 and 1921, the nationalist and democratic movements gained considerable strength in Gilan in the north, which was led by the Jangalis, and in Azarbayjan in the northwest, which was controlled by the Democratic Party of Azarbayjan. Also in 1920, the Communist party was formed. These movements began to challenge the supremacy of the British as well as large local merchants and landlords.

The reformist movements, having gone far beyond the initial objectives of the Constitutional Revolution and now combined with the "menace" of Communism, was a concern to merchants, landowners, and the British alike. All these interests thus began to support the creation of a centralized government capable of withstanding the threat of a social revolution in Iran. This historical juncture determined the political fortune of Reza Khan, a cossack brigade commander. Backed by the British general William Edmund Ironside, Reza Khan and a group of Anglophiles headed by Sayyid Zia ud-Din Tabataba'i carried out a coup in February 1921. In his ascent to power, Reza Khan was also assisted by the dominant classes and the ulama. In particular, 256 prominent merchants of the bazaar of Tehran sent Ahmad Shah, the last shah of Qajar, a petition to appoint Reza Shah as the prime minister.[31]

Reza Shah was therefore successful in building a new centralized monarchy because his regime rested on the dominant interests in the country. However, his policies were shaped by the secular discourse dominant in society. When he so daringly outlawed the veil (which covered women from head to toe) as well as traditional ethnic clothes, obliged the people to wear Western-style dress, expelled the ulama from the state bureaucracy, and initiated many other secular reforms, he did so not simply because of his leadership capability and military might. It was the constitution of the Reza Shah's rule by and through the secular discourse whose adherents were both inside and outside the polity, and this included both the flatterers of the monarchy as well as his critics. The Shah was supported by his critics on these measures, although on the whole they expressed ambivalent attitudes about him.

When his rule abruptly ended, history somewhat repeated itself. The peasants, workers, and ethnic minorities attempted to get what they had been unable to gain a generation earlier. The British and the merchants, landowners, and diverse politicians once again united in suppressing them as they had before. This time, however, there was one major difference. These movements were suppressed without the presence of a brutal and capable dictator. Why then did they fail yet again? The Left often attributes these defeats to a British conspiracy that persuaded the "national bourgeoisie" to participate in the suppression of the movements, or it simply resorts to its standard argument that when the national bourgeoisie face the movement of the masses, they take the reactionary side. However, to implement a plot does require some degree of organization, and it is highly unlikely in the chaotic situation of the 1940s that British agents had managed to infiltrate all the major political institutions. Nor is it clear that these movements were fundamentally against the interests of the national bourgeoisie. Thus if the conservative politicians, the Court, and the military were able to lead the reaction against the ethnic minorities and the peasants and the workers, it was because the dominant political discourse must have made their missions acceptable and their arguments quite meaningful to their political rivals (who of course were also operating within the same ideological universe). A broad coalition was formed against the Turks and Kurds precisely because these ethnic minorities, by demanding regional autonomy, violated the most important principle of the secular nationalist discourse—i.e., national unity. They were defying over twenty years of nationalist propaganda.

The major argument advanced against the Turkish autonomy movement was derived from the nationalist ideology. Even the Iran party, which was the most significant democratically oriented nationalist party, attacked the autonomy movement in Azarbayjan on the grounds that "the Democratic Party of Azarbayjan had taken advantage of a favorable international situation. Its birth came about under the supervision of foreigners and through their military support. Many Iranians considered this as an unforgivable sin, especially when the party demanded the protection of the Turkish language and other things that wounded the hearts of the Iranian patriots."[32]

At any rate, the coalition between the dominant forces broke down as soon as the mission was accomplished. Intense conflicts among diverse factions and political groups resumed. However, if the dynamic of nationalist-secular discourse helped defeat the ethnic demands for autonomy and the movements of the dominated classes in the mid- to late 1940s, it subsequently transcended ethnic and class divisions by bringing into focus the British exploitation of Iranian oil. Moreover, the landowners and the merchants were too disgruntled by the arbitrary rule of Reza Shah to allow the rise of another dictator. Whoever among the politicians was able to most effectively articulate the themes of nationalism and restrictions on the arbitrary power of the monarch had a better chance to lead the masses and rally them to action. It was within the discursive field of national interests versus foreign interests, and democracy versus arbitrary rule that the National Front grew to become the strongest political force in the country in the early 1950s.[33]

Oil as the National Issue

This is not to argue that the nationalist ideology covered up the reality of ethnic and class differences by virtue of constituting the dominant discourse. Its transcendental power to a large extent rested on the interest in controlling the country's most important natural resource. The argument that much of Iran's economic difficulties could be resolved if the oil industry was brought under the government's control had considerable support by the public. The nationalist leaders and agitators made effective use of British plundering of Iranian oil in their mobilizing efforts against the British and the Shah.

Iran's grievances against the British-controlled Anglo-Persian Oil Company (APOC) were indeed extensive. First, the oil concession of 1901, which had been granted by the Shah of Qajar to a British engineer, William Knox D'Arcy, was not ratified by the parliament of the postconstitutional period. Some sort of move by the parliament was highly likely, especially when one considers that the concession had left the country's most important resource under the control of the concessionaire for over a half century.[34] Second, to make matters worse, APOC did not consistently follow the terms of the 1901 Agreement. For example, the British government granted a rebate to the Royal Navy in 1920 without the agreement of the Iranians. Furthermore, the Iranians began to demand back payments and royalties that had been discontinued during the war period of 1916–20 as well as a share in the profits of the subsidiaries. The British responded with a bill of over £600,000 in damages to compensate for the severance of their pipeline by Turks during the war. Finally, while the company had made a profit of £200 million by 1933, Iran had received only some £10 million of the £32 million due it contractually. Iran's revenue from the oil was less than one-third of the share to which it was entitled by the concession.[35]

Third, from the Iranian perspective the 1933 Agreement signed between Reza Shah and the British was not much better than the 1901 concession had been. For example, according to Article Nineteen of the 1933 Agreement, prices for refined petroleum products in Iran were based upon average Romanian or Gulf of Mexico FOB prices, whichever was lower, plus actual transportation and distribution costs, less a 10 percent discount. The unfairness of the agreement is evident when one considers that the production cost of oil in the Middle East averaged $1.20 per ton compared to $12.45 per ton in the United States.[36] It has been estimated that the British made as much as a 500 percent profit from the domestic sale of petroleum products in Iran. This policy hampered, if indeed it did not prevent, Iran from establishing manufacturing industries based on oil. The Anglo-Iranian Oil Company (AIOC; formerly the APOC, before the 1933 Agreement) sold oil to Iran at such a high price that Iran had to import oil from the Soviet Union.[37]

The leaders of the National Front questioned the legitimacy of the 1933 Agreement. In response to the Truman-Churchill letter to Mosaddeq in August 1952, which suggested "having regard to the legal position of the parties existing immediately prior to nationalization,"[38] Mosaddeq responded that "the Iranian people have declared the 1933 contract that was forced upon it [*sic*] invalid."[39] They also claimed that the AIOC's labor policy was not satisfactory. While the company had increased the number of foreign employees from 1,800 in 1933 to 4,200 in 1948, it refused to train any Iranian technical staff. The company was explicitly obligated to provide health services and housing for the workers employed in its operations, but more than 80 percent of the Iranian workers in the oil regions were without housing. The houses built in Abadan and other oil centers were occupied mostly by the British staff.[40]

After World War II, Iran's grievances against the AIOC continued to mount. It was indicated that "the profit of the Company in the year 1950 alone, after deducting the share paid to Iran, amounted to more than the entire sum of £114 million cited by the representative of the United Kingdom of the past half century."[41] In the United Nations Security Council, Mosaddeq stated:

> Although Iran produces a considerable proportion of the world's supply of petroleum and has produced a total of 315 million tons during a period of fifty years, its entire gain, according to the account of the former Company, has been only £110 million. To give you an idea of Iran's profit from this enormous industry, I must say that in 1948, according to the account of the former Anglo-Iranian Oil Company, its net revenue amounted to £61 million; but from these profits Iran received only £9 million though £28 million went into the United Kingdom Treasury in income tax alone.[42]

The rise of the Front was also aided by the active involvement of the United States in international politics under the banner of anticolonialism and liberal internationalism, an ideology that was well articulated under the Wilson administration.[43] U.S. support for the nationalist cause in Iran was further reinforced by the conflict between American and British oil companies. This conflict became apparent in 1949 when the British—attempting to cut down on their record dollar drain (i.e., $625 million a year spent to buy and produce oil)—decided to ban imports of fuel oil from the dollar areas until all oil from sterling areas was used up. As a result, U.S. refineries faced a possible drop of 100,000 barrels a day in sales.[44] This somewhat abrupt action by the British concerned U.S. oilmen, who believed that "Britain is less interested in saving dollars than in using its ECA-created oil surplus to drive the U.S. out of existing markets."[45] Secretary of State Dean Acheson declared that "it was and is the U.S. view that the British action [against dollar oil] was taken without adequate consultation with American companies."[46]

In March of the same year, the U.S. government decided "to waggle a big financial stick against Britain."[47] Texas Senator Tom Connally "announced that he would seek to block all further aid to Britain unless it abandons its 'discrimination' against US oil."[48] Furthermore, in comparative terms, the British oil agreement with Iran was more favorable to the British than the American oil agreements with other countries such as Saudi Arabia.[49] Royalties offered the Iranian government by the AIOC came to about 35 cents a barrel, but in Saudi Arabia a U.S. company was already paying that government more than 55 cents a barrel.[50] U.S. oil companies did not want to see the British having a competitive advantage. Therefore, during the initial stages of negotiations with the British, Iranian demands had been backed by the American ambassador, Henry Grady, and by other American officials.[51]

In turn, the Front's leaders were counting heavily on U.S. support for the realization of their democratic and nationalist objectives. The United States was praised by even the most radical members of the Front:

> From the other side of the Atlantic Ocean, from the State of Liberty and from the Land of George Washington, these days we hear the message of affection.
>
> The United States of America that, with its invaluable material and moral assistance, has saved many nations of the world from death and starvation, and the hungry and destroyed Europe from embracing Communism, today is going to assume a much heavier responsibility.

The United States must help us at the mouth of the volcano [imply-
ing the Soviet Union]. . . . We do not interpret the United States' assistance but as a reflection of humanitarianism and feelings of love for
humanity.[52]

The Coup and Its Consequences

The coup of 1953, however, changed the course of Iran's political development. The leaders of the National Front were taking the United
States' avowal of liberal internationalism too seriously, not realizing
that the dominant interests in the region had placed decisive constraints
on U.S. political options. The interests in question were those of the International Petroleum Cartel, consisting of seven large oil companies or
the "Seven Sisters," which were directly threatened by Mosaddeq's nationalization of the oil industry and which benefited from his downfall.
These were Exxon, Texaco, Socal, Gulf, Mobil, British Petroleum, and
Shell.[53] In 1952 these seven companies accounted for one-half of the
world's total crude production, including that of the Soviet Union.[54] In
1949 they controlled 65 percent of the world's estimated crude reserves
and (excluding the United States, Mexico, and the Soviet Union) about
92 percent of such reserves.[55] Furthermore, they controlled 57 percent
of all refining, two-thirds of the word's tanker tonnage and all major
pipelines outside the United States, and the sale of oil throughout the
world.[56] The overall control by the International Petroleum Cartel of
the world's petroleum reserves, productive capacities, and refining and
distribution facilities had led to domination of the world market. In a
variety of ways, the "Seven Sisters" cooperated with each other so that
their steadily increasing control of production, bound together by an
intricate maze of joint ownership and contractual and cartel relationships, gave promise of less difficulty in the future in following a common policy.[57]

To establish the connection between the interests of the "Seven Sisters" and the U.S.-British coalition against Mosaddeq, one should asses
the importance of Middle East oil to these companies. At that time,
Middle East petroleum reserves constituted over 60 percent of all crude
reserves in the entire world. This fortune was divided among the "Seven
Sisters." In the Sheikhdom of Kuwait, for example, a concession lasting
until the year 2026 was divided between BP and Gulf through their
equal ownership of stock in Kuwait Oil Company. In neighboring Iraq,

BP, Compagnie Français de Petroles (a French concern with heavy government interests), and Shell each had a 23.75 percent participation in all that nation's rich reserves. Another 23.75 percent was held by Socony Mobil Oil Company and Standard Oil of New Jersey, effectuated through their joint ownership of the Near East Development Company. In Saudi Arabia, lying to the South, four American concerns—Socony Mobil, Standard Oil of California, Standard Oil of New Jersey, and Texaco, Inc.—together owned Arabian American Oil Company (Aramco), which had concession rights to prolific oil reserves (lasting in some instance until the twenty-first century).[58]

When the Iranian oil industry was nationalized, AIOC was heavily involved in all the other important Middle Eastern oil-producing nations except Saudi Arabia. Furthermore, large international oil companies were partners of AIOC in at least one of these ventures. Moreover, both Standard Oil of New Jersey and Socony Mobil had entered into long-term contractual arrangements with Anglo-Iranian, commencing in 1952 for the purchase of crude oil production from Kuwait or Iran itself.[59] This close affinity among the seven large oil companies in the Middle East had led to a community of interests among them, which placed a premium on price stability, production control, and mutual respect for one another's marketing outlets.

This, however, does not mean that the relationships among these oil companies had always been free of conflict. As noted earlier, the conflict between American and British oil interests was an important factor for the initial U.S. support of Mosaddeq, which was the major concern of the British. According to Anthony Eden: "I was concerned by the extent to which Musaddiq was being aided in the oil dispute by a United States Policy of 'neutrality.' The Government of Iran argued publicly [that] the United States was supporting them. If this current were allowed to swell, it would sweep all away."[60]

Eden indicates that when Secretary of State-Designate Dean Acheson, accompanied by Averell Harriman, first met his British counterpart in Paris in the wake of nationalization, their views regarding the future of Iran were far apart. However, "the American Government were anxious to complete an agreement with him if this were possible."[61] As soon as a concrete proposal was advanced by the British as a framework within which an accord might be reached, the United States allied with the oil companies against Iran, which was apparently in line with British strategy.[62]

Subsequently, U.S. policy toward Mosaddeq changed. Shortly after the nationalization law went into effect, Secretary of State Acheson warned the Iranians to settle their grievances with the British promptly because of the lack of available technicians elsewhere, including the United States, to run the oil industry.[63] When Averell Harriman was in Iran in July 1951, he stated that "the seizure of foreign-owned assets without prompt, adequate, and effective compensation or arrangements satisfactory to the owners constitutes confiscation; that there must be more than willingness to pay, there must be ability to do so; and in order to be able to pay compensation, Iran must have an efficient oil industry with large assured outlets such as was possible under the British proposal."[64] Harriman was apparently threatening the Iranian government that unless Iran accepted the British proposal no aid from the United States was forthcoming. "The United States," so Mr. Harriman stated, "grants aid only to people who help themselves and whose government has the welfare of the people at heart."[65]

In early October 1951, Mosaddeq flew to the United States, officially to participate in the meeting of the UN Security Council, but also to negotiate with the Americans over the settlement of the oil problem. During his forty-day stay in the country, Mosaddeq met American representatives about twenty times and made different suggestions for the settlement of the oil dispute. Some of his aides went so far as to suggest the formation of an international oil distribution company (that is, giving a monopoly over the sale of oil to U.S.-based international oil companies).[66] But the United States government refused to accept these proposals. As Iran's economic difficulties intensified and as the country became more and more desperate, the attitudes of the United States became more and more unyielding. In the spring of 1952, the State Department refused an Iranian request for a $20 million loan on the grounds that the Iranian government had the immediate means of helping itself.[67]

To Mosaddeq's request for economic aid on May 28, 1953, President Eisenhower responded that "it would not be fair to the American taxpayers for the United States government to extend any considerable amount of economic aid to Iran so long as Iran would have access to funds derived from the sale of its oil and oil products if a reasonable agreement were reached with regard to compensation whereby the large-scale marketing of Iranian oil would be resumed."[68] The United States, however, went beyond this "settle or else" policy whereby aid to

Iran was refused as a penalty for its "intransigence."[69] It cooperated fully with the British in placing an embargo on Iranian oil by actively discouraging any transaction over the purchase of oil by American companies. For example, an American firm, Consolidated Brokerage, negotiated an exclusive five-year contract with the National Iranian Oil Company (NIOC) in May 1952 for the sale of Iranian oil in the United States. However, it abandoned its contract on the grounds that this company "had been requested by the State Department to avoid complicating the situation while there was any hope of diplomatic settlement."[70] Similar pressures were exerted on other American companies that were willing to help the Iranian oil industry resolve its technical and personnel difficulties. Lee Factors, an engineering firm, offered to recruit 3,500 trained technicians and to take over the operation of the oil installations, but the offer was withdrawn because of the "furor caused by the original announcement." The contract with Consolidated Brokerage of Denver met the same fate.[71]

The breakdown of W. Alton Jones's mission to Iran in 1952 followed a similar pattern. Jones, the late president of Cities Service Company, arrived in Iran at the personal invitation of Mosaddeq. Following his inspection of the Abadan refinery, he enthusiastically announced that "the Free World knows that the Iranians can manage their own oil industry and operate the refinery."[72] He estimated that full-scale production could be resumed with a minimum expenditure of $10 million.[73] Jones also said that "he might buy oil from Iran irrespective of whether Britain or the Anglo-Iranian Oil Co. would take legal action against his company for handling Iranian oil products."[74] The Jones mission, however, failed. In September 1952 the two companies with which Jones was affiliated, Cities Service and Sinclair, signed long-term contracts for Kuwait oil with the Gulf Oil Corporation. These provided for extremely low prices ($7.40 per ton, as against $12.89 per ton). Subsequently, these two companies received shares in the international consortium that succeeded the AIOC after the coup.[75]

The United States' policy toward Britain contrasted sharply with its policy toward Iran. It cooperated fully with the British in order to ameliorate the economic difficulties besetting the British as a result of the nationalization of its Iranian interests. Nineteen American oil companies were formally invited by the Defense Production Administrator to participate in a voluntary agreement to provide measures to offset the deficit of supplies of crude oil and refined products resulting from the interruption of Iranian petroleum operations. Its provisions guaranteed the British enough petroleum for 1951 to replace the amount that under normal circumstances would have been secured from Iran.[76] American replacement was so successful that, according to a *New York Times'* headline in early 1952, "Loss of Oil in Iran Is Fully Replaced."[77] In fact, the nineteen American companies that participated in the Voluntary Agreement of June 25, 1951, in fact constituted the entire American oil industry operating outside North America.[78]

During this period Mosaddeq was under attack from two sides. From the outside, there were the United States (which by 1952 had abandoned any semblance of neutrality) and the British, which with the former had become "as inseparable as 'tweedledum from tweedlee.'"[79] From the inside, there were pro-British circles within the Parliament and the Court which had begun to intensify their offensive against Mosaddeq. These groups were particularly encouraged by Mosaddeq's failure to return from the United States with some kind of assistance and by the economic difficulties that followed the nationalization of the oil industry. However, these pressures made Mosaddeq firmer and more persistent on his nationalization policy.[80] Frustrated with the Americans' empty friendliness, Mosaddeq "remarked to the United States' Ambassador that the Iranians were not donkeys and could no longer be deceived by professions of friendliness."[81]

Mosaddeq seemed to have realized that he could not count on the United States and that the oil problem was not to be settled soon. He attempted to reorganize the economy independent of oil. In December 1951 he stated in Parliament that "we should assume that like Afghanistan and the European countries we do not have oil, we should reduce our spending and increase our revenues, the nation should tolerate [the burden of hard times] in order to free itself from the yoke of slavery."[82] Four months later, in the early spring of 1952, the oil-less economy became the official economic policy of the government.[83] Although this policy provided Iran with a positive balance of trade,[84] it failed to stabilize and stimulate the economy.[85] Under pressure from below as well as from the Tudeh party and the radical wing of the National Front, Mosaddeq decreed a land reform law according to which all landlords had to give up 20 percent of their share of the crop: 10 percent was to go to the peasants and 10 percent to newly created rural banks that would help the peasants with credit. To collect the unpaid back taxes of the rich, commissions were created throughout Iran that were entitled to jail, and confiscate the property of, those in arrears.[86] This measure antagonized many landowners. To ameliorate economic problems, Mosaddeq nationalized certain enterprises such as bus and telephone companies. To reduce food prices, he opened new bakeries. These measures were opposed by the bazaaris and contributed to the decline in the bazaar's support for Mosaddeq.[87]

Learning that no oil money was forthcoming, the Iranian bourgeoisie had the choice of remaining nationalist, proud, and poor by continuing to support Mosaddeq, or to back his rival, the Shah, with the expectation that the latter would support national industry and commerce. They predominantly chose the latter option. Many of the leaders of the National Front—such as Ayatollah Kashani, Qonatabadi, Makki, and Baqai—who had close ties with the bazaar, abandoned Mosaddeq and established contact with the Shah's forces. On the international level, the United States and Britain had been actively conspiring to overthrow Mosaddeq for some time. In collaboration with the Court, they engineered the coup that brought his downfall in August 1953.[88]

Why did Mosaddeq continue to insist on his policy of national-liberalism, considering the difficulties he was facing? He could have compromised his nationalism by striking a deal with the British or the Soviets (as the Tudeh had insisted), while protecting his democratic government. Alternatively, he could have compromised democracy in favor of nationalism. There had already been one aborted coup several days before the successful one. The Shah fled the country after hearing that the coup had failed. And when the commander of the air force called Mosaddeq, excitedly asking whether he should force the Shah's aircraft to land or shoot it down in the sky, Mosaddeq responded, "Let him go."[89] Furthermore, Mosaddeq could have imprisoned General Zahedi, who later led the coup against him, when it became clear that he was actively conspiring to oust him. To be sure, he arrested the army chief of staff and several military officers. Following the referendum that gave him the mandate, he also dissolved Parliament. Nevertheless, all of these were conducted constitutionally. In principle and in deed, Mosaddeq remained committed to the ideology of national-liberalism. He was its spokesperson. He sacrificed politics for the ideals of nationalism and democracy.

After his ouster, the nationalist-liberal episode was effectively over. That Iran failed to produce again a leader like Mosaddeq, who was deeply committed to democracy and nationalism, was not because the remaining leaders of the National Front lacked his charisma. The National Front and followers of democracy in the postcoup period were unable to produce a leader of Mosaddeq's caliber because national-liberalism failed to become the dominant discourse of the opposition. Because of its affinity with imperialism, the postcoup intellectuals within the opposition tended to belittle the idea of democracy.

The review of events in the precoup period indicates how ideology autonomously contributed to the outcome of class conflict and contention for power. As was noted, the absence of an overarching revolutionary ideology was a factor in the defeat of the ethnic minorities and the decline of the peasants and workers movement, despite the organizational weakness of the dominant classes and the collapse of the state in 1941. The dominance of the nationalist discourse, which emphasized the themes of national unity and Iran's territorial integrity, provided the ideological context that united the politically divided elites of the 1940s against the ethnic autonomy movements.

The rise of the nationalist-liberal discourse in the 1941–53 period was attributed to a constellation of factors such as the weakness of the state, the defeat of the dominated classes, and the U.S.-British conflict. The themes of nationalism and democracy transcended class and ethnic differences and united the public for restricting the power of the monarch and bringing the oil under the control of the Iranian government. Finally, Mosaddeq was ousted not simply because of the breakdown of the coalition that brought him to power. It was also because the nationalist-liberal discourse had reached an impasse. The political problems Mosaddeq was facing could not be resolved within the framework of national-liberalism.

The coup ended the nationalist-liberal episode. In the postcoup period the United States abandoned its support for democracy in Iran and, along with other advanced capitalist countries, stood firmly behind the Shah. The Shah's economic, social, and cultural policies from the 1950s on, and the connection between his rule and the imperialist powers, provided effective constraints on the ideologies of the opposition movement. As will be explained in forthcoming chapters, the dialectic between the state and civil society generated an extraordinary condition for the rise of Islamic revolutionary discourse.

2

The State and the Problem of National Integration

In a negative sense, the Shah was the leader of the revolution.

Mehdi Bazargan

For many of the existing explanations of the Iranian Revolution, the rule of Reza Shah remains anomalous. In terms of absolutism, patrimonialism, boldness in pursuing a modernization program, and vulnerability to the vicissitudes of the world economy and international politics, there was not much difference between Reza Shah and his son. Why then did the state face a revolutionary crisis in the late 1970s, while no such crisis transpired in the early 1940s despite the collapse of the Pahlavis' central authority and the intensification of social conflict? The explanation offered in this chapter is twofold. First, the 1953 coup was followed by the inauguration of a bureaucratic-authoritarian regime, resulting in a structural separation of the state from civil society, with no significant intermediate organization connecting the two. Second, the state's cultural policies and ideological orientation exaggerated this separation and provided a context for the ideological polarization of society. Therefore, the character of the state, to use Stepan's perceptive remark, affected "the evolution of opposition politics."[1] The next chapter will discusses the state's alliance with international capital and the role of its economic policies in patterning class conflict in the 1960s and 1970s, thereby determining the content of the revolutionary movement that was developed against it.

To stress the point raised in the previous chapter, a revolutionary crisis did not transpire in the early 1940s because an overarching revolutionary ideology was absent. The dominant oppositional discourse stressed the themes of nationalism, secularism, the separation of religion from politics, and the adoption of Western models. These themes also informed Reza Shah's policies. The nationalist leaders were attempting to resolve the existing socioeconomic and political problems according to the parameters of the ideological universe that included the state's discourse as well.

The State versus Civil Society

In the postcoup period, the structure and policy of the state began to change. Two broad policy orientations characterized the Shah's regime: (1) a systematic attempt to exclude all the dominated classes—and, to some extent, the indigenous dominant classes—from major political positions and to prevent them from participating in important economic decision-making; and (2) the adoption of an economic strategy that promoted dependent capitalist development. These political and economic orientations, followed under the aegis of advanced capitalist countries, had great impact on the country's class structure and class politics. These policies reinforced the expansion of the state's bureaucracy and repressive apparatus, hence the growth of a bureaucratic-authoritarian (BA) state. On one hand, state-initiated economic policies highly antagonized the indigenous classes. On the other hand, its systematic disorganization of the collectivities within civil society conditioned the nature and form of the opposition movement.

True, crucial differences existed between the general conditions that preceded the coups in Iran and those that preceded the inauguration of a BA regime in Brazil. For example, Cardoso observes that the Brazilian coup was the consequence of a change in the pattern of class alliance produced by foreign capital infiltration, whereby international capital became economically but not politically dominant. Cardoso relates changes in a political regime to basic changes in the pattern of class alliance. His understanding of the process of "associated-dependent development" sees the coup as the recognition of a fait accompli.[2] Precoup Iran, in contrast, experienced little infiltration of international capital, save for the oil sector.

The U.S.-British oil embargo did produce an economic difficulty by draining the state's major, if not only, source of revenue. The embargo also brought the state's developmental projects to a standstill. The restrictions imposed by the Bank of England on conversion of Iran's sterling holdings in 1961 caused a de facto devaluation of the rial: the United States dollar rose from forty rials in 1950 to 124 rials in 1953. Yet the effect of the devaluation and the embargo proved stimulating to the economy. According to Agah:

1950–3 was a period of industrial recovery. . . . Good crops and larger exports kept up the mass purchasing power, while restrictive measures gave the domestic industry welcome protection. With the return of profits to normal, many factories reopened, new plants were installed and Iran actually became an exporter of manufactured articles such as mill textiles and matches. In textile alone, in these three years eleven new factories with 110,080 spindles and 1,600 weaving looms, were installed.[3]

Iran's sociopolitical condition was also far from a praetorian system, which is claimed to have characterized precoup conditions in Brazil. "In a praetorian system," says Huntington, "social forces confront each other nakedly; no political institutions, no corps of professional political leaders are recognized or accepted as the legitimate intermediaries to moderate group conflict."[4] Under Mosaddeq, however, there were available in abundance both legitimate political institutions and professional leaders. Several political parties existed, whose programs and strategies were more or less defined. The nationalization of the oil industry was accepted by virtually all the existing political parties, except for the conservative groups and the Court. Nor was the coup an attempt by the state to impose "order" on society and to provide stable conditions for the investment and inflow of foreign capital, as O'Donnell argues for the Brazilian case. The 1953 coup was principally the result of the conflict between the international petroleum cartel and the National Front.[5]

Thus in terms of the social conditions and problems facing the popular leaders, there were differences between Iran under Mosaddeq and the conditions preceding the coups in certain Latin American countries. Nevertheless, the concept of the bureaucratic-authoritarian regime is borrowed here because the form and content of class conflict that transpired in the sixties and seventies emanated from the bureaucratic and repressive policies of the Shah's regime as well as from its alliance with international capital.[6]

Depoliticization and Repression

In a crucial respect, the empirical evidence seems to support the Left's argument that the state's repressive policy was to destroy all the political groups and provide stable conditions for the inflow of international capital. Evidently, the Shah, in order to resolve the oil issue in a manner acceptable to his international guardians, needed effectively to silence the nationalist leaders and the Communists. Right after the coup, the political parties and organizations associated with the National Front—including the Iran party, the Iranian People's party, the Party of the Nation of Iran (Pan Iranism party), and the Toilers' party—were all disbanded and their publications discontinued. Members of the Front were either killed, imprisoned, exiled, or co-opted. The suppression of these parties was so pervasive that not only were the communication networks between party leaders and the rank and file broken down but also National Front leaders lost contact with each other. The Tudeh party was repressed with a much higher degree of intensity. After the coup an estimated 3,000 Tudeh militants were arrested. Many Communists were shot and murdered in prison; many professors and students were put in jail after being arrested at night. The organizational power of the Tudeh was effectively demolished when its units in the army were discovered in 1954 and over 500 officers were arrested.[7]

This interpretation is reinforced when one considers the U.S. role in protecting the Shah and assisting the construction of his repressive apparatus. Cottam has indicated that "From 1953 to 1963 Iran could be described not only as an American client state but as an American dependency. The regime required full protection against external aggressor as for its internal survival. Had American support been withdrawn, the regime would in all likelihood have been overthrown."[8] As early as 1957, the CIA and MOSSAD, the Israeli intelligence agency, assisted the Shah in forming a new intelligence organization—SAVAK.[9] It did not take long for SAVAK to become one of the most pervasive and feared secret police in the world.[10] SAVAK gradually expanded its networks, created through the Ministry of Labor an array of trade unions, and scrutinized anyone recruited into the university, the civil service, and large industrial plants.[11]

Nevertheless, brutal repression of dissent has always been a characteristic feature of all ruling despots in Iran. Why then should repression be entirely attributed to the dynamic of foreign economic infiltration in the postcoup period? The Shah's prime objective was to maintain national integration in a manner similar to his predecessors, but under a different historical condition. His father came to power to maintain security and order in the country with the assistance of not only the British but also the merchants, landowners, and the ulama who were fed up by the "chaotic" conditions of the postconstitutional period. And in the period that the nationalist leaders were included in the country's polity, national integration was less problematic, and centrifugal forces such as the Turkish and Kurdish autonomy movements were repressed at a relatively low cost. In the postcoup period these leaders were excluded from politics, and major political decision-making became increasingly concentrated in the hands of the Shah and a few of his close associates. Political process—parliamentary debates, newspaper editorials, political parties' platforms, and opinions of community leaders—gradually lost its relevance in affecting the course of decision-making. Politics became depoliticized. National integration was therefore maintained by brutal force.[12]

Iran's Alliance with the United States and Its Military Buildup

The menace of democracy and pluralism under Mosaddeq prompted the Shah to form an alliance with Great Britain and the United States for the protection of his despotic rule. The alliance was greatly reinforced by America's abandonment of its liberal internationalist ideology—partially as a result of the cold war but also by a host of other factors such as the economic crisis in Britain, the American debacle in Vietnam, and the crisis of the U.S. military industry. These factors began to operate simultaneously by the time the Nixon administration was inaugurated in 1969. In Britain, Prime Minister Harold Wilson, following the economic crisis and devaluation of the pound in 1967, had speeded up the withdrawal of British forces from east of Suez and the Persian Gulf; Washington thus regarded the ensuing "vacuum" as requiring either an American presence or the presence of a powerful ally. At the same time, as a result of American casualties and failure in Vietnam, the U.S. government was unwilling to commit itself directly to maintaining the stability of the region to ensure the flow of oil to the West.

Thus the Nixon administration developed a policy that became known as the "Nixon doctrine." The doctrine was based on the premise that the United States should undertake fewer commitments in world affairs and should assist local states in assuming responsibility for their own defense and that of their region. The United States was to supply arms rather than troops, equipping its reliable allies with large arsenals in crucial areas.[13] As the doctrine was explained in 1970 by David Packard, the Deputy Secretary of Defense: "The best hope of reducing our overseas involvements and expenditures lies in getting allies and friendly nations to do even more in their own defense. To realize that hope, however, requires that we must continue, if requested, to give or sell them the tools they need for this bigger load we are urging them to assume."[14]

The implementation of the Nixon doctrine was expedited by the American arms industry's declining orders from the Pentagon, which was expecting some relief through orders from other countries. Furthermore, in 1971 the U.S. foreign trade balance showed a deficit for the first time since 1893. The need for export was now far more urgent than ten years before (when Secretary of Defense Robert McNamara and Henry Kuss of the Pentagon had first unleashed the Pentagon's salesmen), and the aerospace slump and unemployment added to the problem. In the White House, Nixon discussed how to redress the trade balance and was pressed for both political and economic reasons to relax restrictions on arms sales. Just as the slump in railroad-building in the 1880s had led Edward Vickers and Andrew Carnegie into making guns, so the aerospace crisis of the late 1960s helped to encourage the government and defense companies to sell more weapons abroad.[15]

These political and economic factors provided a foundation for a new relationship between Iran and the United States, as Iran was seen as the power to assist in assuring the stability of the Persian Gulf. It was in this period that the American government articulated its so-called "twin pillar" policy, relying on Iran and Saudi Arabia in the Gulf region to help assure the flow of oil to the West. The new relationship was consummated by the State visit of President Nixon to Iran in May 1972. At that time, agreement was reached to sell Iran substantial quantities of sophisticated military equipment available in the U.S. inventory (excluding strategic weapons) and to provide technicians and advisers for the armed forces.[16]

The Arab-Israeli war and, more important, the quadrupling of oil prices in 1974 increased substantially the demand for arms by countries in the region, particularly Iran and Saudi Arabia. By the summer of 1974 the statistics were making the point: in one year the Pentagon had more than doubled its total foreign sales, from $3.9 billion in 1973 to $8.3 billion in 1974. The world arms trade was transformed beyond recognition.[17]

For the Shah, the Nixon doctrine was a welcome development. When the Senate Foreign Relations Committee published a well-documented report on the Iranian arms buildup, criticizing Nixon's policy in August 1976, the Shah subsequently responded that: "If you do not pursue a policy of standing by your friends who are spending their own money and are ready to spend their own blood, the alternative is nuclear holocaust or more Vietnams."[18]

Table 2.1 summarizes foreign military sales agreements and sales deliveries to Iran for the 1955–78 period. As this table indicates, it was after 1972 that Iran's huge arms buildup started. During 1955–78, Iran agreed to purchase military equipment worth about $21 billion but actually received only about $9 billions' worth of such equipment. It should be noted that sales worth $19 billion (or 92 percent of the total agreed purchases) and $8 billion (again, about 92 percent of the total arms delivered between 1955–78) actually took place during the 1973–78 period.

The militarization of the country was also reflected in the increase in both the size of the armed forces and the military budget. Between 1953 and 1978, the number of men in Iran's military increased from 200,000 to 410,000.[19] In the same period, defense expenditures rose from $67 million to $844 million—an increase of more than one thousand percent; between 1970 and 1977 it rose again by almost the same degree, to $9,400 million. In 1974, a year in which rising oil prices were reflected in a 141 percent increase over the previous year's expenditure, defense spending was 32 percent of the total budget allocations. While

TABLE 2.1
U.S. Military Sales to Iran, 1955–78 (in thousands)

Year	Foreign Military Sales Agreements	Foreign Military Sales Deliveries
1955–68	$ 505,414	$ 145,874
1969	235,821	94,881
1970	134,929	127,717
1971	363,884	75,566
1972	472,611	214,807
1973	2,171,355	248,391
1974	4,325,357	648,641
1975	2,447,140	1,006,131
1976	1,794,487	1,927,860
1977	5,713,769	2,433,050
1978	2,586,890	1,792,892
TOTAL (1955–78)	20,751,656	8,715,810

SOURCE: *Foreign Military Sales and Military Assistance Facts* (December 1978), U.S. Department of Defense, Security Assistance Agency.

this percentage declined somewhat after that, it was estimated that in 1973–78 planned defense expenditure amounted to 31 percent of total planned expenditures, or over 9 percent of GNP.[20] In addition, there is evidence that civilian accounts included sizable military allocations (e.g., approximately 70 percent of the "public housing" outlays during this period went for military construction) that could amount to an additional 3 to 5 percent of the central government's budget.[21] The high priority given to the military in government spending seriously drained state resources and contributed to its fiscal difficulties as well as to the intensification of the infrastructural bottleneck the economy was facing in the 1970s.

The Bureaucracy and the Weakness of Corporativist Structures

In the absence of any major alliance with politically weighty classes and groups, the expansion of bureaucracy became another mechanism for the state's control of civil society and the maintenance of national integration. Bureaucratic expansion was partly the result of the state's intervention in the economy. The weakness of the domestic bourgeoisie and the unwillingness of international capital in providing the infrastructural elements necessary for capitalist development and the accumulation of capital made state intervention a necessity. The state assumed responsibility for the construction of roads, harbors, airports, heavy industry, and the provision of a financial infrastructure (such as state-sponsored banks).[22]

State investments were concentrated mainly in the areas where both domestic and foreign investors were neither able nor willing to invest. These areas were communications and telecommunications, the construction of roads and airports, and services. But in industry and mines, the public sector made fewer investments than the private sector. Nevertheless, the shares of public investments in these areas began to increase in the 1960s and 1970s. According to table 2.2, during the Third Plan, of the R 66 billion invested, R 20 billion (30.3 percent) belonged to the public sector. For the Fourth Plan public investment reached R 125 billion (41.7 percent); and during the Fifth Plan, of the total R 556.4 billion invested, R 246.4 (44.3 percent) belonged to the public sector. The shares of private sector were 69.7, 58.3, and 55.7 percent for the Third, Fourth, and Fifth plans, respectively. However, despite

TABLE 2.2

Private, Public, and Total Investment in Industry and Mining from the Third to the Fifth Plans (in billion rials)

	Third Plan	Fourth Plan	Fifth Plan
Public investment	R 20 (30.3%)	R 125 (41.7%)	R 246.4 (44.3%)
Private investment	46 (69.7%)	175 (58.3%)	310.0 (55.7%)
TOTAL	66 (100.0%)	300 (100.0%)	556.7 (100.0%)
Ratio of public to private investment	0.43	0.71	0.79

SOURCE: Sazeman-i Barnameh (Plan Organization), *Barnameh-ye Panjom-i Omrani-ye Keshvar* [The Fifth Developmental Plan], 1352–1356/1973–1977. The ratios have been computed by author.

some talk about privatizing the economy and reducing the size of the public sector, the proportion of public investment to private investment began to increase from 0.43 in the Third Plan to 0.71 in the Fourth Plan, and finally to 0.79 in the Fifth Plan.

This massive state intervention in the economy resulted in bureaucratic expansion. The development plans of 1960 doubled the ranks of public employees from just under 310,000 in 1956 to over 630,000 in 1977.[23] In the towns, the state expanded to the point that it hired as many as one out of every two full-time employees.[24]

The growth of the bureaucracy, however, could not be solely explained by state intervention in the economy. The overexpansion of the bureaucracy was thought to be responsible for the failure of the government's projects.[25] For example, during the period of the Fifth Plan, "current expenditures were to average 18 percent of overall budget. This meant that from an early stage funds earmarked for capital investment were diverted into the day-to-day running of the government."[26] Political control was another important factor that caused the growth of the bureaucracy. The Shah used the bureaucracy for co-opting the members and leaders of opposition groups. Civil service positions were created and often handed out as political favors and rewards to opposition leaders for their conciliation and compromise with the regime. Furthermore, the Shah frequently resorted to the tactic of divide and rule to insure his control over the bureaucracy by creating new ministries and civil servant posts with overlapping responsibilities. "This overlapping of function," says Zonis,

is not restricted to the gathering of information vital to the survival of the regime. Similar practices exist elsewhere in the bureaucracy.

There is a Ministry of Economy and another for Development and Housing. Labor unions are the concern of the Ministry of Interior and the Ministry of Labor. Responsibility for the Literacy Corps is assigned to the armed forces and the Ministry of Education.[27]

The consequence was the growth of the bureaucracy to an unwieldy size. In 1953, when Mosaddeq was in power, there were eleven cabinet-level ministerial portfolios. In 1960, when Amini was the prime minister, there were sixteen, and in 1975, under the fourth term of the Hoveida premiership, there were twenty-seven.[28]

The expansion of the bureaucracy caused the decline of intermediate organizations such as guilds, *anjumans* (societies), the *dowreh* (circle), the local magnates, the *boneh* (traditional farming organizations), and other aspects of corporate life that had existed in Iran for centuries. These organizations often mediated relations between the state and civil society. To be sure, modern political parties and certain corporativist structures were created by the state in the following decades after the coup. However, the existing political parties did not have much relevance to the real source of political power. Following the ban on all political parties after the coup, the Shah created the Melliyun (Nationalists) and Mardom (People) parties, which were led by two of his most trusted men. Nevertheless, even the controlled electoral competition between the two official parties proved dangerous to the Shah's absolutism. From 1963 until 1975 (when a single-party system was established), the Shah therefore decided to support one major political party, the Iran Novin party, while a number of minor parties such as Melliyun, Mardom, and Khak va Khoon (Land and Blood) were also encouraged. These parties were at best legitimate but limited channels for political expression, mechanisms used to co-opt opposition leaders and, ultimately, to discredit them for participating in the system.[29]

Nor did the state-created corporativist organizations such as rural cooperatives and trade unions enjoy sufficient autonomy to play a meaningful intermediary role between the state and their constituents. As will be explained in the following chapters, the cooperative movements, which emerged as a result of the land reform of the 1960s, were discouraged by the state. Instead, the state began supporting the unpopular farm corporations and agribusiness, a policy that antagonized medium-sized and small farmers. Similarly, while the state created labor unions, these unions were not organized on a national or industrywide scale but were confined to the individual factory. They could not act as meaningful channels for the expression of workers' interests and grievances. Finally, of some consequence for the efficacy of the army during the revolutionary conjuncture of 1977–79 and the postrevolutionary period was the Shah's peculiar administration of the armed forces, which effectively discouraged any horizontal links among the top generals. This undermined the possible development of a corporativist structure within the army. As a consequence, the army began to resemble patrimonial armies that were, in Weber's words, "incapable of any action without the ruler and completely dependent upon him."[30]

The Monarchy-Centered Nationalist Discourse

Thus it appears that the expansion of the bureaucratic and repressive apparatus of the state expanded the gulf between the state and civil society. As the next chapter shows, the state's alliance with international capital antagonized the indigenous classes and helped determine the content of the revolutionary movement of 1977–79. The ideology of the state, in turn, expanded the gulf between the monarch and the society.

The traditional Iranian society was highly religious, and religion was the dominant, if not all-encompassing, medium for ideological thinking. Shi'i Islam constituted an important element in the state's ideological apparatus in the nineteenth century, and the ulama were an integral part of the country's traditional power structure.[31] However, by the turn of the century, modern ideas were penetrating the society through various channels such as travel, translations of modern philosophy, and technological and scientific works. The most important ideological elements in the Constitutional movement was the idea of political democracy.[32] The late nineteenth century also witnessed the growth of Islamic modernism, and a group of the ulama attempted to establish some sort of metaphysical bridge between Islam and modern ideas, and to reconcile Islamic political theory with the constitutional idea. The Constitutional Revolution of 1905–11 was partly produced by and resulted in the growth of secular discourse.

While the idea of democracy was suppressed by the advent and consolidation of the Pahlavi monarchy, secular ideology remained the dominant discourse both within the society and the state. The implementation of Reza Shah's modernization program resulted in an increasing dissociation of state ideology from religion. Although the ulama were instrumental in bringing Reza Shah to power, the official ideology of the new state began to glorify the pre-Islamic kingship and ancient history, overlooking the Islamic period.[33] Reza Shah's regime claimed to represent a revival of the Persian Empire, and at the same time propagated a chauvinist idea about the Arabs whose "barbarism" (*vahshigari Arab*) was blamed for the subsequent ills of Iran.[34] Thus nationalism—not Shi'ism—began to be identified with the nation. The concept of citizenship was substituted for religious allegiance, and discrimination based on religion and religious prosecutions were severely forbidden.[35]

The ideology of the state under Reza Shah and the dominant cultural trend within society by and large belonged to the same ideological universe, and the Shah's campaign against the ulama was reinforced by the anticlerical attitudes and secular orientations of the Iranian intellectuals.[36] However, after World War II, the nationalistic feelings and secularism of these intellectuals were organized in the National Front under the leadership of Mosaddeq. The preemption of the idea of nationalism from the monarchy and the association of the latter with foreign interests during the oil nationalization period were causing serious ideological problems for the second Shah of Pahlavi. What further cast doubt on the nationalism of the second Shah was that his rule was established through the direct assistance of the United States and Great Britain.

Following the coup, the state discourse was directed toward responding to the ideologies of the opposition, national-liberalism and Communism. It attempted to appropriate the idea of nationalism from the first and revolution from the second. Then it took on an increasingly anti-Islamic character and at the same time drifted in a totalitarian direction. In response to Mosaddeq's ideology of negative nationalism, the Shah began to portray his nationalism as "positive"—that is, "a policy of maximum political and economic independence consistent with the interests of one's country."[37] Mosaddeq's nationalism, in contrast, was labeled "destructive" and "pro-Communist." Nevertheless, the idea of "positive nationalism" was too weak to provide a strong defense of the monarchy vis-à-vis the critique of the leaders of the National Front, the Communists, and the ulama. The launching of land reform in the early 1960s changed the course of the ideological disputes to the Shah's advantage, placed the Communists and the nationalists on the defensive,[38] and caused a strong reaction among the ulama.

At this point, the Shah began to portray himself as the champion for revolutionary change. As the Shah proclaimed: "Iran needs a deep and fundamental revolution that could, at the same time, put an end to all the social inequality and exploitation, and all aspects of reaction which impeded progress and kept our society backward."[39] From this period, the Shah associated his rule with the idea of progress, civilization, and equality. These reforms provided a basis for the Shah's ideological campaign against his opposition. Pointing to the ulama-led disturbances of 1963, the Shah frequently used the term "black reaction" (referring to the ulama), and "the red forces of destruction" (referring to the Communists), who combined to paralyze his action.[40] The Shah's ideologues were claiming that the ship of state was steering a proper course, navigated by an experienced captain capable of guiding it through the stormy waters of social change to the threshold of a "Great Civilization."[41] To provide his "revolution" with a sense of continuity, the Shah was periodically adding other principles to what he called "the Shah-People's Revolution." The number of such principles increased from six in 1963 to seventeen in 1975.[42]

To propagate the monarchy-centered national mythology further, the Islamic calendar was changed into a civil calendar, and then into a monarchical calendar, whose beginning was the time when the first system of monarchy was established in Iran. In 1971, the Shah celebrated the 2,500th anniversary of continuous monarchy. This celebration was to establish a historical continuity between the political past and the present. In his interview with Oriana Fallaci, the Shah stated:

> When there's no monarchy, there's anarchy, or an oligarchy or a dictatorship. Besides, a monarchy is the only possible means to govern Iran. If I have been able to do something, a lot, in fact, for Iran it is owing to the detail, slight as it may seem, that I'm its king. To get things done, one needs power, and to hold on to power one mustn't ask anyone's permission or advice. One mustn't discuss decisions with anyone.[43]

Moreover, the importance of religious holidays was downplayed, while new holidays were added to the calendar such as the Shah's and the Shah's son's birthdays, and the date of the implementation of land reform. The state discourse became totalitarianism proper when in 1975 the Shah abruptly dissolved all the "official" political parties and declared that the country now had a one-party system,[44] the Rastakhiz party. "One country, one Shah, and now one party" became the regime's new slogan.[45] The Shah was demanding a total ideological commitment to his rule:

> Iranians had the choice of supporting or rejecting the three basic principles of Monarchy, Constitution, and the White Revolution. Supporters now would join the Rastakhiz party to consolidate and promote these objectives. Opponents could either remain apathetic and be non-participants (in which case they would be denied the fruits of Iran's prosperity); or if they wished to actively oppose these principles, they would be allowed to leave the country.[46]

In principle, there was little difference in the state's ideology under the two shahs, even though the second shah had stretched the monarchy-centered nationalist discourse to its logical extreme. The opposition movement under Reza Shah did not develop into a revolutionary crisis despite the collapse of his authority and the intensification of social and political conflict because its discourse was similar to the Shah's save for his dictatorship. Under his son, the dominant discourse of the opposition was different. The postcoup social critics began to resort to Islam in their attempt to address Iran's problems. The more the Shah insisted on his secular antireligious ideology, the less he was applauded by his critics; and the more his discourse excluded civil society, the more explicit became the domination of his regime over society. However, the question of why Islam became the dominant discourse of the opposition movement requires a basic understanding of the content of the Shah's economic policies and their impact on class politics, and how that led to the decline of secular oppositional ideologies.

3
The State and the Patterning of Class Conflict

While various features of the state contributed to the form of the revolutionary movement of 1977–79, the state's strategy for economic development affected the distribution of wealth, patterned class conflict, and, therefore, determined its content. The main beneficiaries of economic development in the 1960s and 1970s were international capital and the dependent bourgeoisie who, behind the protective shield of the state, were able to dominate the economy and reap substantial profit. The petty bourgeoisie, the merchants, and landowners were antagonized by state economic policies. Industrial development, state policies of various sorts (such as the licensing system), credit allocation, and the establishment of farm corporations and agribusiness undermined the interests of these classes. Consequently, the dependent bourgeoisie and international capital faced the opposition of the indigenous social classes on two levels. On the market level, their increasing dominance over the national market provoked the hostility of the petty bourgeoisie, the merchants, and the landowners. On the production level, the process of capitalist development and the economic difficulties in the mid- to late 1970s brought about capital and labor conflict. These overlapping conflicts underlay the revolutionary conjuncture of 1977–79.

Economic Development

With the state's extensive intervention in the economy, Iran experienced a period of fast capitalist development characterized by the general processes of (1) separation of producers from the means of production, (2) "freedom" of the laborer from precapitalist relationships, and (3) creation of a national market tied to the world market. To be sure, these processes were set in motion as early as the nineteenth century. Nevertheless, it was during the postcoup period that "feudalist" relationships were eliminated and capitalism became the dominant mode of production. Two periods marked the postcoup economic development. The first was from 1953 to 1963, during which international capital began to infiltrate different sectors of the economy, the financial infrastructures for investment were laid, and many large-scale and long-gestation projects were initiated and implemented by the Plan Organization (PO). The second period began with the implementation of a land reform program in 1963 and ended with the revolutionary crisis of 1977–79. In the second phase, Iran experienced remarkable economic growth as measured by conventional indicators. This period was characterized by what Evans describes as "dependent development."[1]

Iran's economic growth during the period covering the Fourth Plan (1968–72) was exceptionally good, amounting to 11.6 percent (higher than the original 9 percent target). With the exception of agriculture and construction, all the sectoral value-added targets were either attained or surpassed. Agriculture had the lowest growth rate, at 3.9 percent per annum; oil and services achieved the highest rates, at 15.2 and 14.2 percent, respectively, with the services growth rate almost twice the planned rate (mainly due to the rapid expansion of government services). Industry grew at an average annual rate of 14 percent in real terms. Moreover, the employment targets were also overachieved, with actual employment increasing by 1.2 million versus the target of only 966,000. Agricultural employment, however, declined by 202,000 compared with a planned increase of 226,000. On the other hand, industrial employment increased more than its planned target (737,000 actual new jobs as against the planned figure of 417,000). Perhaps most significant, employment in the service sector increased by 720,000 or 60 percent of the total increase in employment during the period.[2] The Fifth Plan began in 1973 and was completed at the end of 1977. During this period, the economy grew at a rate faster than that of the Fourth Plan. However, the Fifth Plan did not achieve its projected goals (see table 3.1).

The process of dependent development changed the country's class profile. In alliance with the state, international capital gained a domi-

TABLE 3.1
Economic Growth During the Fifth Plan (in percent)

	Projected	Actual
Gross national income*	25.9	17.0
Non-oil dometic product	15.0	13.3
Value-added in the oil group*	51.5	25.9
Value-added in agricultural group	7.0	4.6
Value-added in industrial group	18.0	15.5
Value-added in service group	16.4	15.3

SOURCE: Bank Markazi Iran (BMI), *Annual Report and Balance Sheet* (1978) p. 15.
  *Including the compensation for valuation of the terms of trade.

nant position over the key sectors of the economy. A dependent bourgeoisie also emerged that was closely tied to, and dominated by, international capital. Consisting of about one thousand families, these included the royal family, the owners of private banks and modern commercial centers, industrialists, and those involved in the agribusiness. These people owned not only many of the large commercial farms but also some 85 percent of the major private firms involved in banking, manufacturing, foreign trade, insurance, and urban construction. The indigenous property-owning classes were the petty bourgeoisie (craftsmen and retailers), merchants, and "feudal" landowners. The merchants, craftsmen, and retailers were mainly (but not exclusively) organized in the bazaar, which had been the commercial focus of the city and its hinterland. Despite its relative decline under the Shah, the bazaar managed to control a third of imports and two-thirds of retail trade. These classes are estimated to number nearly 1 million families.

The feudal class's position was destroyed in the land reform of the 1960s. In its place, a capitalist landowning class emerged in the postreform period. On the eve of the revolution, agricultural holdings were divided into three categories. The first comprised large, medium, and small agricultural holdings, with 5 to 6 million hectares of fertile land in the control of just over 100,000 people. The second was composed of a small group of rich peasants and small rural capitalists who had considerable influence in their own villages. Finally, the third category consisted of 1.5 million small holdings, or landless peasants. The landowners had long had close ties with the merchants and the real estate owners in the urban areas. These groups plus rich farmers constituted the rural bourgeoisie. The new middle class and the working class grew as a result of the country's industrial development and the expansion of the state bureaucracy. The new middle class, consisting of civil servants, teachers and school administrators, engineers, managers, and while-collar workers, was estimated to number 1.8 million in 1977. The working class, consisting of wage earners employed in different industrial sectors, grew rapidly as a result of the economic development of the 1960s and 1970s. In 1977, the size of the industrial work force was estimated at 2.5 million.[3]

The penetration of the Iranian economy by international capital resulted in a change in the structure of its domestic production toward not only an increasingly concentration in external trade but also in the production of oil, the most profitable commodity. This led to the development of an "export enclave" economy characterized by uneven development between international and domestic production, and sectoral disarticulation.[4] Intersectoral disarticulation was characterized by a lack of backward and forward linkages between different sectors of the economy, and intrasectoral disarticulation by a lack of such linkages within each of the main sectors of the economy—agriculture and industry. Small-scale production, dominated by the traditional sector, did not have significant backward and forward linkages with the large-scale state-promoted monopoly sector, the so-called modern sector. The modern sector was vertically integrated with international capital and dominated by the latter. The state's strong support of the modern sector was undermining the traditional sector. Because domestic production was concentrated in exports, both downward and upward movements in export markets generated dislocations in investment, employment, and industrial demand. Iran's economic difficulties in the 1970s, which triggered political conflict, was partly the result of its vulnerability to the destabilizing effects of the world economy.

The state-guided dependent development was shaped by the monarchy-centered nationalist discourse. The state's support of the dependent bourgeoisie, while undermining the interests of the merchants, cannot be explained entirely by the dynamic of its interests. From the viewpoint of economic relations, there was little difference between the merchants and dependent bourgeoisie. What made the difference was that the two classes were constituted by two distinct ideological universes. The members of the dependent bourgeoisie were staunch supporters of the monarchy-centered nationalist discourse, strongly pro-West, and highly critical of the traditional Iranian lifestyle. The merchants, in contrast, were religious and tied to the clerical establishments. Therefore, the fact that the Shah as well as the technocrats, who managed the economy, boldly disregarded the traditional interests and local conditions and began replicating American models in various fields does not transform them into agents of imperialism. The state, acting within the parameters of its own discourse, was biased against the merchants and distrusted the bazaaris as a whole. But there was nothing in the alliance between the state and international capital that prevented the inclusion of the merchants or, in O'Donnell's words, to convert "the duo into a ménage à trios"[5]

This chapter discusses the alliance between the state and international capital, their domination over the key sectors of the economy (agriculture, banking, and industry), and Iran's vulnerability to fluctuations in the world economy. The next chapter will then discuss the impact of dependent development on the indigenous classes.

Agriculture

The Iranian Revolution was urban-based and the peasantry were by and large bystanders. The removal of power from the landowning class was a major political consequence of the state's agrarian policies. Nevertheless, the state failed to maintain its rural popular basis that land reform had generated. The infiltration of international capital in this sector and the state's bias in favor of farm corporations and agribusiness eroded the peasants' active support for the Shah and antagonized the landowners. Moreover, population growth added to the country's agrarian problems. Although the area under cultivation expanded, the agricultural sector was unable to provide the country with self-sufficiency in food, and in the 1970s food shortages were a factor causing considerable dissatisfaction in society.

International Capital and Agrarian Change

On June 1, 1955, the Development and Resource Corporation (D&R) was founded as a joint venture between David E. Lilienthal, the former chairperson of the Tennessee Valley Authority (TVA) and the Atomic Energy Commission (AEC), and Andre Meyer, the senior partner of the banking house of Lazard Freres and Company. This corporation played a crucial role in structuring Iran's agricultural development. The

D&R's underpinning developmental rationale, which later became the unarticulated ideology of the state, was:

> Public initiative and public financing of such facilities as dams, highways, ports, etc. (as well as agricultural education, public health and sanitation measures, etc.), constitute the first wave of development, and essential precondition of economic progress for many countries and regions in the earlier stages of their economic development.
>
> Public development schemes that are practical, and bring the best result to the people themselves are those that provide a basis, or opportunities, under which private business undertakings have a good prospect of success. Unless there is this development of private business, virtually contemporaneously with the first wave of public activity, expenditures for development works are largely wasted.In most of the so-called underdeveloped countries . . . there is an absence of business imagination, character, and creative financial judgment and experience. To aid in bringing such talents, as well as capital, to private development needs and opportunities of such a country is an integral part of the problem of aiding in the economic and social advance of such a country.[6]

In the same year, Abol-Hasan Ebtihaj, head of the PO, invited Lilienthal to Tehran to examine the possibility of establishing a unified regional development scheme similar to the TVA in Khuzistan, Iran's southwest province. After visiting Khuzistan, Lilienthal was convinced that "the Khuzistan region presented the essential elements of a very important regional development."[7] A few days after the informal establishment of D&R, but before Lazard's Wall Street lawyers had even begun to draw up the articles of incorporation, Lilienthal gave World Bank president Eugene Black "a copy of a memo describing the new venture."[8] Black, wrote Lilienthal, "could not have been more pleased and cooperative," and "welcomed the idea, thought it was sound."[9]

But Meyer did not like the idea and told Lilienthal that Lazard was "not going to invest any money in that country."[10] However, he was told by a World Bank man that "it was an interesting part of this particular 'underdeveloped country' that they didn't need money; they had lots of it, lots of it for this development program, $180,000,000 next year, $100,000,000 the next year, and so on. What they needed is management; but how can they get that."[11] Convinced, Meyer acknowledged that the thing about this new venture . . . is that it is real, it deals with real things; and out of such a close knowledge of a country real business opportunities may appear. That is the original part of the Lilienthal idea, bringing the foreign investment picture into intimate and realistic touch with a country, with the local people who can be depended upon.[12]

At any rate, in March 1956, Lilienthal and Gordon R. Clapp, on behalf of D&R, signed the first series of contracts with the Iranian government. By 1959, D&R had won the approval of a plan for the unified development of the natural resources of the Khuzistan region. It called for the construction of fourteen dams, 6,600 megawatts of power production, and hundreds of miles of canals to irrigate an eventual 2.5 million acres—a multibillion-dollar undertaking that was to take many years to complete.[13]

While the dam, powerhouse, and canals specified in the first project were being constructed on the Dez River, the D&R's experts sought a quick showpiece that would convince prospective investors regarding the profitability of large-scale farming and food processing (or "agribusiness") in the province.[14] They found their showpiece in sugar cane. D&R started a cane plantation near Haft Tapeh, north of Ahwaz, and subcontracted with the Brewer Company of Hawaii to manage it.[15] In 1963, two years after its operation had begun, Lilienthal indicated:

> The plantation of Haft Tapeh is already an operating unit, with the necessary common mechanical units, common housing, common technical services. In short, it is about where some of the land reform activities now being gestated will be after a generation of what I hope will be something quite new, i.e., peasant farm corporations.[16]

Three years later, the establishment of farm corporations and agribusiness became the state's official agrarian policy, as the Shah began talking about his unique solution to Iran's agrarian problem.

The Land Reform

The state's alliance with international capital was the context within which the land reform of the early 1960s was implemented and thus structured the country's agrarian development in subsequent years.

Iran had remained primarily an agrarian society under Reza Shah, and the "feudal" landowners were among the most powerful classes in the country. Reza Shah himself was the guardian of the landowning class, ending all talk of land reform, transferring the agricultural tax from the shoulders of the landowners to those of the peasant cultivators, changing the rural custom in favor of the landlords, and rewarding reliable aristocrats with high positions in the Majles (the parliament), the cabinet, the diplomatic corps, and the newly established state enterprises.[17] And when Mosaddeq began to implement certain measures in favor of the peasants, the landowners in response threw their support behind the Shah in the coup of 1953.

Table 3.2 shows the concentration of landed property prior to the land reform. According to this table, 65 percent of the lands were owned by large landlords as compared to 15 percent owned by the peasants. The amount of land controlled by religious institutions was 15 percent of the total, while the state lands and crown estates combined made up 5 percent. According to a government estimate, between 400 and 450 large landlords owned 57 percent of all the Iranian villages.[18] Some of this group were reported to have owned as many as 300 villages. It has been estimated that thirty-seven families alone owned 19,000 villages (i.e., around 38 percent of the total), while another group of landlords, those having from one to five villages, altogether owned roughly 7,000 villages (or about 14 percent of the total).

The continued dominance of the landowning class in the rural areas was not in the Shah's interests, and his chief objective in emancipating the peasants was to stabilize the kingdom. Such a reform was highly overdue considering the economic difficulties of the late 1950s and ear-

TABLE 3.2
Land Ownership Prior to Land Reform

	Number of Villages	Total Area (in hectares)	Percent
Large private estates	32,500	10,400	65
Peasant ownership	7,500	2,400	15
Endowed land owned by religious institutions	7,500	2,400	15
State lands and crown estates	2,500	800	5
TOTAL	50,000	16,000	100

SOURCE: Bahman Nirumand, *Iran: The New Imperialism in Action* (New York: Monthly Review Press, 1967), p. 126. Copyright © 1967 Monthly Review, Inc. Reprinted by permission of Monthly Review Foundation.

ly 1960s and the possibility of a peasant-based revolutionary movement. The latter factor was also the principal U.S. concern in pressuring the Shah to implement land reform.[19] However, the long-term effects of the reform for the stability of the regime remained precarious. Social tensions subsided in the countryside, but was intensified in the urban area.

Nevertheless, the fact that less than two decades later a major revolution occurred does not mean that the reform was a bad idea for the regime's stability. The reform failed, first, because it was incomplete. Not very many peasants received lands. According to the official figures, for the first phase of the land reform between 13,000 and 14,000 villages out of a total of 49,000 villages were distributed.[20] But government statistics remained suspect because "they include many-fold counting."[21] The land reform did not affect the landless peasants, consisting of sharecroppers with only their labor to sell, laborers with regular wages, and casual laborers. This group constituted from 40 to 50 percent in the villages. Only 14 to 16 percent of the villages were distributed by mid-1964, at which time the first phase of the reform was declared complete. Therefore, it is estimated that about 8 percent of the peasants received land in the first phase. In the second phase, based on official figures, it is estimated that another 6 to 7 percent of the total peasant population received at least some land, making a grand total of perhaps 14 to 15 percent of the peasants who became new landholders.[22]

Second, the Shah even failed to form a solid alliance with the newly liberated peasant farmers. His liberal agricultural minister, Hasan Arsanjani, was trying hard to create a class of independent small-scale farmers tied to the government through the newly established rural cooperatives. By the end of 1962, Arsanjani reported that 500,000 hectares of land had been distributed among 35,000 peasant families and 1,080 cooperatives had been formed. Arsanjani made a further move to solidify these cooperatives by organizing the Congress of Rural Cooperatives in early 1963. Some 4,700 delegates gathered in Tehran and, after days of speech-making and meetings, unanimously passed several resolutions that included the farmers' commitment to give their last breath to the protection of the constitutional monarchy, a demand that the government should observe the UN charter on human rights, a call for the unity of the farmers and the rural cooperatives, the unanimous approval of the six laws offered in the referendum by His Imperial Majesty, and an appreciation of Arsanjani for his selfless efforts and sacrifice.[23]

But Arsanjani's liberalism did not go very well with the Shah's despotic style. Had the Shah supported the rural cooperatives, his regime in all likelihood would have been more stable. Pressures from conservative groups and the 1963 disturbances resulted in a considerable "deradicalization" of the land reform program. Moreover, support of the rural cooperatives and the protection of peasant farmers were not the state's prereform nor, as later became evident, its postreform agricultural objectives. The agricultural policies pursued by the state were directed toward establishing and expanding farm corporations and agribusinesses, and it was overlooking the interests of small and medium-sized landowners, if not acting contrary to their interests. Soon Arsanjani was dismissed and given a new appointment as Iran's ambassador to Italy.

With the dismissal of Arsanjani, the government's agricultural policy changed toward supporting large-scale farming and agribusiness tied to international capital.[24] In 1967, legislation on farm corporations was passed, giving the Ministry of Land Reform and Rural Cooperation permission to initiate a five-year experiment with farm corporations. Under the 1967 act, corporations were to be formed, provided that 51 percent of the owners gave their consent. In order to break resistance to the establishment of the corporations and to tighten up the original 1967 provision, a bill enacted in 1975 stated that holdings belonging to those farmers who refused or were unable to join the farm corporations being set up on their lands were to be expropriated and that all lands so taken over were to be placed under the control of the Regional Agricultural Development Organization. Consequently, the number of farm corporations increased considerably. In 1968 there had been fifteen farm corporations with about 24,000 shareholders. By 1976 these figures increased to eighty-nine corporations with 186,000 shareholders.[25]

Peasants received shares in the farm corporations in proportion to the amount of land and property each had placed at the disposition of the enterprise. But each shareholder had only one vote, regardless of the number of shares owned. This voting procedure solidified the state's control of these corporations. On one hand, large shareholders could not affect the decisions of the corporation, and on the other hand, small shareholders could be easily persuaded by the state-appointed manager to vote according to the latter's desires.[26] Thus while farmers owned the corporations, they remained under the control of the state.

The state's objective was also directed toward a creation of large shareholders in the farm corporations. The law concerning the creation of farm corporations indicated that "it is hoped that the holding of each shareholder will be no less than 50 acres of irrigated land, or 100 acres of non-irrigated land."[27] Since the average holding of farmers was in fact less than five acres, every possible means was used to induce the small shareholder to leave. The latter had no alternative but to give up his share to those who remained and to join the ranks of the proletariat.[28]

With land reform removing the resistance of the landowners to the state's agricultural policies and the state's consolidation of its power in the rural areas, no obstacle was left for the further deepening of capitalist development and the involvement of international capital in the agricultural sector.[29] In the Fourth Plan (1968–73), the main emphasis was placed on the creation of large mechanized farming and animal husbandry units. The basic rationale was that small-scale farming by peasants was inefficient. In 1968 the government decided to dispossess the peasants working on some 250,000 preselected acres, "bought out" the peasants in the fifty-eight villages affected, and handed the land over to shareholders in the following domestic and foreign firms: Hashem Naraghi Agro-Industries of Iran and America (20,000 hectares), the Iran-California Corporation (10,000 hectares), Iran Shellcott Company (15,000 hectares), International Agricultural Corporation of Iran (17,000 hectares), Deskar (5,000 hectares), and Dez Farm Corporation (17,000 hectares).[30]

Agribusiness, farm corporations, and other large-scale projects took the lion's share of the government budget allocated for the agricultural sector. Almost all the allocation of the Second and Third plans went for the construction of three dams and other large-scale projects. The largest proportion of the Fourth Plan's agricultural budget ($143 million out of $880 million) was allocated for the establishment of thirty-four agricultural units.[31] Besides the 84,000 hectares devoted to agribusiness, the revised Fifth Plan provided for the allocation of 300,000 hectares of the best irrigated land for such establishments.[32]

Consequently, the number of peasant families possessing lands declined from the mid-1960s. Under phase two of the land reform, about 57,000 peasant households had to sell their lands to the landlords under the provisions of that stage: over half of those were in an area controlled by the powerful Alam family (Asadullah Alam was the prime minister and then the Court's minister). Then, in the transition between phases two and three, another 592,000 families seem to have failed to convert their tenancies into ownership; most of these must have been forced into the proletariat.[33]

The modern agricultural units did not contribute significantly to agricultural production. According to table 3.3, 87.8 percent of the national prerent surplus is contributed by traditional families, while the contribution of modern large-scale farming was 12.2 percent. The share of farm corporations and agribusiness was only 2.4 percent. Considering that 87.8 percent of surpluses coming from the traditional farms was based on the traditional irrigation system, one may conclude that the state's construction of dams had had limited impact on agricultural production. Despite these figures, traditional farmers received little support from the state. Table 3.4 summarizes different sources of credit for Iranian farmers. According to this table, state institutions accounted for 31 percent, commercial banks 20 percent, and noninstitutional sources 49.2 percent of the total agricultural credit. This means that almost 50 percent of the credit was provided by middlemen and private money lenders, who usually charged the cultivators high interest rates. Thus, although during the initial phase of land reform the state attempted to expand its bases of support in the countryside, its agricultural policies after land reform was not favorable to the peasants or to small and medium-sized landowners.

The main beneficiaries of state agricultural policies, on the other

TABLE 3.3
*Contribution to National Prerent Surplus
by Different Farm Units*

Units	Rials (million)	Percent
Traditional	R97,395	87.8
Small*	(47,182)	(42.6)
Medium*	(50,213)	(45.2)
Modern and large	13,462	12.2
Partially and fully irrigated	(10,837)	(9.8)
Corporations and agribusiness	(2,625)	(2.4)
TOTAL	100,857	100.0

SOURCE: Farhad Rezazadeh, "Agricultural Development in Iran: Evaluation of State Planning and Policies in Relation to Agriculture" (Ph.D diss., Iowa State University, 1979), p. 78. Reprinted by permission of Farhad Rezazadeh.

*This includes traditional rainfed, partial, and full irrigation.

TABLE 3.4
Sources of Agricultural Credits for Farmers

Source	Credit (in billions of rials)	Percent
State institutions	R 20.5	31.0
Commercial banks	13.2	20.0
Noninstitutional credit	32.3	49.2
TOTAL	66.0	100.0

SOURCE: Rezazadeh, "Agricultural Development in Iran," p. 92. Reprinted by permission of Farhad Rezazadeh.

hand, were the state bureaucrats, who expanded their control over the rural areas. There were also large international companies such as D&R which benefited substantially from their contracts with the Iranian government, and finally, the managing directors of the agribusinesses and the technocrats of KWPA and those involved in the large-scale projects.[34]

The general performance of the agricultural sector was not remarkable. From 1959 to 1972 the agricultural output improved at an official rate barely superior to the rate of increase in the population: 3.4 percent as against 3 percent. The main beneficiaries of mechanization were not basic food products but industrial crops like cotton, fodder, citrus fruits, sugar cane, and sugar beets. During this period wheat production increased no more than 1 percent per year while barley and wool decreased; milk and red meat increased by only 1 percent and 3 percent per year, respectively. All had a lower growth rate than that of the population, whose consumption needs rose from 10 to 20 percent annually, varying with product. The failure of the agricultural sector to cover the nutritional needs of the country led to an unprecedented dependence on food imports. By the mid-1970s Iran became the leading importer of food and agricultural products in the Middle East. The importation of food during this period was increasing at a rate of 14 percent per annum.[35] The government had to allocate a considerable amount of funds for food subsidies, which drained much of its revenues and contributed significantly to its fiscal problems. The substantial increase in food prices in the world market in the early 1970s, and a decrease in state revenue due to a drop in international demands for oil, reduced the state's financial power to subsidize food imports. The result was a food scarcity in the mid-1970s that contributed to the spread of social discontent.

Industry and Industrial Finance

The state's other major initiative was a remarkable effort to industrialize the country in a short period of time. Iran's industrial development followed a pattern similar to the agrarian changes, promoting a capital-intensive industry designed to produce consumer goods for the upper middle and high-income groups. These policies strongly favored large and modern industrial establishments and ignored the traditional sector and small-scale manufacturers. The high capital-intensive industrialization program did not utilize Iran's large labor surplus.

Similar to the agricultural sector, the basis and framework for industrial development were laid down during the 1953–63 period.[36] These included certain measures taken by the state to encourage, facilitate, and direct the country's industrial development. The first of these measures was the formation of a legal framework for the protection of foreign and domestic capital. In 1955 the "Law Concerning the Attraction and Protection of Foreign Capital Investment in Iran" was enacted, in which Article 3 provided that "should any capital be expropriated in accordance with specific legislation, the Government guarantees equitable compensation for the loss." In addition, investment guarantee agreements with the United States (1957) and Germany (1961) went even further than simple expressions of government goodwill.[37]

The second measure was the provision of physical infrastructures such as the construction of roads, ports, and airports as well as the establishment of heavy industries. The third was the state's provision of financial infrastructures with the objective of providing capital for financing industrial projects. This latter factor was crucial in determining the direction of industrial development in Iran. The lending institutions had strong leverages through their priority classifications and loan policies to orient the country's industrial development. Banks and financial institutions established between 1953 and 1963 provided a framework for industrial development and functioned as the main channel through which foreign capital infiltrated Iran's industry.

International Finance Capital and Industrial Development

Foreign finance capital began to infiltrate Iran's economy as early as 1872, when a concession granted rights of banking, note issues, and mining (except for precious stones and metals) to Baron Julius de Reuter. In 1888 a branch of the New Oriental Banking Corporation (with headquarters in London) opened offices in several cities in Iran. Reuter established the Imperial Bank of Iran with a capital of £1,000,000 in 1889.[38] In 1891, Banque des Prêts with a capital of 1,875,000 gold rubles was founded. In 1899 it became a branch of the Russian state bank. In 1902 its name changed to Banque d'Escompte de Perse. During 1921–23 the British-owned Ottoman Bank opened its branches in Iran. This was followed by the establishment of the Banque Russo-Persane in 1924.[39]

These financial institutions, however, did not have much impact on Iran's industrial development. Nor were they interested in providing financial resources for industrial projects. When the Bank Melli Iran was established in 1927, the roles of the Imperial Bank of Iran and the Banque d'Escompte de Perse gradually declined, and the former's monopoly of note issuing was bought up by the Bank Melli Iran. In sum, prior to the coup, the history of industrial finance in Iran consisted of almost exclusively short-term advances by banks and money lenders. There was no systematic program for long-term industrial lending until the Industrial Credit Bank (ICB) was initiated by the PO in 1955. The following year saw the establishment of the government's Revaluation Loan Fund (RLF), administered jointly by Bank Melli and the Ministry of Industry and Mines.

The active intervention of international finance capital in the country's banking system and hence in industrial finance began in 1959 when the Industrial and Mining Development Bank of Iran (IMDBI), under the sponsorship of the International Bank of Reconstruction and Development (IBRD) and a foreign consortium, was established. IMDBI was a replication of private financing experiments that had been launched under IBRD auspices in neighboring Pakistan, Turkey, and India. The proposal that eventually led to IMDBI originated at the San Francisco International Industrial Development Conference in October 1957, where Ebtihaj discussed the subject with Andre Meyer of Lazard Freres. IBRD entered the plan at an early stage. At the same time, a syndicate of U.S. and West European financial institutions and industrial companies began to crystallize under the leadership of Lazard and the Chase International Investment Corporation.[40]

Of an initial capital of $42.4 million, equity totaling $5.3 million was divided 60–40 between local and foreign investors; IBRD and the Development Loan Fund (DLF) each provided $5.2 million in foreign-exchange loans, and the Iranian government contributed an $8 million interest-free cash advance plus $18.7 million in RLF and ICB loan port-folios, managed by the new bank for an agency fee. Apart from $734,000 invested by American interests, banking interests from Britain, France, Germany, and Italy each subscribed $250,000, while the Netherlands and Belgium accounted for $200,000 each.[41]

On the question of ownership, it was decided to charter IMDBI with 60 percent of initial equity—240,000 shares at $3.2 million—designated as Class A, to be completely subscribed by Iranian nationals. Class A was always to constitute %60 of IMDBI stock and could not be sold or transferred to foreigners. The Lazard-Chase group was allotted 160,000 Class B shares at $2.1 million. As was originally planned, however, the syndicate retained actual control of IMDBI's Board of Directors and Executive Committee (the ultimate loan approval authority) for the first five years.[42] In the following years, the percentage of shares held by the foreign syndicate was reduced from 40 to 20, and then to 15.3 percent. Nevertheless, the absolute volume of the foreign capital actually increased. In 1959 the total value of the shares belonging to these banks amounted to more than $2 million, while in 1977 this amount increased to over $244 million.[43]

Besides their direct control over the Board of Directors and Executive Committee of IMDBI (for the first five years), the dominant position of international finance was further ensured through their loan policies. In 1966, IMDBI received $2.16 million in loans and credits from the PO, $11.76 million from IBRD, and $2.45 million from the Agency for International Development (AID). In early 1975 the total amount of loans received by the bank was increased to $473.68 million. Of this amount, $22.16 million was from the sale of stocks abroad, $171.67 million from the PO and the Ministry of Industry and Mines, $123.65 million from IBRD, $0.31 million from AID, and $155.90 million from other foreign banks. In other words, within a period of less than ten years the amount of long-term loans received by IMDBI increased by a factor of twenty-two.[44] These figures indicate that, first, IMDBI was active in Iran's industrial development, and second, that international banks and financial institutions were the major sources of finance for IMDBI. Such a dependence on international finance capital had naturally enabled the latter to exert considerable control over the bank's industrial policies.[45]

The dominant position of international financial capital was further expanded through its participation in a number of other specialized

TABLE 3.5

Major Commercial and Specialized Banks with Foreign Ownership
in 1975 (ranked according to the date of establishment)

Commercial/Specialized Banks	Date of Estab.	Percent Ownership	
		Iranian	Foreign
Russo-Iran Bank (State Bank of USSR)	1924	—	100
Bank of Tehran (Paribas International, Paris)	1957	65	35
Bank Etebarat Iran (Credit Lyonnais, Paris)	1958	60	40
Foreign Trade Bank of Iran (Bank of America)	1958	60	40
Irano British Bank (The Standard & Chartered Banking Group, London)	1958	60	40
Mercantile Bank of Iran and Holland (Algemene Bank Netherlands, NV)	1959	65	35
The Bank of Iran and the Middle East (The British Bank of the Middle East)	1959	60	40
The International Bank of Iran and Japan (Bank of Tokyo)	1959	65	35
Industrial and Mining Development Bank of Iran (IMDBI)	1959	85	15
Iranian Bank (Citibank, New York, N.Y.)	1959	65	35
Development and Investment Bank of Iran	1973	78	22
Bank Dariush (Continental Bank of Chicago)	1974	65	35
International Bank of Iran (Chase Manhattan)	1975	65	35
Irano-Arab Bank	1975	66	33

SOURCE: U.S. Department of Commerce, *Iran: A Survey of Business Opportunities* (October 1977), table 2, p. 149.

and commercial banks. Table 3.5 summarizes the major commercial and specialized banks with mixed foreign and domestic ownership. According to this table, nine out of fourteen (or 64 percent) of these banks were established between 1957 and 1959. If one disregards the Russo-Iran Bank, which had no significant role in the Iranian economy, this figure would increase to 69 percent,[46] supporting the claim that the 1950s was a period when the financial infrastructures were laid down for the subsequent development of dependent capitalism. The four banks that were established during 1973–75 further reinforced Iran's domination by international finance capital. Although the foreign shares of the mixed banks were restricted to a maximum of 40 percent of the bank's total stocks and the remaining 60 percent was assumed to be bought and controlled by Iranian nationals, the foreign participants could have effective control over these banks through their concentrated shares and because the Iranian shares were dispersed and divided. As table 3.6 indicates, the foreign shares were predominantly

TABLE 3.6
*Characteristics of Iranian Banks with Mixed Ownership
in Terms of the Distribution of Shares*

	Foreign Shares		Iranian Shares	
	Concentrated	Dispersed	Concentrated	Dispersed
Banks	(in percents)		(in percents)	
The International Bank of Iran and Japan	30.0	5.0	16.0	49.0
Bank Etebarat Iran	33.8	6.2	5.0	55.0
Iranian Bank	35.0	0.0	3.2	57.8
The Irano British Bank	39.3	0.7	10.0	50.0
The Bank of Iran and the Middle East	39.8	0.2	6.3	47.7
Mercantile Bank of Iran and Holland	35.0	0.0	0.0	65.5
The Foreign Trade Bank of Iran	40.0	0.0	40.0	20.0
Bank of Tehran	35.0	0.0	1.3	63.7
Development and Investment Bank of Iran	19.0	0.0	6.0	61.4

SOURCE: Safari, Hamid. *Enhesarha-ye Bein-ul-malali dar Iran* [International monopolies in Iran], p. 67. Tehran: Tudeh, 1980.

concentrated and controlled by financially powerful international banks, while the Iranian shares were predominantly dispersed and distributed among a considerable number of shareholders.

Industrial Development

This financial framework structured Iran's industrial development, favoring large-scale industrial establishments and monopolies tied to multinational firms, at the expense of medium and small-scale producers. The IMDBI's loan policies are indicative of this process (see table 3.7). According to this table, only 5.3 percent of the total loans approved by the bank during 1959–77 were small loans—that is, less than R 45 million ($600,000)—while during the same period 90 percent of the total value of the approved loans were for over R 75 million ($1 million). Bias in favor of large loans was accentuated in later years. For example, in 1977–78 less than 1 percent of the total amount of the bank's available credits was allocated to small loans, whereas 97.1 percent was given in the form of large loans. A similar trend can be observed in terms of the number of loans as well. During 1959–77, 44.1

TABLE 3.7
Loans Approved by IMDBI (classified by size)

Size (in millions of rials)	1959–77				1977–78			
	Number of loans	Percent	Amount (in millions of rials)	Percent	Number of loans	Percent	Amount (in millions of rials)	Percent
Up to R 15	150	16.0	R 1,471.7	.9	1	.9	R 13.9	.04
R 15–25	98	10.4	2,114.5	1.3	4	3.5	87.0	.20
R 25–45	146	15.6	5,132.8	3.1	9	7.9	287.2	.70
R 45–75	130	13.9	7,666.6	4.7	12	10.5	719.6	1.90
R 75–150	166	17.7	17,998.6	11.0	28	24.6	3,012.2	8.00
Over R 150	248	26.4	129,226.8	79.0	60	52.6	33,684.2	89.10

SOURCE: Industrial and Mining Development Bank of Iran, Annual Report of the Board of Directors to the General Assembly of Shareholders, no. 18 (1978).

percent of the total number of loans was over R 65 million. The comparative figure for 1977–78 was 77.2 percent. IMDBI was the major channel through which multinational firms infiltrated Iran's industry. IMDBI participated in the establishment of forty-eight industrial, mining, agricultural, and service enterprises,[47] and by the end of the summer of 1978 it had invested $339 million in 155 industrial, mining, transportation, and agribusiness ventures. The multinational monopolies were involved in most of these.[48] From 1956 to 1977 foreign firms invested R 39,410 million ($525.5 million) in Iran. During the 1950s and 1960s these firms invested R 11,197 million ($149.3 million), or 28 percent of the total, while from 1971 to 1977 they invested R 28,213 million ($376.2 million), or 72 percent of the total. These investments were confined to key areas in the industrial sector with high growth rates, such as mining and metallurgy (19.1 percent of the total), rubber (12.2 percent), petrochemical (26.7 percent), electrical and electronic (7.9 percent), automobiles and transportation (6.6 percent), building materials construction (3.5 percent), and other areas (10 percent). Foreign investment in agro-industries and food were 2.7 and 2.1 percent of the total, respectively, which were far less than the amount of investment required to reduce Iran's dependence on food imports.[49]

The monopoly position of multinational enterprises was also reinforced by the licensing system, which erected barriers against the entry of new industries, thus enabling the multinational monopolies to reap substantial profits. The heavy-industry segment (apart from the oil industry) was totally dominated by state enterprises, while the segment for the light-consumer industry was mostly in the hands of Iranian producers, modern or traditional. A large fraction of foreign investment went into consumer durables, which were little more than assembly-line industries. This in fact characterized most joint ventures, which packaged or put together raw materials, intermediate goods, and spare parts imported from abroad.[50]

Dependence and Vulnerability

The growth of the modern sector, due to its capital intensity and technological complexity, was tantamount to increasing Iran's dependence on the import of capital and intermediate goods, spare parts and machinery, and foreign specialized personnel. Moreover, the industrial development of the 1960s and 1970s was accompanied by the country's increasing dependence on the export of oil. Such dependence increased Iran's vulnerability to shortages and breakdowns of equipment[51] as well as to economic fluctuations in the world market.

The industrial development of the 1960s and 1970s did not lead to a reduction in Iran's dependence on foreign trade. The country's trade dependence—measured by the ratio of total foreign trade to GNP— actually increased during the postcoup period. The trade dependence was around 0.27 in the period between 1959 and 1966. This ratio gradually increased to 0.38 in 1973 and then jumped up to 0.62 and 0.67 in 1974 and 1975 respectively, reflecting the effects of the increase in oil revenues on trade dependence (see table 3.8). These figures mean that with economic growth Iran was transforming into an "export enclave" economy instead of becoming a more stable autocentric economy characteristic of the advanced capitalist countries. A particularly destabilizing factor was Iran's increasing dependence on food imports. Measured in absolute terms, in 1970 Iran's food imports came to $111

TABLE 3.8
Iranian Foreign Trade as a Proportion of GNP
(at current prices, 1959–75 in $millions)

Year	(1) GNP*	(2) Foreign Trade	Trade Dependence (2) ÷ (1)
1959	$ 3,703	$ 982	0.27
1960	4,104	1,159	0.28
1961	4,332	1,135	0.26
1962	4,611	1,099	0.24
1963	4,884	1,113	0.23
1964	5,468	1,451	0.27
1965	6,015	1,687	0.28
1966	6,465	1,837	0.28
1967	7,420	223	0.30
1968	8,389	2,565	0.31
1969	9,389	2,887	0.31
1970	10,643	3,229	0.30
1971	13,055	4,554	0.35
1972	16,420	5,470	0.33
1973	24,436	9,317	0.38
1974	41,653	25,850	0.62
1975	46,917	31,362	0.67

SOURCE: Bank Markazi Iran, *Annual Report and Balance Sheet* (various issues)

*GNP was reported in terms of rials. The dollar equivalent of the GNP is obtained by dividing the orginal values by 75 ($1 = 75 rials).

TABLE 3.9

Value of Imports of Foods, 1970–77

(in $millions)

Year	Food and Live Animals	Beverages and Tobacco	Vegetables and Animal Oils	TOTAL	Food Imports as % of GNP
1970	$ 68	$ 1	$ 42	$ 111	1.04
1971	171	3	45	219	1.68
1972	206	4	59	269	1.64
1973	327	5	61	393	1.61
1974	852	13	240	1,105	2.65
1975	1,555	26	291	1,872	3.99
1976	1,232	77	137	1,446	2.37
1977	1,486	130	164	1,780	2.50

SOURCE: Bank Markazi Iran, *Annual Report and Balance Sheet* (various issues).

million, while in 1977 this value increased to $1,780 million. In other words, from 1970 to 1977 the annual average increase in food imports was 48.7 percent. The increase in the country's dependence on food imports is still evident even if the size of the GNP is taken into account. The value of food imports as percentage of GNP increased from 1 percent in 1970 to 2.5 percent in 1977 (see table 3.9).[52]

The Oil Boom and the Economy

Iran's dependence on the export of oil made the state-guided industrialization both possible and problematic. The oil boom of the seventies saved the state from a budget deficit and the economy from a rapidly declining foreign reserve. In the sixties, although Iran had experienced an exceptionally high growth rate, its relative position in the world market (compared to the major capitalist countries of the West) deteriorated. This process of steady deterioration was reflected in Iran's terms of trade. Between 1961 and 1970, the annual average loss due to the deterioration of the terms of trade was $136 million, constituting 15 percent of the actual import volume and 22 percent of the base periods (1958–60 = 100). Between 1968 and 1970, the annual average import loss was $224 million, constituting 17 percent of actual import volume and 36 percent of base period imports.[53]

Iran's declining purchasing power was aggravated in the late sixties when the major Western economies were experiencing expansionary movements accompanied by strong inflationary pressures of a demand-pull and cost-push nature, reaching their peak in 1970. In 1970 the GNP price deflator forged ahead on the average between 4.5 and 6.5 percent in almost all industrial countries.[54] The inflationary developments were particularly noticeable in North America, the European Economic Community (EEC), the United Kingdom, and Japan. Since these countries constituted Iran's major trade partners, the rises in the export price indexes were tantamount to a reciprocal fall in Iran's foreign purchasing power. In addition to this decline, the export price index failed to rise with inflation abroad. In fact, Iran's export price index fell from 116.6 in 1957 to 106 in 1970.[55]

Over the 1963–72 period, the accumulated deficit of the current account amounted to $2,617 million, all of which was financed by long-term loans. By 1970 the situation appeared alarming. Indeed if it were not for the dramatic rise in oil prices during the early 1970s, the adoption of some kind of economic stabilization program would have been inevitable. The Tehran Agreement of February 1971 and the subsequent quadrupling of oil prices in 1973–74, which increased Iran's per-barrel oil revenue from $0.98 in January 1971 to $9.49 in January 1974, not only solved Iran's foreign exchange problems but also presented the state with a golden opportunity to redress the economic and social inequities that its ill-thought-out social reforms and rapid industrialization of the 1960s had created.[56]

With the increase in the oil revenues in 1974–75, the government revised the Fifth Plan and increased its budget to R 4,698.8 billion from the estimated original budget of R 2,461.1 billion. The public sector's share was thus to increase from R 1,548.7 billion estimated in the original plan to R 3,118.6 billion in the revised plan. In other words, the percentage share of the public sector increased from 62.9 to 66.4 percent.[57] Subsequently the volume of imports increased by 39 percent,[58] and the value of imports between 1974 and 1975 increased from $6,614 million to $11,696 million (77 percent).[59]

At the same time, paradoxically, the oil boom enhanced the country's vulnerability to economic fluctuations in the world market. A comparison of the sources of the state budget and the composition of exports for three consecutive periods (1963–67, 1968–72, and 1973–77) demonstrates this process (see tables 3.10 and 3.11). According to table 3:10, in the first period, the oil revenues constituted 48.1 percent of the government's total revenues, while taxes and other sources were 35.2 and 16.7 percent of the total, respectively. In the next period, the

TABLE 3.10

Percentage Share of Oil Revenues and Taxes
in Total Government Budget for Three Periods

Source	1963–67	1968–72	1973–77
Oil revenues	48.1	55.2	77.7
Taxes[a]	35.2	36.5	18.4
Others[b]	16.7	8.3	3.9
Total	100.0	100.0	100.0

SOURCE: Baku, "Oil Revenue and Socio-Economic Development in Iran, 1963–78," p. 88.
[a]Taxes include: direct and indirect taxes, other taxes, customs.
[b]Others include: revenues from the government's monopolies other than oil; domestic and foreign loans/savings; and "other revenues" not specified.

contribution of the oil sector to the total government budget increased to 55.2, the contribution of taxes increased to 36.5, and other contributions decreased to 8.3 percent. During the last period, the contributions of the oil sector jumped to 77.7 percent, while the share of taxes and other sources decreased to 18.4 and 3.9 percent, respectively.

As for the composition of exports, according to table 3.11, in the three consecutive periods, the value of oil exports as a percentage of total exports increased from 78.7 percent in 1963–67 to 82.8 percent in 1968–72, and finally to 96.7 percent during the 1973–77 period. The amount measured in the value of oil exports also increased considerably. This table also shows the dominant position of traditional and agricultural goods among non-oil export goods.[60] One significant change with respect to non-oil export goods was their increasing value from about $801 million to $1,546.1 million, and then to $2,871.5 million in the three consecutive periods. However, it should be noted that these figures were based on current prices, and therefore a portion of the export value increase is due to inflationary prices. Another point is the growth of the new industrial export goods. These goods accounted for only 5.6 percent of the total non-oil export goods in the 1963–67 period. In the following periods, they represented 19.6 and 24.7 percent, respectively, of the total non-oil export goods. But once again, when one looks at the comparative weight of the total non-oil export goods, which represent only 17.2 and 3.3 percent of the total oil and non-oil exports in the respective periods, the role of the new industrial export goods is reduced almost to nil. This is particularly true in the

TABLE 3.11

Value of Iran's Exports According to Production Type, 1963–77

(in $millions)

Export	1963–67		1968–72		1973–77	
	Amount	Percent	Amount	Percent	Amount	Percent
Traditional and agricultural goods[a]	$ 756	(94.4)	$1,242.9	(80.4)	$ 2,160.7	(75.3)
New industrial goods[b]	45	(5.6)	303.2	(19.6)	710.8	(24.7)
TOTAL (Non-oil)	801[c]	(100.0)	1,546.1	(100.0)	2,871.5	(100.0)
		(21.3)		(17.2)		(3.3)
Oil exports	2,967	(78.7)	7,458.6	(82.8)	84,270.0	(96.7)
TOTAL EXPORTS	3,768	(100.0)	9,004.7	(100.0)	87,141.5	(100.0)

SOURCE: Bank Markazi Iran, *Annual Report and Balance Sheet* (various issues).

[a]Minerals and metal ores, carpets, cotton, fresh and dried fruits, skin and leather, caviar, casings, gum tragacanth, cumin seeds, and "others."

[b]Detergents and soaps; glycerine and chemicals; shoes; sweets and cookies; ready-made clothes and textiles; cement, building stones, and mosaic; road motor vehicles; and "others."

[c]BMI's annual report for 1968 does not separate non-oil exports according to traditional and new industrial goods. The figure for this column is arrived at by using BMI's 1973 and 1978 classifications.

post-1973 period, during which the new industrial export goods accounted for only 0.82 percent of total export goods. The corresponding figure for the preceding period, 1968–72, was 3.4 percent.

These figures are indicative of a wider picture. Despite the state's indifference, at best, the traditional sector constituted the major non-oil export. Had the state decided to move away from an export-oriented and toward an autocentric economy, supporting the traditional sector would have been the best option. Moreover, the continued growth of the traditional sector was also indicative of changes in the power relationships between the state and civil society. While in the early phase of the postcoup period, state power tended to increase at the expense of civil society, in the late sixties and thereafter the relationships changed into a positive sum—hence enhancing the resources of the opposition groups. At any rate, during this period the state became increasingly dependent on oil revenues as its major source of finance.

The increase in the petroleum price, however, had two major destabilizing effects on the Iranian economy. On one hand, the sudden abundance of petrodollars overheated the economy, which was reflected in the emergence of many infrastructural bottlenecks and in the growth of effective demand at a much faster rate than total supply. This led to inflation and the scarcity of basic necessities such as food and other vital consumer goods. On the other hand, the increase in the oil revenues was, paradoxically, accompanied by the state's expenditures outreaching its income—hence an increase in Iran's vulnerability to economic fluctuations in the world market. When the already overheated economy received a shock from the international market through a sudden drop in the demand for Iranian oil, economic conditions grew worse.

The World Economic Crisis and the Iranian Economy

Iran's overheated economy and the problems that ensued would probably have been manageable, had the international demand for Iranian oil and the prices of imported goods remained stable. But the world economic crisis, which began in 1973 and continued through 1976, made the situation worse for Iran. In 1974 galloping inflation, shortages of food, and sharp fluctuations in exchange rates imposed great pressures on developing countries.[61] Toward the end of 1974 the pressure of price inflation reached such a level that oil-exporting countries lost about 28.5 percent of their purchasing power.[62]

In spite of the widespread recessions in the major industrial countries in 1973, these countries continued to experience inflationary pressures in 1974. Average price increases in the major capitalist countries reached 13.3 percent. The pressures were more pronounced in the UK, Italy, and Japan. Furthermore, the growth of volume of world trade, which in 1973 was about 13 percent, dropped to 5 percent in 1974. Such a decline was unprecedented since the end of World War II.[63]

Economic recession in the industrial countries was aggravated toward the middle of 1974, and their unemployment rates showed a rapid increase. In 1974 the number of unemployed in the United States, the UK, France, West Germany, and Japan increased by 5.5 million, bringing the total to about 11.5 million. This trend continued in the first quarter of 1975 in the United States. In Europe, too, the situation worsened, and the number of unemployed workers in the UK and West Germany at the end of the first quarter of 1975 reached unprecedented numbers—939,000 and 1 million, respectively. On the whole, the number of unemployed in the EEC countries in March 1975 was about 42.7 percent higher than the figure at the same time a year before. "Stagflation" was a peculiar phenomenon against which the capitalist industrial countries struggled to find an effective economic policy. Fiscal and monetary policies aimed at curbing inflation resulted in increased unemployment and decline in output, while any move to reinvigorate economic activities and measures to expand output escalated the price inflation.[64]

In 1975 economic recession in those industrialized countries that consumed the bulk of oil products, coupled with their implementation of policies aimed at conserving energy, led to a decline in world demand for oil. Therefore, the export of oil from Iran and the value added of the oil sector declined from R 1,388 billion in 1974 to R 1,321 billion in 1975 in current terms, a drop of 11.1 percent in constant prices when compared with increases of 10.4 percent and 1.1 percent respectively in 1973 and 1974. In view of the significance of the oil sector in the country's economy, despite the rapid growth of non-oil production GDP increased by only about 5 percent at constant prices. Furthermore, during 1975 the export price of Iranian oil rose by 6.3 percent, while the prices of various categories of imported goods rose by between 8 and 16 percent. There was thus an adverse effect on Iran's terms of trade of over R 47 billion. As a result of all this, the gross national income increased by only 2.7 percent in 1975.[65] Finally, the contribution of the oil sector to GDP declined at constant prices from 45 percent in 1974 to 38 percent in 1975.[66] The overall balance of payments moved from a surplus of $5.1 billion in 1974 to a deficit of about $1 billion in 1975.[67]

Economic activity and boom conditions gradually revived in the industrial Western countries, resulting in an increase in demand for Iranian oil—an increase of 14 percent in value added for Iran's oil sector in 1976. Nevertheless, the economic difficulties in Iran continued to escalate. While between 1962 and 1970 the economy was experiencing price stability, both in retail and wholesale values, from 1971 on, inflationary pressures started to build up, reaching the high level of 15.5 percent for retail prices and 15.9 percent for wholesale prices in 1974.[68]

One of the reasons for the escalation of prices in 1973 and 1974 was externally induced inflation. International inflation (particularly the worldwide increases in the prices of raw materials and agricultural products, which became intensified during the second half of 1973) continued during the first half of 1974. In fact, the rate of increase of prices of some basic goods such as sugar, soya oil, rice, and wheat rose 211 percent, 75 percent, 40 percent, and 30 percent respectively. On the whole, the annual weighted average of the export price index of the major industrial countries exporting to Iran increased by 28 percent.[69] In 1974 the increase in food prices was the most important factor contributing to the rise of the consumer price index, showing an increase of 19.1 percent against a rise of 8.4 percent in 1973.[70]

In 1975 percentage increases in both retail prices and wholesale prices dropped to 9.9 and 5.3 percent respectively. This drop was partly due to a decrease in the international prices of imported goods. This same year, the import price index increased at the rate of 6.4 percent.[71] However, in 1976 and 1977 the prices began to escalate again. Retail prices increased by 16.6 and 25.1 percent, and wholesale prices increased by 13.5 and 14.6 percent, respectively.[72] Although in 1975 the percentage price increases were considerably lower than in the previous years, overall during 1974–76 price escalation in basic necessities gained unprecedented intensity. In 1976 the housing group index registered a rise of 35.9 percent,[73] and the food group index went up by an average of 12.9 percent (as compared with 5.6 percent in 1975).[74] In 1977 the annual rise in the food group index was 20.6 percent, in the clothing index 21 percent, and the annual average growth in the housing index was 37.8 percent. The transportation and communications index showed an annual average increase of 31.9 percent, and, finally, the annual average increase in the index for medical care was 20.1 percent.[75]

The state's budgetary problems and the infrastructural bottlenecks were also partly caused by the state's defense spending and military buildup. The seventies witnessed a quantum leap in defense spending. The defense expenditures were R 58.4 billion in 1970, R 374.5 billion in 1974, and R 569.1 billion in 1976.[76] Moreover, in 1975 it cost Iran an average $9,000 per month for each American defense personnel stationed in Iran; at that time there were some 20,000 defense and defense-related personnel.[77]

Increasing imports and subsidizing the prices of basic commodities were the policies the government pursued to dampen inflationary pressures.[78] However, this approach soon faced a number of difficulties. First, the increased imports encountered infrastructural bottlenecks of the kind described earlier.[79] Second, although the increase in oil revenues had brought the state a R 140.3 billion budget surplus, the amount of budget surplus in 1975 was reduced to R 12 billion, primarily due to a drop in demand for Iran's oil in the world market. In 1976 and 1977 the Iranian government had deficits of R 37.6 and R 354.9 billion, respectively. To meet the budget deficit in 1976, the government had to resort to international borrowing. It was as much a surprise to the Iranians as to the international community that the situation could change so quickly.[80] To meet the budget deficit, the state began cutting social spending. This, however, increased social discontent. In particular, it further antagonized the ulama since it terminated their payments and the payments to religious schools for grants and scholarships.[81]

The Iranian Economy in a Comparative Perspective

To highlight the argument that Iran's vulnerability to fluctuations in the world economy contributed to its economic difficulties in the 1970s, Iran has here been compared with other OPEC countries and a selected number of Latin American countries; Japan has also been included to provide a contrast with the economy of these countries (see table 3.12). The comparison is made concerning two important aspects: dependence and vulnerability. Three measures of dependence are most frequently used in the literature: the first is foreign capital penetration. This measure is operationalized by Bornschier and Chase-Dunn for 1973 as the ratio of the total stock of foreign investment divided by the square root of the product of domestic capital formation and total population.[82] The second is Galtung's Trade Composition Index, which is intended to measure the relative concentration between raw material exports and manufactured good imports.[83] Countries ranking low on this measure tend to import raw materials and export manufactures (i.e., the developed core countries) while high-ranking countries specialize more in raw material exports and exhibit higher levels of dependence on manufactured imports (i.e., less developed peripheral countries). The third measure specifies the degree to which export production is concentrated by commodity. This variable measures the percentage contribution of 175 individual export commodities to total exports in 1973. The last two measures taken together specify the degree to which domestic production has been distorted to produce an "export enclave" economy that is dependent on the external dictates of international capital and the world economy.

As for vulnerability, since export production is one of the principal economic mechanisms through which peripheral countries become vulnerable to the world economy, fluctuations in total export earnings are employed as a measure of vulnerability. This is calculated using the UNCTAD Index of Export Fluctuation as the annual average percentage deviation of the actual exports from the expected value if the growth or decline in exports was constant for the entire period.[84] This variable is measured during the period 1975–80. Hence:

$$\text{Export Fluctuation} = 100/n \sum \frac{|xi - x'|}{X'}$$

where X_i = The value of exports at
time i X' = corresponding trend value
n = number of years, which in this
case is equal to 6.

Since the magnitude of the effects of export fluctuation are dependent upon both the relative size and composition of the export sector, these values are taken as the ratio to export enclave specialization, using the index measure developed by Sylvan and associates.[85]

A crude measure of political conflict is also provided in order to show a connection between vulnerability and political conflict. It is a combination of several indicators. The first is based on the annual number of protest demonstrations and political strikes. A protest demonstration is defined as "a nonviolent gathering of people organized for the announced purpose of protesting against a regime,"[86] while a political strike is "a work stoppage by a body of industrial or service workers or a stoppage of normal academic life by students to protest a regime."[87] The second indicator concerns state repression and is operationalized as the annual incidence of sanctions implemented by the state to counter political opposition. According to Taylor and Jodice, a government sanction is "an action taken by the government to neutralize, to suppress, or to eliminate a perceived threat to the security of the government, the regime, or the state itself."[88] Finally, the incidence of political violence is measured as the number of riots ("a demonstration or disturbance that becomes violent")[89] and armed attacks ("an act of violent political conflict carried out by [or on the behalf of] an organized group with the object of weakening or destroying the power exercised by another organized group . . . typically a regime, a government, or a political leader").[90]

As table 3.12 indicates, Iran was ranked ninth in terms of investment dependence, seventh in terms of the trade concentration index, third in terms of the commodity concentration index, third in terms of vulnerability, and first in terms of political conflict. Considering that the theoretical boundary for the trade concentration index is between -1 and $+1$ and the boundary for the commodity concentration index is between 7.56 and 100, Iran could be categorized among the countries with the highest trade dependence in the world. Japan has the lowest values on all these measures, representing a highly stable and autocentric economy.

The occurrence of political conflict in many of these countries in recent years is partly attributed to their economic dependence and vulnerability. Upswings in the demand and price for exports increase state revenues, adding to the capacity of the state for economic intervention and increasing resources available to expand the apparatus of coercion.[91] Moreover, export expansion may also generate conflict over how the export revenues are to be distributed.[92] And finally, enclave growth facilitates the mobilization of opposition groups by increasing the industrial concentration of the labor force, by providing an organizational framework for the formation of opposition groups within the occupational hierarchy, and by adding to the economic resources available to opposition groups. Downswings in export markets are even more likely to trigger political conflict among the peripheral societies.[93] Declining revenues undercut the capacity of the state to manage the economy effectively, leading first to the adoption of coercive policies

TABLE 3.12
Dependence and Vulnerability for a Selected Number of Countries

Country	Foreign Investment	TCI[a]	CCI[b]	Vulnerability	Political Conflict
OPEC countries[c]					
Algeria	77.40	.628	71.0	497.11	0.16
Ecuador	25.98	.799	54.0	189.17	0.62
Indonesia	7.32	.753	51.7	509.86	−0.55
Iran	44.52	.723	80.4	1231.43	1.44
Iraq	31.94	.781	38.5	649.87	0.33
Liberia	103.00	.756	65.1	167.01	1.11
Libya	104.00	.811	98.5	710.38	0.86
Nigeria	20.70	.581	44.0	274.50	0.46
Saudia Arabia	102.00	.885	91.2	1049.90	0.40
Venezuela	103.00	.844	68.2	761.34	−0.28
Selected Latin American countries					
Argentina	61.37	.375	29.2	2505.39	0.51
Brazil	67.12	.399	29.8	430.47	−0.33
Chile	101.00	.559	69.5	1814.39	0.97
Mexico	43.48	.447	19.6	149.24	0.04
Japan	3.13	−.551	23.9	141.27	−0.32

SOURCES: World Bank (1984); Volker Bornschier and Christopher Chase-Dunn, *Transnational Corporations and Underdevelopment* (New York: Praeger, 1985); Thanh-Huyen, Ballmer-Cao, and Jürg Scheidegger, *A Compendium of Data for World-System Analysis*, in Volker Bornschier and Peter Jeintz, eds. (Zurich: Sociological Institute of the University of Zurich, 1979); Michael Michaely, *Trade, Income Levels, and Dependence* (Amsterdam: North-Halland, 1984); Charles Taylor and David A. Jodice, *World Handbook of Political and Social Indicators*, 3d ed. (New Haven: Yale University Press, 1983); and UNCTAD, *Yearbook of International Trade Statistics* (New York: United Nations, 1979).
[a]Trade Composition Index (Range: −1 to +1).
[b]Commodity concentration Index (Range: 7.56 to 100).
[c]Relevant data for Qatar, United Arab Emirates, and Kuwait were not available.

to restimulate investment, accumulation, and growth, and second, to the reduction of resources available to maintain the apparatus of coercion. This weakens the state relative to its opposition by further eroding both its legitimacy and the capacity to effectively oppose civil unrest through coercion.

Nevertheless, the correlation between vulnerability and political conflict is 0.289—that is, vulnerability accounts for only about 8.4 percent of the total variations in political conflict.[94]. Therefore, for explaining political conflict, it is inadequate to confine the analysis to the macrostructural effects of world economy on the political conditions of these countries. After all, it was only Iran that experienced a major revolution. Further, the economic difficulties of the 1970s were not strong enough to paralyze the state and the economy. Had the state enjoyed the support of the indigenous classes, in all likelihood it would have been able to control some of the problems besieging the economy. Thus it is important to analyze how class struggle, the opposition movements, and the state-initiated economic development interacted to produce the revolutionary conjuncture of 1977–79.

This chapter has attempted to make several important points. First, the coup marked the beginning of a new era in Iran's economic history. Second, in the postcoup period international capital dominated key sectors of the economy. Third, functionally related to international capital were the dependent bourgeoisie who were the product of the state-initiated economic development. This class consisted of the owners of (mixed developmental) banks who had often shared ownership with, and been dominated by, foreign banks; those who had invested in farm corporations and agribusiness; the owners of modern factories engaged in the production and assembling of consumer goods; and the modern commercial bourgeoisie (excluding the merchants of the bazaar). Included among the members of this class were the royal family, top state bureaucrats, and high-ranking military personnel. Finally, it was also noted that the Iranian economy was highly dependent on foreign trade and in particular on the export of oil. Such a dependence led to Iran's vulnerability to economic fluctuations in the world market, which contributed to the economic difficulties of the seventies.

4

The State and the Indigenous Classes

Dependent and vulnerable as it was, the fall of the monarchy was far from being a fait accompli. Nor does domination of the economy by international capital and its internal ally, the dependent bourgeoisie, by itself make the occurrence of revolution inevitable. To explain why the Iranian version of dependent development ended up with a major revolution, I shall now focus on the other side of the dialectic of class conflict. I will trace the trajectory of class struggle since the nineteenth century to uncover its specific features and will show how these features interacted with the postcoup economic and political circumstances to contribute to the making of the revolution of 1977–79.

Iran's substantial capitalist development after the coup was consequential to the form and intensity of class struggle in this period. On one hand, the merchants and petty bourgeoisie came under pressure and the "feudal" class was destroyed. On the other hand, it led to the growth of the working class and the new middle class.[1] Although state policies were highly biased in favor of large and modern industrial establishments tied to international capital, these policies were paradoxically promoting small-scale industry and, to some extent, reproducing the traditional social classes. For state-initiated and state-directed industrialization was capital intensive, producing consumer-durable goods for the upper middle and high-income groups, and thus serving a relatively small section of the population. Nonetheless, sufficient space in the labor and consumer market was left for the petty bourgeoisie and the merchants, who were predominantly organized in the bazaar, to conduct their economic activities.

To say that the bazaar had played an important role in many protest and revolutionary movements of nineteenth- and twentieth-century

Iran is simply to reiterate the established historical scholarship. What have been overlooked, however, are the specific mechanisms underlying the bazaar's political dynamics. This chapter specifies three such mechanisms. First, the bazaar rested on some sort of de facto coalition between the merchants and the petty bourgeoisie. Except for the Reza Shah period, this coalition had been reproduced since the nineteenth century. Second, the bazaar's practical experiences have had direct bearing on the politics of religion. Third, while the bazaar had often acted in defense of its economic interests, its strategies of action were shaped by the kind of discourse dominant in society. In the nineteenth century, the bazaaris' protests were shaped by the Shi'i oppositional discourse. In the early to mid-nineteenth century, their actions were constituted through the secular discourse. Finally, during the course of the Iranian Revolution and the postrevolutionary period, Islamic revolutionary discourse played a crucial role in shaping the bazaar's political action.

This chapter presents an historical analysis of the politics of the petty bourgeoisie, the merchants, and the working class. It will be argued that these classes were dissatisfied with the state's economic policies. However, neither their grievances nor their organizations and resources by themselves explain their revolutionary action against the state. As the next chapter will attempt to demonstrate, it was Shi'i revolutionary discourse that shaped the action of the members of these classes in a revolutionary direction.

The Petty Bourgeoisie and the Merchants in the Nineteenth Century

One of the shortcomings of classical Marxism was its emphasis on class polarization as a condition for revolution. Contemporary class theory has departed from the class polarization model to emphasize the importance of class coalition as an explanatory variable in determining the cause and outcomes of social revolution. In Moore's work, "no coalition, no revolution" is a principal dictum. In convergence with Moore's conceptual scheme, one of the specific features of class politics in Iran was a coalition between the merchants and the petty bourgeoisie against the dependent bourgeoisie and international capital. Besides the presence of a common enemy, these classes belonged to the same ideological and cultural universes, which made their unity a historically distinctive phenomenon frequently reproduced during the course of the nineteenth and twentieth centuries. Chapter 6 below will provide a detailed analysis of the conflictual relationships between the merchants and the guilds in Egypt to signify the merchant–petty bourgeois alliance in Iran as a central factor underpinning the singularity of both Iran's class politics and its religious experience.

The Structure and Organization of the Petty Bourgeoisie

The concept of the petty bourgeoisie is applied to "small-scale production and ownership, independent craftsmen and traders."[2] More specifically, the petty bourgeoisie are those small-scale handicraft producers and retail traders who are self-employed, own and control the means of production based on routine technology, and have limited control over investment and labor process. In the context of Iran, the members of this class consist of those engaged in metalworking crafts, woodworking crafts, building and ceramic crafts, textile and leather crafts, food-treating crafts,[3] and retail traders.

Craftsmen and retail traders, along with small farmers, were among the most stable and populous classes in nineteenth-century Iran. The division of labor among handicraft producers was extensive, and thus considerable differentiations existed in the type of commodities they were producing.[4] However, the technical division of labor within a single workshop was quite low. Marx has noted that the low level of technical divisions within handicraft production is the result of the fact that "if circumstances called for a further division of labor, the existing guilds split themselves up into varieties, or founded new guilds by the side of old ones; all this, however, without concentrating various handicrafts into a single workshop. Hence the guild organization . . . excluded division of labor in the workshop."[5] In all likelihood such was also the case in precapitalist Iran.

Thus, there was little social differentiation within the handicraft workshops. The craftsman owned the means of production and also worked in the workshops—hence, a unity between ownership and labor, although the craftsman did employ apprentices. Undoubtedly, there was some degree of exploitative relationship between master and apprentice, but the fact that they both worked in the same workshop made the character of their relations different from those between the landlord and the peasant. This work was also a determining factor in the development of an identical worldview between masters and apprentices. Master-apprentice solidarity was reinforced by kinship ties, for the apprentices were usually recruited from the craftsman's family. The apprenticeship system provided the workshop with a hierarchical division of labor based on skill. Starting as a child-apprentice, acquiring the necessary skills over many years and usually gaining recognition in his late twenties, the artisan developed a strong sense of craft identity. His craft name followed his own name as a sort of surname. Based on shared skills, this identification was one of the main elements of solidarity among artisans.[6] Moreover, the long years of apprenticeship training necessary to acquire the skills and expertise provided the craftsman with some degree of job security, for it made it difficult to replace artisans.

Craftsmen and retail traders were organized into guilds by type of occupation. A guild consisted of "a group of townspeople engaged in the same occupation, who elect their own chief and officers, who pay guild taxes, this group having fiscal and administrative functions."[7] Two factors are believed to be responsible for the emergence of the guilds in Iran: first, "craftsmen and traders by their association together were more easily able to resist demands by the government, in other words, the guild organization was a measure of self-help; and secondly—and here a parallel is to be sought with the Byzantine empire with its autocratic centralization—the gild organization was, somewhat paradoxically, encouraged by the government to facilitate its control of economic life, the collection of taxes, and the performance of corvèes."[8] The guilds were thus taxed as a corporate body. The quota was fixed each year after negotiations between the government representative and the guild leaders.[9] As for pricing, the guild leaders, convened by the market superintendent (*muhtasib*), would determine prices at the beginning of each month.[10] In many guilds, the office of guild head tended to be hereditary. In some cases the government of the day directly appointed the guild head, thereby having closer control over the guilds. In any case, the appointment of the guild head was subject to the approval of the government.[11] Guild leaders had some judicial powers in guild matters, especially if these concerned disputes among guild members. The guilds to some degree protected themselves against competition by requiring that anyone wishing to start a shop should be approved by the guild head.

Lambton believes that the guilds existed well before the nineteenth

century and were "highly organized," having "clearly defined association in the cities."[12] Furthermore, she observes that "most of the craft
gilds had their own bazaars, which fact no doubt [sic] strengthened
their sense of corporate life. Throughout the Middle Ages craft gilds
played an important part in the life of the cities."[13]

Such was the structure and organization of Iran's petty bourgeoisie, a
class that provided the backbone of many of the country's protest and
revolutionary movements in the nineteenth and twentieth centuries.

The Social Organization of the Merchants

In general, (Marxist) historians agree that merchant capital existed
long before the dawn of capitalism. Marx observes that "not commerce
alone, but also merchant's capital, is older than the capitalist mode of
production, is, in fact, historically the oldest free state of existence of
capital."[14] Merchant capital was characterized by the circuit of the
conversion of money into commodity by purchase and of conversion of
commodity into money by sale. Thus the sphere of merchant capital lies
outside the production process.

Iran's geographic location and a well-developed system of petty com-
modity production were conducive to the expansion of commerce in
precapitalist Iran. Around 1800, Iran's main trade partners were
Afghanistan and the principalities of Central Asia, Turkey, and India.
Trade with India consisted mainly of native products on both sides, the
East India Company's export of British goods to Iran being very small.
Trade with Afghanistan and Central Asia included a large amount of
European goods reexported from Iran, and that with Turkey also comprised a substantial amount of such goods, coming through Constan-
tinople or Baghdad.[15] John Malcolm estimates total trade for Iran
around 1800 at £2,500,000; this figure is the sum of imports, exports,
and reexports (the last item accounting for over half the total).[16]

The consolidation of state power under the newly established Qajar
dynasty at the turn of the century no doubt contributed to Iran's commercial stimulation. Prior to this period, Iran had been experiencing a
century of political turmoil—between the fall of the Safavids and the
rise of the Qajars—created by recurrent wars for political supremacy
between a number of major tribal groups, such as the Afshars, Zands,
Qajars, Bakhtiyaris, and the Afghans. The rule of the first two shahs of
Qajars (1796–1834) was one of rapid recovery from the devastations of

the previous century,[17] followed by some improvement in the economic conditions of the peasants.[18] Therefore, trade increased with extraordinary rapidity during the early part of the reign of Fath Ali Shah—the second shah of Qajar—because of both greater security and the greater attention paid by the government of India to Persian Gulf trade. Whereas around 1784 annual imports of Indian chintz through Bushire averaged 60–70 bales, by 1811 they had risen to 500–600 bales. The available evidence also shows a rapid growth in Persian Gulf trade between the 1780s and the 1820s and perhaps a doubling again by 1860. The trade of Tabriz also increased considerably. Russian trade with Iran, expressed in gold rubles, about doubled between the early 1830s and mid-1860s. All together, it seems unlikely that total trade around 1860 could have been much below £5,000,000.[19] In southern Iran, largely due to the influence of trade between Iran and India that was carried on through the Persian Gulf port of Bushire, the agricultural economy changed from one designed overwhelmingly to meet the needs of local consumption to one that to a large degree was geared to meeting the demands of expanding foreign markets.[20] In short, in real terms, trade rose about threefold between 1800 and 1850 and quadrupled again by 1914, a total rise of about twelve times during the whole period under review.[21] In Issawi's view, the outstanding feature of this period was the rapid growth in international trade.[22] This expansion, as we shall see, brought with it considerable class conflict.

The merchants were actively involved in this economic endeavor. The word "merchant" is the translation of the Persian term *tajir* (pl. *tujjar*), referring to a wholesale merchant.[23] The merchants were engaged in long-distance and relatively large-scale domestic and international trade. In each city a few merchants dictated economic life.[24] The merchants also played an important part in financing the activities of the government, and the payment of the revenue quota due from a provincial governor had in some cases to be guaranteed by a merchant before the governor designate set out for his government.[25]

It was not, however, their economic position that was the sole factor in the constitution of the merchants as a class. Shi'i Islam and Iran's traditional culture were also important factors in defining the merchants' class identity, factors that made their cooperation with the postcoup regime problematic, and that added an ideological dimension to their conflict with the dependent bourgeoisie. In traditional Iran, the merchants occupied a high position in the distribution of social honor.

Their prestige was rooted in the Islamic culture. Pristine Islam is favorably disposed toward commerce and commercial activities. Torrey observes that the Quran manifests everywhere a lively interest in matters of trade and that words commonly found in a trade or commercial context are often used to express relations between God and man.[26] Torrey observes that these terms (such as "reckoning," "weights," "measures," "payments," "loss," "gain," "fraud," "buying," "selling," "profits," "wages," "loans," and "security") occur about 370 times in the Quran[27] and thus "impart a certain commercial tone to the whole."[28] Observing the presence of a striking uniformity in the numerical distribution of commercial words throughout the Quran, Torrey concludes that "the mutual relations between God and man are of a strictly commercial nature."[29]

Besides the Quran, many eulogistic formulations about commercial activities can be found in the dicta attributed to the Prophet and in other religious texts. It is reported that the Prophet said: "The merchant who is sincere and trustworthy will [at the Judgment Day] be among the prophets, the just, and the martyrs." Or: "The trustworthy merchant will sit in the shade of God's throne at the Day of Judgment." Or: "Merchants are the messengers of this world and God's faithful trustees on Earth." According to holy tradition, trade is a superior way of earning one's livelihood: "If thou profit by doing what is permitted, thy deed is djihad [a holy war]." The taste for business that was characteristic of the Prophet and of the Caliphs, his first successors, was reported with tenderness. Umar is alleged to have said: "Death can come upon me nowhere more pleasantly than where I am engaged in business in the market, buying and selling on behalf of my family." "If God let the dwellers in Paradise engage in trade," the Prophet is claimed to have said, "they would trade in fabrics and in spices." Or, again: "If there were trading in Paradise, I should choose to trade in fabrics, for Abu Bakr the Sincere was a trader in fabrics."[30] It is recorded, says an eighteenth-century commentator on Ghazali, that Ibrahim an-Nakha'i, a pious authority of the first century AH, was asked which he preferred: an honest merchant or a man who has given up all forms of work so as to devote himself wholly to the service of God. He is said to have replied: "The honest merchant is dearer to me, for he is in the position of one waging a holy war."[31] Finally, Lambton observes that "Jahiz in an essay in praise of trade and censure of the service of sultans . . . maintains that merchants were held in high estimation and that people of discrimination considers them to be the most pious members of the community and their life to be the most secure; they were in their houses like kings on their thrones, the people seeking them out to satisfy their needs."[32]

In light of Islam's promerchant tendency, it is hardly surprising to observe that nineteenth-century Iranians considered the merchants to be "more respectable than any other social class."[33] The merchants were also among the better-educated section of the population. For instance, in northern Iran more than half, sometimes even 90 percent, of the merchants could read and write.[34] "It is, therefore, no wonder that they were considered notables of the city in which they lived. Every small-scale trader or even a prosperous money-dealer wanted to become a merchant as soon as possible, for 'it was the best occupation there is.'"[35] Fasa'ie's description of the influential individuals in Shiraz frequently mentions with reverence the names of merchants whose basic characteristics were honesty and sincerity. His description also indicates that that city's high-ranking *mujtahids* and the merchants were often related.[36]

Area specialists differ on the question of whether the merchants were organized into guilds. Lambton points to the presence of merchant guilds but concedes that it was "a late growth in Persia and not widely found until the late nineteenth century."[37] Floor, on the other hand, claims that the merchants did not form guilds. But the merchants did enjoy an exclusive class consciousness, which was reflected in the lives of many merchant families. The merchants as a class cultivated the public esteem and kept strictly to a certain way of life. Any merchant deviating therefrom stood to loose his standing in the merchant community. In most cities, especially in the second half of the nineteenth century, the *tujjar* were headed by a *Malik ut-Tujjar* or chief merchant [38]

The Politics of the Bazaar

The merchants, craftsmen, and retailers were organized in the bazaar, which had been the commercial focus of the city and its hinterland.[39] The bazaar was not merely a market-place for economic transactions in the modern sense of the term. It was also a type of community center. The bazaar area included one, or several, mosques, public baths, religious schools, *karavansiras,* and many teahouses. The religious idiom was the basic common denominator in the bazaar and functioned to create crosscutting ties and bonds among bazaaris of different guilds and professions.[40] The bazaar constituted the major source of support for the ulama and religious institutions, and the ulama and bazaaris were often related through family ties. Since the mid-nineteenth century, the bazaar has been the major source and center of support for oppositional politics. Underpinning the bazaar's political dynamism was the coalition between the merchants and the petty bourgeoisie, which made the bazaar a powerful force in the opposition movements.

The specificity of Iran's historical development as the principal factor for the merchant–petty bourgeoisie alliance must be underlined, because from the viewpoint of the structure of economic relations one may argue that there are grounds for potential conflict between these two classes. The merchants were engaged in the domestic and international circulation of goods and raw materials according to the well-known principle of "buy cheap and sell dear." Having a monopoly over the supply of raw materials for the traditional industries and over the purchase of the finished goods produced by the craftsmen, the merchants were naturally interested in turning the terms of exchange to their own advantage vis-à-vis the craftsmen by forcing the latter to sell their products to the merchants below the value they themselves would have preferred. Moreover, under certain conditions, the craftsmen's guilds own protective policies and price controls could be in conflict with the merchants' desire for an open-door policy. Thus the guilds' exploitation by the merchants through trade,[41] and the two classes' divergent trade-policy orientations, offer objective grounds for conflict between the merchants and the petty bourgeoisie.

Such was the case in Western Europe where the conflict between craft guilds and merchants became ubiquitous as soon as the tempo of primitive accumulation and capitalist development was set in motion from the fourteenth century and on. Before this period, in England for example, merchant guilds generally contained no more than a fraction of the townsmen, and craftsmen did not appear to have been excluded from them.[42] But "the class of merchants, as soon as it assumed any corporate form, was quick to acquire powers of monopoly, which fenced its ranks from competition and served to turn the terms of exchange to its own advantage in its dealings with producer and consumer."[43] This marked the beginning in fourteenth-century England of an organized trading interest in the towns distinct from handicraft. Similar historical patterns could also be observed in other parts of Western Europe later.[44] The exploitation of handicraftsmen through trade by the merchants, the decline of the system of petty-commodity production, and the pauperization of the small producers were all considered as conditions of, and pari passu with, primitive accumulation and the development of capitalism. The occurrence of conflict between these two classes is well documented in the historical writings on this period. The industrial revolution put a decisive end to this battle in nineteenth-century Europe.[45]

Iran's capitalist development in the course of the nineteenth and twentieth centuries experienced little conflict between the merchants and the petty bourgeoisie, even though there was an economic basis for such conflict between them. The merchants and the petty bourgeoisie were able to maintain their de facto alliance over many historically significant issues that appeared on the political scene in this period. This alliance was conditioned by foreign economic infiltrations that undermined the interests of merchants and petty bourgeoisie alike.

The Bazaar and the Shi'i Discourse

Beginning in about the second quarter of the nineteenth century, the merchants and craft guilds faced strong competition from European and Russian concerns.[46] Foreign companies gradually took over a greater part of the Iranian commerce. Notwithstanding the economic recovery and commercial boost associated with the consolidation of the Qajar's political order, Iran's primitive accumulation (according to the then existing international scale) was too little and too late. Iran had neither the economic resources nor the political power to successfully meet the challenge from Europe and Imperial Russia. For one thing, Iranian merchants lacked the organizational and administrative capabilities as well as the capital necessary to finance and run their affairs on the same scale as the Europeans.[47] For another, the situation was exacerbated by the very different manner in which European governments and the Iranian government treated their domestic interests. Equipped with unprecedented new military technology, European governments were largely the gendarmes for their own native economic interests. In contrast, the Qajar state—sandwiched between the competition of the British and the Russian empires for regional domination and weakened by its repeated defeats in the Perso-Russian wars in 1813 and 1828—not only left its domestic trade unprotected but also granted concessions to other foreign concerns.

As a result, the merchants and the guilds began to engage in protest activities against the state and international capital. Initially, they directed their actions toward either an attempted boycott of foreign goods or petitioning the monarch to implement some sort of protective measures. These tactics failed. Given that Muslim interests were in conflict with the non-Muslim, Islamic discourse became an effective language for addressing the problem of Western domination and a generally callous state. By invoking religious principles, the merchants not only overcame the anticipated charges that they were acting out of self-interest but also transcended their conflict with the British by turning it into a confrontation between Muslims and infidels, thereby effectively mobilizing the people against foreign economic intervention.

The first sign that European influence had penetrated and was resented by the Iranian mercantile community was about 1830, when "the quality of English and Masulipatan chintzes alarmed the manufacturers so much that they petitioned the king to put a stop to the importation."[48] When in 1837 the trading house of Ralli opened a branch in Tabriz, the first of many protests against European merchants occurred.[49] This was followed by a ban on the consumption of tea, which was issued in Tabriz and Tehran against the Russian Georgians, "who have the principal traffic in that article, whereas native merchants have none."[50] Three years later the British consul reported that "Persian merchants had asked the government to prohibit imports of European manufactures 'on the ground principally of the ruin Persian manufacturers are reduced to by the constant and immense importation of foreign goods.' This attempt was, however, unsuccessful, and the combination formed by the merchants for that purpose was dissolved."[51] Similar and equally fruitless attempts were made by "traders and manufacturers of Cashan [Kashan] . . . and other manufacturers and traders."[52] According to K. E. Abbott, the British consul in 1844, "a memorial was presented to His Majesty the Shah by the traders and manufacturers of Cashan praying for protection to their commerce which they represented as suffering in consequence of the introduction of European merchandise into their country."[53] Again, in 1849, he reported from Kashan that "the manufacturers have however rapidly declined for some time past in consequence of the trade with Europe which has gradually extended into every part of the kingdom to the detriment or ruin of many branches of native industry."[54] In 1864 there was another unsuccessful attempt against European trade.[55]

The Qajars' tax policies further undermined the merchants because they had to pay higher taxes than the Europeans.[56] The British consul in Iran in 1851 reported that "the position . . . of the Persian Merchant compared to that of the European may be understood by the following statements; The European importing a load of Sugar of the value of 10 Tomans—pays his 5 per cent once for all and may re-export it to Tehran. The Persian pays for the load . . . 14 per cent and if he re-exports to Tehran is charged Rohdarlik [custom duties] at Meeana, Zenjaun, Kazveen and Tehran."[57] Similar differential taxes were applied on the manufactures. The same report then concludes that "unless these duties are not [sic] considerably reduced the natives must abandon Commercial pursuits, and the Trade will then be reduced in amount, and remain entirely in the hands of Europeans."[58]

Finally, the concessions granted by the monarch to foreign companies further intensified economic pressures on the bazaaris. The concession-hunting era was inaugurated in 1872 through what Curzon describes as an "international bombshell." The first major concession was granted to Baron Julius de Reuter, a British citizen, for £40,000 and 60 percent of profits on the customs in return for the exclusive rights to finance a state bank, farm out the entire customs, exploit all minerals (with the exception of gold, silver, and precious stones), build railways and tramways for seventy years, and establish all future canals, irrigation works, roads, telegraph lines, and industrial factories.[59] "The agreement," Curzon commented, "contained the most complete surrender of the entire resources of a kingdom into foreign hands that has never been dreamed of, much less accomplished, in history."[60] Due to some opposition, the Reuter concession was withdrawn. The sales of concessions, however, continued. Reuter retained mining and banking privileges that developed later into the Imperial Bank of Persia, a financial monopoly that continued to irritate the merchants for many coming years.

Inflation and other economic crises had drastic effects on Iran. Caught between spiraling expenses and stagnating incomes, between the need to find additional revenues and the political dangers of levying new taxes, Naser-ud-Din Shah of Qajar increasingly resorted to the sale of titles, patents, privileges, concessions, monopolies, land *tuyuls* (the right to collect taxes on crown lands), and most detrimental of all, of high offices such as judgships, ambassadorships, governorships, and even ministerial offices.[61] As one modern historian has commented, hardly a day passed in the court without a sale of something to someone for some price.[62]

Gradually, the merchants lost their hold on the domestic markets. By the end of the nineteenth century they were completely dominated by foreign companies. In the north the Russian merchants had about half of the foreign trade in hand, and in the south the British merchants handled "the bulk of transaction."[63] Not only was Iranian trade seriously hurt by the Western impact, but also its industry was virtually ruined.[64] In his report, a tax collector in Isfahan noted the deteriorating conditions of the weavers' guilds:

> In the past, high-quality textiles were manufactured in Isfahan since everyone—from the highest to the lowest—wore local products. But in the last few years, the people of Iran have given up their body and soul to buy the colorful and cheap products of Europe. In doing so, they incurred greater losses than they imagined: local weavers, in trying to imitate imported fabrics, have stopped buying Iranian textiles; and many occupations have suffered great losses. At least one-tenth of the guilds in this city were weavers; not even one-fifth have survived. About one-twentieth of the needy widows of Isfahan raised their children on the income they derived from spinning for the weavers; they have now lost their source of livelihood. Likewise, other important guilds, such as dyers, carders, and bleachers have suffered. Other occupations have also been affected: for example, farmers can no longer sell their cotton for high prices.[65]

In the course of the nineteenth century, many merchants bought land, and they, along with some traditional landlords, began to meet Western demand by using their lands increasingly for export crops like cotton and opium, the result of which was their vulnerability to the economic fluctuations in the world market.[66] The international fall in agricultural prices, which started in 1871 and continued to the end of the century, brought insecurity to many Iranian exporters: for example, the price per bushel of wheat declined from $1.50 in 1871 to $0.23 in 1894. The volume of wheat exported from Bushire increased by 80 percent, but the realized value failed to rise significantly. Finally, the introduction of European capital and the capitulations granted to European businessmen created outside the bazaar a comprador bourgeoisie.[67]

The government's failure to support domestic commerce and industry, coupled with the interference of the Russian and British governments on behalf of their mercantile interests in Iran's internal affairs, made the Iranian merchants for the greater part dependent on the European firms, not as equal partners but as agents (*dallal va dastkar*) and hired hands (*muzdur*) whose best asset was their personal honesty.[68] The Iranian merchant who at the beginning of the nineteenth century had had the reputation of a liberal, freethinking man within a bigoted nation, became in European eyes a scoundrel whom one could not trust and whose favorite pastime was to outdo and deceive foreigners.[69] The gradual decline of the merchants' economic position as well as their social esteem naturally led to their resentment against foreigners and the state. These processes provided the merchants and the petty bourgeoisie a common political platform. This alignment was decisive for the supremacy of the bazaar in the tobacco rebellion of 1890–92, the Constitutional Revolution of 1905–11, and the revolution of 1977–79.

The protest activities of these classes against the state first culminated in the tobacco movement of 1890–92, one of the most celebrated events of nineteenth-century Iran. The movement was a rebellion against a concession granted by the Shah of Qajar to Major G. F. Talbot, a British citizen, in 1890 for the monopoly of buying, selling, and manufacturing all the tootoon and tobacco in the interior or exterior of the Kingdom of Iran for fifty years in return for an annual rent of £15,000, and a quarter of the annual profits after the payment of all expenses and of a 5 percent dividend on the capital.[70] The concession was particularly damaging to the merchants and retail traders whose income depended on the tobacco trade. Had it come to force, the concession would have had affected the livelihood of about 200,000 people in Iran. Tobacco was one of the country's major exports, and it was not so easy to cut off Iranian merchants from this profitable trade.[71] The period between March 20, 1890, when the concession was signed and late January of 1892 when Naser ud-Din Shah was forced to repudiate the concession was characterized by intense conflicts between the British company and the Shah, on one hand, and a merchant-led resistance movement that included a group of the ulama, on the other.

The merchants of Tehran were the first group to protest the concession. Before the concession was publicly announced, these merchants wrote a protest letter to the Shah. An underground leaflet criticizing state policies was also distributed in the city. Pointing to the concession, the leaflet stated that "tobacco belongs to Iranians, the buyers and consumers are Iranians, why should then tobacco trade be monopolized by foreigners?"[72] Following Tehran, the merchants of Fars stood up against the concession. Tobacco trade in Fars was under the control of sixty well-known and influential merchants, who began sending telegrams to the Iranian prime minister and the Shah against the concession. At the same time, they attempted to gain the support of the ulama (although unsuccessfully at the beginning).[73] As a result of government repression, for which the British Embassy and the tobacco company were thankful, the movement in Shiraz subsided.[74]

However, it reemerged with greater strength and on a larger scale in Azarbayjan. Unlike Fars, Azarbayjan was not a tobacco-growing region. Foreign trade of tobacco, however, was under the control of the merchants. This explains why here also it was the merchants and retail traders who organized the movement, while the ulama were initially reluctant to participate.[75] Following Tabriz, Isfahan began to rebel. One of the distinctive features of the tobacco rebellion in Isfahan was that it was here that the idea of boycotting the consumption of tobacco was contemplated and executed for the first time. Like other places, the tobacco movement in Isfahan initiated with the merchants. The rebellion began with the effective cooperation of two leading ulama, Aqa Najafi and his brother Shaykh Mohammad Ali. Aqa Najafi was a large landowner and an influential *mujtahid* whose power matched the governor's. Shaykh Mohammad Ali was an able preacher.[76] In Mashhad the tobacco movement was not as strong as it was elsewhere. The tobacco merchants and traders were not able to attract the cooperation and support of the ulama. Only a few of the ulama—such as Va'ez Sabzivari, Mirza Abdorrahman, and Sayyid Mohammad Kalati—and a group of *tullab* (sing., *talabih;* students of religion) joined the movement. The tobacco company, on the other hand, was successful in gaining the support of Khorasan's governor, Fath Ali Khan Sahibdivan, and the leading ulama.[77]

Meanwhile, as a result of these rebellions and the flood of petitions and protest letters he was receiving, the Shah began to contemplate the idea of canceling the concession. The tobacco company and the British government were naturally resisting this idea. The British embassy, however, began to realize that the tobacco monopoly was not going to work and that its forced imposition did not seem to be in British interests in Iran. The Russians were also active against the concession, although their role in the tobacco movement was by no means central.

Given this background, another wave of protests was necessary to break the balance of forces in favor of the resistance movement. The idea of a tobacco boycott had already been tested with some success in Isfahan. By late November 1891, talk about a boycott became popular among the people in Tehran. Then it was rumored that a *fatva* regarding the boycott of tobacco had been issued by the eminent Ayatollah Mohammad Hasan Shirazi and sent to Isfahan. By early December 1891 it was announced that the *fatva* had arrived and that the original copy of the *fatva* was at the disposal of Ayatollah Ashtiyani, a leading *mujtahid* of Tehran.[78] The *fatva* read: "To the name of God, the Merciful and the Forgiving. As of now, the consumption of tobacco and tootoon in any form is tantamount with a war against the Imam of the Age."[79] The *fatva* was then quickly copied and distributed throughout the country. The tobacco movement hence culminated in a nationwide tobacco boycott. As it turned out, however, the *fatva* was not real but a fabrication by a group of merchants (including Haj Kazim Malik ot-Tujjar and with the cooperation of Mirza Hasan Ashtiyani).[80] When news about the boycott reached Ayatollah Shirazi, he was prudent enough not to question its authenticity. The universality of the boycott, followed by a huge demonstration at the Shah's palace that left many people dead or wounded, eventually forced the Shah to repudiate the concession by the end of January 1892.

The Bazaar and the Constitutional Revolution

If the West can be blamed for the intensification of social conflict in the late nineteenth century, it was also responsible for the invasion of Iranian culture by modern ideologies. Through translations, travel, and the infiltration of various artifacts of Western culture, Iran's leading intellectuals, social critics, and political activists became aware of an alternative way of organizing social life and were consequently increasingly attracted to ideas of constitutionalism, secularism, and nationalism. As Abrahamian has aptly summarized: "The first, they argued, would destroy the reactionary power of the monarchy. The second would eliminate the conservative influence of the clergy. And the third would eradicate the exploitative tentacles of the imperialists."[81]

Prominent among these intellectuals were Sayyid Jamal ud-Din al-Afghani, a pioneer of Islamic modernism, and Mirza Malkum Khan, a liberal and reformist thinker. Even though he was a prominent Muslim ideologue, al-Afghani regarded the mediocrity of the existing religious establishment to be the cause of the decline of the Islamic nations. "It is clear that wherever it became established," said Sayyid Jamal, "this religion tried to stifle science and was marvelously served in its design by political despotism."[82] The ideology of the monarchy, in contrast, emphasized the divine nature of the monarch's absolutism, rejected the notion that the temporal ruler was a usurper of the power of the hidden Imam (while stressing that he was the shadow of God on earth), and called for the subjects' total submission to his authority to prevent social chaos.[83]

Therefore, modern political discourse contradicted the ideology of the monarchy at its very roots, and its increasing dominance in civil society was tantamount to the intensification of the revolutionary crisis. This is quite important because, prior to the modern period, the Iranian people had resisted their kings. Their resistance, however, had always been expressed within the parameters of the state's ideological universe. Successful rebellions against the shah had usually ended up generating the same type of political system. But when resistance to Qajar absolutism and protests over foreign domination began to be expressed in terms of the modern secular discourse, they took a new, revolutionary direction. Modern forms of social organizations and political parties were created, and new resources for political mobilization were defined and discovered. A new mode of historical action thus emerged on Iran's political scene, and its dynamics produced the Constitutional Revolution of 1905–11.

Merchants, retailers, and craftsmen widely participated in this revolution. Inspired by the new democratic order in Istanbul, Baku, and Bombay, the merchants demanded democracy and nationalism, "democracy because it gave them greater access to power, and nationalism because it would lead to the ouster of foreign domination."[84] After the approval of the new constitution by Mozaffar ud-Din Shah in 1906, the merchants and guilds played an influential role in the first parliament. The merchants and the guilds together made up 41 percent of the representatives in the first Majles, while the guilds alone constituted the largest single group (26 percent of the representatives). However, the influence of the guilds began to decline and by 1909, when they were barred from representation in the Majles, the guilds completely lost power.[85] Never again did they acquire the same political influence. The guilds produced no important political leader. They acted cohesively in politics only as long as their political patrons had a common basis for cooperation.[86]

The merchants' representation in the Majles did not decline under Reza Shah. And the Shah's economic policies more or less satisfied the large merchants and landowners, while antagonizing the artisans and retail traders. State control of foreign trade hurt private traders and even caused bankruptcies; taxes on income and consumer goods prompted them to complain that the new army and railway projects were too expensive. Also, modern textile factories destroyed many handicraft workshops; thus, in general, economic centralization antagonized the provincial bazaar. Paradoxically, Reza Shah further antagonized the guilds by abolishing taxes on 216 of them—for the abolition took away from guild elders the power to determine how much each guild member paid in taxes, and thus paved the way for the weakening of the organizations of the bazaar. As a spokesman for the bazaar later admitted, elimination of the guild tax was a kiss of death designed to sap the control of craft and trade masters over their apprentices, artisans, journeymen, and wage earners.[87] The guilds' organizational autonomy also came under direct governmental control. Whenever guild members wished to hold meetings, they had first to report this fact to the local police station, and a policeman would be deputed to attend the meeting. The government also used the guilds to implement most of these policies, and since these were dictated by the government's higher authority the guilds were bereft of consultation or discussion.[88]

Reza Shah's unfavorable policies toward the guilds, combined with his modernization policies that undermined ulama influence in society, provided the context for the eruption of two major protest demonstrations in 1927 and 1937. The first was triggered by the enactment of Ali Akbar Davar's secular laws and the conscription of urban youth into the military. While the ulama of Tehran took sanctuary in Qum, the guilds organized a general strike in Tehran, Qum, Qazvin, Isfahan, Shiraz, and Kerman. The second upheaval was restricted to the city of Mashhad. On July 10, 1935, the anniversary of the Russian bombardment of the Mashhad shrine in 1911, the main preacher at the shrine took advantage of the emotional occasion to denounce the "heretical innovations," the high consumer taxes, and the prevalence of corruption in high places. This was followed by a massive demonstration from the bazaar and the neighboring villages against Reza Shah.[89] However, none was strong enough to have any major impact on the state's policies.

The Bazaar under the Second Shah

The forced abdication of Reza Shah in 1941 by the Allies and the subsequent emergence of a favorable political atmosphere relaxed many governmental restrictions on the guilds. The guilds regained their autonomy, and, according to a law enacted in 1948, they were once more taxed as a corporate body.[90] Under Mosaddeq there was an upsurge of guild activity in politics and street demonstrations. The merchants were also quite influential in the politics of this period. The bazaar as a whole served as a social base for the National Front. As early as 1944, in the fourteenth parliamentary elections, the bazaar supported Mosaddeq, giving him the largest number of votes for any representative. Mosaddeq's nationalist economic policies in turn helped promote certain local industries and expanded the export of local products.[91] At the same time, the nationalist-liberal discourse provided the ideological context for the formation of the Society of Merchants and Guilds (*Jaami'ih-ye Bazarganan va Pishevaran-i Bazaar*), which was in turn used as a vehicle for the mobilization of the bazaaris against the Shah and for the nationalist cause. The guilds' and the merchants' political influence was short-lived, however. The coup of 1953 changed the state's economic policies toward the bazaar, and the state's alliance with international capital undermined the interests of the guilds and merchants.

Once again the guilds came under the direct control of the government. A 1957 law provided the guilds with legal status, stipulating formation of the High Council of Guilds (*shura-ye ali-ye asnaf*), consisting of representatives from different guilds.[92] The law also determined that the governor general would be the honorary chairperson of the High Council. The most important points of discussion between the guilds and the government centered around the guilds' annual taxes, foreign imports, and starting modern factories.[93] While these discussions failed to produce policies in favor of the guilds, the state's stabilization program, which led to recession in the early 1960s, intensified pressures on the bazaar.

The state's overtly hostile policies towards the petty bourgeoisie, coupled with the implementation of land reform, provided a back-

TABLE 4.1
*Social and Class Composition of a Sample
of the Participants in the Demonstrations
of June 1963*

Background	Number	Percent
Workers	*128*	*22.1*
Industrial workers[a]	52	9.0
(*Factory workers*)	(*17*)	(*2.9*)
Construction workers	15	2.6
Traditional workers[b]	39	6.7
Type of work not specified	22	3.8
Peasants	*22*	*3.8*
Petty Bourgeoisie[c]	*249*	*43.0*
(*the new petty bourgeoisie*)	(*17*)	(*2.9*)
Apprentices[d]	*34*	*5.9*
Merchants	*1*	*0.2*
Students	*72*	*12.4*
Ulama	*52*	*9.0*
Housewives	*5*	*0.9*
Unemployed	*16*	*2.8*
TOTAL	579	100.1

SOURCE: Dahnavi, *Qiyami-i Khounin-i Panzdah-i Khordad bi Ravayat-i Asnad* [The bloody uprising of the fifteenth of Khordad according to the documents] (Tehran: Rasa Institute of Cultural Services, 1981).

[a]Factory workers, mechanics, (carpet) weavers, turners, welders.

[b]Tailor workers, (cab) drivers, dry-cleaning workers, porters, workers in public bath houses, servants.

[c]Wide range of traditional occupations with varying incomes such as yogurt makers, liver sellers, teahouse workers (Qahveh-chi), ice cream sellers, vegetable sellers, cloth sellers, shoemakers, carpenters, tailors, builders, blacksmiths, grocers, drapers, glass-blowers, (petty) brokers, "radiomakers," iron sellers, "bicycle makers," and similar occupations.

[d]Apprentice iron sellers, furniture makers, drivers, cloth sellers, cooks, bakers, and barbers.

ground for the outbreak of bloody street demonstrations in which members of this class extensively participated. Table 4.1 summarizes the class composition of a sample of the participants in the June 1963 demonstration in Tehran.[94] According to this table, out of a sample of 579 individuals who were involved in the incident, 128 (22.1 percent) were workers, 22 (3.8 percent) were peasants, 249 (43 percent) were involved in petty bourgeois–type occupations, 34 (5.9 percent) were apprentices, 1 (0.2 percent) a merchant, 72 (12.4 percent) were students, 52 (9.0 percent) were ulama, 5 (0.9 percent) were housewives, and 16 (2.8 percent) were unemployed.

The data in this table reveal several points. First, there were very few peasants involved in the incident, despite the religious opposition's at tempts to mobilize them in the areas surrounding Tehran. At that time, the Shah was able to attract the support of the peasants through the implementation of his land reform program. Second, the participation of industrial workers was quite limited, only 9 percent of the total.[95] Of this group only seventeen (2.9 percent of the total) were factory workers. There were fifteen construction workers (2.6 percent of the total), and thirty-nine traditional workers (6.7 percent of the total). Third, as the description of their occupation indicates, traditional workers as well as apprentices were employees of the petty bourgeois–type trades, and there is not much evidence to indicate that their political outlook and occupational aspirations were significantly different from their masters. (In all likelihood, an apprentice of, say, a tailor would wish to become a tailor in the future.) Thus, it may make sense to group these workers with the petty bourgeoisie rather than with modern industrial workers (in this case, the numerical weight of the petty bourgeoisie would increase to 322—or 55.6 percent of the total).[96]

The above conclusion is reinforced when one compares the data in table 4.1 with an estimate of the percentage distribution of the size of classes in Tehran (see table 4.2).[97] According to this table, 7.1 percent of the total population of Tehran was estimated to be members of the "upper" class, while only 0.2 percent of the participants in the June 1963 riot were identified as "upper" class members. Similarly, the estimated size of the new "middle" class was 9.7 percent of the total, while only 3.9 percent of the participants in the riot were identified with this class membership. For the working class, these values were 46.4 percent and 37.3 percent, respectively. On the other hand, the estimated size of the petty bourgeoisie was 37 percent of total, while among the participants in the riot this value was as high as 58.8 percent. This comparison thus seems to indicate that among the participants in the demonstration, virtually all the classes, in differing degrees, were underrepresented, except for the petty bourgeoisie who were overrepresented.

Later the Shah admitted his contempt for the bazaaris: "The bazaaris are a fanatic lot, highly resistant to change because their locations afford a lucrative monopoly. Moving against the bazaars was typical of the political and social risks I had to take in my drive for modernization."[98] It is, therefore, hardly surprising to see how the government's industrial and financial policies reflected such an antibazaar attitude. The licensing system and credit policies were designed to favor members of the Iranian dependent bourgeoisie and foreign capital. Subsi-

TABLE 4.2
*Tehran's Class Structure vs. Class Composition of the Participants
in the Demonstrations of June 1963*
(in percent)

Class Background	Estimated Class Size*	Participants in the Uprising**	Difference	Z-test	Probability
Sample size	1,189.0	434.0			
"Upper" class	7.1	3.9	5.8	4.58	.0000
New middle class	9.7	3.9	5.8	4.58	.0000
Traditional petty bourgeoisie	37.0[a]	58.5[b]	−21.5	−7.82	.0000
Working class	46.4[c]	37.3[d]	9.1	3.32	.0005
TOTAL	100.0	100.0			

SOURCES: *Asef Bayat, "Farhang va Ravand-i Prolter Shodan-i Kargaran-i Karkhanedjat-i Tehran" [Culture and the process of proletarianization of factory workers in Tehran], *Alefba* 4 (Fall 1983): 92–93.
**Same as table 4.1.
[a]Small traders, sellers, and handicraftsmen (24.1%), and peasants and farmers (12.9%).
[b]Traditional petty bourgeoisie and peasants from table 4.1.
[c]Skilled, semi-skilled, and unskilled workers, and agricultural workers.
[d]Workers and apprentices from table 4.1.

dized rates considerably below the market price were available only to large enterprises, whereas small shopowners and craftspeople were starved even for unsubsidized bank credits.[99] Moreover, small entrepreneurs did not have the time, the knowledge, or the resources to follow long and complicated governmental procedures, and operating outside the licensing system did not encourage the establishment of links between large producers and small workshops to supply their needs. Small firms had suffered from the limitation of their markets due to the low level of income in agriculture, and from the fact that they had no real possibility of obtaining government orders. Furthermore, the linkages between small-scale production and the modern industrial sector was either weak or nonexistent. It has been indicated that in large industrial establishments, dependence on imported intermediate goods was very high, not so much for basic raw materials as for parts and components. There were grounds for believing that the balance of choice between importing and buying local was more easily tipped toward the former in large modern industries, for the obvious reason that there were strong tendencies to cooperate on a technological and commercial basis with the foreign firms that provided the technology.[100]

Jazani aptly summarizes the deterioration of the economic conditions of the small producers and the guilds as a result of the dependent development:

> With the growth of an industrial comprador bourgeoisie, the small bourgeoisie and traders who, with their system of workshop production, were engaged in making consumer goods, came face to face with rivals that began to flood the market with consumer goods. . . . The rapid increase in imports during the previous two decades, coupled with the subsequent establishment of dependent industries and their rapid growth, forced these sections under pressure to retreat from their position and take up those trades that had not as yet been threatened. At every stage of retreat a considerable number of people lost their source of livelihood and joined the reserve army of labor. With the import of the Pepsi Cola factory, all lemonade workshops disappeared; with the growth of factories engaged in the production of household goods, the furniture and other workshops closed down; with the setting up of shoemaking factories, shoemakers went out of business. This process is still continuing. Today, not only the urban markets but also markets in villages and even small hamlets are closed to the products of the artisanal system of production.[101]

The merchants, albeit to a lesser extent, were also undermined by state policies. Expansion in the banking system, other state credit institutions, and a modern commercial sector caused some decline in the power of the bazaar (although in the late 1970s it still controlled a third of imports and two-thirds of retail trade).[102] Figures for 1977 show that carpet exports, the main non-oil export, declined by 13 percent in both value and volume compared with the previous year. In the same year, exports of cotton, the next largest revenue earner after oil and carpet exports, fell by 45 percent in volume and by almost 50 percent in value. The largest cotton textile mills, including factories in Isfahan and elsewhere, were having difficulties staying in business and competing with cheaper imports flooding in from foreign countries.[103]

Moreover, the Shah even went as far as to endorse the physical destruction of the bazaar itself and the establishment of new shopping centers outside the bazaar. This was done in two ways:

> firstly by building new state schools, new housing and new shopping centers outside the Bazaar, while within the Bazaar streets were "widened"—a euphemism for imposing a modern grid-iron pattern of roads on the old narrow alleyways. . . . Secondly it was done by

the modernization of the banking system. . . . To cut out the Bazaari middlemen, in 1976 the government sought to improve the nation-wide distribution of foodstuffs, and conceived of building a new market in Tehran, based on London's New Covent Garden.[104]

As was mentioned in the previous chapter, a sudden drop in the international demand for oil, externally induced inflation, and the rise in the demand for various commodities that overwhelmed supplies created considerable economic difficulties for Iran. The state's strategy to manage these economic problems further deteriorated its relationship with the bazaar. To control inflation, the state launched a nationwide anti–price-gouging and antiprofiteering campaign, which was intensified in mid-1975. The bazaar was particularly singled out as a scapegoat for inflation, and a major price-regulation campaign was directed against it. In 1974–75 the anti-inflation campaign was launched using the guilds as an enforcement mechanism. When the chamber of guilds proved to be less than cooperative in implementing the government's measures, the Minister of Commerce dismissed seventeen top guild leaders from the Chamber of Guilds of Tehran and dissolved most of the guild members throughout the country. Price levels were lowered by fiat from Tehran, and price lists were posted in shops and printed in newspapers. Indeed, the government's imposition of price controls over goods and services in 1975 was another blow at the economic interests of small-scale trade and artisan capital. In the subsequent two years, over 20,000 small businessmen were fined or brought to court on charges of speculation and the violation of price regulations. The price-control campaign had only a short-term effect: official indexes went down for six months, but black-market prices for essential commodities rose sharply. On the whole, the campaign proved to be quite ineffective. But it considerably enhanced the merchants' and guilds' hostility toward the state.[105]

Nevertheless, conflict of interests is not a sufficient cause for the bazaar's mobilization against the state. The bazaar was stratified. The merchants made considerable gains in the sixties and seventies, even while being systematically harassed by various forms of government regulation. The petty bourgeoisie, on the other hand, was under considerable pressures. Moreover, the bazaar did not enjoy the privilege of having a viable nationwide organization. The postcoup regime dissolved the Society of Merchants and Guilds, which had been the bazaar's major vehicle for mobilization under Mosaddeq. In addition, the guild organizations were controlled by the government and their activities closely monitored by SAVAK, the Shah's intelligence organization. The bazaar was also divided politically. The merchants and landowners were predominantly following Ayatollah Shari'atmadari and other grand ayatollahs in the Qum establishment, who tended to be more moderate within the religious opposition. Members of the petty bourgeoisie and less fortunate bazaaris tended to follow the ayatollahs Khomeini, Shirazi, and Taleqani, the radical faction among the ulama.[106]

Workers and Revolution

Industrial workers are considered latecomers to the revolutionary movement of 1977–79. This statement, however, should not be taken to imply that the workers' movement did not start until the late seventies. Nor does it presume that the bazaaris demanded the revolutionary overthrow of the state from the very beginning of their protest activities. The timing of these protest actions for both the bazaaris and the workers was more or less the same. The sequence of labor unrest, spontaneous strikes, and work stoppages in major industrial units (those having one hundred or more workers) began as early as 1975 and continued to rise afterward. If workers were latecomers to the revolution, it was because their dissatisfaction with present conditions was expressed in terms of revolutionary discourse much later than that of the bazaaris. Nevertheless, given their concentrations in major cities and their strategic location in the economy (e.g., the oil and steel industries), participation of the industrial workers proved crucial to the success of the revolutionary movement of 1977–79.

Capitalist Development and the Growth of the Proletariat

Capitalism presupposes the existence of a proletariat. Capitalist development and proletarianization are two aspects of the same historical process whereby, on one hand, there is the growth and concentration of a new form of productive wealth over the ashes of the old form in the hands of a few; but on the other hand, there is the destruction of the traditional system of production, which separates peasants and petty commodity producers from the means of production—hence, the creation of a reserve army of labor in the cities. The proletarianization process in Iran did not depart from this general historical scheme.

The late growth of capitalism meant the late growth of a working class. The first nucleus of the Iranian working class had been formed between the late nineteenth and early twentieth centuries, not in Iran but in the rich oil fields of the Caucasus, in southern Russia. About 5 percent of the total workers of this region and 50 percent of the workers in the Baku oil establishment were Iranian immigrant workers. On the verge of the Constitutional Revolution, major strikes occurred in Baku, and subsequently thousands of workers were fired, including many Iranians who had to leave their work and return to Iran.[107] With the discovery of oil in Khuzistan in southwest Iran and the establishment of an oil refinery in Abadan, the first major concentrated nucleus of an Iranian working class emerged. As a result of the limited capitalist development under Reza Shah during 1930–40, the working class continued to grow. By the beginning of World War II, the number of industrial workers was estimated at 650,000.[108]

The number of industrial workers continued to grow rapidly in the sixties and seventies, reflecting the impact of both land reform and industrial development. Between the 1956 and 1966 censuses, the population of urban centers (i.e., those with a population of not less than 5,000 inhabitants) grew at a rate of 5.5 percent per annum, as compared with a rate of 3 percent for the whole country. In other words, during this decade 2 million persons left the countryside (and their only partially gainful agricultural or rural occupations) to settle in one of the 249 urban centers. The influx of rural immigrants toward the largest towns was even more rapid. Accordingly, the rural labor force increased by only 19 percent while the economically active urban population increased by 47 percent. In the 1960s rural-urban migration transferred 400,000 job seekers from rural areas to the towns.[109] The sudden population increase in the urban areas is more a reflection of the effect of capitalist development on the process of proletarianization than of a natural growth in the population. Table 4.3 shows the growth in employment in major industries during the 1956–72 period. Employment in utilities, government services, mining and manufacturing, and construction (with 500, 158, 123, and 111 percent increases, respectively) had the highest growth rates. Employment in commerce, the oil industry, and banking exhibited a medium rate of increase (83, 60, and 55 percent, respectively). Employment in transportation and communica-

TABLE 4.3

Employed Population by Major Economic Sectors, 1956–72

(in thousands)

Sector	1956	1966	1972	% increase (1956–72)*
Agriculture	3,326	3,774	3,800	14
Oil	25	26	40	60
Mining and manufacturing (including handicraft)	816	1,324	1,820	123
Construction	336	520	710	111
Utilities	12	53	60	500
Commerce	355	513	650	83
Transport and communications	208	224	255	23
Government services	248	474	640	158
Banking and other services	582	650	900	55
TOTAL (fully or seasonally employed)	5,908	7,558	8,875	50

SOURCE: Adapted from International Labor Office, *Employment and Income Policies for Iran*, p. 31, table 5. Copyright © 1973 International Labour Organization.

TABLE 4.4

Employment in Selected Industries, 1970–76

Industry	1970	1976	Percent increase (1970–76)*
Dairy products	1,191	2,205	85
Vegetable shortening	4,176	5,993	44
Alcoholic beverages	1,445	1,858	29
Nonalcoholic beverages	2,335	5,137	120
Tobacco	6,882	9,024	31
Spinning and weaving	60,122	68,413	14
Leather	1,426	1,611	13
Machinemade shoes	4,419	8,062	82
Petrochemicals	3,018	4,318	43
Paints	757	1,479	95
Pharmaceuticals	1,957	3,170	62
Cosmetics and soap	2,014	3,449	11
Automobile tires	1,305	3,001	130
Glass sheets	773	1,597	107
Cement	4,360	7,227	66
Basic metals	3,312	6,616	100
Household appliances	8,586	13,585	58
Radio, television, and telephone	3,810	6,294	65
Electrical appliances	1,777	4,532	155
Automobiles	9,125	20,270	120
TOTAL	122,800	177,841	45

SOURCE: Bank Markazi Iran, *Annual Report and Balance Sheet* (1975), p. 182; and (1977), p. 142.
  *Percent increase is computed by author.

tions and in agriculture, with increases of 23 and 14 percent respectively, had the lowest growth rate. But the rapid growth of employment in the modern industrial sector as a whole in the early 1970s is evident from table 4.4. From 1970 to 1976, total employment in these industries increased by 45 percent.

The level of concentration of the labor force in the manufacturing sector, however, was quite low. For example, of 1,461,000 estimated workers employed in the manufacturing sector in 1968, 164,000 (11 percent) were employed in industrial units with fifty workers or more, while 87,000 (6 percent) were employed in medium-sized units of ten to fifty workers. The remaining 1,210,000 (83 percent) were employed in small units of under ten workers. As for the concentration of industrial workers on the eve of the revolutionary movement, it was estimated that the industrial work force was to increase to 2.5 million by the end of 1977. Of this number, 720,000 (29 percent) were to be employed in large and medium-sized units.

The lack of considerable industrial concentration is a direct result of the late and limited development of heavy industry. Capital-intensive industrialization did not encourage a high concentration of the labor force (hence limiting the numerical strength and political capacity of workers), while on the other hand, it generated surplus labor that was not absorbed by the industrial sector—thus, simply adding to the army of the destitute whose dwellings were around the big cities in shantytowns and slum areas. Their occupations were those of unskilled laborers in the construction field, street vendors, domestic servants, and load carriers (with or without mules). The expansion of shantytowns, slum areas, and squatter settlements around the major cities became a widespread phenomenon in the 1960s and 1970s. A survey of Tehran's squatter settlements in 1972 showed 428 settlement units with 3,780 households.[111]

The State and the Working Class

The state's orientation toward the merchants and the petty bourgeoisie was at best outright neglect of their interests (which meant that they were left unprotected against competition from international capital and the dependent bourgeoisie), and at worst was consciously directed toward undermining their economic interests and organizational power. State policies toward the working class, in contrast, contained elements of long-term planning. This was so possibly for two major reasons. First, contrary to the bazaar, the proletariat was a growing class that the state could not afford to antagonize. Outright economic and political repression of workers was counterproductive for the regime's stability. Second, the success of the state's industrial policies was to some extent contingent upon a contented working class.

These considerations underlay the evolution of the regime's policy toward the working class. In the mid-1940s, the workers were organized in the Central Council of the Unified Trade Unions of Iranian Workers, which claimed to have a membership of 400,000 workers with 186 affiliates. In the aftermath of the Mossadeq period, the regime suppressed all unions. Even the shadowy official ones were banned in 1957. This cleared the way for a new regime-directed program aimed at the working class: the 1959 Labor Law specified that unions could be established if recognized by the Ministry of Labor, and the 1960 special insurance and 1963 profit-sharing laws established the basis for a system of benefits to selected workers.[112]

However, the workers' right to collective bargaining and to strike was not recognized by the 1959 Labor Law. The law also forbade the unions to engage in political activity. Instead, the state-run unions approached some sort of corporatist structures, in the sense that they were, in Schmitter's authoritative statement,

> "singular, non-competitive, hierarchically ordered, sectorally compartmentalized, interest associations exercising representational monopolies and accepting (de jure or de facto) governmentally imposed or negotiated limitations on the type of leaders they elect and on the scope and intensity of demands they routinely make upon the state."[113]

To be sure, corporatism in Iran did not develop as extensively as it did in Latin America. The state-run labor organizations did not enjoy much power and influence, if any. Nevertheless, these organizations could be considered a variant of corporatism, containing two important elements—ideological and organizational. Ideologically, the state's propaganda machine was categorically rejecting the idea of class conflict while emphasizing "class compromise" under the rubric of "national unity."[114]

In his book, *The White Revolution*, the Shah claimed that "whereas in some countries the workers syndicates are opposing the state or management to fulfill their legitimate demands, today in our country, because of the resolution of the social and economic conflicts and contradictions, these [labor] organizations are moving forward not in opposition to the state but in the same direction."[115] Similarly, Hoveida, the prime minister, stated: "Fortunately, in Iran we neither have a class struggle nor do we believe in it. We are all united as one nation, attempting to achieve the goals of the great Iranian Revolution [referring to the "Shah-People's Revolution"]."[116]

Organizationally, the state encouraged the formation of fragmented unions. These unions were not industrywide but confined to individual factories. By the early seventies, according to one report in 1972, workers' syndicates under the direct supervision of the state were set up in virtually all modern industries, numbering over 574.[117] Another source indicated that in 1971 there were 397 state-run workers' unions and 168 employees' unions. By 1978 the number of these unions increased to 1,023.[118]

Parallel with the setting up of the state-run unions, and to promote further divisions in the working-class movement, the state adopted certain measures to increase the income of workers in selected industries. The first was a profit-sharing scheme, which was assigned as the fourth principle of "the Shah-People's Revolution." The profit-sharing scheme applied to workers in enterprises with ten or more workers, but excluded those in the oil, railway, and tobacco industries. Workers were to receive up to 20 percent of a company's profits, which was to be distributed according to seniority and wages. The law called for agreements between workers and management to determine what the profits were, in return for increased productivity. Another measure was the worker-share scheme, introduced in 1975; like the first one, it was designed to raise productivity.[119] Undoubtedly, these policies (coupled with the Shah's often working-class rhetoric) undermined the workers' revolutionary politics. While state policy inadvertently contributed to the political unity of the bazaar (i.e., the alliance of the merchants and the petty bourgeoisie), it produced a fragmented working class whose organizational weakness and lack of experience constituted a principal factor for the failure of the social revolutionary movement in postrevolutionary Iran (see chapter 8 below).

The Shah's labor policy had some success, however, as reflected in the occurrence of only a few major strikes and little in the way of protest activities in the 1960s and early 1970s. However, the economic difficul-

TABLE 4.5
The Number of Major Strikes in Large
Industrial Establishments in Iran, 1975–77

Year	Number of Strikes[a]	Mean Length (days)[b]
1975	27	5.5
1976	27	5.5
1977	49	Not available

SOURCE: *Navid* (publication of the Tudeh Party of Iran; 1981, various issues).
[a]The quality of data for the number of strikes is fair.
[b]The quality of data for the mean length of strikes is poor.

ties of the seventies, such as inflation and a scarcity of basic necessities, brought down real wages and stimulated protests by industrial workers. Beginning with the oil boom of 1973, strikes in major industrial establishment began to increase from just a few in the 1971–73 period to over twenty-five or thirty a year from 1975 on.[120] According to table 4.5, there were about twenty-seven major strikes per year in 1975 and 1976. In 1977 the number of strikes increased to forty-nine. In 1976 public employees and white-collar workers began to strike, and by the end of 1978 strikes were widespread and infested all sectors of the economy. Strikes in the factories and in the oil fields were initially over economic issues, but then became directly about political matters. Although the regime might have been able to repress the demonstrations by brutal force, as it did in 1963, it could not at the same time end workers' strikes.

The economic difficulties of the mid-seventies, and the specific manner in which the state attempted to resolve these difficulties, provided the background for a de facto unity of the dominated classes against the Shah. This background, however, hardly explains the emergence of coordinated political actions by the members of these classes, their fascinating harmony in demanding the overthrow of the monarchy, and the establishment of an Islamic alternative. An analysis of class interests at the point of production or the market does not provide this missing link. Nor does an organizational/resource mobilization model account for the mobilization of the people against the Shah. Organizational analysis is particularly inadequate in light of the fact that the preexisting organizations of the dominated classes were undermined by the state.

In the following chapter, it will be argued that the process of the people's mobilization against the state, the transformation of economic difficulties and social discontent into a revolutionary crisis, and the effective paralysis of the state's repressive machine occurred through Shi'i revolutionary discourse.

5

The Rise of Revolutionary Islam

To summarize what has been said so far, the 1953 coup effectively ended the national-liberal episode of the post–World War II period and was followed by the inauguration of a bureaucratic-authoritarian state. The state's repressive policies depoliticized politics, and its bureaucratic expansion undermined the preexisting organizations that had mediated the relationship between the state and civil society. The state's ideology further expanded the gap between the state and society, while the state's alliance with international capital antagonized the bazaaris and the landowners. Iran's vulnerability to the destabilizing effects of the world economy, externally induced inflation, and the increased demand for various commodities that overwhelmed supply led to the economic difficulties of the 1970s and produced social discontent.

While all these factors may explain the content of Iran's revolutionary development, they do not account for the emergence of the revolutionary crisis in the late seventies. As will be argued in this chapter, Shi'i revolutionary discourse transformed social discontent into a revolutionary crisis. This chapter first discusses those specific features of the postcoup episode that account for the rise of Shi'i Islam as the dominant ideology of the opposition. Second, it argues that Shi'i revolutionary discourse was not simply a preexisting ideology rooted in the political theory of early Shi'ism or in the institutional development of the ulama in the nineteenth century. Rather it was produced by diverse Islamic intellectuals as a result of the problems they faced in the postcoup (1953) episode. Finally, this chapter will explain the role of the Shi'i discursive field and ritual practices in systematically negating the ideology of the monarchy and in orienting the actions of the discontented groups and classes in a revolutionary direction. I will also show how Shi'i metaphors, symbols, and ceremonies offered an effective channel of communication among participants in the revolution, thus providing a necessary mechanism for the political mobilization of the masses against the state.

The connection between religion and the political concerns of various groups and social classes has been a recurrent phenomenon in nineteenth- and twentieth-century Iran. The bazaaris have often used religious rituals and symbols in their mobilization efforts to change or resist unpopular policies initiated by the state. In its turn, the state has also resorted to religion to justify its actions. There have been occasions in which the ulama's theological hair-splitting paralleled mundane political conflicts in society. However, the rise of Islam as the dominant discourse of the opposition is a special phenomenon of the 1960s and the 1970s. The episodic context commences with the coup of 1953, which resulted in the defeat of the nationalist-democratic movement and the Shah's resumption of power. The broad environmental conditions that provided the context for the growth of revolutionary Islam were characterized by the ulama's unity against the state (which paralleled the antistate alliance of the bazaaris and landowners), the decline of secular ideologies, and the ideology of the state.

State, Class, and the Problem of Ulama Unity

The ulama were a group of learned scholars and jurists, whose religious status made them members of the elite. Their positions gave them significant material wealth as well as social prestige and political power, and they had been an integral part of the polity in procapitalist Iran. The ulama were disciples of a particular school of Shi'ism, the Usuli, whose somewhat exclusive domination in society became established in early nineteenth-century Iran. Up until that time, there had not been much consensus among the ulama regarding the nature of their role in society. They were divided among three competing schools. The first was the Akhbari school, which denies any independent ruling on the part of the ulama above and beyond what is left from the Traditions of the Prophet and the Imams. The Usuli school, on the other hand, asserts the legitimacy of the function of the *mujtahids* in interpreting law and doctrine and in making independent judgments. Finally, there was Sufism, which is basically more concerned with esoteric matters than with the law. The essence of Sufi beliefs has to do with moral contrition and the detachment of the soul from material things. Sufism, like Akhbarism, rejects the validity of any ulama interference in worldly affairs, while claiming that the Sufi doctrine is identical with the esoteric knowledge of the Imams. The Usulis emerged victorious from this ideological struggle.

Noteworthy in this process was that the ulama's internal feud was intertwined with the rise of the Qajar dynasty. As the Qajars consolidated their political power in different parts of the country, the Usuli ulama established their own exclusive religious domination at the expense of the Akhbaris and the Sufis. Such an association between the Qajars and the Usuli ulama was not mere historical accident. The rise of the Usulis to the position of exclusive religious domination and the rise of the Qajars turned out to be two mutually reinforcing historical processes. The Qajars were of nomadic descent, and for them the administration of the country was far more complex than that of a tribe. The leaders of the Qajars faced the tasks of building a bureaucratic-administrative apparatus and establishing legitimacy to their rule. The tribal background of Qajar leaders provided neither the legitimacy nor the administrative structure necessary to rule a country. The new Iranian rulers had to break away from their tribal methods of administration and at the same time transform themselves from being the leaders of a tribe to being the leaders of a nation.

The growth of the Usuli ulama was thus reinforced by their ability to perform educational, judicial, and legitimation functions for the Qajar state. The ulama held a monopoly over the educational apparatus. The judicial system of the Qajar state was divided into two parts—the *'urf* and *shar'* courts. While the 'urf courts covered the areas related to state administration and crimes against the state, shar' courts covered the areas of civil laws and disputes. The ulama had full control over the shar' courts, which seem to have gained considerable importance as general economic conditions in the country began to improve in the early nineteenth century.[1] The development of Shi'i political theory under the Qajars also reflected this process. Arjomand persuasively argues that these two forms of political and religious domination began to represent "the twin functions of imamate—supreme political and religious leadership of the community."[2]

The ulama were interested in maintaining religious and doctrinal uniformity in society, protecting institutional interests, and controlling the traditional educational institutions and the shar' courts. Yet being pressured by conflicting interests in society, they seldom had a unified basis for political action. These conflicting interests were dictated by historical relations between the state, the landed interests, and the bazaar. As a result, diverse factions existed within their own ranks. The specific form of capitalist development, and the state's policies from the 1960s on, provided the bases for ulama unity against the state. Moreover, the ulama's political actions in different periods were also shaped by the kind of discourse dominant in society at the time. To demonstrate this, I shall analyze the role of religion in various political crises of nineteenth- and twentieth-century Iran.

The Ulama and the Tobacco Movement: The Tobacco Movement of 1890–92 is perhaps the first vivid example of a major political division among the ulama. They were torn between supporting the Shah and the concession or siding with the merchants. The available evidence seems to suggest that the variations in their political behavior were related to variations in their sources of support. In Isfahan, for example, the leading ulama became actively involved in the movement because they were connected to the landed interests and the concession had affected their income from tobacco trade. Keddie also concedes that ulama hostility to the concession partly "reflected their ties to merchant families and merchant guilds and their interest in tobacco grown on their private or *vaqf* land"[3] In Tehran, on the other hand, Ayatollah Behbahani was bribed and became allied with Amin us-Sultan (the prime minister), and so refused to participate in the movement.[4] In Azarbayjan, while the merchants and retail traders organized the movement, the ulama were initially reluctant to participate.[5] According to the British Consul: "I am informed from the most reliable sources that it is not true that the Mollahs have been preaching in the mosques against the Regie. In the bazaar and in private houses it is the all-engrossing subject of conversation, but no amount of inquiry elicited the information that the matter has been referred to in the mosques."[6]

The ulama's reluctance to join the movement prompted the anti-Regie activists to distribute an anonymous placard, which was posted up in Tabriz in reply to a notice issued by the tobacco company:

Ulemas [*sic*] of the town! Law is the law of religion and not the laws of the Europeans!

Woe to those Ulemas who will not co-operate with the nation! Woe to those who will not spend their lives and property! Any one of the Ulemas who will not agree with the people will lose his life. Woe to anyone who may sell one muskal of Tobacco to the Europeans! Woe to the Europeans who may wish to enforce these customs of the Infidels. We will kill the European first, and then plunder their property. Woe to the Armenians, who will be killed, and will lose their property and their families! Woe to those who will keep quiet!

We write this in answer to the Notice.

Curses on the father of anyone who may destroy this Notice![7]

In Mashhad, the tobacco merchants and traders organized opposition to the concession, but were unable to attract the cooperation and support of the ulama. Only a few of the ulama—such as Va'ez Sabzivari, Mirza Abdorrahman, and Sayyid Mohammad Kalati—and a group of *tullab* (sing., *talabih*, students of religion) joined the movement. The tobacco company, on the other hand, was successful in gaining the support of Khorasan's governor, Fath Ali Khan Sahibdivan, and the leading ulama. Kennedy reported that "the Governor-General and the principal Ulemas [*sic*] are endeavoring to the best of their ability to allay the excitement which still continues at Meshed [*sic*]."[8] Included among these ulama were Mirza Ahmad Razavi, Haj Shaykh Mohammad Taqi, Sayyid Habibullah, and Shaykh Mohammad Rahim who all sent a telegram to the Shah which read:

These tobacco sellers and some ruffians who know nothing about the affairs of the state and the nation, and do not understand all aspects of the issue, behaved ignorantly, causing the disappointment of His Majesty, the protector of Islam. . . . While praying for the Shah's well being, we began calming down the people; thanks to God . . . and to the intelligence and competence of Sahibdivan, the people were calmed down and dispersed. In every respect, we consider obeying the orders of the Islam protector Shahan-shah our necessary duty.[9]

In Kerman, when people boycotted smoking (after hearing the news about the *fatva*), the merchants reported that smoking had not yet been prohibited by the city's *mujtahids* and ulama. It should be noted that the faction among the ulama that participated in the movement seems to have gained much popularity and recognition, since it reflected a general dissatisfaction present in society. The existence of two opposing factions within the ulama vis-à-vis the issue, however, is a matter of historical fact.

The Ulama and the Constitutional Revolution: The movement that brought about the Constitutional Revolution was largely shaped by a modern political discourse whose central themes were nationalism, secularism, and democracy. The idea of political democracy was at the center of social thought in this period and made up the strongest ideological element of the constitutional movement.[10] These themes were also reflected in the actions of the ulama and in their justifications for a constitutional regime. The ulama demanded a strong and well-organized government, under the protection of which the merchants and craft guilds could run their businesses in peace, domestic industry and trade could be encouraged, and foreign penetrations could be terminated.[11] Among the ulama leading the Constitutional Revolution were Ayatollah Behbahani, Ayatollah Tabataba-i, and Hasan Modarris. There were also ulama like Malekol-Motekallemin, who had ties with the social democrats' circles.

The ideological polarization of society between the followers of monarchical absolutism and the constitutional regime cut through the ranks of the ulama and produced two ideologically opposed factions. The anticonstitutionalist and royalist ulama were led by Shaykh Fazlullah Nuri, who had initially joined Behbahani and Tabataba-i during the early stages of the constitutional movement but later turned against it. He assisted the royalist Imam Jum'eh of Tehran in organizing the Society of Muhammad and called upon devout Muslims to gather in the large Canon Square to defend the *shari'a* from the "heathen" constitutionalists. Evidently, Nuri's counterrevolutionary action was in line with anticonstitutionalist Mohammad Ali Shah. The Shah proclaimed that as a good Muslim he could accept the Islamic term *mashru'* (lawful), but not the alien concept *mashrut* (constitutional).[12]

Shaykh Fazlullah considered the Constitutional Revolution to be a great sedition that had evolved in three stages: discourse and presentation; writing and declaration; and practice and test. He argued that the call for the first stage had been favorably received by all, literate and illiterate, because it was presented in a pleasant way. The second stage involved the writing of the constitution and freedom of the press. Such freedom would allow one to write against religion and religious people and against the ulama (and therefore could not be scripturally sanctioned). In the third stage, the constitutionalists would begin to practice whatever oppression they could. He further added that the drafting of a constitution had involved three innovations, all of which were against Islam and forbidden: the writing of a law apart from Islamic law; forcing subjects to obey a law that was not present in the *shari'a;* and punishing subjects for their failure to obey the written law. Many followers then gathered around the absolutist ulama and seriously threatened the position of the constitutionalists.[13]

The modernist ulama, on the other hand, attempted to reconcile Islam with constitutionalism. For example, Sayyid Mohammad Tabataba-i, a prominent constitutionalist *mujtahid,* spoke favorably of a constitutional government: "I have not seen constitutionalism. But according to what I have heard, and been told by those who visited the constitutional countries, constitutionalism will bring security and prosperity to the country. Therefore, I also became an enthusiast of constitutionalism and interested in setting up a constitutional system for Iran."[14]

A more compelling Islamic argument for constitutionalism was advanced by Ayatollah Mirza Hosein Na'ini:

Once these three points are clear, there remains no room to doubt the necessity of changing a despotic regime into a constitutional one. This is true, because the former consists of three sets of usurpations and oppressions: 1) It is usurpation of the authority of God and injustice to Him; 2) it is usurpation of the Imam's authority and oppression of the Imam; 3) it also involves oppression of the people. By contrast, a constitutional system is only oppression of the Imam, because his authority is usurped. Thus, a constitutional regime limits three sets of oppression to one; consequently it is necessary to adopt it.[15]

Parallel to the ideological debates between the pro- and anticonstitutionalist ulama were intense fights and armed confrontations between the constitutionalists and the royalists. The royalists and their supporters among the ulama were eventually defeated, and Shaykh Fazlullah Nuri was executed.[16]

The Ulama and the Pahlavis: The Constitutional Revolution did not lead to democracy, and Reza Shah ruled in an arbitrary manner. Nevertheless, the themes of secularism and nationalism remained central features of the dominant cultural trend in society. As was mentioned in chapter 1, the leading social critics and intellectuals, both within and outside the polity, considered religious establishments, communal sectarianism, and tribalism to be the real obstacles to Iran's development and progress. The secular nationalist discourse also shaped, and at the same time was reinforced by, Reza Shah's modernization policies. The state's ideology under Reza Shah and the dominant cultural trend in society belonged to the same ideological universe.

This ideological context partly explains Reza Shah's success in implementing his modernization policies. Although the ulama were instrumental in his ascendance to the throne,[17] as soon as the Shah consolidated his power he launched severe attacks on their power and privileges. Under his rule, the ulama gradually lost all their seats in the Majles as well as control of the educational and judicial institutions. He brought the *Owqaf* (religious endowments) under government control. Considerable changes in people's clothing styles (including prohibition of the veil) were initiated and enforced. The importance of Shi'i Islam was downplayed, while the Shah's ideologues glorified pre-Islamic Iranian kingship and culture.[18] Obviously, the ulama did not like these policies. Nevertheless, these anti-ulama measures did not provide a natural background for the ulama's united opposition to the state. The ulama's response to modernization was contradictory. Some of them withdrew their support of the Shah and engaged in oppositional activities (these included Ayatollah Kashani, Haj Aqa Nurrollah Isfahani, Sayyid Hasan Modarris, Shaykh-ul Eslam Malayeri, and Shaykh Naser Rasouli). But another faction among the ulama submitted to Reza Shah's rule and thus gained wealth and position (these included Hairi-Zadeh, Mohammad Tadayyon, Shaykh Asadullah Mamqani, Shaykh Ali Dashti, Sayyid Ya'qub Anvar, Sayyid Ahmad Behbahani, Mirza Hashem Ashtiyani, and Sayyid Hasan Taqi-zadeh).[19]

The ulama's impotence vis-à-vis Reza Shah also correlated with the divergent political orientations of their various class bases—the landed aristocracy, the merchants, and the petty bourgeoisie. As indicated in the previous chapter, the Shah's economic policies by and large satisfied the merchants and the landed aristocracy, while undermining the petty bourgeoisie. The latter did constitute a base for some ulama-led political protests against the Shah in 1927 and 1935.

Reza Shah's repressive effectiveness and military power may also explain the absence of a major ulama-led opposition movement. This factor, however, did not seem to be a decisive one, for after his downfall in

1941 the ulama's orientation toward the state was not predominantly oppositional. On the contrary, a sort of ulama-monarch alignment was formed that lasted until 1959.[20] The conservative ulama (such as Ayatollah Sayyid Mohammad Behbahani, Shaykh Baha-uddin Nuri, Shaykh Mohammad Ali Lavasani, and Falsafi, the preacher) supported the new Shah (Mohammad Reza Shah) and participated in religious ceremonies organized by the court and the army to pray for his health and well-being.[21] The main supporter of the Shah was the sole *Marja' Taqlid* (the source of emulation), Ayatollah Burujirdi. The Burujirdi family had close and friendly relationships with the Pahlavis. Abdul Hosein, the leader of the family, once told Reza Shah that "we have always been the protectors and guardians of the monarchy, and have repeatedly shown our attachments to the Pahlavis."[22] Burujirdi supported the Shah when he changed the Constitution in 1949 that expanded his power,[23] and even went so far as to organize a convention in Qum in which the ulama passed a resolution that prohibited the clergy from joining political parties or taking part in politics.[24] By doing so, the Left and nationalist leaders have long argued, Burujirdi became the court's accomplice, for he attempted to prevent young clergymen from participating in the nationalist movement.

To be sure, a relatively small group of influential ulama participated in the National Front. Ayatollah Kashani was a leading *mujtahid* who supported Mosaddeq's nationalization of the Anglo-Iranian Oil Company. Ayatollah Mohammad Taqi Musavi Khvansari, in an implicit reference to Burujirdi (and in response to questions from a number of merchants in the central bazaar of Tehran), cited the Prophet Muhammad as saying that he who, upon waking up in the morning, does not concern himself with the affairs of Muslims, is not himself a Muslim. The faithful had no choice but to unite and support the position advanced by Kashani regarding the nationalization of the AIOC, declared Khvansari.[25] Another left-oriented *mujtahid* was Ayatollah Ali Akbar Burgha'i, who was a member of the National Front and the International Partisans of Peace.[26] He also stood for female enfranchisement. But the most influential *mujtahid* among the three was Ayatollah Kashani, who was popular among the second echelon and lower-ranking members of the ulama as well as with the mosque congregations and the itinerant preachers.[27]

However, considering the dominant political discourse in society, the ulama-Shah alignment may not be too hard to understand. The National Front was not only secular but also democratic. For the ulama, the secularism of the past two decades had been bad enough. Now, combined with democracy in the National Front, it threatened to lead to a total decline of their power and resources. The religious establishment frequently protested secularism and irreligiousness in society, and the conservative ulama often blamed the nationalist leaders for the prevalence of "social corruption." In the fall of 1947, religious extremists began harassing and attacking unveiled women and, in certain cases, threw acid at their faces. They threatened to punish bazaaris who let these women shop at their stores. They also attacked and murdered several Baha'i families. A religious terrorist organization, the Feda'iyan-i Islam, was also formed in the mid-1940s to fight all forms of irreligion, and its first act was to assassinate Ahmad Kasravi. The assassins were acquitted, however, because of lobbying by religious leaders.[28] Therefore, Ayatollah Burujirdi's alliance with the Shah was not indicative of his opportunism and indifference to the nationalist cause. His major aim was to protect the religious establishment. As his politically active colleagues also discovered a few months before the coup, alliance with the Shah against the menace of democracy and secularism seemed, at the time, the best option. Shaykh Fazlullah Nuri, during the course of the Constitutional Revolution, had reached the same conclusion. It is thus hardly surprising to find the ulama offering predominant support for the Shah in the 1953 coup:

> Not only Kashani and his followers became the enemy of the [nationalist] movement, but also the *Marja' Taqlid* and the ulama who followed the Court and the reaction were all united to defeat Mosaddeq. . . .
> [Burujirdi] and other religious leaders, in their opposition to Mosaddeq, went so far as to call for mourning in the mosques to show their grief for the Shah's departure from Iran. On August 19, 1953, Burujirdi sent a cable to the Shah pleading: "come back since with your return to Iran religion and order will be protected in the country." Later on, in his response to a cable from Zahedi, he wrote: shall almighty God help you in your protection of Islam and in the elimination of the nation's enemies. . . . In addition to Burujirdi and Kashani, Ayatollah Behbahani was one of the most active reactionary *mujtahids* who was in direct contact with the Court.[29]

Given this pro-Pahlavi orientation of a large section of the ulama in the 1953 coup, why did they turn against the Shah in unison at a later time? What historical processes provided the basis for the unity of the ulama?

It is evidently inadequate to argue that the ulama-Shah encounter occurred because the Shah was perpetrating a modernization scheme
aimed at the very citadel of ulama occupational interests. The modernization of social institutions and the centralization of power were first
launched by Reza Shah, and at that time the ulama's political response
was not predominantly oppositional. What did change under the second Shah (in addition to further changes in the ideology of the state in
an anti-Islamic direction) was the convergence of the politics of the
classes constituting the historical bases of the ulama—the petty bourgeoisie, the merchants, and the landowners. State economic policies
strongly in favor of large establishments in the agricultural, industrial,
and commercial sectors tied to international capital highly antagonized
these classes—hence the emergence of an objective basis for the ulama's
unity and expansion of power.

Up until the implementation of land reform, the conservative faction
of the ulama (Burujirdi and Behbahani) continued to support the Shah.
When talks about land reform became popular, these ulama began to
voice their disagreement. Referring to the land reform bill of late 1959,
Ayatollah Burujirdi in February 1960 wrote to Sayyid Ja'far Behbahani,
stating that for some time there had been rumors that the size of landed
estates was to be limited, and that he had informed the prime minister
personally (and the Shah in writing) that such a step would be contrary
to the law of Islam.[30] The ulama were also concerned about the threat
of land reform to their own property and to land belonging to the religious institutions. Historically, some of the ulama constituted an important component of the landowning class. Although under Reza
Shah religious institutions and the ulama lost much of their land, until
the implementation of land reform in the early 1960s the ulama still
owned considerable landed interests. (As table 3.2 shows, before land
reform 15 percent of all land was controlled by religious institutions.)[31]

The Decline of Liberalism and Communism

At the same time the ulama found themselves united against the Shah,
the National Front and the Tudeh party began to experience considerable internal dissensions and splits in the postcoup period. As a result,
the ideological framework and concepts derived from national-
liberalism and Tudeh-style Communism increasingly lost their appeal
and relevance to the intellectuals and activists. A combination of effec-

tive state repression, the growth of a radical faction among the ulama, and tactical errors and disorganization of the existing secular political groups provided the climate for an extraordinary mass "conversion" to Islam as an alternative revolutionary ideology to both Communism and national-liberalism.

The growth and consolidation of the bureaucratic-authoritarian state in the postcoup period had debilitating effects on the secular opposition. The National Front was a heterogeneous movement, consisting of diverse parties and influential individuals with varying degrees of militancy. The most militant members of the Front, besides Mosaddeq, were Fatemi, Shayegan, Razavi, and Karimpur Shirazi. The less militant members were people like Sanjabi, Saleh, Hasebi, Zirakzadeh, Zanganeh, and Parsa. In between were people like Foruhar, the founder of the National party, and Maleki, the head of the Third Force (whose name after the coup was changed to *Jame'eh-ye Sosyalist-ha-ye Iran*— the Society of Iranian Socialists). The Front also contained a religious faction consisting of people like Bazargan, Ayatollah Taleqani, and others. In 1954, these groups formed the National Resistance Movement (*Nahzat-i Moqavemat-i Melli*).

During the course of its activities between 1954 and 1961, the National Resistance Movement failed to effectively challenge the Shah's dictatorship.[32] On one hand, the radical members of the Front were repressed brutally. Mosaddeq was sentenced to three years' imprisonment and strict house arrest for life. Fatemi was executed, and Karimpour Shirazi was murdered in prison. Shayegan and Razavi, released after three years' imprisonment, were put under continuous surveillance and not allowed to have contacts with their colleagues. On the other hand, the less militant members of the Front (who were gradually released from prison) were strongly pro–United States. Saleh, a top leader of the Iran party, accepted the Eisenhower doctrine, which had assigned the United States the leading role in defending "the free world and combating Communism."[33] It should be remembered that the growth of the liberal-nationalist movement in the post–World War II period was to a considerable extent aided by the United States, which was portraying itself as the champion of peace, democracy, and the anticolonial movement. The United States' image in Iran was also enhanced by the existence of conflict between British and U.S. oil interests in the region. The Iranian nationalists counted heavily on U.S. support to build a democratic and independent Iran. But in the post-1953 period, the situation was quite different. The United States had proved to be a callous ally for Iran's nationalist movement under Mosaddeq. And the idea of democracy and pluralism was too closely associated with imperialism to prevent the intellectuals from advancing a causal argument that since the West had betrayed Iran, Western-style democracy was an inappropriate model for the country's development and independence. Therefore, the leaders of the National Front's persistent attempts to gain U.S. support was a tactic that became increasingly ineffective, if not counterproductive. The United States' effective support of the Shah constituted an insurmountable anomaly for nationalist-liberal thought.

The inauguration of the Kennedy administration and subsequent pressures on the Shah to relax police control and to implement land reform ushered in a short "breathing period" (to use Jazani's phrase) for the opposition between 1960 and 1963.[34] Consequently, the nationalist-liberal politicians began to engage openly in political activities, chanting again the early fifties' slogan that the Shah should reign not rule and that the principles of the constitutional monarchy be observed. The National Resistance Movement gave way to the Second National Front in this period. Dissatisfied with the Front, but not in opposition to it, Bazargan and Taleqani, assisted by a group of Muslim intellectuals and activists, founded the Freedom Movement of Iran (*Nahzat-i Azad-i Iran*), which became the main party of the Second National Front. The Front soon experienced internal disputes over tactical and organizational matters. The Freedom Movement argued for close cooperation with the ulama, while the dominant faction preferred the slogan "Land Reform Yes, Dictatorship No." The radicals in the Front demanded waging ideological struggle against the Shah, while the liberals, predominantly from the Iran party, preferred attacking the regime on concrete issues such as the lack of democratic freedom and the continued house arrest of Mosaddeq. There were also organizational problems. To control the radical elements, the liberals who had occupied key positions in the Second National Front attempted to transform the Front into a party under their own control, demanding the dissolution of all the parties and the participation of their members in the Front as individuals, not as party representatives. The opposing faction, including Mosaddeq himself (who had still maintained secret contact with the Front's leaders and other parties), argued that the Front must remain an alliance of parties and groups and that its executive organs and leadership should reflect this fact. The latter prevailed, and the leaders of the Second National Front resigned. The Third National Front, based on an alliance of parties, was formed in 1965. At any rate, except for the publication of a few placards (including an open letter to U Thant, then the General Secretary of the United Nations, regarding the violation of human rights and the lack of democratic freedom in Iran), the Front was unable to play a leading role in the opposition movement.[35]

The Tudeh party was even more debilitated by state repression. Founded in 1941, the Tudeh gained considerable strength in the post–World War II period, especially under Mosaddeq. Its strength declined drastically after the coup, as a result both of the Shah's effective repression and of the extensive psychological and propaganda warfare waged against it. The Tudeh was further undermined by a number of splits and defections between the late 1940s and the early 1960s. The first was a split led by Khalil Maleki, Anvar Khameh-ei, Jalal Ale-Ahmad, and others. The second split (1965) was caused by the Sino-Soviet dispute, when two senior Central Committee members—Ghulam Foroutan and Ahmad Qasemi—left the Tudeh and formed a pro-Chinese organization. In addition to state repression, considerable propaganda warfare was waged against it by virtually all the organizations and parties within the opposition, which accused the Tudeh of sacrificing national interests for the Communist International,[36] of being reformist and revisionist,[37] and of betraying the National Front.[38] It was also blamed for the failure of the nationalist movement under Mosaddeq. Evidently, these extensive ideological attacks did not leave much breathing space for the Tudeh.

By the early to mid-1960s, the National Front and the Tudeh party were in serious trouble. The state for the most part used every means to ensure the organizational destruction of both movements. By doing so, it left a void in the realm of ideological production and dissemination; thus, there was no real competition against the radical Islamic intellectuals and new converts such as Ale-Ahmad (see below) in formulating an alternative claim to control over the polity.

Noteworthy in the liberal-nationalist period (1941–53), nonclerical Islamic intellectuals and activists were also involved in the National Front. People like Mehdi Bazargan and Muhammad Nakhshab were members of the Iran party. However, their deep anti-Communism prompted them to withdraw from the party in the mid-forties because the Iran party had allied itself with the Tudeh party. In this period, Bazargan formed an Islamic Student Society at Tehran University, which was intended to stem the influence of Communism.[39] The society, however, had little appeal to most student activists before 1953, but did gain some ground after the coup since it was the only nongovernment organization permitted to function on the university campus.[40] Similarly, Nakhshab formed the Movement of God-Worshipping Socialists (*Nahzat-i Khoda Parastan-i Sosyalist*). In short, Islamic political ideas were not popular among the nationalists and political activists in this period. Even Bazargan's mingling of religion with politics was considered a nuisance both during his student life in Paris as well as during his activities in the National Front under Mosaddeq.[41]

Revolutionary Islamic Discourse

To repeat what was said in chapter 2 about state ideology, in many crucial respects considerable similarities existed between Reza Shah's ideology and that of his son—but there was one major difference. The dominant cultural trend within civil society and Reza Shah's cultural policies belonged, in principle, to the same ideological universe: secularism and nationalism. The Shah's modernization policies were supported by his critics, although on the whole they were ambivalent about his rule. But under his son, the ideology of the opposition began to change. The postcoup social critics and ideologues began to resort to Islam in their attempt to address Iran's problems. The more the Shah insisted on his secular antireligious ideology, the less he was applauded by his critics; for the insistence on his discourse widened the gap between state and civil society, and the domination of his regime over society became more explicit.

It should be emphasized that revolutionary Islamic discourse was not simply a preexisting ideology resting on the political theory of early Shi'ism or in ulama institutional development, ready to be used by discontented groups and classes against the Shah. Rather it was produced by diverse ideologues such as Ayatollah Khomeini, Ale-Ahmad, and Ali Shari'ati, who were all inspired by the problems of political repression, the state's policies, and the highly uneven distribution of resources. In producing the imageries of an alternative Islamic society, these ideologues were constrained not only by Islamic concepts but also by the state ideology itself. Islamic Revolutionary discourse was produced in contradistinction with the state ideology because for them, whatever the state ideology was was not right. Therefore, what was said about an ideal Islamic state to a significant extent was a reaction to what the Shah was saying about the desirability of his rule. However, the Islamic movement was itself heterogeneous, consisting of various Islamic ideologues with diverse backgrounds, interests, and political agendas. Yet it appeared as a single movement by virtue of its relation to one common enemy—the Shah.

The call for the overthrow of the Shah on the part of the ulama was a gradual process. In the early 1970s, only a faction among the ulama under the leadership of Ayatollah Khomeini was fighting for the establishment of an Islamic government under the exclusive control of the supreme religious leader (i.e., the *faqih*). The growth of this ideology among the ulama seems to have been the result of changes in the triadic relationship involving the state, various classes, and the ulama in the sixties and seventies. The state not only definitively broke with the ulama but also antagonized the members of the classes that had historically close ties with the ulama. This situation, therefore, made ulama unity an objective possibility and at the same time shifted the balance of forces in favor of the radical ulama, for they were the ones who had developed a specific political agenda.

Nevertheless, the transformation from objective possibility to wished-for actuality was not an unproblematic process for the ulama in their attempts to gain unity and total power. Granted that they were being antagonized by the policies of a hostile state and that all the classes constituting their bases had turned against the state— nonetheless, these conditions (while setting up the necessary conditions for ulama unity) do not by themselves sufficiently explain how unity among the ulama for the establishment of an Islamic government actually transpired. Nor was there an intellectual precedent for the establishment of such a political institution. For one thing, the Usuli position simply called for the ulama's independent judgments on those matters not directly specified or left unclear in the religious texts; it did not call for the specific establishment of an Islamic government under the ulama's exclusive sway. For another, the ulama and their devout followers had to be convinced that their claim to total power was not only consistent with the political teachings of Shi'ism but also—and this was crucial—that it was practical. Only then could one expect the ulama to act harmoniously for the achievement of an ideologically justified common goal. It was within this context that Ayatollah Khomeini's political theory for the establishment of an Islamic government was produced and gained increasing attention.

Khomeini articulated his arguments for the establishment of an Islamic government based on *velayat-i faqih* (governance by the jurisprudent) by gearing these toward the antistate and antiforeign orientations of the bazaar. Khomeini would first present his view of the problem, blaming the "imperialists" and their "agents" for the imposition of the "unjust economic order" on the Muslim people:

> Through the political agents they have placed in power over the people, the imperialists have also imposed on us an unjust economic order, and thereby divided our people into two groups: oppressors and oppressed. Hundreds of millions of Muslims are hungry and deprived of all form of health care and education, while minorities comprised of all the wealthy and powerful live a life of indulgence, licentiousness, and corruption. The hungry and deprived have constantly struggled to free themselves from the oppression of their plundering overlords, and their struggle continues to this day. But their way is blocked by the ruling minorities and the oppressive governmental structures they head.[42]

Therefore:

> How can we stay silent and idle today when we see that a band of traitors and usurpers, the agents of foreign powers, have appropriated the wealth and the fruits of labor of hundreds of millions of Muslims—thanks to the support of their masters and through the power of the bayonet—granting the Muslims not the least right to prosperity? It is the duty of Islamic scholars and all Muslims to put an end to this system of oppression and, for the sake of the well-being of hundreds of millions of human beings, to overthrow these oppressive governments and form an Islamic government.[43]

Khomeini's central political objective was to identify Islam with the ulama by attempting (1) to indicate the consistency of his views with Shi'i political theory; and (2) to define a true Muslim emphatically as anyone who believed in the authority of the ulama. Khomeini argued that Islam gives, in the Quran and Tradition (*Sunnat*), "all the laws and principles needed by man for his happiness and perfection."[44] But, "their execution and implementation depend upon the formation of a government."[45] The ulama's governance would be "an institution for ensuring the rigorous application of Shari'a to Muslim society."[46]

Therefore, the jurisprudent (i.e., *faqih*) "has the same authority that the Most Noble Messenger and the Imams had," except that his authority does not extend to other jurisprudents.[47]

Khomeini's attempts to champion the cause of the ulama by equating ulama power with both Islam and the integrity of Iran are evident in many of his writings.[48] Khomeini's attack on the secular Shi'i movement was indeed based on his conviction that one cannot be a Muslim if one does not recognize ulama power.

Although Khomeini attempted to establish some consistency between his views and Shi'i political theory, many of his ideas were simply his own invention, and their growing acceptance was principally due to the specific socioeconomic and political context of the 1960s and 1970s. This is so because the functions of the ulama, in Rose's apt assessment, "have been formalized and institutionalized in Khomeini's thought to a degree that renders them, frankly, things different from the functions undertaken traditionally by jurisprudents."[49]

If the ulama's ideological attack on the Shah was all that was going on in the postcoup Islamic opposition, then there would be no real need to treat Islam as an autonomous discourse. The idea of Islamic government could simply be treated as an organizational ideology produced by the ulama in response to state challenges to their authority, and its growth attributed to the hostilities of the bazaaris and landowners to the Shah's economic policies. Such, however, was not the case, for many leading secular intellectuals in the period under consideration also began using Islamic discourse in order to address Iran's socioeconomic and political problems. Islamic political discourse was indeed a constitutive feature of the postcoup development of oppositional activities.

Two lay intellectuals were to play prominent roles in popularizing revolutionary Islam among the educated people. The first was an ex-Communist, Jalal Ale-Ahmad, and the second was Ali Shari'ati, who in his youth had been a member of the Movement of God-Worshipping Socialists. Ale-Ahmad was from a clerical family. His father, Shaykh Ahmad was a clergyman and Ayatollah Taleqani was his paternal uncle. Ale-Ahmad completely broke with religion by joining the Tudeh party, and his works at that time, particularly *Did-du Bazdid* and *Seh Tar*, had an explicitly antireligious tone. In 1947, Ale-Ahmad, with his friend and mentor Khalil Maleki, left the party. He returned to political activity during the oil nationalization period. With Maleki, he allied with Muzzafar Baqai's Toilers' party (*Hizb-i Zahmat-Kashan*). When Baqai withdrew his support of Mosaddeq, both Ale-Ahmad and Maleki split from the Toilers' party and established the Third Force (*Niru-ye Sivvum*). Three months before the coup, Ale-Ahmad withdrew from the Third Force, after which he never joined any organized political movement.

Ale-Ahmad attempted to reexamine the causes of the defeat of the nationalist and democratic movement, to understand the roots of Iran's underdevelopment and its domination by imperialism, and to rethink the ideological resolutions offered by Iranian intellectuals. In his relatively short lifetime, Ale-Ahmad produced about forty-five books, articles, and translations. Three major works are directly related to the above issues and reflect the core of his sociopolitical thoughts: *Seh Maqaleh-ye Digar* [Three more essays], *Gharbzadegi* [Plagued by the West, or Westoxication], and *Dar Khedmat va Khianat-i Roushanfikran* [Concerning the service and betrayal of the intellectuals]. Ale-Ahmad viewed these works as parts of a single self-study of Iranian history and culture. *Gharbzadegi* represents a turning point in Ale-Ahmad's intellectual life, for it marks the beginning of his departure from Marxism toward an appreciation of the significance of Islam in the Middle East. At the outset, he begins with the observation that Iran is not industrialized.

> But, forced by economics, politics, and that global confrontation between poverty and wealth, we must be polite and servile consumers of the products of western industry, or at best we must be satisfied, subservient, and low-paid repairmen for whatever comes from the west. It is this last which necessitates that we re-shape ourselves, our government, our culture, and our everyday lives into some semblance of a machine.[50]

The root of the problem is the contradiction between Islam and Western culture:

> The West, in its dealing with us, not only struggled against this Islamic totality (in the case of the bloody instigation of Shi'ism of Safavid times, in the creation of friction between us and the Ottomans, in promoting the Baha'i activities in the middle of the Qajar period, in the crushing of the Ottomans after the first World War, and finally in the opposition to the Shi'ite clergy during the Constitutional Revolution and afterwards. . .), but it also tried to as quickly as possible

tear apart that unity which was fragmented from within and which only appeared whole on the surface. They tried first to turn us into raw material, as they did the natives in Africa, and afterwards bring us to their laboratories. It was because of this that among the many encyclopedias produced in the West, the *Encyclopedia of Islam* is the most important. We are still asleep but the westerner in this encyclopedia has brought us to his laboratory. India was almost the same as Africa, with its "confusion of tongues," and the diversity of its races and religions. Then again, South America was completely converted to Christianity under the swords of the Spanish, and Oceania was a collection of islands, i.e., the best geography for sowing division. It was our lot then to be the only ones, both in the guise and the reality of an Islamic totality, to stand in the way of the advance of European civilization (read: colonialism; Christianity), i.e, in the way of the drive to market western industry. The stopping of Ottoman artillery outside of the gates of Vienna in the nineteenth [*sic*] century was the end of a prolonged event which had begun in 732 in Spain (Andalus). How can we view these twelve centuries of struggle and competition between East and West as anything but a struggle between Islam and Christianity?[51]

The emancipation of Iranian history and culture from Western cultural domination is Ale-Ahmad's solution. This emancipation involves a relentless attack on the secular intellectuals who have been the bearers of Western culture in Iran. Since the West is in conflict with Islam, it is clear that defending Islam is the only way to liberation and development. In his defense of Islam and critique of the West, Ale-Ahmad even argues that the execution of Shaykh Fazlullah Nuri during the Constitutional Revolution marked the triumph of Western domination over Iran:

> I agree with Dr. Tondar Kiya who writes that Shaikh Nuri was not hanged as an opponent of the Constitutional movement (for in the beginning he was in fact a defender of it), but as a proponent of "the rule of the *Shariat*" and, I will add, as a defender of the integrity of Shi'ism. It was for this reason that in the wake of his death everyone was waiting for a writ to be issued from Najaf. And this was going on at a time when the leader of our west-stricken intelligentsia, Malkom Khan, was a Christian and Talebof was a social democrat from the Caucasus. In any case, from that day on we were marked with the

brand of westitis. I consider the corpse of that great man [Nuri] hanging from the gallows, to be a banner bearing the emblem of the final victory of westitis over this country after 200 years of struggle.[52]

Therefore, in Ale-Ahmad's view, those who translated the French constitution for Iran and those who sacrificed Iran's national interests for the Communist International are of the same type, responsible for the decline of Iran's historical and cultural identity.[53]

In *Dar Khedmat va Khianat-i Roushanfikran*, Ale-Ahmad developed a more detailed and sophisticated critique of the intellectuals. At the outset, he indicates that the book was provoked by the bloody demonstration of 1963, which was led by Ayatollah Khomeini, and by the indifference of the intelligentsia vis-à-vis the event.[54] Ale-Ahmad attributes five characteristics to Iranian intellectuals: (1) having a Western lifestyle, (2) being irreligious or antireligious, (3) being educated, (4) being alienated from their local and traditional environment, and (5) having a scientific worldview.[55] Ale-Ahmad argues that the antireligious orientation of the Iranian intellectual is a simple imitation of their European counterparts and is not rooted in Iranian culture or history. Critiques of religion in Europe, says Ale-Ahmad, were rooted in the Enlightenment (which culminated in the French Revolution); caused by the industrial revolution and the development of science and technology; reactions to the close association between church and state; and stemmed from the fact that a comprehensive system of laws on commerce and politics is absent in Christianity. In Iran, on the other hand, there has been no Enlightenment movement, no industrial revolution, and no significant connection between the state and religion. Moreover, Islam offers guidelines on virtually all aspects of social life. Finally, while the European intelligentsia have had vast intellectual resources, a tradition of discovery and inventions in laws, science, and philosophy, the Iranians have had none of these. Therefore, they (Iranian intellectuals) are not authentic but uprooted imitators.[56] Ale-Ahmad then concludes his critique by suggesting that

The intellectuals must decide between two alternatives:
— Either putting an end to the westoxication, and in its stead attempting to understand the native environment and problems, and making serious efforts, worthy of an intellectual, to solve these problems by means of the latest scientific methods; or,

— continuing the westoxication to the extreme, that is, a total reorganization of the Iranian society according to the moral, political and social standards of the West. This will result in a complete spiritual, national and cultural annihilation of Iran from the face of the world.

In other words, the choice is between resisting colonialism or completely submitting to it. Submission to the western cultural domination is of course easy and beneficial. But resistance is hard and demands many sacrifices.[57]

That Ale-Ahmad's understanding of Iranian history was inadequate, if not flatly wrong, and that it reflected, in Adami'yat's apt assessment, a "confusion in historical thinking" is beside the point.[58] After all, when history becomes relevant for political action, it is not the kind of history that is based on what actually happened but is often based on what political actors think happened. In the absence of an effective secular organization, this kind of distorted history found a large and interested audience in the public.

At any rate, Ale-Ahmad was followed by a leading Shi'i ideologue, Ali Shari'ati. Like Ale-Ahmad, Shari'ati was born into a clerical family. Shari'ati's father, Muhammad Taqi Shari'ati, was one of the Iranian ulama. In his youth, Shari'ati was a member of the Movement of God-Worshiping Socialists and of the Center for the Propagation of Islamic Truth. After receiving a B.A. in Arabic and French from the University of Mashhad, he won a state scholarship to study in France. In 1959 Shari'ati began his graduate work in sociology at the Sorbonne in Paris, where he joined the Freedom Movement and the Confederation of Iranian Students.

In many respects, Shari'ati begins where Ale-Ahmad leaves off: a criticism of the intellectuals' critique of religion. He sympathetically quotes 'Abduh, who had said, "Europe abandoned religion and made progress, we abandoned religion and went backward."[59] Struggle against religion in Iran, says Shari'ati,

is different from the opposition of the educated people of Europe to religion. Opposition of the intellectuals to religion in Europe was rooted in their own experiences and knowledge of religion, the Middle Ages and the Church. The opposition of Iranian intellectuals to religion is rather based on a blind mimicking of the Europeans. . . . Our contemporary educated people understand neither Islam nor its history. They know only a European language and have translated the Europeans' judgement about their own religion [into Persian], and then imitation.[60]

For Shari'ati religion is the most effective weapon to fight imperialism and Western cultural domination. He even began challenging Fanon on the question of religion and revolution. Shari'ati says:

> Franz Fanon, whom I know personally and whose books I translated into Persian, was pessimistic about the positive contribution of religion to social movement. He had, in fact an anti-religious attitude until I convinced him that in some societies where religion plays an important role in the culture, religion can, through its resources and psychological effects, help the enlightened person to lead his society toward the same destination toward which Fanon was taking his own through non-religious means.[61]

In his attacks on Marxism, Shari'ati goes beyond Ale-Ahmad's critique of the Stalinist version of Marxism. While drawing upon concepts and categories from liberalism, Marxism, and existentialism, he claims that Islam transcends all these ideologies:

> Humanity arrived at liberalism, and took democracy in place of theocracy as its key to liberation. It was snared by a crude capitalism, in which democracy proved as much a delusion as theocracy. . . .
> The desire for equality, for liberation from this dizzying whirl of personal avarice, so horrifyingly accelerated by the machine, led humanity into a revolt that resulted in communism. This communism, however, simply represents the same fanatical and frightening power as the Medieval Church, only without God. It has its popes, but they rule not in the name of the Lord but in the name of the proletariat.[62]

This kind of criticism of Marxism was evidently in line with the Shah's policy of anti-Communism. The regime began publishing his works on this topic in a series of articles entitled "Man, Marxism, and Islam" in the daily newspaper *Kayhan* between February and March 1976. These articles most probably contributed to the rise of Islamic revolutionary discourse. At any rate, Shari'ati's teachings of revolutionary Islam contributed to the emergence of Islamic revolutionary groups. An important organizational offshoot of his discourse was the emergence of a new form of religious gathering called *Hoseinieh-e Ershad*. In this forum, Shari'ati gave lectures on various facets of Islam, and these became quite popular among the educated public. The *Hoseinieh Ershad* in turn provided an organizational context for the growth and propagation of revolutionary Islamic organizations.

As it grew, the Islamic revolutionary discourse increasingly conditioned the political actions of secular groups in the opposition. Different leftist groups began to emphasize the role of religion in the struggle against the Shah, attempting to forge alliances with the Islamic opposition. Too desperate in its efforts to overthrow the Shah, the Left downplayed its ideological differences with these Islamic intellectuals and began approaching Islamic groups as possible allies. After the Khomeini-led bloody demonstration of 1963, this tendency became quite strong within the Left. For example, Mostafa Shoa'ie'yan, a leftist activist, suggested the use of religious tactics for a revolutionary mobilization of the masses. He indicated that the ulama were among those having extensive propaganda facilities. Since the leading ulama such as Ayatollahs Khomeini, Millani, and Taleqani were actively engaged in the opposition movement, argued Shoa'ie'yan, the use of religious tactics would gain an added significance. He then suggested that the ulama should issue *fatvas* to boycott basically every thing which had to do with the government, adopting a religious tactic similar to the tobacco boycott of the late nineteenth century.[63] Similarly, having failed in their efforts to forge an alliance with the National Front for over a decade, the leaders of the Tudeh party changed tactics and began approaching the religious opposition. For many years, the Tudeh was boasting that it was one of their Central Committee members who recorded Khomeini's speech against the Shah in 1963 and subsequently broadcasted it through their clandestine radio station.[64]

In sum, revolutionary Islamic discourse was produced and formed, as it were, as a result of the propaganda warfare and back-and-forth argument between the state ideology and the opposition within the changing conditions of the postcoup period. It should be remembered that when secular-nationalist discourse was the dominant ideology in civil society, Iran's underdevelopment and economic backwardness was attributed to clerical influence, tribalism, communal sectarianism, and the undemocratic nature of the monarchy. The solution was sought in the separation of religion from politics, the strengthening of the democratic institutions, and national integration. Western democracy was also envied and emulated. Secular ideology had also left its marks on religion as a group of ulama attempted to reconcile Islam with the idea of constitutionalism and democracy during the Constitutional Revolution, and then to depoliticize Islam altogether in the late forties. Considering changes in the socioeconomic and political climate of the postcoup period, revolutionary Islam became the dominant discourse of the opposition, and different themes gained significance: (1) the idea that underdevelopment and economic inequality is connected to Western cultural domination; (2) the idea that religion and politics are inseparable and that Islam is a revolutionary and anti-imperialist ideology; (3) the anti-Islamic nature of the institution of monarchy; and (4) the rejection of the political systems of both the West and East.

The Shi'i Discursive Field and Ideological Mobilization

In the 1960s and 1970s, the Shah apparently did not need to worry about the possibility of a serious revolutionary challenge to his rule. His kingdom seemed politically stable. The Left and the National Front had been effectively undermined, and after the suppression of the Khomeini-led rebellion in 1963, the religious opposition was unable to organize a similar reaction. It was a period of rapid economic growth and industrialization with no noticeable economic problems. Therefore, the monarchy-centered nationalist ideology had some degree of efficacy. However, when the country began to experience economic difficulty, the association of the monarchy with progress, economic development, and prosperity became increasingly weak. The monarchy became ideologically vulnerable. Furthermore, the state's policies to resolve the economic problems, such as its antiprofiteering campaign and the cut in social spending, backfired and contributed to the general social discontent . The inauguration of the Carter administration and the increasing international pressure on the Shah to ease political control led the opposition leadership to believe that the time for open political activities was ripe.[65]

Some of the specific policies the government pursued in 1977 further contributed to the outbreak of protest activities. To curb inflation, Prime Minister Jamshid Amouzegar moved to impose price controls. As mentioned in the previous chapter, the government's antiprofiteering and price-control campaign began in 1975, and the subsequent arrest and fining of over 20,000 merchants and retailers provided a context for the bazaar's unity against the government. Amouzegar's action produced additional feelings of hostility in the bazaaris. Another policy was to eliminate payments to the clergy in order to balance the budget. This action is believed to have caused dissatisfaction among the clergy.[66] The government's plan to cut social spending had begun a year earlier. The Shah, in a highly publicized press conference in October 1976, attacked workers for their high wages and low productivity, demanding that people should work harder and reduce their expectations. Subsequently, Minister of Labor Manouchehr Azmoun, tied profit-sharing to a high level of productivity.[67] Finally, to appease critics of the regime, Amouzegar released several hundred political prisoners.

These actions probably explain the intensification of antigovernment activities by diverse classes and groups in the latter half of 1977. The bazaaris revived the Society of Merchants and Guilds that had been outlawed following the coup of 1953 under the new name of the Society of Merchants and Guilds of Tehran Bazaar.[68] The activist followers of Khomeini in the bazaar such as Khamoushi, Asgar-Owaldi, Pour-Ostad, and Rafiq-Doust also stepped up their organizing efforts. As early as 1975, industrial workers also began to strike more frequently than in previous years. Their dissatisfaction was caused by an increase in inflation and a scarcity of basic necessities. The cut in social spending further stimulated labor unrest, and by mid-1978 workers began demanding the overthrow of the monarchy. Thus the simultaneity of the struggle of the bazaaris and workers against the state was the central factor for the success of the revolutionary movement of 1977–79. For comparison, one may attribute the failure of the 1963 demonstration against the Shah to, among other things, the absence of the workers' participation. With relative ease, the Shah singled out the ulama as supporters of the landed aristocracy, and as against progress and modernization. His pro-poor rhetoric, backed by his implementation of land reform, had placed the Left and the National Front on the defensive. In the late seventies, the situation was quite different. The reform had not provided Iran with agricultural self-sufficiency. To be sure, the destruction of the "feudal" class had provided favorable conditions for the growth of some rich peasants, who had considerable influence in their own villages.[69] On a few occasions, the government had mobilized the peasants in certain areas to attack anti-Shah demonstrators and members of the opposition. However, the state's connection to the peasants was too weak to seriously combat the urban revolutionary forces. Nevertheless, how the grievances of the bazaaris and workers were translated into a revolutionary movement cannot be deduced solely from their economic interests or the level of their solidarity structure.

At any rate, the most important political events of the mid-seventies were the protest activities of the intelligentsia, lawyers and judges, writers, and former leaders of the National Front. Several highly critical letters were sent to the Shah and high-ranking government officials. A series of nighttime poetry readings was also organized by the Iranian Writers Guild in Tehran that was attended by several thousand people. These events gained remarkable national and international publicity. The poetry readings stimulated protest demonstrations and rallies in Tehran during which several people were wounded or killed. In the 1977 protest movements, secular groups were quite active and visible.

Nevertheless, the revolutionary crisis did not seem to have emanated from the logic of these events. It is hard to claim that the demands of the dominated classes and the intelligentsia were totally incompatible with the institution of monarchy. Nor does it seem to be correct to argue that the revolution succeeded because of the government's failure to act against it. According to Bill, careful research indicates that an estimated 10,000 to 12,000 persons were killed and another 45,000 to 50,000 injured during the fourteen-month revolutionary upheaval.[70] Even if one assumes that the government had lost its will to repress people, it is not altogether clear that participants in the revolution were aware of this fact or would have believed it.

Rather, the Shah's regime was thrown into crisis, and the social discontents were transformed into revolutionary movements by and through Islamic discourse. The revolutionary crisis transpired when the revolutionary ideology began to take over the protest movements. This is because the themes of the monarchy's ideology and of the Islamic opposition were somewhat mutually exclusive. Thus when the public became dissatisfied with the Shah and gradually joined the Islamic opposition, their dissatisfaction was transcended and expressed in terms of Islamic discourse. Given that revolutionary Islam was negating the monarchy's ideology, the action of the discontented became shaped in a revolutionary direction. At the same time, Islamic revolutionary discourse, by posing the problem in terms of the conflict between Islam and the infidels, transcended class differences and social divisions in a communitarian rotation—that is, the Muslim community (i.e., *ummat*) was pictured as fighting the boundless tyrant (i.e., *taghut*).

Several specific ways can be identified through which the discursive field of revolutionary Islam was expanded and ideological mobilization took place. The first was the transformation of the politics of the clerical establishments and its reconstitution in terms of Islamic revolutionary discourse. This was important because alternative courses of action have always been available to the ulama in pursuing their occupational and religious goals. And the idea of the revolutionary overthrow of the state and the establishment of an Islamic government was by and large Khomeini's own invention.[71] No ideological precedent had existed to justify the ulama's direct rule in society. Indeed many grand ayatollahs disagreed with Khomeini's political views. In particular, Ayatollah Abol-Qasem Kho'i argued that no direct ulama governance existed. Khomeini's first crucial revolutionary task was therefore to convince his colleagues of the necessity of establishing such a rule. In his response to Ayatollah Kho'i, Khomeini instructed his followers (not without sarcasm) to "present Islam to the people in its true form,"

> so that our youth do not picture the *akhunds* as sitting in some corner in Najaf or Qum, studying the questions of menstruation and parturition instead of concerning themselves with politics, and draw the conclusion that religion must be separate from politics. This slogan of the separation of religion and politics and the demand that Islamic scholars not intervene in social and political affairs have been formulated and propagated by the Imperialist; it is only the irreligious who repeats them.[72]

Even in the initial stage of the revolution, the first priority for Khomeini and his followers consisted of the radicalization of the ulama, by pressuring them to take an active part in the revolution.[73]

Second, the discursive field generated by revolutionary Islam—that is, its symbolic structure, its rituals and calendar, and its theme of martyrdom—played a crucial role in providing an effective channel of communication between the leaders and the led, providing occasions for people to gather and mobilize against the Shah, therefore perpetuating the revolutionary crisis. The revolutionary crisis proper seems to have begun in January 1978, when several thousand Khomeini supporters in Qum began to protest the publication of an article in *Ittila'at,* in which Khomeini was portrayed as an Indian Sayyid (*Sayyid-i Hindi*) who was being used as a tool by the red and black colonialists, referring to the Communists and the British.[74] The significance of the event does not seem to lie in the fact that Khomeini was insulted, or that the religious protest in Qum was brutally repressed. After all, the regime had frequently attacked the ayatollah since he had been expelled to Iraq, and there had been many violent protest demonstrations in Qum at least once a year (the last major one being in June 1975, the twelfth anniversary of the Khomeini-led mass demonstration in 1963). None of these had been followed by a show of support for Khomeini and for solidarity among the various discontented groups and classes.

The protest demonstrations in Qum in January 1978 gains significance, however, when judged against the secular groups' experiences in the previous year's protest activities. The open letters to the Shah and high-ranking officials of the government, the nights of poetry readings, and the rallies that ensued all pointed to the emergence of a new opportunity for political action. Because of international pressures on the regime, the existence of economic difficulties, and the prevalence of corruption in high places, the Shah had to listen. But at the same time, there were serious limits to these actions. The writers of the open letters and the organizers of the nights of poetry readings were treated harshly. They were badly beaten-up by the SAVAK's organized gangs, or explosives were planted in their houses.[75] The demonstrations had ended with violence, leaving several people wounded or dead. The impotence of the protest movements vis-à-vis the regime's might seemed clear. Another occasion was needed around which the opposition could mobilize its forces against the Shah. The article against Khomeini and the violent repression of his supporters constituted such an occasion. Not only did the leading ulama in Tehran and other major cities express their outrage at the regime's violent behavior but so did the Society of Merchants and Guild of Tehran Bazaar, the Isfahani and Tabrizi bazaaris in Tehran, the National Front, the Toilers' party, and the Left.[76] In the same way that the monarchy's ideology shaped the ideology of the opposition, the state's repressive policy was partly responsible for making Khomeini the leader of the revolution.

The 1978 demonstration strengthened the connection between the secular and religious forces within the opposition, and at the same time aided Khomeini and his followers to establish a hegemony over the rest of the opposition. The secular groups, including the Left, by and large accepted and had often used religious tactics to mobilize the people against the Shah. As mentioned earlier, this tendency had begun much earlier, when leftist forces were attempting to forge an alliance with the religious opposition. The clearest instance of the ideological compromise made by many secular groups was the acceptance of the idea that women, while participating in street demonstrations, should wear the veil as a symbol of resistance to the Shah's Westernization policies. Whether the veil at the time represented a symbol of resistance or an instance of the patriarchal nature of the Islamic opposition is of course a matter of one's interpretation.[77] What seems clear is that the tactic epitomized the total invasion of Islamic revolutionary ideology into the field of secular discourse (in this case, women's rights). However, the enhanced power of Shi'i revolutionary discourse did not simply stem from the tactical necessity of the struggle against the Shah. It motivated people to action precisely because Shi'i ideology meant different things to different contenders. As became quite clear in the postrevolutionary period, there were as many interpretations of the teachings of Shi'i Islam on practical issues as there were Islamic groups. Highly educated women who had proudly worn the veil for the sake of the revolution probably had no idea what Khomeini and his followers would end up doing to women's liberty in the postrevolutionary period. Likewise, the Tudeh and other groups within the Left had accepted Khomeini's hegemony because in their view he was either a revolutionary democrat or petty bourgeois anti-imperialist, but overlooked the fact that the Ayatollah was equally anti-Communist. The leaders of the National Front, as well, do not seem to have contemplated the incompatibility of their democratic ideals with those prescribed by revolutionary Islam.

In any case, the 1978 Qum incident unleashed a chain of ideologically constituted events whose dynamics were responsible for the continuation and intensification of the revolutionary crisis. The events in question were produced by the Islamic ritual for the dead. This ritual includes, among other things, memorial services and commemorations of the deceased which are to occur on the fortieth day after the death. The performance of this ritual for those killed in anti-Shah demonstrations led to the killings of some of those participating in the ritual, which in turn provided another occasion for performing the memorial services for them forty days later, and so on. The sequence started in Qum on January 9, 1978, when tens of people got killed. The next major anti-Shah demonstration occurred in several cities on February 18—that is, forty days after January 9. In Tabriz, in particular, this occasion sparked serious riots, resulting in violent clashes between troops and demonstrators that left a dozen killed and twice as many injured. Forty days later on March 29, during the commemoration for those killed in Tabriz, scattered riots erupted in several major urban centers, again leading to a number of deaths (particularly in Yazd). The next fortieth was May 8–9, and there were disturbances in some thirty-four towns. Hence, there came to be no need for revolutionary leaders to tell the public when and in what form they should demonstrate against the Shah. The cycles of these religious rituals set the exact dates and reasons to engage in protest activities, autonomously contributing to the mobilization of the people against the state. This cycle more or less continued until 1979.[78]

Third, the Islamic calendar provided not only a means to negate and contradict the ideology of the monarchy but also periodic occasions for the people to mobilize against the Shah. By observing the rituals and ceremonial practices associated with religious holidays and disregarding the state-specified civil holidays, the opposition undermined the ideology of the monarchy. Furthermore, the major mass demonstrations against the Shah often transpired in the holy months and were initiated in the mosques. The month of August 1978, for example, coincided with the lunar month of Ramadan (the month of fasting), a time when religious activities and evening sermons were particularly paramount. The religious opposition effectively used these occasions to attack the Shah and to prepare the first massive demonstration to occur on the day following the end of Ramadan—*Id-i Fitr* (a religious holiday). Following the prayers and sermons, mass demonstrations occurred during which people handed out flowers to the soldiers [79]

These protest demonstrations produced the government's first major retreat. In August 1978 the Shah replaced Amouzegar with Jafar Sharif-Emami, whose clerical background was meant to assist in the formation of a government of "national reconciliation." To appease the opposition, Sharif-Emami relaxed the state's control of the press, raised the salaries of the government's employees, abolished the monarchical calendar and reinstated the Islamic calendar, and released several hundred political prisoners.[80] These concessions by and large met many of the demands that had been raised by the secular groups during the protest activities of 1977. But why did the opposition in mid-1978 categorically reject Sharif-Emami's government of national reconciliation and demand the overthrow of the monarchy? There was nothing inherent in the interests of the bazaaris or the workers or in the nature of their organizations and solidarity structure that necessitated the revolutionary overthrow of the state. Even the influential leaders of the opposition such as Bazargan and Ayatollah Shari'atmadari were willing to take Sharif-Emami seriously. Shari'atmadari even announced that he would give the government three months to prove its good intentions. Then what caused the shift in the opposition's attitudes toward the government to a revolutionary direction?

To be sure, there were a number of small radical groups, such as the Feda'iyan and the Mojahedin-i Khalq, that had demanded the overthrow of the monarchy and the redistribution of wealth much earlier than this date. Khomeini and his followers had also resolved in the 1970s that the monarchy ought to be overthrown and an Islamic government established. But at that time the radical groups had been debilitated by state repression, many of their leaders had been either killed during armed clashes with the security forces or imprisoned, and the remaining cadres and members were too few to be able to mobilize the masses along the social revolutionary line. Also, in 1977 Khomeini and his followers had not yet established their hegemony over the protest movements.

Therefore, Sharif-Emami's failure does not seem to be a result of the logical progression of class conflict or contention for power. Rather, by the time he became prime minister in mid-1978, the Shi'i revolutionary discourse had taken over the movement, and the social discontent of the people had become transformed into a real revolutionary crisis. The forty-day cycles of religious rituals for the dead had continued unabated for several months, and hundreds, if not thousands, had been wounded or killed in virtually all the major cities. Political changes were now occurring according to the direct actions of the masses (not according to the specific intentions of the leaders), shaped by the internal dynamics of Shi'i revolutionary discourse. Society was polarized into two mutually negating discourses that basically left no room for compromise. No matter how sincere the Shah's and Sharif-Emami's intentions were, the national reconciliation policy was bound to fail. Khomeini categorically rejected Sharif-Emami's concessions as a propaganda ploy and demanded the overthrow of the Shah. To stop the revolutionary movement, the government resorted to outright repression. It banned all public gatherings. In a massive demonstration that occurred in Jaleh Square a few hours after the announcement of the curfew, the troops fired at the demonstrators, killing several hundred. The government also detained the opposition leaders and pressured Iraq to expel Khomeini.

This additional repression proved ineffective. The month of Muharram provided an even more effective context for mass mobilization against the Shah. In Shi'i tradition, Muharram is a month of mourning and ceremonial practices commemorating the martyrdom of Imam Hosein, the third Shi'i Imam. In their mobilization efforts, the religious opposition invoked the theme of martyrdom. They vowed to make Muharram "the month of victory of blood over sword." On November 6, the Shah replaced Sharif-Emami with General Azhari, and martial law began. In defiance of the dusk-to-dawn curfew imposed by the military government, men in white shrouds (signifying their readiness to be martyred) went into the streets. Another mobilization tactic was that millions of people, again in defiance of the curfew, went to the roofs of their houses in virtually all the cities in the evening and repeatedly shouted "Allah-o Akbar" (God is Great).[81] The ninth and tenth of Muharram (December 10 and 11, 1978) saw the largest demonstrations yet, taking place in Tehran and other major cities, in which several million people participated. Resolutions passed in these demonstrations designated Ayatollah Khomeini as the leader of the nation and demanded the overthrow of the system of monarchy as well as the establishment of an Islamic government.[82] The resolution of the ideological conflict between the state and the religious opposition ended the first stage of the Iranian Revolution. Henceforth, Islamic discourse set the framework for the resolution of political and social conflicts in the postrevolutionary period.

On December 29, 1978, the Shah replaced Azhari with Shahpour Bakhtiyar, a member of the National Front. On January 16, 1979, the Shah left Iran. Although Ayatollah Khomeini did not call for armed struggle against the government and, along with the leaders of the National Front, was busy negotiating with the government for the transfer of power, the revolutionary dynamic nonetheless culminated in an armed confrontation between revolutionary groups and the Imperial Guard that thrust Bakhtiar from power on February 10 and 11, 1979.

This chapter has treated Shi'i ideology as the dominant political discourse in the postcoup period. First, it discussed the causes of the growth of Islam as the dominant political discourse of the opposition, after several decades of extensive secularization. These were the complex interactions between the state's changing structure, policies, and ideology vis-à-vis similar changes in class politics and religious institutions—or, more specifically, the alliance of the classes that had constituted the historical bases of the ulama against the state, the ulama's expulsion from the state bureaucracy, the ideological aspect of the state that glorified pre-Islamic kingship and culture while overlooking Islam, and the state's effective destruction of the National Front and the Tudeh party (thereby creating favorable conditions for the growth of Islam as the dominant ideology of the opposition). As this chapter showed, Islamic revolutionary discourse was not simply a preexisting ideology rooted in Shi'i political theory or in the ulama's institutional development in the nineteenth century; rather it was produced by diverse ideologues in response to the problems they faced in the 1960s and 1970s. Finally, the role of Shi'i ideology in the revolutionary conjuncture of 1977–79 was discussed, and it was argued that Shi'i metaphors, symbols, and ceremonies transformed the general social discontent into a revolutionary crisis by providing not only an effective channel of communication between participants in the revolution and their leaders but also a mechanism for the political mobilization of the masses against the state.

6

Contrasting Cases: Islam and Politics in Egypt and Syria

The analysis of the causes of the Iranian Revolution advanced in the previous chapters should stand, or fall, by virtue of the logical consistency of its theoretical framework and the adequacy of its historical documentation. However, contrasting Iran with Egypt and Syria may further illuminate the causal mechanism that this work has suggested underpinned the Iranian Revolution. Egypt, Iran, and Syria display many similar structural characteristics and historical experiences. Besides their inclusion in the same geopolitical region, they all have, by and large, a similar class structure based on an export-enclave economy, thus occupying a dependent position in the world capitalist system. The emerging indigenous dominant classes—a combination of landowners and merchants—at the turn of the century were prevented by the colonial powers from establishing a viable hegemony in their respective countries. Traditional Islamic institutions have been predominantly connected with the bazaar and landed interests. Islamic radicalism has been an important component of revolutionary movements in all these countries, following a period of liberal politics. One can no longer speak of the existence of a monolithic and conservative corps of religious scholars engaged in a defense of the status quo. Islam, to use Gismondi's assertion about the church in Latin America, has become a "contested terrain."[1] Islamic tenets have been diversely interpreted by different and even opposing Islamic political organizations.

Despite these similarities, Iran is the only country to have experienced a major revolution shaped by Islamic revolutionary discourse. However, Egypt was the first to experience the upsurge of religious revolutionary movement in the twentieth century, under the leadership of the Muslim Brothers, and the overall politics of Islam in this country displayed two diverse tendencies. In contrast with the Muslim Brothers, the ulama associated with the orthodox Sunni establishment were either apolitical or strongly in favor of the existing regime. But like Iran, the Islamic movement in Syria was predominantly revolutionary, though sectarian; a movement within the Sunni community (constituting about 70 percent of the country's total population), it was directed against the predominantly non-Sunni Syrian leaders.

The comparative strategy used in this chapter is based on what Tilly has defined as *individualizing comparison*.[2] Here it involves contrasting certain key features of Iran with Egypt and Syria in order to grasp the singularities of the Iranian case. First, Iran is contrasted with Egypt, in terms of state structure and policies, and in the pattern of alliances involving the state and various social classes from the nineteenth century to about the mid-twentieth century. The intent of the comparison is to explain the contrast between the rise in the power of the Iranian ulama and their influential role in the politics of this period, and the decline in power of the Egyptian ulama in the course of the nineteenth century and the emergence of a politically divided Islam in Egypt. In Iran, the alliance between the merchants and the petty bourgeoisie against the state and international capital is considered the central factor underpinning the oppositional role of religion. In Egypt, as will be argued, no such alliance was formed. Before the advent of Muhammad Ali in the early nineteenth century, the artisans and retailers were followers of popular Sufi brotherhoods. The merchants and the ulama were allied with Ottoman-Mamluk rulers. Under Muhammad Ali, the old landowning class was effectively destroyed and the system of landownership was changed. The autonomous institutions of society such as the guilds, village administrations, and ulama religious institutions came under the government's control. Nevertheless, the pattern of alliance remained similar as Muhammad Ali allied with large merchants and a group of conservative ulama who submitted to his authority. The breakdown of his system of monopolies in the mid-nineteenth century, the state's fiscal crisis under his son Ismail Pasha, and a change in the Ottoman law regarding the ownership of private land led to the sale of state lands to private individuals. The nationalist revolution of the early twentieth century brought considerable political power for the Egyptian dominant classes and the ulama. The artisans, in contrast, were undermined by the process of social change. Throughout the course of the nineteenth century, the influx of cheap Western goods plus a change in the tax law destroyed the artisanal guilds. Further deterioration of the economic conditions of the petty bourgeoisie between the two world wars, and the decline of liberal politics, provided a context for the growth of the Muslim Brothers. Thus it seems that the division within the Islamic movement in Egypt between orthodox ulama and the radical Muslim Brothers broadly paralleled the pattern of alliances between the state and the indigenous social classes.

Second, Iran is contrasted with Syria in the 1960s and 1970s. Like Iran, the Syrian state's intervention in the economy and the implementation of such radical measures as the nationalization of most business and land reform provoked strong reactions from traditional social classes—the landowners, merchants, and petty bourgeoisie—as well as the ulama. Moreover, the state's socialist ideology and its antireligious orientation structured the ideology of the opposition and helped the rise of revolutionary Islam. In contrast to Iran, however, the Syrian state maintained a strong basis of support among workers, and more so, among peasants; these provided a defensive shield against the urban challenge as well as a source for military conscription. Furthermore, beginning in the seventies, the Syrian political elites took a favorable orientation toward the merchants and at the same time attempted to play down their ideological differences with Islam. Thus it seems that these policies undermined the development of a revolutionary conjuncture in Syria.

Egypt: A Divided Islam

The coalition between the merchants and the petty bourgeoisie constituted the distinctive feature of class politics in Iran and the central factor underpinning the singularity of the country's religious experience. In the twentieth century this coalition was undermined by Reza Shah's somewhat pro-merchant and pro-landowner policies, but Mohammad Reza Shah's policies in favor of the dependent bourgeoisie and international capital caused the hostility of the merchants, the landowners, and the petty bourgeoisie—hence, an objective condition for ulama unity against the Shah. In Egypt, these classes have had diverse political orientations in the nineteenth and twentieth centuries. Between the two world wars the orthodox Sunni ulama were allied with the monarch vis-à-vis the nationalist groups who were organized in Egypt's first modern political party, Wafd. The petty bourgeoisie, on the other hand, provided the core basis of support for the Society of Muslim Brothers (*Al-Ikhwan al-Muslimun*). Founded by Hasan al-Banna in March 1928, the Society grew to become one of the most important politico-religious organizations in the country by the late 1930s. This social group began to engage in revolutionary activities as Egypt's economic conditions began to deteriorate in this period. Egypt's economic instability emanated chiefly from its export-oriented character, which made it quite vulnerable to fluctuations in the world market.

Export-Enclave Economy: Socioeconomic changes involving the transition to capitalism began in Egypt in the late eighteenth century. An important aspect and consequence of capitalist development was the country's integration into the world capitalist economy, which transformed the structure of domestic (yet subsistence) production under which Egypt had lived for centuries into an export-oriented economy.[3] Eighteenth-century exports of coffee (from Hejaz), textiles to France, and rice and sugar to the Ottoman Empire became limited to massive trade with Europe strictly based on European need—and was thus less diversified.[4] In this process, cotton cultivation and export became the single most important commodity upon which the country's economy rested. Thus like Iran, Egypt's capitalist development was accompanied by an increasing vulnerability to economic fluctuations in the world market.

Egypt's economy, however, was not stagnant, and throughout the nineteenth century it continued to expand. As the result of a highly developed system of irrigation, lavish use of fertilizer, and labor-intensive production techniques, land under cultivation continuously expanded—from 3,050,000 *feddans* (a *feddan* is 1.04 acres) in 1813 to 4,743,000 *feddans* in 1877, and then to 5,658,000 *feddans* in 1911.[5] Parallel with the increase in agricultural production was the growth in foreign trade. In 1800 exports represented a mere £E 288,000. In 1850 they had risen to £E 2,302,000, an increase of more than eightfold.[6] Much of this increase was owing to cotton exports. Until 1821 exports of cotton were negligible. Most of the cotton grown in Egypt at that time was used in the local textile industry. By 1836, however, cotton had become the most important item in the country's exports. Out of this year's total export of £E 1,336,831, cotton represented £E 1,114,903 (86 percent of the total).[7]

The American Civil War gave the first big boost to cotton production in Egypt. The war disrupted cotton production in the United States, and as a result Egypt faced a high demand for its product. The boost was then followed by the Great Depression of 1870, which hit Egyptian as it hit European agriculture. Egypt did not stand up to the economic shocks and incurred an enormous debt, which was a factor triggering England's invasion of the country.[8] The British occupation of Egypt in 1882 reinforced a one-crop economy. The insatiable cotton mills of Lancashire and Egypt's foreign debt were two good reasons for Lord Cromer to direct the country's economy toward cotton, and the large landowners who thereby made great profits were only too happy to comply—until, ultimately, the former "granary of Rome" was forced to import grain for its own local consumption.[9]

Between 1882 and 1914, large-scale works were undertaken in the Nile Valley (construction of the Aswan Dam, extension of irrigation to Lower and Middle Egypt). Agricultural production showed a yearly increase of 1.6 percent—equal to the growth rate of the rural population.[10] The rapid increase in agricultural output through expansion of the cultivated area, which had characterized the previous hundred years, came to an abrupt end with the First World War; henceforth production rose more slowly and only thanks to costly irrigation works and intensification. The sharp fall in world prices of primary products in general, and cotton in particular, in the 1920s and 1930s led to a deterioration of Egypt's terms of trade and a decline in the real value of exports.[11] Given that landed property was very unevenly distributed and that its income was derived from cotton,[12] such a decline meant the further impoverishment of the masses and a new climate for the intensification of class conflict. Thus similar to Iran in the seventies, it seems that Egypt's economic difficulties in the twenties and thirties partly stemmed from economic dependency and vulnerability to fluctuations in the world economy.

The State: The consolidation of a unified state administration in nineteenth-century Egypt, as well as the kind of policies the state pursued and the problems it faced, had far-reaching consequences for the massive social changes that were sweeping the country in this period, which in turn broadly set the stage for class conflict in the twentieth

century. Like the case of Iran, the Egyptian state played a crucial trans-
formative role in society by extensively intervening in the economy and,
hence, patterning class conflict. However, in Egypt radical Islam
emerged within the context of the Constitutional Monarchy of the
post-1922 period, in which the state rested on an uneasy alliance between the monarch, the nationalist elites who were tied to the dominant
classes, and the British. The orthodox Sunni ulama tended to support
the monarch vis-à-vis the nationalist groups. During the course of the
struggle for independence (1919–22), national-liberal discourse transcended class differences by mobilizing the society against British domination. Nevertheless, the decline of liberalism (as a result of a set of factors ranging from the decline of liberalism in general in Europe, to the
monarch-British conspiracy, to the persistence of economic difficulties)
was paralleled by the rise of the Muslim Brothers. Since the conservative ulama and the dominant classes were part of the power bloc, the
radical Islamic movement in Egypt remained mainly a petty-bourgeois
phenomenon, and the Islamic movement as a whole remained politically divided.

We may begin by considering the conjuncture of national and international events that in the early nineteenth century facilitated the
growth and consolidation of a new political order under the leadership
of Egypt's first modernizer, Muhammad Ali. In 1517, when Sultan Se-
lim I defeated the Mamluk rulers of Egypt, the country became a province of the Ottoman Empire. For almost three centuries, political power
was divided between three rival elites: the viceroy, or governor, who
represented the imperial authority; a body of Janissaries, ostensibly established to serve the imperial military force but actually there to
checkmate any dangerous ambitions of the viceroys; and the Mamluk
Beys, who had declared their allegiance to the Sultan and were therefore
appointed governors of various provinces in Egypt. The decline of the
Ottoman Empire in the course of the centuries brought increasing autonomy for Egypt, so that by 1700 the Turkish Viceroy in Egypt was a
mere pawn in the hands of the local Mamluk Beys.[13] The French Occupation of Egypt (1798–1801) overthrew the despotic rule of the
Mamluks. But Napoleon was unable to establish a pro-French government in the country, and his evacuation of Egypt in 1801 left the country in a state of chaos produced by the constant struggle for political
power among rival Mamluk and Ottoman forces.

The native notables, and in particular the ulama, remembered only too vividly the tyranny of Murad and Ibrahim Beys (1775–89) to allow a restoration of the Mamluks to power in their country.[14] Therefore, they began rallying behind Muhammad Ali, an ambitious young officer who had come to Egypt in 1801 with an Albanian detachment in a Turkish expeditionary force against the French. Through the support of the ulama and the merchants, Muhammad Ali became the wali of Cairo in 1805.[15] By 1810, Muhammad Ali was able to successfully defeat all his rivals and secure order in the country.

Muhammad Ali's consolidation of power, however, did not mean a restoration of the Mamluk-type system of government. He soon initiated the formation of a new set of administrative apparatus, bringing under the firm control of the government such institutions of traditional society as the semiautonomous guilds, village administrations, the Sufi orders, and orthodox religious establishments.[16] Along with the maintenance of security and order at home, military aggrandizement became Muhammad Ali's central purpose. Allied with the rich import-export merchants and a group of the ulama, Muhammad Ali unleashed a series of military campaigns against his neighbors.[17] He created a navy, expanded and intervened in foreign trades, dispossessed the land-owning class (who were largely the Mamluks), and reformed finances in order to increase revenues for his military expeditions. Muhammad Ali became for all practical purposes politically, economically, and financially independent of the Ottoman Empire, even though he continued to pay tribute to the Imperial Ottoman Treasury.[18]

Muhammad Ali's political independence, however, was short-lived. He was balked by the colonial powers, especially the British, in 1840. The decline of state power in Egypt paralleled the increase in British influence in the country. British occupation of the country in 1882 (instigated by the impotent Egyptian rulers, the Khedive Tawfiq, to help quell the Urabi rebellion) changed the picture. From then on Egypt came to be dominated by the British consul general, Lord Cromer, who set up a system known as the Veiled Protectorate, by means of which Egyptian executive authority was abrogated and replaced by that of the British Resident and the British advisers in Egyptian service.[19]

It was not the first time that Egyptians had been formally dominated by an external power. But their struggle for independence became distinctively revolutionary by virtue of its constitution in terms of liberal-nationalist discourse. The broad environmental conditions that promoted the rise of national-liberalism were characterized by: the growth of the bourgeois-landowning class; the state's fiscal crisis under Ismail Pasha and his successor Tawfiq Pasha; the promotion of Arabic as the official language of the country; and the emergence of educated elites. Similar to Iran, and, broadly speaking, for the same reasons, nationalism and liberalism became the governing ideologies of the struggle against British and Turkish domination. Nationalist struggle culminated in Egypt's first modern revolution, resulting in the formation of a constitutional government. Egypt was officially recognized by Britain as an independent sovereign state in 1924 (although in practice the British maintained considerable military and administrative influence in the country). Between the two world wars, Egypt's polity was divided between three rival political institutions. One was the Palace, headed by King Faruq (whose power had been curtailed by the constitutional revolution). The second was the Wafd party, led by Egypt's indigenous dominant classes. Finally, the third was the British, who sided with the king or against him as circumstances dictated. Thus, two factions had to combine against a third in any given political situation in order to prevail. It was these dominant classes' direct access to power, perhaps for the first time in Egypt's modern history, that underlay the difference between Egypt's and Iran's Islamic opposition movements.

Class Politics and Ideological Outcomes: Like Iran, Egypt's geographic location was favorable to commercial expansion. The country was situated at the meeting point of two continents, Asia and Africa. The Valley of the Nile had been the site of the first ancient civilization and a center of flourishing economic activity. From the beginning of the second millennium B.C., Egypt had succeeded in establishing trade contacts with Southern Arabia and East Africa and was able to draw on the produce of India through the mediation of the Southern Arabians, whose chief port, Aden, was a great entrepôt for international trade.[20] Despite a decline in Egypt's role in international trade (as a result of Portuguese fleets under the Mamluks sailing around the Cape of Good Hope), trade remained an important economic activity in the country. And it gained even more significance with the development of an export-oriented economy in the nineteenth century. Egyptian merchants were engaged in importing and exporting goods manufactured or grown outside the country, both for sale in domestic markets and for shipment to markets in Turkey, North Africa, and Europe.[21]

In the course of the nineteenth century the economic functions and the internal social composition of Egypt's dominant classes began to change. By the early twentieth century, the most important component of the country's dominant classes became the large absentee land-owners (this group had increased rapidly in the latter half of the nine-teenth century as a result of both state policies and the changes in pri-vate land ownership and capitalist development). Tied to trade and industry were artisans and retail traders, whose members were orga-nized into guilds and were among the most politically conscious groups in Egyptian society.[22]

While in Iran the merchants, artisans, and retail traders were united against the state and international capital, the relationship between rich import-export merchants and artisans in Egypt was characterized by a conflict of interests and diverse political tendencies. Before the ad-vent of Muhammad Ali in the early nineteenth century, the merchants were the allies of the Mamluks, who kept order, and of the ulama, who kept the population quiescent.[23] The artisans, on the other hand, had a close but exploitative relationship with the Janissaries (an elite corps of Turkish infantry), which peaked around 1670–1700. The latter "pro-tected" the artisans and exploited them by becoming their "partners," but at the same time they did assure their security and tempered the ex-actions levied on them by the Mamluks. Around 1750, when the Janis-saries began to lose their influence to the Mamluk Beys, the picture changed, and the more tempered exploitation of the urban producers was replaced by the severe financial exploitation of the Mamluks.[24]

This political change was an added burden for the artisans, who had already been economically declining since around the 1700s because of various factors, including the increase in European imports, competi-tion from Syrian merchants who had killed off the textile trade in order to export raw materials to Europe, and the outbreak of plague and fam-ine in the last two decades of the eighteenth century.[25] All these factors were responsible for the occurrence of many protest activities and vio-lent rebellions during the turn of the century. Beginning in about 1777, popular revolts in Cairo started to be more frequent and more serious than they had been before. Those associated with the city's guild organ-izations participated in these revolts in greater and greater numbers to-ward the end of the century.[26] The poorer ulama and the artisans began to make increasingly better use of the most important organizational resource available to them—the Sufi brotherhoods—to influence do-mestic political affairs. Toward the end of the eighteenth century, "popular" Sufi brotherhoods (*turuq*) proliferated throughout Egypt. These *turuq* reinforced the influence of local religious practices and teachers, while threatening the social position of the elite ulama associated with al-Azhar University in the capital.[27] These *turuq* orders in fact had a history of rebellion against the city's rulers, when conditions warranted, and they had close ties to Cairo's artisan guilds.[28]

There seems to have been certain mutually reinforcing relationships between class and religious movement in Egypt. This is because the diverse political leanings of the merchants and the petty bourgeoisie paralleled the presence of two rival Islamic institutions. The first was an orthodox Islamic institution centered in al-Azhar and led by the ulama. For up until the advent of Muhammad Ali, the ulama had constituted an integral part of the government and had formed exceptionally close political and social ties with their Ottoman-Mamluk rulers. They were participants in the government, not outsiders, and their own influence and wealth, the well-being of their entire corps, and the influence of Islam in general depended upon the close relations the ulama were able to maintain with their powerful rulers.[29] The second institution, consisting of a less learned religious group, was the Sufi order. The existence of these large popular orders, which engaged in social protest and propagated heterodox religious views, was an ever-present threat to the merchants and the ulama as well as to the Mamluk elites.[30] Again this phenomenon lends credence to the argument presented in this work that concrete political and ideological factors are important in the constitution of a class. While in Iran the unity between the merchants and the petty bourgeoisie was reinforced by a common ideological tendency (because both classes were allied with ideologically uniform yet diverse factions of the ulama), the availability of two rival Islamic institutions in Egypt reinforced the existing conflict of interest between the merchants and the craft guilds.

However, there were historical occasions in which both the merchants and the petty bourgeoisie pursued a similar kind of politics. In such situations the politically minded ulama found themselves in a formidable position to lead the popular opposition to the state. Three major revolts between 1798 and 1805 are examples of such occasions. The third revolt was directed against the governor of Egypt (who had been appointed by the Ottoman Sultan) and placed Muhammad Ali on the viceregal throne.[31] The merchants and artisans supported Muhammad Ali for different reasons. The merchants saw him as the exponent of law and order who would bring stability to the country and restore the military-mercantile alliance of the past. The artisans and the masses probably saw in Muhammad Ali the possibility of a return to an earlier artisan-military alliance.[32]

In their turn, the ulama deposed the governor on religious grounds, for Umar Makram, one of the leading ulama, argued that "Those set in authority are the ulama, and those who uphold the sharia and the righteous sultan. This man [the governor] is a tyrannical man, and it is the tradition from time immemorial that citizens depose a wali if he be unjust."[33] The role of the ulama and the guilds in Muhammad Ali's ascendance to power was thus crucial,

> for Muhammad Ali's troops were divided among themselves and were constantly defecting because of lack of pay, so that it was the people, who, armed by the *ulama*, did all the fighting. Town-criers went round calling on the people to arm and report for action in response to the call of Sayyid 'Umar Makram and the *ulama*. . . . 'Umar Makram, assisted by the head of the greengrocers' guild, organized combat groups which took over whenever Muhammad 'Ali's forces deserted their posts, which happened fairly regularly. . . .
>
> For one brief glorious moment the *ulama* had taken the initiative and had posed as the rulers of the country, rousing the people into a resistance movement. 'Umar Makram levied a contribution from the wealthier citizens and bought arms to supply the populace, and even paid the poorer artisans a daily wage, as indemnity for leaving their trade and turning soldiers. As a result, he could call upon nearly 40,000 armed men.[34]

Muhammad Ali's ascendance to power ushered in a new era in Egypt. His consolidation of political power resulted in a gradual decline of the economic and political power of the artisans and the ulama (for the latter, both as landowners and political leaders). Between 1810 and 1815, the Egyptian government began to create a comprehensive system of state trading monopolies whose purpose was not only to augment the state's revenues from economic activities but also to establish some sort of discipline among the artisans and small traders of the cities and towns.[35] Muhammad Ali's government also created a modern industry replete with iron foundries, tanneries, bleaching establishments, a printing press, and twenty-nine cotton factories in 1837.[36] It is evident that government monopolies severely limited the activities and profits of the country's artisans, both in the capital and in the provinces.[37] Economic dislocation—resulting from the infiltration of European goods into the Egyptian market, government centralization, and its policies of various kinds (such as conscription, corvées, and new taxes)—provided a basis for the outbreak of several uprisings against Muhammad Ali in Cairo in 1814 and in the Upper Egypt in 1820–25. These uprisings, which were largely the revolts of disgruntled artisans and pieceworkers of the textile trade and peasants, often took the air of millinary or chiliastic movements.[38]

Muhammad Ali also drastically changed the system of land ownership, an act that greatly contributed to the decline in ulama power at the same time that it preconditioned the rise of Egypt's landowning class in the last quarter of the nineteenth century. Under the Ottomans, land had been regarded as the property of the crown, but for administrative and economic purposes it was parceled into tracts called *iqta* and *iltizam,* which were tax-farmed either by public auction to a *multazim,* or given to a Mamluk Bey or the head of the Ottoman regiments as reward for services rendered.[39] The advent of Muhammad Ali and the establishment of his new ruling dynasty in the early nineteenth century displaced the Mamluks as the largest group of landowners with the new royal family. Muhammad Ali annulled the *iltizam* system as a wasteful means of collecting taxes (thereby cutting out the middleman, the *multazim*) and substituted the state as direct tax collector.[40]

Thus *multazim*-cum-ulama were gradually squeezed out of the alliance, unless they accepted the redistribution of land resources. Some ulama accepted their secondary role, while others like Makram sought to block it (and in so doing lost more than their land).[41] Those ulama who submitted to Muhammad Ali and became the "propagandists of his regime,"[42] gained wealth and influence. Here the similarities between ulama politics in Egypt and in Iran under Reza Shah are striking. In neither case was the ulama's response to modernization unified. In both cases, a faction of the ulama supported the state, while another tended to engage in oppositional activities. When Muhammad Ali's power was curtailed in the 1840s, and when Reza Shah was overthrown in 1941, there was no unified opposition on the part of the ulama to regain the social and economic privileges they had lost to the government. Instead, diverse factions of the ulama allied with different class-based political groups. This observation in fact reinforces my argument that the cause of the growth of religious opposition to the state in Iran should be sought in the political and social (i.e., class) alignments of the postcoup (1953) period, not in the modernization process itself or the specific features of Shi'i political theory.

At any rate, what happened to the rich import-export merchants? The available historical writings indicate (though not invariably) that the merchants were experiencing favorable political and economic treatment under Muhammad Ali. These merchants constituted the chief historical allies of the Egyptian rulers. To be sure, the government's new trading monopolies threatened to dislodge the rich import-export merchants of Cairo from their predominant position in the economic affairs of the country. Not only did these monopolies prevent the merchants from being able to increase their hold within the country's economy as domestic order was restored around 1810, but also the state's new workshops were often in direct competition with those merchants who made their livelihood from the import of cheap manufactured goods from Europe and India.[43] However, it is a mistake to assume that these government monopolies ruined the country's merchants across the board. Instead, they effectively ruined the poorer merchants, especially the poorer ones in the provinces, while benefiting the more influential and wealthier ones in each region and in the capital. Moreover, the rich import-export merchants were involved in the state's activities not only as administrators for Muhammad Ali but also as his representatives in international trade and commerce.[44]

Had these merchants allied with the artisans, Muhammad Ali would have had a difficult time in not only effectively undermining the power and privileges of the ulama but also establishing his system of monopolies. Given the conflict of interests between these two classes, and given that the merchants and the artisans tended to ally respectively with the Mamluks and Janissaries—two rival military groups— no historical precedent existed for such a coalition. Despite Muhammad Ali's alliance with the merchants, however, they could not escape the disorganizing effects of the Khedive's economic policies on their class. Because while the merchant's role as economic agent remained intact, the internal composition of his social class began to change as Muhammad Ali encouraged European or Levantine merchants to participate in the bureaucracy and to settle in Egypt.[45] As a consequence, the number of foreigners increased from about 3,000 in 1836 to over 68,000 in 1878.[46] In the course of time, these merchants were "Egyptianized" and by the twentieth century constituted an important branch of the country's large bourgeoisie class.[47] Thus, while in Iran the merchants were somewhat uniformly Muslims, the Egyptian merchants became ideologically fractionalized—hence the further erosion of ulama power in Egypt.

A more crucial factor affecting the making of Egypt's dominant classes was the change in the structure of domestic production toward a cash-crop economy, which began under Muhammad Ali and continued in this direction thereafter. Although the transformation of property relations in Egypt that led to the appearance of private ownership of land occurred long before the famous reforms of the nineteenth century,[48] the emergence of large privately owned landed property began in the latter half of the nineteenth century. The breakdown of Muhammad Ali's monopoly system,[49] and the state's fiscal crisis under Ismail led to the sale of state lands to individual buyers.[50] Since the largest landowners had access to credit, they were able to buy these lands and further enlarge the size of their holdings. This process was reinforced by an 1858 Ottoman land law that also applied Egypt, and from then on land could become privately owned in return for proof that taxes had been consistently paid over a five-year period; on presenting such proof, title deeds were accordingly issued.[51] The expansion of the large estates was also carried out at the expense of the small owners, many of whom were forced to sell because they incurred huge debts.[52] The British also encouraged large land ownership by deliberately selling state lands in large blocks so that only wealthy individuals could buy them.

Similar to the changes in the internal composition of the merchant class, the new element in the landowning picture was the advent of foreign landowners, land companies, and members of local minority groups, especially the Copts. The rise of these groups as landowners occurred with the British occupation. Foreign landlords, however, never formed more than 0.5 percent of the total, although their holdings covered large tracts of land and in 1932 reached a total of 700,000 *feddans*.[53] By the end of the nineteenth century the landowners had become a powerful class in Egypt, and the newly emerged small industrial bourgeoisie did not challenge their economic and political power. On the contrary, a close link between the two was forged, and individuals with double class membership (i.e., landowner/industrialist or landowner/merchant) became the rule. Marsot observes that "the links among political activity, economic enterprise, and landowners were positive and strong, and explain why there was no challenge to the power of the landowners from the new industrial elite, for they were to a large extent one and the same, or wanting to be."[54]

Concurrent with Egypt's integration into the world capitalist economy, the indigenous dominant classes were formed and at the same time benefited from this process. Landed property derived its basic income from cotton; even the leading industries dealt with or were related to cotton: spinning, weaving, ginning, and pressing. Although cotton was the most expensive crop to plant in terms of labor and capital outlay, it brought in the highest financial returns.[55] The landowning class, however, was continuously menaced by arbitrary governments, especially in a hydraulic economy where irrigation was controlled by the government and could be manipulated in a way that could make or break a large landowner. Naturally, the dominant classes, the landowners in particular, pushed for a constitutional government, where they would have a majority voice. And indeed the establishment of a constitutional monarchy in Egypt considerably expanded their power and influence in the government. The commission responsible for drafting the constitution consisted of eighteen members, of whom eleven (61 percent) were large landowners. Similarly, of the total of thirty-two members of the Constituent Assembly, twenty (62 percent) were large landowners.[56]

Under the impact of the nationalist revolution, Egypt's first modern mass party, the Wafd, emerged. The leadership of the Wafd reflected the dominant class members of Egyptian origin (rural and urban, Muslim and Coptic) who had conflicts with the British, the large landowners of Turkish origin, and/or the Palace. At the outset, it consisted of a small group of bourgeois notables who, representing themselves as the "delegates [Wafd] of the nation," demanded independence for Egypt. Its principal adherents (including Sa'ad Zaghlul), having been deported by the British authorities, became the focus of the anti-British movement of national unity (which extended from the extreme north to the extreme south of Egypt and included all sections of the population from the dispossessed masses to the big landowners—except for the aristocracy of Turkish origin).[57]

For the Wafd party and its leadership, Western-style democracy was the desirable model of government for Egypt. Such an ideological resolution fitted quite well with the religiously fractionalized dominant classes as it made possible the inclusion of the powerful Coptic community (the largest Christian minority in Egypt) into a unified nationalist movement against British domination. Like Iran during the Constitutional Revolution, the liberal and nationalist movement in Egypt made its mark on Islamic political thought, hence the growth of the modern Islamic movement. Islamic modernism was an ideological innovation that was made possible by the massive social changes Egypt had experienced as a result of its close contact with the West. Modern Islamic ideas suggested by al-Afghani and his disciple, 'Abduh, gained an extensive reception in Egypt. The relative success of Islamic modernism in Egypt was most probably related to its resonance with the interests of the Egyptian Muslim dominant classes. Abduh's disciples and supporters were the Egyptian landowning bourgeoisie—a social group that fell economically between the workers/peasants and the Turco-Circassian elites. Many became wealthy from buying state lands after the British occupation. This ideology attempted to reconcile Islam with liberal ideas and to liberate it "from the shackles of a too rigid orthodoxy, and to accomplish reforms which will render it adaptable to the complex demands of modern life."[58] This kind of Islam made peaceful coexistence between ideologically diverse members of Egypt's dominant classes possible. The leaders of Islamic modernism and the nationalist movement were closely associated. Among 'Abduh's disciples was Sa'ad Zaghlul, who attained great distinction in modern Egyptian political life. In the years following World War I, Zaghlul gained an international reputation as the spokesperson for Egypt's political aspirations. Zaghlul's relation to Muhammad 'Abduh was very intimate in character. He was not only a pupil as many others were, he was a "disciple" (*murid*), like the initiate of the Sufi orders who submits himself unquestionably to the direction of his superior. 'Abduh treated Zaghlul like a son and devoted the kind of time and attention to his training in religious, literary, and political matters that he gave to none of his other pupils.[59]

In contrast with the dominant classes, the artisans and the guilds in general were undermined by the process of social change. The decline of this social group was not simply, or even principally, the result of the country's industrial development, for it was on too small a scale. Rather, it was caused by the state's policies and the country's integration into the world economy. The first blow to the guilds came from the growth of state monopoly under Muhammad Ali. In addition, throughout the century the influx of cheap Western goods killed off various artisanal guilds while the changes in tax collecting finished off the rest. In 1890 a law passed that taxed workers and employers individually and established the principle of freedom to practice any trade or profession.[60] The number of traditional craftsmen in the cities and villages fell from 150,000 in 1914 to 95,000 in 1937, and then to 60,000 in 1958. Meanwhile, the number of new artisans increased only very slowly—from 380,000 in 1907 to 715,000 in 1958 (an annual growth rate of 1.3 percent). On the other hand, with the expansion of administrative activities and various social services, the number of the petty bourgeois functionaries, those in the liberal professions, intellectuals, and technicians and engineers increased.[61]

The petty bourgeoisie, like workers and peasants, were hard hit by economic hardship between the wars. As Issawi notes, the petty bourgeois class, consisting of government officials, employees, tradesmen, the less successful members of the professions, and the upper layers of artisans were passing through a severe crisis. The spread of education, together with the halting of economic expansion, produced a vast number of the "intellectual unemployed." In 1937 it was estimated that there were 7,500 jobless baccalaureate holders and 3,500 jobless graduates of the universities or high schools. In 1942 the Minister of Social Affairs gave a total unemployment figure of 10,000, the brunt of which was borne by the petty bourgeoisie.[62]

Fluctuations in export prices in the world market had a debilitating effect on economic activity between the two world wars. The total value of various crops in Egypt in 1924 was £E 115.5 thousand. This value declined to £E 77.0 thousand in 1929, then to £E 44.3 thousand in 1937, but was up again to £E 117.9 thousand in 1942.[63] Similarly, indexes of the volume and value of production was 83 and 145, respectively, in 1924. While the volume index increased to 93, the value index declined to 118 in 1929. In 1933, both volume and value indexes declined to 92 and 78, respectively. In 1937 both rose to 103 and 97, then declined again to 93 and 89 in 1938, then rose again to 94 and 94 respectively in 1940.[64] These sharp fluctuations and deteriorating economic conditions provided the climate for an outbreak of many protest movements during this period.

Similar to Iran in the 1970s, the economic difficulties in Egypt between the two world wars contributed to the growth of the Islamic opposition movement. But unlike Iran, Egypt's religious movement remained largely a middle-class phenomenon. The key to the difference between the two countries seems to have been the diverse patterns of class alliance. While the Iranian ulama and the indigenous dominant classes were excluded from participating in the state's decision-making, their Egyptian counterparts had direct access to state power. However, the Wafd party, the major political institution of the dominant classes, which had galvanized a grass-root movement against the British occupation and had promised independence for Egypt, was unable to deliver on its promises because of British intransigence.[65] Considering that the Wafd constituted the major institutional basis for liberal-nationalist politics, its inability to solve the country's socioeconomic problems was tantamount to the decline of the significance of this ideology for addressing Egypt's problems. Nor were the ulama in a position to lead the opposition movements because, as Marsot has observed:

> The people could not turn to their erstwhile natural leaders, the ulama, for over the past century the latter had been coopted into the state apparatus. The Sufi leaders had also fallen by the wayside. The Bakri and Sadat movements . . . had united through intermarriage, and were headed by a man who felt more at home when speaking English than when speaking Arabic.[66]

It was within this context of a highly politicized middle class, an impotent ruling class, and the decline of liberalism that the Society of the Muslim Brothers found extensive interested audiences for its messages. The anti–dominant class attitudes of the Muslim Brothers were reflected in sanctioning their members to avoid involvement with "notables and names" and "parties and societies."[67] Mitchell's analysis of the occupational background of some of the leaders and activists of the Muslim Brothers led him to conclude

> That this membership largely represented an emergent and self-conscious Muslim middle class is obvious. Sundry aspects of the Society's ideas and programmes demonstrated this clearly. Hostility to foreign economic control which limited the prospects of the new bourgeoisie, a hostility which extended to the local minorities, is one of the most obvious which comes to mind. Another is the political struggle against imperialism (which sustained foreign economic control) and its "agents"—the internal imperialists, the ruling classes—who buttressed their economic and political power by co-operating with and depending on imperialism. A similar element from a different angle is the "national unity" theme which so dominated the Society's thinking. In a religious and cultural sense this meant, of course, the re-establishment of Islam as the beacon to guide the nation's destiny; in more secular terms, it was a political call for unity of purpose to protect national sovereignty and to achieve national

goals; it was also a call for the unity of classes expressed in the theme of harmony between labor and management, and landowner and peasant; themes which have become the hallmark of the middle-class conservative reformism in the Arab world.[68]

Class was of course only one factor, albeit a major one, for the rise of the Muslim Brothers. Their growth was also initially assisted by the British, the right wing of the Wafd, and the king, who considered them a useful instrument against Communism and the left-leaning faction within the Wafd. The Muslim Brothers, in their turn, did not attack the British presence in Egypt until the mid-1940s. And while they listed fifty demands in one of their Epistles, which included an attack on colonialism couched in general terms, there was no mention of independence for Egypt nor anything about the withdrawal of British troops from Egyptian territory, a very odd omission.[69] Furthermore, the Brothers wholeheartedly joined the anti-Communist campaign launched by the pro-king Sidqi government, and their press reported the course of the governmental campaign in a daily column entitled "The Fight Against Communism." The intelligence of the Society passed on information useful to the government in its continual roundups of real and suspected Communists, especially in labor and university circles.[70]

The Society of the Muslim Brothers was not a revolutionary organization in its initial stages of development. Nor did it have a clear idea about its role in society. The ideology of the Society was developed and articulated in the course of the first ten years of its activities. It was at the fifth conference (which was also the tenth anniversary of the movement) that the Muslim Brothers offered a general sketch of their programs. Moreover, only after the government blocked their participation in the 1942 election (and rigged the 1945 election against the Brothers as well as the Wafd) did the Brothers begin to engage in revolutionary activities, which included the assassinations of several government figures. The government's dissolution of the Society in 1948 seems to have pushed the Society even further toward extremism.[71] Nevertheless, while the state's policies significantly affected the political orientations of the Muslim Brothers, one cannot argue that ideology did not matter. The Brothers' deep commitment to Islamic fundamentalist ideas prompted them to define liberalism and Communism as their immediate enemies—definitions that in all likelihood underlay their complicity with the conservatives and the king. Strictly from the viewpoint of class interests, it would have made more sense for them to coalesce with the left wing rather than with the right wing.

Syria and a Sectarian Islamic Movement

Egypt's divided Islamic movement broadly paralleled the division between the dominant classes and the petty bourgeoisie and was at the same time an element in the makeup of these classes in the nineteenth and twentieth centuries. The orthodox Sunni institutions were closely tied to the landed and commercial interests, and the ulama constituted an integral part of the polity in precapitalist Egypt. The Islamic extremism of the Sufi brotherhood, on the other hand, was predominantly adhered to by the artisans and retail traders. In the modern period, Islamic modernism began to resonate with the interests of the newly constituted Muslim indigenous dominant classes, while the Society of the Muslim Brothers was chiefly associated with middle-class politics. The role of Islam in the precapitalist area that is now the state of Syria was quite similar to that of Egypt. But the opposition of the traditional social classes—the landowners, merchants, and petty bourgeoisie—to the consolidation of an authoritarian socialist-oriented regime in the 1960s and thereafter unleashed considerable social resources for the growth of an Islamic opposition similar to the Iranian religious protests early in the same decade.

The Economy: Like Egypt and Iran, the integration of Syria into the world capitalist economy resulted in the development of an export-oriented economy vulnerable to fluctuations in the international market. In precapitalist Syria, agriculture and commerce were the mainstays of the economy. Syria's commercial expansion was principally due to its central position in the old world as a great junction for overland and sea trade routes from Further Asia and India to the Mediterranean, Africa, and Europe as well as for exchanges between its neighbors, Mesopotamia, Egypt, and Anatolia. Some of the routes developed in prehistoric times. By 3,000 B.C. caravan trade was so well established that its methods were standardized, and commercial exchanges regularized.[72] Incorporation into the Ottoman Empire in 1516 brought Syria an empirewide market and made it the main communication link between the Eastern empire and Europe. Aleppo developed as the Levant's chief market city where European merchants established their trading stations and consulates. Damascus flourished as the principal staging area for the annual Haj (pilgrimage) to Mecca, for which it supplied the provisions and transport.[73] Beginning in the seventeenth century, which marked the decline of the Ottoman Empire, the infiltration of the Syrian market by European mercantile interests gradually changed the structure of the country's domestic production. The principal instrument of foreign economic invasion does not seem to have been the mechanism of unequal exchange. Rather, it was political in the form of the treaty of capitulations, which limited Ottoman customs duties on imports from the states to which the concessions were granted and accorded various extraterritorial privileges. Consequently, European goods paid very low customs duties on entry into the empire, while Syrian and other Ottoman goods seeking to enter Europe were subject to prohibitive duties or barred outright. Such concessions very probably inhibited the accumulation of capital and so blocked the growth of a bourgeoisie.[74] The commercial treaties signed by the Ottoman rulers in 1838 were applied to Syria and further reinforced the already great advantages enjoyed by foreign merchants under the capitulations.

Parallel with the decline of traditional industry and commerce was the growth of an export-enclave economy. The merchants' purchase of land and changes in the Ottoman law in favor of the establishment of private ownership of land facilitated the growth of Syria's landowning class in the course of the nineteenth and early twentieth centuries. Cash crops gradually became the country's most important export, considerably benefiting the landowner/merchant class. A period of rapid economic growth began in the 1930s, accelerated in the 1940s, and lasted until the late 1950s. Growth was primarily based on the opening of new land to cultivation, financed largely by wealthy urban merchants (particularly from Aleppo).[75] Until the early 1970s, raw cotton had been the country's main export. As a result of price increases, oil overtook cotton as the chief export in 1974. Whereas in 1973 oil exports had been valued at $67 million, in 1974 they amounted to $412 million. In the same years, cotton exports totaled $116 million and $195 million, respectively.[76] Taken together, petroleum and cotton accounted for 81 percent of the total exports in 1976.[77] Fluctuations in export prices constituted the major destabilizing factor for the economy, which contributed to the intensification of political conflicts in Syria.

The State: The creation of a modern centralized state in Syria is a mid-twentieth-century phenomenon. For centuries, beginning in 1516, Syria had been part of the Ottoman Empire. The Ottomans ruled Syria through pashas, despots appointed by, and ultimately responsible to, the Sublime Porte.[78] The first experience of a centralized government, judicial reform, and regular taxation occurred during Egypt's occupation of Syria between 1831 and 1839. But Ibrahim Pasha, son of the Egyptian ruler Muhammad Ali, became unpopular with the landowners because of the limitations he placed on their influence, and with the peasants because of conscription and the taxes he imposed. Syria achieved a brief moment of independence in July 1919 when the General Syrian Congress declared Syria sovereign and free. In March 1920, the Congress proclaimed Faysal the king of Syria. Faysal and his Syrian supporters established Arabic as the official language and proceeded to have school texts translated from Turkish. But France and Great Britain refused to recognize Syrian independence, and the Supreme Allied Council, meeting in San Remo, Italy, in April 1920, partitioned the Arab world into mandates. Arab resistance was crushed, and on July 25, 1920, the French marched into Damascus. Faysal fled to Europe and did not return to the Middle East until he was made the king of Iraq in 1921.[79]

Despite the fact that under the Mandate a Muslim nation was formally dominated by a non-Muslim Western power, Syria's struggle for independence did not take place within an Islamic ideological framework, a situation similar to Egypt's. This fact indeed questions the validity of the argument that seeks a direct correspondence between Western domination and the outbreak of the Islamic opposition movement. Here also nationalist ideology dominated the political scene. The objective for all the nationalist groups was to form a Western-style parliamentary democracy. In 1925 a People's party was formed, which was basically the amalgamation of several existing nationalist groups.[80] In 1928 the People's party was transformed into a nationwide front that came to be known as the *kulta,* the Nationalist Bloc, whose common bond was a militant attitude toward the Mandate. Its leaders included most of the older nationalists, men who had worked for Syrian independence during the Ottoman era. Among them were representatives of the influential landholding families.[81]

The nationalist struggles, coupled with favorable international circumstances, culminated in Syrian independence when the Soviet Union in July and the United States in September 1944 granted Syria and Lebanon unconditional recognition as sovereign states. British recognition followed a year later. These Allied nations brought pressures on

France to evacuate Syria. The French acceded, and by April 15, 1946, all French troops were off Syrian soil.[82] Postindependence Syria experienced a sequence of parliamentary democracy (1946–49), military dictatorship (1949–54), and parliamentary democracy again (1954–58), followed by a brief period of unification with Egypt in the United Arab Republic (1958–61). As long as this sort of semiparliamentary democracy was present, Islamic fundamentalism was but one among many political currents in society, as was the case in Iran between 1941 and 1953.

The rise of Islamic ideology as the dominant ideology of the opposition movement in Syria is a post-1963 phenomenon, when the coup of March 1963 brought the Baath to power and effectively ended the nationalist-liberal episode. The Baath seizure of power heralded new political and economic orders in Syria. The socialist-oriented bureaucratic-authoritarian regime inaugurated after 1963 antagonized the traditional landowning, mercantile, and artisan classes in the country—hence the formation of a strong basis for the growth of an Islamic opposition. Thus a similar kind of class coalition that was behind religious opposition in Iran began to form in post-1963 Syria. The Syrian regime pursued three major economic aims: to initiate a land reform program that would eliminate the concentration of land ownership; to destroy the monopolistic merchant families and their businesses by nationalizing most of the organized business sectors; and to give the government a more decisive role in managing the economy through planning. By 1965 these three objectives had been more or less achieved.[83] The state's extensive intervention in the economy was associated with the expansion of the bureaucracy. The first government, announced within a week of the takeover, was made up of twenty-six ministers, of whom thirteen were Baathists and the remainder were Nasserites, Arab Socialists, Communists, and independents. This was already the largest government Syria had known since independence in 1943. Subsequent re-shuffles increased the number of ministers to thirty (but the balance between Baathists and non-Baathists remained unaltered).[84]

Similar to Iran, the ideology of the state (here formulated by the Baath party) encouraged the growth of an Islamic opposition. In the mid-1950s, Baath ideology was essentially a nationalist doctrine that viewed the Arab as a "single eternal nation." While Islam was acknowledged as the basis of the most glorious phase of Arab history, it was considered a past that had now become part of the heritage of Christian (and other non-Sunni) Arabs as well.[85] In the 1960s the Baath moved toward socialism. Arab unity was relegated to a secondary position in its doctrine. A significant element of Marxist-Leninist ideas and terminology was integrated into Baathist thinking, and with it a more radical concept of socialism.[86] A Baathist ideologue even began attacking religion in an article (published in an army magazine) in which it was urged to sweep away all the traditions of the past—feudalism, capitalism, colonialism, God, and religion; in their place the author proposed "absolute belief in man's ability." The publication of the article produced a considerable furor among the ulama and, for the first time, among Christian clergymen. The government quickly backed down and attributed the article to an "imperialist conspiracy."[87]

These changes in state structure, policies, and ideology led to the opposition of Syria's traditional social classes. By 1965, diverse Islamic groups were involved in protest activities. From this period, Syria's political history departs from Egypt's and begins to approach Iran's. Nevertheless, the Syrian religious movement was unable to overthrow the regime. Differences in class politics between Iran and Syria may provide the clue as to why the Syrian Islamic movement failed to achieve its goal.

Class Politics and Ideological Outcomes: The making of Syria's dominant classes in the late nineteenth and early twentieth centuries followed a pattern by and large similar to Egypt's. Here also these classes were benefited by the 1858 Ottomans' land code, which had been devised to ensure the occupiers' stability in their holdings, and thus to provide a basis to increase tax revenues. The development of a profitable cash-crop economy, and the decline of the role of Syrian merchants in international trade (which had prompted them to invest in land), were two major factors for the growth of the landowner/merchant class. The French also encouraged the growth of private latifundia, facilitating the private appropriation of land, especially by those who collaborated with the Mandate. State and *vaqf* lands were sold to large landowners, concession companies, and tribal chiefs.[88] The result was a high concentration of landed property. Until 1958, big estates that covered 45 percent of the irrigated areas and 30 percent of the rainfed land were held by only 2.5 percent of the total number of landowners. Moreover, about two-thirds of the big estate owners were absentee landlords who, for the most part, were not themselves farmers but merchants who had invested their earnings from trade in agricultural land. Finally, about 70 percent of the rural population did not own any land at all but subsisted either as sharecroppers or laborers.[89] In the twentieth century, some "feudalists" began adopting capitalist methods or investing their land rents in industry. Big merchants became agricultural and industrial entrepreneurs. Tribal chieftains, landowners, and merchants often bought shares in industrial corporations. A number of middle-class merchants and businessmen established modern industries. A modern capitalist class was gradually developed within the traditional ruling class of wealthy landowners and traders.[90]

These classes played a leading role in both the nationalist movement for independence and in the postindependence period, and until their power and privileges were taken away by the socialist-oriented Baathist leaders in the mid-1960s, state power was the instrument of this class. Primarily Sunni Muslims, the landowning and industrialist class of Aleppo, Damascus, Hama, and Homs had until the mid-1960s dominated the politics and economy of Syria. Prominent among the members of this class were about fifty families who had possessed wealth for a number of generations and those who had gained it since World War I, primarily in industry. Families of both backgrounds had extensive holdings in the agricultural and industrial sectors.[91] Among the leaders of the nationalist bloc were representatives of the landholding families. In the parliamentary politics of the post–World War II period, political parties were generally personal followers of individuals who were drawn from the landed interests and the professions: doctors, lawyers, teachers, and merchants.[92] Landowners and tribal chiefs consistently formed the highest group of Syrian deputies in the 1919–59 period. Their numerical superiority had precluded legislation designed to modify the existing economic inequality and thus explains the steadily growing gap between the government and the needs and desires of the masses.[93]

The concentration of productive wealth in a few hands was accompanied by an increase in the number of the impoverished masses. The French were partly responsible for this because despite regulations adopted in the mid-1920s to distribute state property to small landholders, they allowed this land to be sold or leased to big landlords. Moreover, the landlords who were the principal recipients of loans from State Agricultural Banks, simply re-lent the money to the *fellahin* at much higher interest rates. Small and landless peasants had to turn to moneylenders, merchants, and landlords, all of whom charged exorbitant rates, which in periods of bad harvests could reach 150 percent.[94]

The army, however, became a major channel for the upward mobility of the members of the dominated classes and the chief mechanism by which they began to influence the future of Syria. The attitudes of the members of the dominant classes were a central factor in this process, for, despite their formal control of the state bureaucracy and political parties, the ruling landed and merchant families were reluctant to control the armed forces. According to Seale,

> After 1946 the great majority of cadets at the Homs military college came from the lower middle class, moulded no doubt in their schooldays by one or other of the doctrinaire youth movements which had sprung up in the 1930s and 1940s. The Muslim landed families, being predominantly of nationalist sentiment, despised the army as a profession: to join it between the wars was to serve the French. Homs to them was a place for the lazy, the rebellious, the academically backward, or the socially undistinguished. Few young men of good family would consider entering the college unless they had failed at school or been expelled. The conservative "right" in Syria neglected the army as a source of political power, with disastrous consequences, as it was the army, an eager and indoctrinated instrument, which later destroyed the power of the landed families and urban merchants, with the result that a veteran Syrian politician of the 1940s would find little to recognize or approve of in the political scene fifteen years later.[95]

This process was reinforced by the French themselves also. Their military recruitment had focused heavily on the dissident rural communities, which the French administration considered to be less nationalist than the urban Sunni.[96] At any rate, the social background of army officers, coupled with the economic polarization of society, were two major factors for the success of the Baathists and Communists in seizing state power. By 1955 the balance of forces in society began to swing in favor of left-wing elements, notably the Baath party and the Communist party.[97] The rise of the Baath to power resulted in a virtual transformation of the Syrian power structure. An elite predominantly recruited from the Sunni landlord/merchant bourgeoisie was displaced by a new one of rural, lower middle class, and disproportionately from Islamic minority origins.[98]

The Baath seizure of power in the coup of 1963 and the kind of policies it pursued was highly consequential for the development of Islamic opposition to their rule. True, the ulama had long been a political force in Syria, and other Islamic organizations such as the Muslim Brothers were active in the forties and fifties. Nevertheless, the growth of Islam as the major political force with considerable followers was a phenomenon of the sixties and thereafter. As was the case in Iran and Egypt, class and the state significantly determined the growth or decline of Islam as the dominant ideology of the opposition. Moreover, revolutionary Islamic discourse in Syria was shaped as a result of the back-and-forth propaganda warfare between the state and its opposition. This is so because before the advent of the Baath party to power, the Brothers had no clear strategy on socioeconomic and political matters. When socialist and Communist ideas were popular in the opposition movement in the late forties and fifties, the Muslim Brothers often flirted with the idea of Islamic socialism.[99] Mubarak, the head of the Syrian branch of the Muslim Brothers, once declared that the Brotherhood was a "Marxist beverage in an Islamic cup."[100] It is interesting to note how a dominant political discourse affects the discourses of other ideologies. During the period of intense socioeconomic contradictions and the popularity of socialist ideas, the Muslim Brothers were also utilizing socialist idioms to attract followers, in the same way that in the post-1963 period the Iranian secular political groups, including the Left, began utilizing religious tactics in their mobilizing efforts against the Shah. This is not to say that power contenders are simply opportunists who bend ideological principles to fit their political objectives. It is rather the force of the dominant political discourse that imposes its own Weltanschauung on other ideologies so that political leaders find it necessary to use its idioms and concepts to communicate their goals and agenda to the masses in a meaningful fashion.

The presence of a multiple party system reflecting the interests of diverse groups and classes in society also hindered the growth of a unified Islamic opposition. The big merchants and landowners of Damascus threw their principal weight behind the People's party and the National party, but they and their supporters also voted for the Muslim Brothers, not out of sympathy for them but out of their fear of the Communists and the Baathists.[101] Otherwise, liberalism was a rival political discourse for the Muslim Brothers. And the Brothers' use of the concept of "Islamic socialism" was highly suggestive that, with their leftist compatriots, they shared the belief that, as Ajami has aptly stated, "liberalism had become anathema, another word for Western colonialism."[102]

However, with the ascendance of the Left the picture began to change. The Muslim Brothers first excised the term "Islamic socialism" from their political vocabulary altogether. Such an act in all probability was a calculated move. And by then they had a pretty good idea as to where the sources of extensive support for the pursuit of their religious goals were to be found. The growth of a bureaucratic-authoritarian regime, similar to Iran's, with its policy of systematically disrupting and disorganizing all the political parties ideologically opposed to the Baath party was an important factor for the rise of Islamic opposition. Moreover, the state's economic policies and ideology helped the Muslim Brothers to define their own concrete political agenda. Finally, deprived of their own political parties and organizations, the landowners, merchants, and artisans found in Islam a strong ideology to express their opposition to the regime.

Thus in the 1964 uprising against the state, the Muslim Brothers and notable merchants were clearly in the forefront. The opposition movement began to create disturbances in each of Syria's major cities. In Hama, the Brothers, the ulama, and certain notable families led an uprising that included attacks on government buildings, the erection of street barricades, merchant strikes, and public denunciations of the "godless" Baath from the mosques. The merchants' strikes and disturbances spread to Aleppo, Homs, and Damascus. In the capital, the Chamber of Commerce called for the repeal of restrictions on foreign commerce and a guarantee against further nationalization. The government responded with tanks against the barricades and with artillery against the mosques in Hama, while in Damascus Baathist militants forcibly opened shops and clashed with the Muslim Brothers. In 1965, Baath radicals launched a major assault on the urban establishment, nationalizing most of the modern industrial sector and all foreign trade plus segments of the wholesale internal commerce as well as speeding up land reform.[103]

These policies further unified Islamic opposition groups and strengthened their connections with the landowners/merchants and artisans. The 1980 program of the Brothers reflected the interests and the outlook of the urban Sunni trading and manufacturing classes, which included outright criticisms of the socialist measures undertaken by the regime. Their ideological attack on the Baath party, however, took on a sectarian character. Given that the Alawis, an Islamic religious minority, were overrepresented among the Syrian leaders, the new program of the Muslim Brothers addressed the "wise men" of the Alawi community, stating that 9 or 10 percent of the population cannot indefinitely dominate the majority in Syria. The Muslim Brothers thus put themselves forward as the natural representatives of the Sunni community and defined their contention with the Syrian rulers as a conflict between the Sunnis and the Alawis.[104] Clashes between the regime and the Muslim Brothers continued in the seventies and eighties. Encouraged by the success of the Iranian Revolution, Syrian Islamic militants accelerated their attack on the regime. Assassinations and sabotage were stepped up. In June 1979 a massacre of more than fifty military cadets took place in Aleppo. In the spring of 1980, the Islamic opposition staged a major offensive in northern Syria, which took on the character of overt urban guerrilla warfare against the government.[105]

Nevertheless, despite its intriguing similarities with the Iranian religious movement, Syria's Islamic opposition failed to overthrow the regime by means of demonstrations and armed struggles. Why? The clue may be sought in the contrasting relations of the Iranian and Syrian states with their dominated classes. As was discussed in chapters 3 and 4, the Shah was not so much interested in expanding the state's power bases into the rural areas. And his agricultural policies of expanding agribusiness and farm corporations, tied to and dominated by international capital from the mid-1960s on, eroded any serious foothold the state had in the countryside. Moreover, despite his pro-workers rhetoric, the Shah was not truly concerned with defending the interests of the working class. Inflation and the food scarcities of the 1970s considerably antagonized the workers—hence their participation in the revolutionary movement of 1977–79.

The policy of the Syrian state was quite different in this respect. The Baath party was socialist and since its inception (along with its ally and sometime rival, the Communist party) had had systematic connections with the peasants and workers. In marked contrast with Iran, Syria had experienced strong peasant movements for years. These movements grew out of the conditions of the poor peasants, who in the early 1950s were still mainly landless and lived under a form of tenancy that amounted to serfdom. The movement in the Hama region, however, included some of the better-off peasants as well as the poorest. From the early 1940s on, the Hama movement began to force changes in Syrian society through militant activity in the countryside and the vigorous political representation of Akram Hourani, its leader.[106] When Hourani and his peasant-based populist movement joined the Baath party in the late 1940s, the party's connections to the peasant movement was considerably strengthened.[107] A working-class movement, although relatively small, had also been present in Syria for some time. Beginning in 1926, the workers' struggle for a wage increase, a minimum wage, and an eight-hour workday led to the formation of the Federation of Trade Unions of Syria in 1938. By the mid-1950s the labor movement had begun to call for assistance to the unemployed, protection for agricultural workers, and an economic development program for Syria. It also became active in opposing alliance with the West, and especially worked against the Baghdad Pact. Militancy increased within the movement, forcing the government to adopt some of the workers' demands. By this time the Baath had gained some influence in the unions, and Communist influence was also growing.[108]

When the Baathists seized power, the peasants considerably benefited from their land reform program. The nationalization of industry and tax policies were favorably predisposed toward workers and the urban poor.[109] Thus when conflict broke out with the Islamic opposition, the Syrian regime, in addition to its well-organized party bureaucracy and military, enjoyed the support of the peasants and workers. In the rural areas, the Alawis in particular began defending the regime, while in the cities Baathist militants forcibly opened shops and clashed with members of the Muslim Brothers.[110] The Muslim Brothers, in contrast, had scarcely any foothold in the countryside, despite their vitality in Damascus and other Syrian cities.[111] Moreover, the Syrian Islamic movement probably lacked the populist appeal needed to mobilize the whole Society against the Baath. Indeed, even today the secular Left, organized workers, the peasantry, and the salaried middle class are bound to be wary of any change likely to return power to the merchants and landlords.[112]

Finally, Syria's religious and ethnic diversity was also a factor affecting class politics, simultaneously enabling and constraining the collective capacity of both the opposition and the state. For example, 82.5 percent of the country's population speak Arabic, and 68.7 percent are Sunni Muslims. In language and religion, the Arab-speaking Sunni Muslims constitute a numerical majority of 57.4 percent of the whole population. The major religious minorities in Syria are the Alawis (11.5

percent), the Druzes (4 percent), the Isma'ilis (1.5 percent), and the Greek Orthodox Christians (4.7 percent), who constitute the most important Christian community in Syria (14.1 percent).[113] It is interesting to note that the Sunni and Christian confessions cut across the urban-rural gap, while the Islamic heterodox sects are chiefly rural and traditionally deprived (particularly the Alawis).[114] Thus when the Baathists took power, they could (given the diversity of religious minorities represented among their leaders) rely heavily on the corresponding co-religious rural peasants. Because of the Alawis' strong distrust of the Sunnis (who had so often been their oppressors),[115] they tended to defend the government in the face of the Sunni's revolutionary challenge. On the other hand, the same diversity of religious minorities in top government positions made the Baath's rule in the cities quite problematic.[116] At any rate, the government's secular reforms received considerable support, in the rural areas especially.[117]

Finally, in contrast to the Shah's policies in the 1970s, the Syrian state in this decade took a favorable orientation toward the merchants, while at the same time attempting to play down its ideological differences with Islam. In the previous chapters, it was pointed out that the ideological polarization of society and the growth of Islam as the dominant ideology of the Iranian Revolution was partly due to the Pahlavi state's own ideology. The Shah's glorification of pre-Islamic kingship and ancient history was basically an attempt to overlook and undermine the influence of Islam in society. This ideological orientation was intensified in the seventies when the Shah changed the Islamic calendar and invented a monarchical calendar. This insensitive policy contributed to the shaping of Iran's Islamic opposition. Moreover, during the economic crisis of the seventies, the Shah singled out the bazaar as a target responsible for inflation and scarcity, an act that further antagonized the bazaaris. The situation in Syria turned out to be somewhat different. While in many respects the Baath's socialist ideology helped define the Islamic identity of the opposition movement, in the seventies the Syrian rulers began taking a more conciliatory approach toward Islam. In particular, when Hafiz Asad came to power in 1971, he pursued policies to mute the secularism of his predecessors. He tried to portray himself as a pious Muslim, reintroduced the abolished religious formulas into public ceremonies, and cultivated the ulama with honors and higher salaries.[118] Asad also launched an economic liberalization program in the seventies designed both to appease the merchants and to stimulate economic growth—a policy that very probably reduced tensions between the state and the merchant class.[119]

The foregoing analysis of religion and politics in Egypt and Syria seems to provide additional support for the theoretical framework advanced in this work. Variations in the religious movements in Egypt, Iran, and Syria were related to variations in class politics, patterns of class alliance, and the state and its policies. Egypt's divided Islamic movement paralleled the political divisions between Egypt's indigenous dominant classes (the landowners and the merchants/bourgeoisie) and the petty bourgeoisie—while religious populism in Iran paralleled the political unity of these classes in their opposition to the state in the 1960s and thereafter. Syria's Islamic movement was based on a class coalition similar to Iran's. Yet the Syrian and Iranian states had different relationships with the dominated classes—the workers and peasants. While the Syrian state had a popular base among the workers and peasants, the Shah's regime did not enjoy much support among these classes. Furthermore, Iran's economic difficulties in the 1970s considerably antagonized workers, hence their participation in the revolution of 1977–79. In terms of the state's orientation toward the traditional social classes, and in terms of a class basis for the religious opposition movement, Syria's religious movement in the sixties and seventies was by and large similar to Iran's in the early 1960s.

PART TWO

The Outcomes of the Iranian Revolution

7

Islamic Discourse and Postrevolutionary Conflicts

That the revolution succeeded so quickly and—
seemingly, at the first superficial glance—so radically, is
only due to the fact that, as a result of an Extremely
unique historical situation, absolutely dissimilar currents, absolutely heterogeneous *class interests,* absolutely
contrary *political and social strivings have merged, and in*
a strikingly "harmonious" manner.
Lenin, Letters from Afar, *First Letter.*

February 11, 1979, is the celebrated date of the Iranian Revolution. It
followed a day of armed confrontation between the Imperial Guard and
mutinied air force–support personnel aided by two major urban guerrilla organizations, the Mojahedin-i Khalq and the Feda'iyan-i Khalq.
The armed struggle, however, was quickly concluded when the army's
Supreme Council decided not to intervene in the political conflict. In a
referendum in March, the public overwhelmingly endorsed the formation of the Islamic Republic, and in December of the same year they endorsed the constitution of the Islamic Republic, in which the doctrine of
velayat-i faqih (governance by the jurisprudent) was central. In the fall
of 1979, the U.S. embassy in Tehran was seized. In January 1980, Abul
Hasan Bani-Sadr was elected Iran's first president; in April the leaders
of the Islamic Republic launched a cultural revolution; and in September Iraq invaded Iran. This was followed by a period of intense internal
conflict within the Islamic Republic that developed into a reign of terror
in the summer of 1981, after which the followers of Ayatollah Khomeini expelled all their rivals from the government and successfully
consolidated power. In the same period, class conflict also intensified. It
revolved around three major issues: land reform, labor law and the
question of labor control of production, and the nationalization of foreign trade. These issues were eventually resolved in favor of the merchants and landowners.

The sequence of these events were manifestations of two intertwined yet analytically distinct processes. The first was a political revolutionary process directed toward the formation and consolidation of a new political order—i.e., an Islamic Republic. The second was a social revolutionary process directed toward transforming existing economic relationships. With the departure of the Shah from Iran; the subsequent downfall of his prime minister, Shahpour Bakhtiyar; the weakening of the state's repressive apparatus (mainly due to soldiers deserting the army); and the mass uprisings and armed struggles, a political revolution was under way in Iran. The Pahlavi monarchy was overthrown; the structure, form, and ideology of the state were considerably transformed; and, finally, the class bases of those now in power differed from those they replaced. But a social revolution failed to materialize in Iran. There is today little difference, in terms of economic structure and distribution of resources, between pre- and postrevolutionary Iran.

This chapter will explain the dynamics underlying these events and the resolution of the issues involved in terms of the interaction between class, politics, and ideology. Conventional models explain revolutionary outcomes in terms of the kind of resources and opportunities available to the contending groups and classes within the context of international structure and the exigencies of world historical development. While these factors remain significant in determining the nature of postrevolutionary accomplishments, this chapter argues that the resources and opportunities available to the contending groups and warring classes (and their capacity to act) were conditioned by the dynamic of Shi'i revolutionary discourse. The themes of Shi'i discourse as the dominant ideology of the revolution and its conceptual framework set up a revolutionary dynamic that produced certain postrevolutionary events and shaped others. It structured the kind of opportunities available to, and the legitimacy of the claims advanced by, diverse power contenders and social classes.

I shall begin by first focusing on the rise of the new political order, and then consider the social revolutionary and counterrevolutionary movements. Finally, I will identify some of the basic features of the postrevolutionary political order.

The Rise of a New Political Order

How was the postrevolutionary state—the Islamic Republic—consolidated? How did the ulama followers of Ayatollah Khomeini establish their political domination over the rest of society? So far I have attempted to establish that, historically, ulama politics have been conditioned by the dominant political discourse in society and the presence of diverse factions in their ranks connected to the merchants, the petty bourgeoisie, and the landowners. When these classes turned against the Shah in the postreform period, an objective basis for ulama unity was formed. Not too surprisingly, these classes, particularly the merchants, played decisive roles in determining the economic policies of the Islamic Republic. This phenomenon strongly suggests a causal link between the prerevolutionary class alliances and postrevolutionary political and economic outcomes. This does not, however, suggest that the dynamic of ulama politics was directly reducible to mere class politics. For one thing, the ulama in and of themselves did not make up a class or even part of a class. Nor were they the conscious champions of their own historical class bases. Also, the ulama's objective was to establish an Islamic Republic under their own exclusive control. Therefore, the ulama are best conceived as *state builders,* i.e., "politicians struggling to consolidate and use state power."[1] Although Ayatollah Khomeini was regarded as the undisputable leader of the revolution, the establishment of the governance by the jurisprudent was far from certain. The ulama followers of Ayatollah Khomeini were facing revolutionary and counterrevolutionary challenges from other power contenders; therefore, their actions were dictated by the exigencies of meeting these challenges. On the other hand, these ulama were constrained by class pressures as well as by the structural limits of Iran's dependent economy. Yet despite all this, they were able to establish their exclusive control over the polity. To understand their success, it is important to consider how Shi'i revolutionary discourse affected the course of political conflict, having a determined impact on the contour of the new political order.

The Contenders for Power

The revolutionary dynamic set by Shi'i discourse remained unabated for several years after the overthrow of the monarchy. A distinctive feature of the Iranian Revolution was the unanimity and harmony of the public in demanding the Shah's expulsion. The regime was brought down by the largest protest demonstrations ever seen in human history (over 2 million on one occasion in Tehran, millions more in other cities) and probably the most prolonged and successful general strike in world history as well.[2] As long as the Shah (i.e., the common enemy) was present, diverse Islamic groups were united and the Islamic alternative to the monarchy's ideology seemed uniform and remarkably consistent. But when concrete plans began to emerge as to precisely how to construct an "Islamic" political and economic order, harmony went out the window and intense ideological disputes among diverse Islamic groups came in. Of notable significance were the following rival political groups:

The Ulama Followers of Ayatollah Khomeini. The central objective of Ayatollah Khomeini and his followers (the so-called *Line of Imam*) was the establishment of the *velayat-i faqih*, under which the *faqih* would have the ultimate authority over all crucial matters facing the government and parliament. The ulama and their laymen supporters were organized mainly in the Islamic Republican party (IRP), founded right after the revolution by Ayatollahs Beheshti, Mousavi-Ardabili, and Bahonar, and Hojatuleslam Hashemi Rafsanjani and Ali Hosein Khameneh-ei. The party soon began to organize Islamic associations in factories, offices, educational institutions, and military bases. Their views were reflected, although not exclusively, in the daily *Jomhouri-ye Islami*. The IRP faced the opposition of other power contenders, including the liberals, the Mojahedin, and the Left.

The Liberals. Known as the bourgeois-liberals in the postrevolutionary political jargon, the liberals were predominantly the remnants of the National Front of the early 1950s. As was mentioned earlier, the Front consisted of a loose coalition of like-minded reformers and nationalists. While it had been effectively repressed during the 1953 coup and never regained its former power and popularity, the Front nevertheless managed to survive during the postcoup period and reemerged now and then under different names: the National Resistance Movement (1954), the Second National Front (1960–63), and the Third National Front (1965). Among the many groups affiliated with the Front, the Freedom Movement of Iran (*Nahzat-i Azad-i Iran*) was to play the most important role in the revolution. Led by Mehdi Bazargan, a skilled and experienced politician, the Freedom Movement remained the most dynamic representative of liberal politics in the postrevolutionary period. The Freedom Movement owed its success to its close link with the ulama, and to the fact that it was considered the most acceptable alternative for the United States. After the revolution, liberals obtained key positions in Bazargan's provisional government.[3] The liberal politicians of postrevolutionary Iran, however, were not confined to the descendants of the National Front. People like Bani-Sadr, Sadiq Qotbzadeh, and Ayatollah Mohammad Kazem Shari'atmadari were also considered liberals because of the similarities of their political and economic views with the provisional government.[4] Tied to Ayatollah Shari'atmadari was the newly formed Party of the Muslim People of Iran (*Hezb-i Khalq-i Mosalman-i Iran*). The liberal views were expressed mainly in *Inqilab-i Islami, Mizan,* and the publications of the Freedom Movement of Iran.

The Mojahedin. The Organization of the People's Mojahedin of Iran, known during part of its history as the Islamic-Marxists, was a radical Islamic organization. The Mojahedin, originating in the 1960s, came mostly from the left wing of the Freedom Movement. The Freedom Movement was intended to link Shi'ism with modern liberal ideas.[5] The leaders of the Mojahedin changed the Freedom Movement's liberal interpretations of Shi'ism, deciding that true Shi'ism opposed not only despotism but also capitalism, imperialism, and conservative clericalism. One Mojahed ideologue, Reza'i, argued that the realm of unity (or monotheistic order—*Nezam-i Towhid*) the Prophet sought was a commonwealth fully united by virtue of being "classless" and striving for the common good as well as by the fact that it worships only one God. Furthermore, "the banner of revolt raised by Shi'i Imams, especially 'Ali, Hasan, and Hosein, was aimed against feudal landlords and exploiting merchant capitalists as well as against usurping Caliphs who betrayed the *Nezam-i Towhid*."[6] In 1975 a faction calling itself Marxist-Leninist split from the Mojahedin, but was not able to attract many followers. The rest of the Mojahedin, while still using Marxist categories, remained Islamic, analyzing politics through the nationalistic-religious struggle against all forms of foreign influence. During the course of the Iranian Revolution and the subsequent postrevolutionary period, the Mojahedin grew rapidly and became a strong nationwide political organization.[7]

The Left. The major leftist political organizations were the Tudeh party and the Organization of the Iranian People's Feda'iyan Guerrilla (known as the Feda'iyan).

Founded in 1941, the Tudeh party gained considerable strength in the post—World War II period, especially during the time of oil nationalization. As was mentioned in chapter 5, the Tudeh party declined drastically after the 1953 coup, and by the late 1950s the party was a mere shadow of its former self. Yet despite defections and splits in the 1960s, psychological warfare waged against it by the Shah's regime, and extensive repression of its organizations and members, the Tudeh managed to survive and even regain some ground during the 1970s. In contrast with the Tudeh, the Feda'iyan was a much younger leftist organization. The nucleus of the first Feda'iyan gained a national reputation on February 8, 1971, when thirteen young men armed with rifles, machine guns, and hand grenades attacked the gendarmerie post in the village of Siahkal on the edge of the Caspian forest. Using guerrilla warfare tactics, the Feda'iyan launched armed attacks on the Shah's regime for almost a decade. Although they suffered heavy losses as a result of their confrontation with SAVAK and the police, Feda'iyan managed to survive to play an active role in the revolution. When the revolution began, Feda'iyan surfaced as an experienced armed organization eager to challenge the military might of the Pahlavi state.[8]

Stages in the Ulama's Political Consolidation

Political conflict and ideological disputes in the postrevolutionary period drifted increasingly in an extremist direction. This extremism, however, was not simply the logical outcome of contention for power or the result of class conflict. It primarily emanated from the internal logic of the Shi'i discourse itself. The postrevolutionary political change began with what may be called the revolutionary-democratic stage. The major political events that contributed to state building at this stage were (1) the referendum on the political system in March 1979, which resulted in the endorsement of the Islamic Republic; (2) the ulama's successful campaign in persuading the public to accept the idea of assigning a group of individuals (who constituted the *Majles-i Khebrigan*—Assembly of Experts) the task of drafting a new constitution, and the election of the members of the Assembly in August 1979; and (3) the referendum on the new constitution in December 1979. This period is considered revolutionary-democratic because all the power contenders were enjoying certain democratic freedoms in expressing their political views, holding open meetings, and so on. These contenders, however, acted in a revolutionary manner according to their own conception of the proper political and social order rather than according to any formal legal framework. On the popular level there was considerable mass participation in the state institutional process. "Ordinary people" were somewhat directly involved in attempting to influence the course of events and the state's policies in their own favor. There also existed a democratic atmosphere in the schools and universities, which were centers of the activities of diverse political groups. During this period, the ulama followers of Ayatollah Khomeini openly used democratic means to consolidate their power, while they covertly engaged in the repression of their political rivals.

The second stage of ulama political consolidation was the period of open political conflicts among diverse power contenders. In this period, the initial consensus among various Islamic groups was gradually replaced by discord and conflict. This period began with the first presidential election in January 1980 and developed into a reign of terror in the summer of 1981. The third stage has been the reign of terror itself, which began in the summer of 1981 and has continued to the present (although its intensity has fluctuated). During this stage the ulama have resorted to open violence and direct repression of the members and organizations of opposition groups. In this third stage, the leaders of the Islamic Republic abandoned those aspects of the Constitution designed to check the power of the government and instead chose to pursue their policies in an arbitrary manner. Each step in the process of state building has excluded one or more of the power contenders from the polity.

The Revolutionary-Democratic Period

The political leadership that emerged during the revolutionary conjuncture of 1977–79 consisted of a coalition of the liberals and the ulama, all recognizing the leadership of Ayatollah Khomeini. The coalition was primarily based on tactical considerations by both sides. The ulama needed the liberals because of their skill in international diplomacy, knowledge of Western politics, and for their assurance to the U.S. and European governments that the post-Shah Iranian state would be friendly. On the other hand, the liberals, who failed to establish a solid nationwide network of support for their cause, sought their political fortune by allying with Khomeini.

Such was the context within which Ayatollah Khomeini endorsed the provisional government under the premiership of Bazargan. The liberals' dominance in the provisional government was indicated by the fact that an overwhelming majority of the members of Bazargan's cabinet were either active members of the National Front or adhered to liberalism.[9] The alliance, however, was uneasy, for the ulama and the liberals had quite different political agenda. For the liberals, a Western-style democracy (with the exclusion of the Left) within the existing capitalist relationships, but now guided by the moral values of secular Islam, was all that was achievable and indeed suitable for Iran. Now that the system of despotic monarchy had been overthrown, the corrupt officials of the old regime should be expelled from the government; law and order should be established in the factories and the rural areas to prevent any possible reduction in production; the fugitive industrialists had to be encouraged to return to the country to run their enterprises; and the ulama were to leave politics to the politicians and continue their moral guidance of the nation from the pulpits of the mosques. For Khomeini and the IRP, on the other hand, the overthrow of the Shah was simply the first stage of the "Islamic" revolution. Several decades of secularization had to be halted and reversed. Liberalism, Marxism, and all other such ideologies belonged either to the West or to the East and had no place among the Muslim people of Iran. Society should be reorganized according to the teachings of Islam; and Islamic associations should be established in the factories, government, military, and the rural areas. The ulama were the guardians of Islam and the people. Their exclusive control of the government would ensure the total application of Islam in all walks of life and prevent any deviation from it. Open conflict between the ulama and the liberals was thus imminent as soon as the provisional government was inaugurated.

Shi'i ideology was an important factor that aided ulama political consolidation at this initial stage. Thus when the ulama pushed forward the issue of establishing an Islamic Republic, they received overwhelming support from the public in the referendum of March 1979. At this time, the specific content and form of the Islamic Republic was unknown to the majority of the voters. The IRP made every effort to downplay the doctrine of *velayat-i faqih*. The idea of an Islamic Republic meant different things to different people, and diverse groups supported the idea in the referendum according to their own readings of the political teachings of Shi'i Islam. After all, it was under the banner of Shi'ism that the class-divided popular masses justified their participation in the revolution and sought an alternative to the Shah's regime.

However, the change from the monarchy to an Islamic Republic was not without some acrimonious disputes. Feda'iyan demanded a "People's Democratic Republic," which was summarily dismissed by Khomeini. And to the notion of establishing a "Democratic Islamic Republic," suggested by the National Democratic Front, Khomeini responded that it was a Western idea and therefore should not be followed.

The referendum set the stage for the subsequent political discourse. Since the country's political system was defined as "Islamic," the Communists and those who wanted to dispense with the idea of an Islamic Republic were defined as outsiders by default and excluded from the pool of qualified candidates for membership in the polity. With the overthrow of the "enemy" of Islam (i.e., the Shah), and the mass endorsement of the Islamic Republic, the course of the ideological dispute revolved around the question of what would constitute the socioeconomic and political content of Islam.

Khomeini's attempt to implement the doctrine of *velayat-i faqih* was a source of tension between his followers and other political groups. Should such a principle be included in the constitution, other Muslim political groups feared that they would be excluded from sharing political power unless they accepted the unquestionable authority of the *faqih*. Opposition to Khomeini's and the IRP's attempts to "monopolize" Islam thus began to mount. Prominent in this regard was Ayatollah Shari'atmadari, who as early as the spring of 1979 had warned the public about the dangers of a monopoly of power, a single-party system, and the possibility of a dictatorship.[10] As for the necessity of the *velayat-i faqih*, he claimed that such a system of rule was suitable only under exceptional circumstances:

> *Velayat-i faqih* is for when there is no legitimate ruler in society like our situation right after the fall of the Shah. Under such a condition, therefore, the *faqih* determines the government. But if there is already a president and a parliament, and the president forms his cabinet and receives the vote of confidence from the parliament, then the constituted government is legitimate and may begin its work. In other words, the people's sovereignty is exerted through the parliament. In our revolution such a channel of exerting sovereignty was not available to the people. Therefore, the *faqih* determined the [provisional] government. Thereafter, with the election of the president and members of the parliament, the future government would begin its work

with the vote of confidence from the parliament, and fall should the parliament vote otherwise.[11]

Under pressure, Khomeini and the IRP then made a tactical retreat by downplaying the doctrine of *velayat-i faqih* in the first and even second drafts of the constitution. Instead, they came up with the idea of setting up an Assembly of Experts, consisting of a relatively small number of representatives, to write the constitution.[12] Despite the existence of a considerable resistance to this idea, they were able to successfully hold elections for the members of this assembly in August 1979. As was expected, the election resulted in a total victory for the followers of Khomeini.

Thus with the Assembly of Experts under the control of the IRP, the inclusion of the *velayat-i faqih* in the constitution seemed certain. As a result, opposition to the establishment of a theocracy continued to escalate. For their part, the ulama were also facing the difficulty of convincing the public in regard to the legitimacy of their demand and its suitability for Iran. It was one thing to argue that an Islamic Republic was the most desirable political system for the country. But it was quite another thing to convince the voters that Iran and Islam were best protected under the governance of a *faqih*—and that the Islam of other contenders had deviated from its proper course. Evidently, the issue was not to be quickly and favorably resolved within the realm of theological debate.

The subsequent events produced by the dynamic of Shi'i revolutionary discourse contributed to the resolution of this conflict in favor of the followers of Ayatollah Khomeini and against the liberals and moderates in and outside the government. One of the foremost functions of Shi'i discourse was the signification of the idea of counterrevolution. This is quite important because in a real sense the Iranian Revolution did not have a counterrevolution. According to the official figure, 98.2 percent of the public in a referendum endorsed the establishment of the Islamic Republic. Although the figure was overestimated because many people in the rural and tribal areas did not vote, the support for the idea of an Islamic Republic was nevertheless quite extensive. Externally, the United States and its allies, who had been the prime supporters of the Shah, somewhat reluctantly accepted the revolution. Many commentators believed that Carter's human rights policy acted as a catalyst for the Iranian Revolution. To be sure, the U.S. government was apprehensive about the nature of the postrevolutionary regime, and the Iranian Left had every reason to define U.S. concern as counterrevolutionary. But for the revolution as a whole, one cannot identify the presence of organized interests either inside or outside the country who had aimed to overthrow the Islamic Republic. Between February 11 (celebrated date of the revolution) and November 4, 1979 (the date the U.S. embassy in Tehran was seized), only three high-ranking members of the Islamic Republic (General Valiullah Qarani, Ayatollah Mortaza Motahhari, and Sayyid Mohsin Behbehani) were assassinated, and there was one assassination attempt on Hashemi Rafsanjani. This is far too few incidents for a government that had summarily executed several hundred of the top members of the Shah's government during the same period. What is more, no evidence existed connecting these assassinations to the United States.

Therefore, the idea that the revolution was under attack and constantly being undermined by the diabolical machination of the United States was primarily a product of the dynamic of the Islamic revolutionary discourse. Indeed the seizure of the U.S. embassy in Tehran was dictated by the revolutionary ideology itself. The post factum explanations that the ruling clerics supported the embassy takeover because they wanted to get rid of the liberals in the provisional government and that the move was triggered by the admission of the Shah to the United States do not seem to be adequate. This is because the provisional government had already decided to resign before the embassy takeover, and the ruling ulama were aware of it.[13] Furthermore, the plan to seize the embassy was contemplated well before the Shah entered the United States. None of these reasons can be construed to be the cause for the seizure of the embassy.[14] Rather, the Shah's admission to the United States was a circumstance that the revolutionary ideology fed on and defined as part of a U.S. counterrevolutionary conspiracy. When Ayatollah Khomeini proclaimed that the seizure of the embassy was tantamount to a second Islamic revolution even greater than the first, and demanded that the counterrevolution, the "Great Satan," be exposed and disarmed in its "spy nest,"[15] he was acting as spokesperson for the revolution. As Bazargan has aptly commented, if before the revolution the objective was the overthrow of the monarchy and the establishment of an Islamic system, now revolution itself had become the prime goal that should expand on the international scene against imperialism, particularly against the United States.[16] The historic mission of the Iranian Revolution, for Muslim revolutionaries, went beyond the Iranian borders.

At any rate, for Khomeini and the IRP, the embassy takeover produced two major political benefits. First, it usurped an important anti-imperialist platform from the Left that was growing continuously. For the Left, on the other hand, the seizure of the embassy was a welcome opportunity to push forward the social revolutionary process currently under way in the country. Both the Tudeh and the Feda'iyan supported the action. Second, it discredited the provisional government. Bazargan was planning to resign as a protest to the undemocratic activities of the Muslim extremists. But now the provisional government had to fall because the seizure of the embassy was incompatible with its political outlook and long-term strategy of maintaining a friendly relationship with the United States. Bazargan fell, it appeared, not because he protested the imminent dictatorship but because he was willing to compromise with imperialism.

The IRP and other religious radicals, however, continued to attack the liberals. They selectively published the documents seized from the embassy pertaining to the liberals' connection with the United States and the Shah. The speaker of the Bazargan government, Amir Entezam, was arrested for allegedly spying for the U.S.[17] Other documents were also published regarding the connection of Bazargan, Ayatollah Shari'atmadari, and other liberals to the Shah.[18] Based on these documents, *Jomhouri-ye Islami* demanded the liquidation of the Party of the Muslim People of Iran, which was tied to Ayatollah Shari'atmadari.[19] With the liberals thus exposed as "pro-Americans" anxious "to collaborate with imperialism," and the Left excited by the fall of their historic enemy (but unprepared for Khomeini's next move), the Assembly of Experts seized the opportunity and passed the doctrine of the *velayat-i faqih* as the central feature of the new Constitution of the Islamic Republic. The IRP then used the mass agitation following the seizure of the American embassy to establish itself as the uncompromising leader of the revolution, quickly set up a referendum on the new constitution, and received mass endorsement in December 1979. The ulama's revolutionary ambition was thus realized.

The Constitution of the Islamic Republic gave the ulama unprecedented power. This was institutionalized in the Council of Constitutional Guardians. The council consisted of twelve members, of whom six were to be ulama experts on Islamic laws (i.e., *fiqh*) and were also to be selected either by Khomeini (as long as he was alive) or by the Council of Leadership (whose members were also to be selected). The other six were to be lawyers (specializing in different areas of the law) elected by the parliament. The six ulama were also supposed to determine the conformity of any law passed by the parliament. But all twelve members of the Council of Constitutional Guardians were responsible for interpreting and determining a law's conformity with the constitution. The council was also to supervise both presidential and parliamentary elections, and to hold referenda.[20] Legally, not only did the ulama establish themselves as the sole guardians of the people but also the constitution represented an unprecedented change in the clerical establishment in the direction of the formal centralization of religious authority.

With the approval of the constitution, the first stage of political consolidation was over. Bazargan and Shari'atmadari were discredited not because they resisted the constitution but because of their willingness to collaborate with the Americans. The Mojahedin, who boycotted the referendum on the constitution, were labeled as hypocrites (*monafeqin*) and, along with other non-Moslem political groups, were excluded from membership in the polity. Later on, Khomeini disqualified the presidential candidacy of the Mojahedin leader, Masoud Rajavi, on the grounds that his organization had opposed the constitution.

The Period of Open Political Conflict

Islamic revolutionary discourse further conditioned political conflicts. The intermeshing of ideological disputes with contentions for power was reflected in the way conflicts over the control of the state bureaucracy proceeded. The result of Iran's first presidential election was a serious defeat for the IRP and a resounding success for the second group of liberals, who had managed to stay "clean" of pro-imperialist charges. Bani-Sadr was elected president with a huge margin, over 10 million votes. Evidently, the fall of the provisional government did not eliminate liberalism from the country's political scene. A new group of liberals such as Bani-Sadr, Qotbzadeh, and Ibrahim Yazdi carried the revolution forward by attacking the provisional government and supporting the seizure of the embassy. They acted the part of uncompromising revolutionaries to fit their political ambitions. Plausibly, this tactic brought Bani-Sadr success in the presidential race. IRP extremism was also relevant in this process because it led to its declining popularity among voters (particularly among the members of the new middle class). Indicative of the IRP's declining popularity was that the second presidential contender, Admiral Madani, who received over 3 million votes, also had a secular background. Equally important in the IRP's defeat was its support for a "wrong" candidate: Jalaledin Farsi.[21] Virtually all the ulama followers of Ayatollah Khomeini rallied behind Farsi's candidacy, and Ayatollah Khameneh-ei went so far as to claim that "if Farsi is not elected, there is no guarantee for the continuation of the revolution."[22] Farsi, however, was disqualified on the grounds that he was foreign-born.[23] With only a few days left to the election, the IRP had little time to campaign for its second choice, Hasan Habibi, who was in consequence unable to attract many votes.

Soon, however, the dynamic of revolutionary ideology helped tip the balance of forces in the government to the IRP's favor. The contradiction between Islam and the West (one of the major themes of Islamic discourse) was the ideological dynamic underlying the cultural revolution launched in April 1980. To be sure, the initial objective of the cultural revolution—over which both the IRP and the liberals were united—was to expel the Left from the universities and colleges. To this end, the Revolutionary Council of the Islamic Republic issued a three-day deadline to all these groups to shut down their offices in the universities.[24] The minister of education, Mohammad Ali Reja-ie, claimed that "closing the offices of the political groups in the universities was the demand of the great masses of the people."[25] However, as it turned out, the influence of the Left within academia was another circumstance that the revolutionary ideology fed on. When both the IRP leaders and the liberals agreed to the idea of cultural revolution through direct action of the people who were mobilized to march on the university campuses, they were acting according to the dictate of the dynamic of revolutionary ideology, namely, the eradication of all the vestiges of the anti-Islamic policies implemented by the Pahlavis. It was a further expansion of the discursive field of revolutionary Islam toward the Islamization of all aspects of social relationships.

The cultural revolution, however, meant different things to its diverse executioners and worked to the advantage of the IRP vis-à-vis the liberals. For the liberals it was a means to get rid of the leftist agitators in the public institutions, the factories, and the rural areas, so that economic and political stability could be restored in the country. They were therefore interested in carrying the revolution to the point where the Left was totally impotent. The IRP, on the other hand, went beyond this objective by pursuing the cultural revolution to its extreme. The IRP leaders wanted to eliminate the liberals as well.

Tied to the IRP were the bands of *chomaqdars* (club wielders) who called themselves the *Hezbullah* (the Party of God). The fanaticism of the *Hezbullah* was evident from its slogan: "Hezb faqat Hezbullah; rahbar faqat Ruhollah" (The only legitimate party is the party of God and the only legitimate ruler is Ruhollah [Khomeini]). The bands of the *Hezbullah* invaded the universities, injured and killed members of the political groups who were resisting the cultural revolution, and burned books and papers thought to be un-Islamic. The ulama, however, attributed the fighting to the agents of the capitalist and socialist camps. The IRP charged that "the line connected to the West and the line connected to the East have arisen against the cultural revolution."[26]

The IRP pursued an "Islamization" program whose goal was to eliminate all forms of cultural resistance to ulama rule. The government kept closed all the universities and colleges for over three years, during which the university curricula were rewritten. By 1984, according to one report, nearly 15 percent of all the required courses for a bachelor's degree were in the area of (Shi'i) religion.[27] Similar changes were also made in the content of elementary and high school curricula. Courses dealing with evolution and portions of biological and geological courses were omitted from the school curriculum. In turn, the number of required courses on religion increased considerably.[28] Thousands of school teachers and university professors were purged. With the conclusion of the cultural revolution, the Left was effectively expelled from the educational institutions, while the ulama were able to establish a firm grip on all the institutions of cultural reproduction. The liberals, however, did not benefit much from their partnership with the IRP.

The cultural revolution also facilitated the IRP's organizing efforts in forming Islamic associations in diverse public and private institutions throughout the country. In the parliamentary elections that took place in March and May of 1980, the IRP managed to win a majority. Learning from its defeat in the presidential elections, the IRP was quick to form a coalition with other Islamic extremist groups. The coalition resulted in the IRP's winning a majority in the parliament.[29] IRP success, then, set the stage for the first serious conflict *within* the Islamic Republic. With the liberal Bani-Sadr as the president, and the IRP dominating the parliament, the selection of the prime minister and the members of his cabinet became the subject of intense disputes between the president and the IRP. The latter scored the first victory by successfully appointing its candidate, Mohammad Reja-ie as prime minister, despite Bani-Sadr's stiff resistance. The appointment resulted in the emergence of two opposing factions in the bureaucracy of the Islamic Republic.

At stake was political power, and each of these men was trying hard to fill the cabinet posts with his own supporters. The ideological dispute between the president and the prime minister revolved around the proper qualification criteria according to which the new members of the state bureaucracy were to be selected. For Bani-Sadr and his liberal supporters, technical competence and specialization in different fields of science were to be the proper criteria. For the IRP, on the other hand, one's degree of religiosity, familiarity with religious matters, and commitment to the *Maktab-i Islam* (school of Islam) were to be given priority. Reja-ie, for example, argued that:

> A series of false needs are created in [our] society . . . and have made our tasks difficult. We should immediately return to ideology. Society is waiting for us to discuss welfare matters. This is not correct. Our concerns are more with the *Maktab* than the availability of, say, oranges and grapes. In the previous regime these things were provided, even though they were imported. But the thing which was not provided [by the previous regime] was the *Maktab*. We are pursuing the *Maktab*.[30]

Bani-Sadr, on the other hand, was emphasizing that Iran's major problem was a lack of experts and specialized personnel to occupy the state bureaucracy. Bani-Sadr argued:

> Was our dependence on the west in the past two to three centuries due to our technical knowledge or lack of it? If we had science and technology and could produce [our own machineries], then for the purchase of a simple part of a machine we did not have to go through so much trouble. If we had technical knowledge, we did not have to leave our doors open to foreigners.[31]

IRP leaders, in contrast, argued that "morality" would take precedent over "science," and "value" over "knowledge." Therefore, it was only through hiring the devout Muslim that Iran could gain its true independence and self-sufficiency.[32]

The ideological dispute between the liberals and the IRP was accompanied by the *Hezbullah*'s frequent attacks on Bani-Sadr's supporters, who were now receiving the same treatment as had the Mojahedin and leftist opposition. The *Hezbullah* frequently disrupted Bani-Sadr's speeches, even calling him a General Pinochet, the Chilean dictator (*Sepahsalar Pinosheh, Iran Shili Namisheh*). The conflict between the two factions was getting more and more intense by the day.

Bani-Sadr did not have a nationwide organization and was quite vulnerable to the attacks of the *Hezbullah* . The Mojahedin, on the other hand, were highly disciplined with a nationwide organization but had no significant connection in the government. For them (who by now had defined the IRP as their principal enemy and the major pillar of the counterrevolution), an alliance with Bani-Sadr was a welcome opportunity.

Bani-Sadr and the Mojahedin defined freedom and democracy as their prime issues, while downplaying concrete issues related to the interests of the working class and peasants (see the section on class struggle in this chapter, below). The Mojahedin's critique of the ulama and the IRP, however, went beyond the latter's antidemocratic nature. The Mojahedin labeled the followers of Khomeini as petty bourgeois and argued that Islam had been distorted and ridiculed by the petty bourgeoisie, and particularly by the traditional petty bourgeoisie.[33] The Mojahedin claimed that there was only one real Islam. "All other kinds of Islam . . . are the slogan of the declining forces and classes . . . whose ideal system is capitalism or petty capitalism."[34] The Mojahedin criticized "petty bourgeois" understanding of Islam on the grounds of: "defending private property and exploitation"; "confirming the coexistence and friendships between exploiting and exploited classes"; "being dogmatic and narrow-minded"; "having idealistic understanding of man and society and without dialectical perspective"; "overlooking or ignoring the realities and the objective economic bases of society and social development"; "denying the necessity of relying on the most deprived and progressive social classes (presently, workers and peasants) for the realization of divine objectives"; and "negating the social orientation of Islam in the direction of eliminating classes."[35] Therefore, "the petty bourgeois understanding of Islam, from 'socio-economic' viewpoint is based upon the acceptance of exploitation and social duality, and thus we consider it a manifestation of *shirk,* invalid and empty of *towhidi* content."[36] In response, an IRP ideologue argued that the Islam of the Mojahedin was eclectic and influenced by Marxism. In the Mojahedin eclectic philosophy, said an IRP commentator, history has substituted God; and concepts such as "reactionary" and "progressive" are used, instead of using categories such as "right" and "wrong" in evaluating social groups and movements.[37]

The Reign of Terror

These charges and countercharges concerning whose argument was in tune with the spirit of revolutionary Islam were not resolved within the realm of ideological debate. Soon the IRP called for the arrest and prosecution of the leaders of the Mojahedin. The Mojahedin in turn launched an armed attack on IRP leaders and members. It is hardly defensible to argue that the "truth" or "falsity" of the claims advanced by these ideologies had an impact on the success or failure of the power contenders who were advancing them. Nevertheless, it is plausible to suggest that the effectiveness of the symbols and the workability of the metaphors used by these power contenders to mobilize support against their adversaries had a certain contribution (albeit to a limited extent) to the outcome of the conflict. Considering that Shi'i revolutionary discourse, as the dominant ideology, had defined "world imperialism" and the "Great Satan" as the main enemies of the revolution, the Mojahedin's academically informed critique of the ulama—while perhaps exciting the educated members of their middle-class supporters—was too abstract to rally the public to action in their support. The idea of democracy and individual freedom, raised by Bani-Sadr and the Mojahedin, had already been discarded as being too closely associated with the West. In short, the metaphors used by these leaders simply "misfired," to quote Geertz.[38] On the other hand, the ulama and the IRP utilized popular idioms and rhetoric to condemn Bani-Sadr and the Mojahedin. The bombing of the IRP's headquarters in June 1981, which resulted in the death of Ayatollah Beheshti (IRP chairman) and many other leaders and cadres of the IRP, provided the ulama with their excuse to unleash a reign of terror against the opposition unheard of in Iran's contemporary history. To rally their supporters and to elicit anger against Bani-Sadr and the Mojahedin, the ulama alluded to the Hosein tragedy by claiming that the number of casualties resulting from the bombing was seventy-two (the same number as those killed in Karbala). According to the *Jomhouri-ye Islami*'s headline: "Iran Cries Blood in Mourning 72 of the Imam's Comrades."[39] The armed struggle between the contending groups resulted in the defeat of Bani-Sadr and the Mojahedin. Thousands of the leaders and members of the Mojahedin were either killed during armed confrontations with the regime or executed by the revolutionary guards while in captivity.[40]

It is noteworthy that the ulama's political consolidation was also aided by splits and dissensions within the Left. The Tudeh claimed that the ulama followers of Ayatollah Khomeini were representatives of the petty bourgeoisie. The petty bourgeoisie, they argued, was anti-imperialist and the ulama, as their representatives, were revolutionary democrats, anti-imperialists, anti–large capitalists and landowners, and disposed toward the common people. In their view, these ulama seemed likely to follow noncapitalist modes of growth by nationalizing foreign trade, expanding the state sector, implementing land reform, breaking up ties of dependency with the imperialist countries, and establishing close relationships with the socialist countries. Furthermore, in one article (entitled "Which Is the Prime Issue: Anti-Imperialist Struggle or the Struggle for Freedom?") the Tudeh argued that:

> With the consideration of the priorities, any revolutionary of our time, and in our country, should fight for the following objectives:
>
> 1. The most important of all, struggle against world imperialism (led by U.S. imperialism) for the achievement of real independence of the country as a basic condition of solving [Iran's] other problems.
>
> 2. Struggle against the remnants of reactionary and exploitative systems and for the provisions of democratic rights of the masses of the people and the establishment of social justice.
>
> 3. Struggle for the realization of social and political freedom.
>
> According to this ranking of priorities, if a regime is sufficiently attempting to realize the first and second objectives but has taken an undesirable position toward the third, it still deserves the support of revolutionary forces because such a regime is fulfilling the prime aspects of our revolutionary tasks.
>
> In regard to the Iranian case and the leadership of Imam Khomeini, in our view this leadership has a national character (anti-imperialist) that is favorable toward the people (defends the rights of the toilers). In respect to the issue of freedom, one cannot argue that this leadership is in favor of political repression because factual evidence points to the contrary. The Imam has repeatedly expressed his opposition to dictatorship.[41]

Thus the Tudeh pursued the policy of defending Khomeini against the challenges of the liberals and the Mojahedin. The Feda'iyan, on the other hand, did not follow a consistent policy. Initially, when the Revolutionary Guards and the military were engaged in the violent repression of the Kurdish autonomy movement and Turkman-Sahra's peasant movement, the Feda'iyan actively participated in armed struggle against the regime. But soon, disillusioned with the tactic of armed struggle which they had unsuccessfully pursued under the Shah, the Feda'iyan began to reexamine their past activities and reformulate their policies to suit the new conditions, which led to a split in the Feda'iyan. A minority faction argued that the Islamic Republic was an institution based on a coalition between two segments of the country's new dominant class—the industrial bourgeoisie (represented by the liberals) and the commercial bourgeoisie (represented by the IRP). Thus the regime was reactionary and should be overthrown. The Feda'iyan minority considered the Mojahedin revolutionary democrats and sided with them.

The majority faction of the Feda'iyan, on the other hand, argued that the Islamic Republic was predominantly controlled by petty-bourgeois elements and was therefore revolutionary and progressive. This group then took several steps toward merging with the Tudeh. Both the Feda'iyan majority and the Tudeh, in their defense of the Islamic Republic, went as far as calling the leaders of the Mojahedin traitors who had collaborated with imperialism and the reactionary states in the region. In their turn, the Mojahedin and the Feda'iyan minority called the Tudeh and the Feda'iyan majority traitors who had betrayed the working class. The Islamic Republic effectively utilized this conflict within the Left. It first destroyed the Feda'iyan minority and the Mojahedin by brutal force, while the Tudeh and the Feda'iyan majority were softly criticizing the government for its "excesses." Over a year later, the Islamic Republic launched a surprise attack on the Tudeh during which thousands of its leaders and cadres were arrested. Many of these people were either executed or sentenced to long prison terms. The Feda'iyan majority received a similar treatment in a later period.

True, coercive power did play a crucial role in shaping events as rival contenders manipulated ideology to fit their goals. Nevertheless, all this took place within a context of Shi'i revolutionary discourse that structured the form of political conflict. Shi'i discourse dictated political change through revolutionary action, glorified martyrdom and self-sacrifice, emphasized unity within the Islamic community, and warned of the immanence of the counterrevolution. Any diversion of view was considered a sign of danger, the infiltration of the counterrevolution and of U.S. agents into the ranks of the Muslim people. It must be effectively suppressed. If fact, the ideological resolutions of each side of the dispute questioned in essence the Islamic nature of the other, meaning that the deviants had not only lost the right to be members of the polity but also the right to exist. The victor had no difficulty in accusing the defeated of being the *Mofsid-i fil Arz* (corrupt on earth), which is/was punishable by death. Had the national-democratic ideology been the dominant discourse, as was the case under Mosaddeq, competitions among political groups would have taken quite a different form.

The Iran-Iraq War

The outbreak of the Iran-Iraq war expedited the process of the concentration and centralization of power and the evolution of the instrument of repression, strongly supporting Skocpol's argument on the significance of interstate military competition and conflict for the massive rebuilding of state power in the postrevolutionary period.[42] The rapid reorganization of the state's bureaucracy and its repressive apparatus under the exclusive control of Khomeini and his followers echoes Tilly's assertion that "war makes states."[43] Nevertheless, it is crucially important to realize that the way the war contributed to the process of concentration and centralization of power in Iran was mediated by the revolutionary ideology. Shi'i revolutionary discourse was a factor contributing to both the cause of the war and its continuation. The war, in turn, channeled ideology away from class issues, affecting the outcome of the social revolutionary struggle (see the next section).

Tensions between Iraq and Iran revolved around two basic issues of dispute: (1) control over the Shatt-al-Arab waterway, and (2) control over three strategic Gulf islands—Abu-Mousa, and the Greater and Lesser Tunbs. The Shatt-al-Arab dispute was rooted as far back in history as the days of military competitions between the Safavids and the Ottoman Empire in the seventeenth century, and it resurfaced several times in the nineteenth and twentieth centuries. Under British patronage, Iraq became independent in 1932 and subsequently began pressing its claims on the river as well as some disputed parts of the border land. This resulted in armed clashes between the two countries. The dispute was settled in 1937. But with the overthrow of the monarchy in Iraq by the army in 1958, relations between Iran and Iraq cooled considerably. Years later the Shah unilaterally abrogated the 1937 Frontier

Treaty with Iraq. The border disputes were further complicated when the Shah, following the British withdrawal from the Gulf in 1971, took over the strategic islands of Abu-Mousa and the Greater and Lesser Tunbs, at the entrance to the Strait of Hormuz, further straining relations between Iran and Iraq.

At any rate, these disputes had never led to full-scale war between the two countries. Indeed the political arrangement in the prerevolutionary period favored a peaceful coexistence between them. The Iraqi regime did not have the military capability to confront the Shah's army, and even if it had, the Gulf states would not have supported a war between the two countries: Saudi Arabia and Iran were partners in curbing revolutionary movements in the region; Kuwait preferred Iran over Iraq because of the latter's territorial claim to Kuwait; the Sultan of Oman needed the Shah for his own protection; and even Iran and Iraq needed each other's cooperation to control and suppress the Kurdish autonomy movements in both countries. Generally speaking, there was a balance of forces among all the dictatorial regimes of the Persian Gulf, many of which were repressing their own people without the immediate concern of a revolutionary upheaval from within their own or neighboring countries.[44]

Then came the Iranian Revolution, which brought sudden changes in the country's political system and many uncertainties. A counterrevolutionary force in the region was replaced by a government whose intention of exporting its own version of revolutionary Islam was real. The neighboring countries began to receive waves of instability generated by the Iranian event. In Saudi Arabia about 200,000 Muslims of the Shi'i sect rioted, carrying signs and pictures hailing the Ayatollah. It was also reported that in Oman there were indications that political dissent was growing in the northern provinces (as distinct from the struggle that had been going on in the Dhoffar province for many years).[45] The Iraqi leaders viewed the victory of the revolution with mounting anxiety. To make matters worse, Ayatollah Baqir Sadr, Khomeini's counterpart in Najaf (Iraq), in his congratulatory message to Khomeini, said that "other tyrants have yet to see their day of reckoning," which was believed to be an undisguised reference to Iraqi's leaders.[46] Khomeini then called upon the Iraqis to overthrow the Baath regime. Given that the Baathist party was dominated by secular-minded Sunnis and that 55 percent of the Iraqi population was Shi'i, the threat of a Shi'i uprising in Iraq was felt to be imminent. Naturally, the threatening results of the unfolding revolution, and at the same time Iran's military disorganization, were giving impetus to the Iraqi temptation to end the rule of the Ayatollah by means of a military invasion. Indeed Iraq expected that an attack on Iran, the occupation of Khuzistan, and perhaps the installation of a puppet government in that region could be quickly realized.[47]

At the time of the invasion, Iran's military was in disarray, produced by the purges of its high-ranking personnel[48] and, of more importance, by antimilitary propaganda from the Left that called for a total dismantling of the military and the creation of a people's army. Moreover, contrary to the current sociological wisdom, the war did not result in an immediate settlement of the Islamic Republic's internal feud. The factional conflict between Bani-Sadr and the IRP was now extended to include the questions of who should control the country's armed forces and how the war should be fought. Bani-Sadr attempted to consolidate his control of the army and defense planning "by holding meetings, as commander-in-chief, with his military commanders in an American-style national security council."[49] On the other hand, referring to Bani-Sadr's supporters, Ayatollah Montazari warned that the devout Muslim should prevent the "infiltration of elements that do not believe in the Islamic revolution into sensitive positions within the armed forces."[50] Prime minister Reja-ie, in his interview with a West German reporter, defined this group as only "a small segment of the military and an infinitesimal group of so-called intellectuals oriented toward the West, headed by Bani-Sadr."[51] To countervail Bani-Sadr's power in the army, the IRP managed to increase its membership in the Supreme Defense Council. However, the factional dispute was manifested in a seven-month stalemate on the battlefront, which seemed to have worked against Bani-Sadr.[52]

The way the leaders of the Islamic Republic prepared for the war, their attitudes, and the continuation of the war after the Iraqi forces were pushed back to the prewar borders may not be fully understood without considering the role of Shi'i revolutionary discourse. As was mentioned earlier, the seizure of the U.S. embassy was dictated by the dynamic of Shi'i ideology. The revolution was to go beyond Iran's borders (i.e., be exported), and the Muslim people had set out for themselves the task of fighting imperialism (*istikbar-i jahani*). Thus, Iraq's invasion of Iran became another circumstance that the revolutionary ideology fed on. The war was perceived in Iran as a plot engineered by the United States and executed by the Iraqi regime to destroy the Iranian Revolution. Saddam Hosein was portrayed as an American agent. The leaders of the Islamic Republic were quick to pronounce that the war was a gift from the West that they had been expecting, and that given their historic revolutionary mission, they were proud to welcome it and meet the challenge of the counterrevolution.[53] The self-fulfilling prophecy that a contradiction existed between Islam and the West was confirmed.

The war led to a further consolidation of the IRP's political power. The initial victory of the enemy at the front brought to the fore the urgent question of defending the revolution and the country and thus shifted attention away from the issues of democracy and freedom raised by the liberals and the Mojahedin. Furthermore, the Revolutionary Guards (the armed wing of the IRP), previously under pressure to be dismantled or incorporated into the military, were now demanding heavy weapons to fight the war, a demand that was gaining increasing support in the government due to the military's inability to resist the invading forces. The army was portrayed as being a left-over from the old regime that could not be trusted. Although the ouster of Bani-Sadr and the subsequent purges of some military personnel left no significant rival in the army,[54] the Guards were more trusted by the ulama and favored over the armed forces.[55] The leaders of the Revolutionary Guards were almost all related to the ulama, and their rank and file were mostly ethnic Persians.[56] To mobilize volunteers to join the Revolutionary Guards, the IRP effectively utilized "Islamic fervor and Iranian nationalism" provoked by the invasion.[57] At the same time, the ulama set up an Ideological and Political Bureau of the Armed Forces (*Dayere-ye Idi'olojik va Siasi-ye Artish*) to monitor the activities of military personnel. The soldiers, Guards, and volunteers were especially encouraged to report anything they thought suspicious going on, particularly among the regular (high-ranking) military officers. It did not take much time for the ulama to promote their own men in the army. Indeed, "the military officers chosen for command positions were young, ambitious, motivated, and dedicated to Islam."[58] Furthermore, in order to ensure the army's loyalty at the front, the Guards "were positioned behind the regular troops, ostensibly to prevent the troops from withdrawing or deserting."[59]

The reconstruction of the military under the ulama's total control was so successful that by early fall of 1982 the Iranian forces were able to push the Iraqis back to the original borders. The effect of the war, however, was mediated by revolutionary discourse as it strengthened the Revolutionary Guards and similar organs within the armed forces. The ideological dynamic was also responsible for the continuation of the war as the leaders of the Islamic Republic began to pursue their objectives of overthrowing the Iraqi regime and establishing an Islamic republic in Iraq, conquering Jerusalem and destroying Israel, and beating the "Great Satan" overseas. Since Saddam Hosein was portrayed as an infidel (*kafir*) and the agent of imperialism, any peace negotiation with him was tantamount to the betrayal of Iran and Islam.[60]

Revolution and Counterrevolution

An exclusive focus on state building does not adequately explain all the features of the postrevolutionary outcomes. While Iran's political revolution was successful, the move toward a social revolutionary transformation was effectively stopped, and then reversed. In the postrevolutionary period, the economic policies of the Islamic Republic shifted from a somewhat revolutionary to an outright counterrevolutionary orientation. To explain such changes, I shall focus on the class struggle which, as will be argued, placed decisive constraints on the range of economic and political options available to the ruling ulama. Class politics explains not only crucial features of the social revolutionary and counterrevolutionary processes in Iran but also the economic policies of the Islamic Republic as well. However, as it affected the outcomes of the contentions for power, ideology conditioned class conflict as well. It shaped the capacity of the warring classes for action and structured the legitimacy of the arguments advanced by the diverse classes to protect and expand their interests.

Class Struggle in the Postrevolutionary Period

The overthrow of the monarchy shattered the unity among the classes that had participated in the revolution, but the disorganization of the state's repressive apparatus opened the gate for a possible social revolutionary transformation. The initial years of the postrevolutionary period were punctuated by events favoring a major structural change directed against landowners and capitalists. However, a reverse trend soon gained momentum. At first, it was able to halt the move toward social revolution. Then it began to undo what had been done in the previous phase. The complex sequence of events that followed the overthrow of the Shah fell into two phases: the first was a social revolutionary phase, and the second was its reversal, characterized by a systematic repression of the demands of the working class, the peasants, and ethnic minorities, on the one hand, and the consolidation of the economic and political power of the merchants and landowners, on the other.

Class struggle in the postrevolutionary period revolved around three major issues: land reform; labor law (including labor's control of production through the newly formed labor councils); and the nationalization of foreign trade. Resolving these issues determined the economic policies of the Islamic Republic. During the social revolutionary phase workers and peasants struggled against the capitalists and landowners. The merchants of the bazaar were busy filling the void that had resulted from the expulsion of international capital and the flight of many industrialists and bankers from the country. To the extent that the workers' and peasants' movements were directed against the dependent bourgeoisie, the merchants and landowners were not directly threatened. The provisional government, which was trying to save the prerevolutionary class structure and distribution of social resources, did not last very long, and the radicalization of the dominated classes was facilitated by its fall. Then the merchants and landowners came under direct attack, but they managed to control the social revolutionary movement and successfully pushed forward their counterrevolutionary economic policies.

Class Background of the State-Builders

Insofar as the seizure and consolidation of state power were concerned, the followers of Ayatollah Khomeini were pursuing one goal—namely, the establishment of an Islamic government under which supreme religious leader(s) would preside over the positions of ultimate authority. However, diverse economic options were available to these politicians. Does the socioeconomic background of the ruling elites of the Islamic Republic tell us anything about the kind of economic policies they initially pursued?

An analysis of the occupational background of 263 members of the first parliament of the Islamic Republic indicates that 134 (51 percent) were the ulama, sixty (22.8 percent) were teachers, seventeen (6.5 per-

TABLE 7.1

*The Occupational Background of Members
of the First Parliament of the Islamic Republic
(N = 263)*

Occupation	Number	Percent
Ulama[1]	134	51.0
Teachers	60	22.8
Students[2]	17	6.5
Professionals[3]	33	12.5
Bazaaris[4]	8	3.0
Government employees	8	3.0
Farmers and workers	3	1.2
TOTAL	263	100.0

SOURCE: Islamic Republic of Iran: *Negarish Be Avvalin Majlis-i Shura-ye Islami* [A glance at the first Islamic parliament], Tehran, 1364/1985.
   [1] Includes ulama and students and religious schools.
   [2] Includes both university students and two high school students.
   [3] Includes university professors, experts and lawyers, and medical doctors.
   [4] Includes merchants and businessmen (*kasabih*).

cent) were students, thirty-three (12.5 percent) were professionals, eight (3 percent) were bazaaris, eight (3 percent) were government employees, and there were only three farmers and workers or 1.2 percent of the total (see table 7.1). The first three groups—the ulama, teachers, and students—may be classified as some sort of intellectuals, because they were all involved in the production and dissemination of ideas. Moreover, the category of the professionals consisted largely of university professors, experts, and lawyers. In this respect, they shared considerable intellectual characteristics with the above three categories. Therefore, it may be argued that an overwhelming majority of these representatives (244, or 92.8 percent) were either intellectuals or people for whom intellectual pursuits constituted an important aspect of their daily activities. But one cannot deduce any *specific* class interests from these occupational positions. Thus, what could be said about these ruling elites is that they were primarily interested in the construction of a new political order according to Khomeini's vision of revolutionary Islam. Yet the effect of class on the economic and social outlooks of these representatives might have worked through the occupational background of their fathers. Table 7.2 reports the occupations of the fathers of 260 representatives. Of this number, eighty-nine

TABLE 7.2
*The Occupational Background of the Fathers
of Members of the First Parliament
of the Islamic Republic (N = 260)*

Occupation	Number	Percent
Farmers	89	34.2
Bazaaris[a]	76	29.3
Ulama	65	25.0
Government employees	22	8.5
Professionals	4	1.5
Workers	4	1.5
TOTAL	260	100.0

SOURCE: Islamic Republic of Iran: *Negarish Be Avvalin Majlis-i Shura-ye Islami* [A glance at the first Islamic parliament], Tehran, 1364/1985.
[a]Includes ten merchants and sixty-six *kasabih*.

(34.2 percent) were farmers, seventy-six (29.3 percent) were bazaaris, sixty-five (25 percent) were the ulama, twenty-two (8.5 percent) were government employees, and there were four workers and four professionals, each with 1.5 percent of the total.

Unfortunately, due to the limitations of the data, the specification of the class backgrounds of these elites was not possible. The description of these occupational categories and their specific characteristics were not reported in the source. In particular, the occupational categories of farmers and bazaaris (constituting 63.5 percent of the total) were vaguely defined, and the degree of internal differentiation was unknown. However, it is clear that only a very small proportion of these representatives had a working-class background or had come from an extremely wealthy family. It is thus plausible to state that these representatives were predominantly from the petty bourgeois or small bourgeois classes.[61]

The Revolutionary Phase

The above findings are not insignificant and probably explain why the architects of the Islamic Republic did not appear to be unsympathetic to the cause of the class-divided popular masses during the initial years of the postrevolutionary period. Among other things, they favored such radical measures as land reform, the formulation of a progressive labor law, and the nationalization of foreign trade. Nevertheless, this is all that can be said about the probable effects of the class backgrounds of the ruling elites on their social revolutionary outlooks. For during the reversal phase they began to abandon one by one their promises of social justice and economic equality. Whether their initial proclamations of social equality and defense of the poor was genuine or a tactical move to mobilize support to consolidate their power is a matter that cannot be judged according to existing historical materials. This work, however, attempts to explain the changes in the economic policy of the ruling clerics according to the class struggle and the balance of revolutionary and counterrevolutionary class forces within the context of Shi'i revolutionary discourse.

The Peasant-Landlord Struggle. During the early phase of the postrevolutionary period, the countryside was the scene of confrontations between peasants and landowners. Peasant self-assertion was initially directed toward the seizure of land in the large estates and then expanded to include the smaller holdings. The first targets of the movement were those estates that belonged to the members and associates of the old regime who had fled the country during the revolution. In certain regions such as Turkman-Sahra, Kurdistan, West Azarbayjan, and the northern provinces, the organized movements of peasants were more successful than in the rest of the country.[62] The land seizures, however, were not initiated by peasants only. In parts of Khorasan, and in areas where semitribal forms of social organization persisted (such as Kurdistan, Fars, and Baluchistan), the khans and the landlords sought in the general disorder to reclaim lands they had lost under the Shah's land reform. Elsewhere, landlords laid claim to disputed properties or pasturelands lying in the public domain.[63]

In sum, depending on the specific conditions of the area, peasant movements were generally involved in one or more of the following: first, the seizure of the holdings of the fugitive landlords; second, the seizure of the holdings of large or even medium landowners (where for a variety of reasons there had been conflict and hostilities between landowners and peasants); third, the seizure of the nationalized forest and pasturelands; fourth, the dissolution of farm corporations and agricultural production cooperatives by the shareholders and the reclaiming of the lands they had to incorporate in these institutions under the Shah; and, fifth, the peasants' refusal to pay the installments for the lands they had received during the land reform, or for the loans they had obtained from the cooperatives, banks, and usurers.[64]

Clashes between villagers and landlords took various forms, ranging from the use of stones, clubs, and chains to organized armed conflict. The intensity of the crisis was manifested in three hundred outbreaks of rural conflict by mid-November 1979 that left one hundred people dead.[65] According to one survey, in seventy-five of these three hundred rural incidents (25 percent), landless peasants were involved; in ninety-six (32 percent), peasants with less than two hectares of land were involved; and in seventy-six (25.4 percent), peasants with two to five hectares of land were involved. The middle peasants, whose holdings ranged between five and ten hectares, were involved in forty-three cases (14.3 percent), and the rich peasants, with ten to thirty hectares of land, totaled only ten cases (3.2 percent). If we define small peasants as those with less than five hectares of land, then this group covers 172 cases (57.4 percent). The same study also reported that peasants' actions were directed against the landowners and the government authorities in the overwhelming majority of cases: in ninety-eight of 242 cases (40.5 percent), peasants directly clashed with the landlords; and in ninety-four cases (39 percent), they confronted government authorities. In thirty-seven cases (15.2 percent), peasants were fighting among themselves, and, finally, in thirteen cases (5.2 percent) they were in conflict with other groups.[66]

The reaction of the authorities to these developments tended to vary from locality to locality. In certain areas, the Revolutionary Guards and local clerics took the side of the peasants while in other areas they sided with the landowners. In general, the provisional government was against the land seizures and tried to secure order in the countryside and protect private property. It launched military attacks on the peasants, and in certain areas such as Sistan and Baluchistan, Kurdistan, Fars and Azarbayjan, it began arming the landlords and the khans.[67] At the same time, the government engaged in an extensive propaganda campaign against the land seizures, arguing that these would cause a decline in agricultural production. It also began downplaying the inequalities in land ownership. Agriculture Minister Mohammad Ali Eizadi claimed that "there is no feudal landowner in Iran,"[68] that "no one in this country owns a whole village," and that "all the lands were divided among the peasants under the Shah's land reform."[69] (*Ittila'at*, however, rebutted Eizadi's claims by indicating that 85 percent of the lands under cultivation were still controlled by the "feudal" landowners.)[70]

The government's attempts to calm the anxious climate, however, were hindered by the pro-poor rhetoric of Ayatollah Khomeini and the IRP leaders. Ayatollah Khomeini repeatedly proclaimed that "the country belongs to the slum dwellers. The poor are the resources of this country."[71] Ayatollah Beheshti stated that "the line of the revolution is anti-imperialism, anticapitalism, and antifeudalism."[72] Ayatollah Bahonar, a member of the Revolutionary Council, announced that "regarding large land ownership, the aim of the Revolutionary Council is to be able gradually to give these lands to those who work on them. . . . Our policy in resolving the country's agrarian problem is oriented toward giving land to those who till it."[73] Finally, Ayatollah Dastghaib, Imam Jom'eh of Shiraz, in his defense of the peasants, went so far as to encourage "the youth and farmers not to wait for the state to give them land. They, themselves, should act, seize the land from the feudals and landowners, and cultivate these lands behind the banner of Islam."[74]

Evidently, this rhetoric had the immediate effect of weakening the liberal government and, at the same time, of enhancing the popularity of the ulama among the peasants. The formation of over 15,000 Islamic associations in the villages toughened the organizing efforts of the leftist forces, which were trying to mobilize the peasants in a socialist revolutionary direction. Given that the formulation and implementation of the land reform coincided with the seizure of the U.S. embassy, the leadership of the Islamic Republic was able to preempt another social revolutionary initiative from the Left.[75] More crucial, however, was the fact that the pro-peasant rhetoric of these ulama placed the debate over land reform within the context of Islam. This meant that any land reform had to be Islamic. However, the question of just what constituted an Islamic land reform was subject to conflicting interpretations among the diverse factions of the ulama. Given that a majority of the leading ulama were economically conservative and had often defended landed property, a radical land reform—now that they had considerable political power and influence—would have faced insurmountable ideological obstacles.

With the fall of the provisional government, a radical land reform gained support. Many liberal politicians, including Eizadi, were replaced by men who were committed in varying degrees to radical economic change. A radical Muslim, Reza Isfahani, the new under secretary for land affairs in the Ministry of Agriculture, became closely identified with the next land reform law. Isfahani announced that the revolutionary land reform would begin with the distribution of the large holdings to the landless and small peasants. He emphasized that land distribution would begin in Kurdistan and Turkman-Sahra,[76] perhaps a tactical move to lessen the influence of leftist forces in these areas. The landowners strongly reacted to this announcement, and, as a result of their concerted efforts and with the help of their supporters in the government and among the conservative ulama, the Revolutionary Council managed to wrangle over the new bill for a relatively long time without coming to a decision one way or the other. The council's inaction, on the other hand, incurred the protests of the pro–land reform ulama such as Ayatollah Dastghaib. "Regarding the agrarian problem," warned the ayatollah,

> a conspiracy is about to happen. Some elements under the guise of Islam, in cooperation with the feudals and the Khans, are acting in the direction of weakening the bases of the Islamic Revolution. The silence of the Revolutionary Council is by no means justifiable. The people must be much more alert, and should not allow the large landowners to infiltrate the revolutionary institutions, and under the cover of religion stop the seizure of their lands.[77]

If landowners and the conservative ulama could no longer block the action of the Revolutionary Council, they were able to change the content of the bill so drastically that the new version (which was announced in mid-March of 1980) hardly satisfied the proponents of the reform. Soon huge peasant demonstrations for land were organized in Tehran and other major cities, supported by workers and other sympathetic elements within and outside the government.[78] As a result of considerable pressures from below, Ayatollah Khomeini assigned ayatollahs Montazari, Meshkini, and Beheshti to deal with the problem. After several meetings, these ayatollahs ended up endorsing a progressive land reform bill which was then approved by the Revolutionary Council in mid-April of the same year, and the Ministry of Agriculture was charged with implementing the law.[79] "The law," says Bakhash,

> provided for a sweeping land distribution. It limited landowners who directly cultivated their land to three times the acreage that in each district was considered sufficient for the maintenance of one peasant family. Absentee landowners who had no other source of income were limited to twice this amount. Since seven hectares was regarded

as an average subsistence holding, this implied the breakup of the middle-sized and even small enterprises. Provisions for the compensation of landlords subject to distribution were vague; and landowners were in any case to be compensated only after their debts to the government and their outstanding religious dues—also vaguely defined—had been deducted. These provisions for compensation, the exemption of livestock enterprises, and the allowance made for absentee owners were the only concessions to critics of the first draft of the bill. The law also provided that mechanized farms would be retained as units and transferred to groups of farmers on a cooperative basis.[80]

To undertake the task of land distribution, the law provided for the establishment of a Center for the Transfer and Revitalization of Land in the capital and seven-member committees (hay'atha-ye haft nafareh) in other cities. The center was formed in May 1980 and, in the course of a few months, thirty-six seven-member committees were set up in different cities. These committees recruited Muslim youth activists who were quite sympathetic to the peasants. They were authorized to determine the local upper limit on landholding, designate the properties subject to distribution, and determine who was to receive land. In eight months, until the suspension of the land reform law in November 1980, the land transfer committees distributed 150,000 hectares of barren land and 35,000 hectares of arable land among small and landless peasants. The committees also transferred 60,000 hectares of barren land to the Organization for the Expansion of Productive Services for the formation of rural production cooperatives by high school and college graduates. Finally, 850 hectares of disputed lands were leased to the peasants on a temporary basis.[81]

The Labor Movement. While the countryside was the scene of peasant-landlord conflict, growing labor unrest prevailed in the major industrial cities. The industrial workers, and particularly the oil workers, played an important role in defeating the Shah's regime in the final stage of the revolution. In late 1978, the Common Syndicate of the Employees of the Iranian Oil Industry (*Sandika-yi Moshtarak-i Karkonan-i Sana'at-i Naft-i Iran*) announced its participation in the revolutionary movement by indicating that:

> In unity with the fighting people of Iran, the purpose of our strike is to destroy despotism and eliminate the influence of foreigners in our

country, and create an independent, free and progressive Iran. These goals are the indisputable rights of the people. The people shall utilize all the means of self-sacrifice to achieve these goals.[82]

On December 20, 1978, the oil workers stated that "we know that our strike was the decisive factor [in overthrowing the Shah's regime]. We control the country's economy."[83] Strike committees were the major coordinators of the working-class movement during the revolution and constituted the nucleus of the subsequent workers' councils in different industrial units. A keen observer remarks:

> The councils were created in the following ways: (1) through the committees created to coordinate strikes within a production unit, which gradually, especially following the overthrow of the shah, prepared the ground for council elections; and (2) in those production units where the capitalist had fled, in the villages where the landlords had escaped, at the military bases where the former order had collapsed, in the ministries where the officials had gone into hiding—in short, wherever the former power structure had disintegrated and the workers had been affected by the propaganda and agitation of the conscious and advanced elements, councils were formed to assume responsibility for the affairs of the operations. These councils represented a new form or a new type of government initiated by the masses—the nuclei for people's rule.[84]

These councils assumed the management of factories. In many cases, workers were able to reduce working hours, obtain a more favorable job evaluation and classification, fire corrupt managers, hire additional workers, obtain across-the-board pay raises, lower managers' salaries, and be given regular health examinations.[85] Reportedly, there were as many different instances of "workers' control" as there were factories in Iran.[86]

The nationalization of many private enterprises in the summer of 1979 also contributed to the workers movement. The Revolutionary Council first nationalized the banking system and then fifteen insurance companies. Finally, the council passed the Law for the Protection and Expansion of Iranian Industry, which provided for the nationalization of industry in three broad categories: (1) "heavy" industries, including metals, automobile assembly, chemicals, shipbuilding, aircraft manufacture, and mining; (2) industries owned by fifty-one specifically named individuals, who had allegedly acquired their wealth illicitly through influence with the outgoing regime; and (3) industries in economic difficulty whose liabilities exceeded their net assets.[87] By 1982 the properties of over 230 large capitalists were nationalized, which altogether constituted over 80 percent of all private industries.[88]

The upsurge of the workers movement in the summer of 1979 continued into the fall, with workers demanding higher wages and profit-sharing, and protesting the firings of especially progressive workers. In Khuzistan and Azarbayjan, both of which had fairly large working classes, workers concentrated on establishing a minimum wage, a forty-hour work week, and independent councils and syndicates.[89] Workers also took steps toward forming regional unions. In Gilan by March 1980, thirty-one factory councils had formed a coordinating council that incorporated 20,000 workers. Another coordinating council was formed by eight factory councils in Tabriz.[90] In Fars, the Islamic councils of workers organized their first congress, which passed several resolutions calling for the continuation of the anti-imperialist struggle; the expulsion from the government of the liberals and those who had collaborated with the United States and its allies; the establishment of a progressive labor law; and the participation of workers' councils in management decisions.[91]

In sum, during this period workers were able to reduce working hours, increase their wages, gain better working conditions, exert some control over the production process, and set up their independent labor organizations.

The Merchants and the Nationalization of Foreign Trade. The prerevolutionary economic difficulties grew worse after the revolution. Many factors contributed to the intensification of this situation: disorganizations in the system of production and distribution as a result of the flights of capital and industrialists from the country and the nationalization of many private enterprises; political conflict within the government; the deterioration of the relationship between Iran and the advanced capitalist countries that had constituted the country's major trade partners; and the outbreak of the Iran-Iraq war. Skyrocketing inflation and the scarcity of basic commodities expedited the need for the government's intervention in the areas of both domestic and foreign trade. The provisional government went so far as to suggest the establishment of centers for the provision and distribution of commodities with the direct participation of the private sector, particularly the merchants.[92] This measure was by no means taken to weaken the economic power of the capitalist class.

With the fall of the provisional government, the question of the nationalization of foreign trade, its relationship with the domestic distribution of commodities, and the role of cooperatives in domestic trade became the subject of intense debates within and outside the Islamic Republic. The interval between the parliamentary debates on the nationalization of foreign trade in early fall of 1980 and the eventual demise of the nationalization bill (approved by the parliament but later rejected by the Council of Constitutional Guardians in late fall of 1982) was a period of acute struggles between proponents and opponents of the bill.

Demand for various goods overwhelmed the supply and led to hoarding and overcharging by the commercial sector as a highly attractive way of making money. Major newspapers began reporting the list of items being hoarded,[93] and both hoarders and profiteers were labeled as "economic terrorists, traitors" and "counterrevolutionaries," who were enriching themselves at the expense of the people by exploiting the crisis.[94] Anticapitalist and antimerchant propaganda was widespread. Angered by the scarcity of everyday necessities and by exorbitant prices, the people began demanding the implementation of the principle of the nationalization of foreign trade (which was already a part of the constitution).

In mid-October 1980, a draft was submitted to the parliament by twenty representatives, who gave the government three months to draw up a plan for the nationalization of foreign trade. About two months later, the draft was approved by the parliament in its first round of discussion; in its second round of discussion in mid-March 1981, the parliament came up with a two-month deadline for the government to formulate its plan for nationalizing the country's foreign trade. Consequently, in May 1981 the Reja-ie cabinet submitted a nationalization bill to the parliament according to which foreign trade was to come under the government's control over the next four years. In late November of the same year, the parliament, in its first round of discussion, approved the bill in principle.[95] Eventually, in April 1982, after about nineteen months of debates within and outside the parliament, the parliament overwhelmingly passed the nationalization bill.[96] It was stipulated that the consumption cooperatives would gradually take over the task of the domestic distribution of commodities. These cooperatives had been formed during the revolutionary struggle against the Shah to ameliorate the scarcities that had resulted from it. These cooperatives were often centered in the mosques. Shortly after the revolution, in Tehran alone 460 cooperatives were established and were publicly financed and staffed.[97] By early 1982 there were 12,387 cooperatives nationwide with a membership of 6.5 million and R 53 billion in capital.[98]

The Reversal Phase

In mid-1980, the social revolutionary movement could claim scores of victories: a radical land reform was being implemented; workers' councils were consolidating their power and establishing a nationwide network; the power of the capitalist class had been curtailed by the nationalization of many industries; and the nationalization of foreign trade had been made a part of the constitution and its implementation seemed certain. However, the revolutionary and counterrevolutionary struggles were far from over. Workers' and peasants' revolutionary gains were one thing, but consolidating these gains so that the social revolution would reach an "irreversible" state was quite another. Peasants and workers were not able to hold on to their achievements, and soon the forces of the landowners and merchants swept them away.

Landowners continued to resist the implementation of land reform. They accused the seven-member committees in charge of land distribution of being extremist and vengeful and of dispossessing some landowners who should not be affected by the law. They petitioned Ayatollah Khomeini and filed many complaints in courts against these committees.[99] Some landowners went as far as to send threatening telegrams to Ayatollah Khomeini's office.[100] Tremendous pressure was thus exerted by the landowners, the merchants, and the conservative ulama to stop the implementation of the reform.[101] The outbreak of the Iran-Iraq war provided the excuse for Ayatollah Khomeini "temporarily" to halt it. Subsequently, the land reform law was reviewed and revised by the parliament, which considerably retreated from the original objectives of the law passed by the Revolutionary Councils. Yet the revised law was still rejected by the Council of Constitutional Guardians, which by then had become an open "champion" of the economic interests of the dominant classes. With the change in the state's agrarian policy, the seven-member committees also came under attack.[102] Lands given to or seized by the peasants were reclaimed by the landowners, who were now backed by the armed forces of the Islamic Republic.[103] Workers' achievements were also undermined. As with its treatment of the peasants, the provisional government was fundamentally against workers' councils. Bazargan assailed radical political groups who "say that the army must be destroyed so that the councils can run the affairs of the nation, and that people must be in a state of revolution all the time. If this goes on we will have no alternative but to resign."[104] In the same vein, his labor minister expressed his opposition to the councils by threatening that "the Ministry of Labor is either my place of work or the councils'."[105] Nor were these achievements favorably received by Ayatollah Khomeini and his followers. Although Khomeini had called workers the pillar of the revolution, in practice the Islamic Republic did not tolerate the autonomy of the labor councils, believing that these councils ought to be Islamic and should be controlled by the Ministry of Labor. Given that the ulama were denying the existence of class conflict in society, these councils were supposed to include both the employers and employees of a given industrial unit, but where such councils were established workers were not allowed to form an independent labor union of their own. Finally, in the same way that the war provided an excuse for Ayatollah Khomeini to suspend implementation of the land reform program, it also provided an occasion to disarm the working class of its most effective weapon: the right to strike. Using as justification the fact that the "citadel of Islam" was in danger due to "the war imposed by the United States and Iraq," and that there was an urgent need to increase production, the ruling clerics organized a gathering in February 1981 consisting of the "representatives" of 170 Islamic associations of factories to condemn any form of labor strike.[106]

Some influential members of the Islamic Republic, however, went far beyond prohibiting labor strikes. The labor minister, Ahmad Tavakkoli (a staunch anti-Communist), and his assistant, Motamed Reza-ie, formulated a draft bill on labor relations in the fall of 1982. The draft was biased strongly in favor of management as it rejected the workers' rights to conduct collective bargaining to maintain job security, and to strike. Tavakkoli argued that Islamic labor law was based on the freedom of contract between the manager and the individual worker. Thus, there was no need for collective bargaining, and the idea of "a workers' representative" was superfluous. He further argued that if a contract contained the word "representative," that contract would be invalid. The draft also contained terminology that was quite new to the country's labor law. The Tudeh party charged that the draft and the terminology were inspired by the labor theory of Nazism,[107] and the draft bill created considerable controversy within and outside the government. However, united action by the workers, perhaps for the first time since the revolution, forced Tavakkoli out of office. Nonetheless, the damage he had caused workers' organizations during his tenure was considerable. *Ittila'at* in 1983 reported that out of the three hundred active workers' councils that had existed nationwide in 1982, only eighty were left. Even among these, many had become inactive as a result of pressures from both the government and the capitalists.[108] In short, in the postrevolutionary period the working class did not score any better than its allies in the rural areas.

The bill to nationalize foreign trade, the third social revolutionary measure, had the same fate. The measure failed as a result of the merchants' resistance and active lobbying against it. The merchants' greatest victory was in the Council of Constitutional Guardians, which vetoed the bill on the grounds that it was contrary to the law of Islam.[109] With the increasing domination of the merchants over the economy, the consumption cooperatives were weakened to the point where it became very difficult for them to procure supplies or bring about price stability.[110] It was reported that the cooperatives were being undermined because the wholesalers "were refusing to provide them with supplies. If this process is continued the local cooperatives will all be ruined."[111]

To summarize, massive as were the popular forces behind the social revolutionary movements, they were not able to defeat the counterrevolution, and by the spring of 1983 these forces had been effectively suppressed or contained within the existing structure of economic relationships. By this time, the moves toward a radical land reform, the formulation of a progressive labor law, and the nationalization of foreign trade had been not only defeated but also removed from the government's agenda. The leaders of the Islamic Republic still claimed, of course, that they were defending the oppressed people of Iran, but at the same time, the measures these dominated classes had demanded for the amelioration of their economic conditions were completely forgotten. As far as the existing distribution of economic resources was concerned, one could find few differences between pre- and postrevolutionary Iran.

Islamic Discourse and the Constitution of Class Capacity

What factors account for the failure of the social revolutionary movement? Why and how did the ruling ulama turn away from the social revolutionary option? The currently dominant models on policy outcomes cannot adequately explain the Iranian case. The failure of workers and peasants cannot be entirely attributed to state interests and its dynamic. Workers and peasants failed despite the fall of the provisional government, Bani-Sadr, and Qotbzadeh, who had supported the bazaaris and the landowners. To be sure, one may argue that Khomeini and his followers were mainly concerned with political power and the institutionalization of governance by the jurisprudent, and that their initial support of the social revolutionary measures taken during the initial phase of the postrevolutionary period was consistent with their struggle against the liberals. However, after their rivals had been expelled from the government and the challenge of the Left was effectively suppressed, there were no serious contenders for power against which they had to mobilize the popular forces. The Iran-Iraq war (while assisting the process of state building) also contributed to the triumph of the counterrevolution. Nevertheless, this argument is not totally satisfactory because the leaders of the Islamic Republic abandoned these measures just at the time they needed popular support in their war effort with Iraq.

Likewise, the Marxian model faces difficulty explaining the demise of the social revolutionary movement. While the organizational power and class capacity of the warring classes were crucial variables that determined the social outcomes of the revolution, class organization and capacity were not primarily rooted in the structure of class relations or the preexisting organizations of the classes involved. What decisively changed the balance of forces in favor of the merchants and landowners was the ideological context in which class conflict transpired. By structuring the legitimacy of the claim advanced by diverse classes and selectively promoting certain organized activities, Islamic revolutionary discourse operated in favor of the merchants and landowners vis-à-vis workers and peasants. Controlling for the variable of ideology, it seems that both dominated and dominant classes had serious organizational weaknesses.

Incapacity of Workers and Peasants. "In the vast ocean of the petty bourgeoisie, the industrial concentrations represent only small islands." This is a well-known saying among Iran's labor activists, and it is not without substance. In Tehran alone there were about 750,000 merchants, middlemen, and retail traders. This city had 800,000 shops and 420,000 guild units in 1980.[112] According to a 1977 estimate, there were 163,819 small industrial enterprises (those with nine or less employees) in the urban areas with a labor force of 315,143 people. Of this number, only 103,422, or 33 percent, had paid employees. The rest were operated by the owners and their families. In other words, 67 percent of these workshops could be classified as the petty bourgeois proper.[113] On the other hand, according to 1982 statistics, there were 7,531 large industrial enterprises (with ten or more employees) in operation, employing 426,000 blue-collar workers and 60,000 white-collar workers. Of this number, 6,738 (89 percent) had less than one hundred employees. Noteworthy is that 4,628 (62 percent of the total) had less than nineteen employees. But 793 workshops (11 percent) had more than one hundred employees. Of this amount, only 233 (3.1 percent) had more than five hundred employees. Thus the country's industrial workshops were dominated by small-scale production units.[114] The small size of the enterprises was an important factor hindering the development of an organized workers' movement.

Despite their size, the industrial workers had some latitude for effective collective action—first, because of the oil industry's strategic location in the country's economy and, second, because the industrial units were concentrated in a few major cities (Tehran province alone had 49.7 percent of the total large industrial enterprises, followed by Mazanderan with 7.5 percent, Isfahan with 5.8 percent, Central province with 5.1 percent, Azarbayjan with 4.8 percent, and Khorasan with 4.6 percent). The rest of the country held the remaining 22.5 percent.[115] Therefore, workers could have paralyzed the economy had they gone on a prolonged general strike. Such a unified class action was, however, contingent on the existence of a solid organization. Workers did not have a nationwide union, and the prerevolutionary state-run unions were fragmented and controlled by the secret police. Workers movements had often been spontaneous and lacked long-range strategies. Lacking a tradition of labor union activity, the postrevolutionary labor movement was quite inexperienced.

Nor was the peasants' collective capacity any better than that of the workers. The geographical dispersal of villages, the persistent threat of raiding nomads, and the absence of a middle peasantry are considered factors hindering the peasants' collective power.[116] Furthermore, the state's policies in the 1960s might have added to the peasants' political weakness not only by destroying traditional farming organizations (i.e., *boneh*) but also by undermining the newly emerged nationwide cooperative movement in this period.[117] Peasant movements, when they did appear with some strength, did so because they were aided by two essential factors. First, radical peasant uprisings were grounded in ethnic divisions (e.g., Azarbayjan, Kurdistan, Turkman-Sahra). Second, the extensive commercialization of agriculture in the 1960s and 1970s provided favorable conditions in certain areas for the upsurge of peasant movements.

These factors probably explain why Turkman-Sahra and Kurdistan were the scenes of radical peasant movements in the postrevolutionary period. Turkman-Sahra, an area of cotton and wheat cultivation, was not covered by the land reform of the sixties. The farms were extensive, the agriculture mechanized, the owners absentee, and the land worked by agricultural workers. Subsistence farms existed alongside the large estates; many local farmers worked their own land and hired themselves and members of their family out as wage laborers to the large landowners. The plantation was the dominant economic organization of commercial farming in this area.[118] The existing agrarian structure, combined with the region's distinctive ethnic characteristics, facilitated the emergence of a radical peasant movement. Right after the revolution many peasant councils emerged that soon culminated in the formation of the Central Organ of the Peasants' Councils of Turkman-Sahra. These councils were in power in the region for nearly one year, during which they were attacked twice by both the military and the Revolutionary Guards. Soon the leaders of the council were arrested by the Guards and, along with ninety-four council members, murdered by Ayatollah Khalkhali.[119] In Kurdistan the peasants were also organized by the Communists and the Kurdish Democratic arty. In this region the Islamic Republic also launched a military attack on the movement. Had the peasants and ethnic minorities of other parts of the country displayed a similar degree of radicalism, one might expect that there would have been a stronger social revolutionary movement in the country.

In addition to the workers' and peasants' organizational weaknesses, there were dissension and even opposing tendencies among the labor activists. The early proliferation of workers' and peasants' councils should partly be credited to the organizing efforts of both the Communists and left-oriented Islamic organizations. However, in the course of the postrevolutionary period, these groups were not only unable to come up with a commonly accepted general strategy (or what Lenin called a *minimum program*) for advancing the social revolutionary movement, they also persisted in following opposing policies that rendered any real cooperation impossible. Crisscrossing ideological and tactical differences among these groups undermined their organizing efforts.

The Mojahedin, the minority faction of the Feda'iyan, and other smaller leftist organizations rejected the social revolutionary potential of Ayatollah Khomeini and his followers, calling for the overthrow of the Islamic Republic. On the other hand, the Movement of Muslim Fighters (*Junbish-i Musalmanan-i Mubariz*), the Tudeh, and the majority faction of the Feda'iyan based their strategy on the belief that the ruling clerics were truly revolutionaries. Moreover, within each of these tendencies there were still ideological differences. The Mojahedin were devout Muslims who believed that their version of Islam transcended both capitalism and socialism. However, the Mojahedin alliance with Bani-Sadr strained their relationships with their leftist allies. The presence of diverse tendencies in the other camps was no less telling. The Movement of Muslim Fighters, while committed to its own version of Islamic socialism, was highly critical of the Communists, in particular the Tudeh. It does not require too much imagination to recognize the destructive effects of these opposing tendencies on the peasants' and workers' organizations. While the coordinating councils of workers in Tabriz and Gilan were being organized by the Feda'iyan, the Congress of the Councils of Islamic Workers in Fars was organized largely by the Movement of Muslim Fighters. The oil workers in the south were believed to be under the influence of the Tudeh. Under the relentless attack of the counterrevolution, these organizations had little time to learn from practical experiences and put aside their differences. Whatever its cause, the consequence of this political hodgepodge among the labor activists was a further fracturing of the workers' and peasants' movements, which aided the triumph of the counterrevolution.

The Collective Capacity of the Dominant Classes. Organizational problems among landowners and merchants were no less telling. The landowners as a class were effectively undermined by the Shah's land reform of the 1960s. On the eve of the revolution, the agricultural holdings were divided into three broad categories. The first comprised large, medium, and small agricultural holdings with the population of over 100,000 controlling 5 to 6 million hectares of relatively fertile land. The second was composed of a small group of rich peasants and small rural capitalists who had considerable influence in their own villages. Finally, the third category consisted of 1.5 million small and landless peasants.[120] The internal structure of the first category consisted of about 9,500 large landowners (with more than one hundred hectares each) who owned over 3.5 million hectares of the best-quality lands; and several tens of thousands of medium owners (with from fifty to one hundred hectares each) and small owners (with from thirty to fifty hectares each) who together owned close to 3 million hectares. Large, medium, and small landowners had historically close ties with the merchants and the real estate owners in the urban areas. These groups plus rich farmers constituted the Iranian rural bourgeoisie. With the upsurge of the peasants' movement, these landowners were threatened and took a counterrevolutionary position.[121]

However, no nationwide network existed in the postrevolutionary period through which the landowners could have mobilized support against the land reform. To be sure. they skillfully took advantage of a law concerning the establishment of agricultural councils passed by the Revolutionary Council in April 1979. The law was a response to the pressures from the Left for the formation of the councils of peasants and agricultural workers to supervise production; however, the councils of landowners were instead formed for the defense of their common interests. With the aid of Eizadi, the agricultural minister under Bazargan, these councils were set up in Tehran and all the provinces. They held two general congresses in Tehran and launched an extensive campaign against land reform. They sent hundreds of letters, petitions, cables, and leaflets to grand ayatollahs and governmental authorities. The resolutions and declarations issued by the congresses were directed against the "un-Islamic" nature of the reform and the activities of the seven-member committees, and defended private property in agriculture. The congresses also received support from the conservative ulama.[122] However, with the fall of the provisional government, the landowners lost an important ally, and these councils by themselves did not seem to have been strong enough to undermine the influence of the peasants' movement within and outside the government.

Nor did the merchants enjoy having a nationwide union in prerevolutionary Iran. The chamber of guilds was controlled by the state and often used as a vehicle to implement its policies. The Society of Merchants and Guilds was the most significant organization of the bazaar in the oil nationalization movement and was tied to the National Front. However, it was outlawed after the coup and never regained its former power and influence in the bazaar. In the late 1970s, it was reestablished illegally under the name of the Society of Merchants and Guilds of Tehran Bazaar (SMGTB). However, SMGTB was one of the three major bazaar-based political organizations. The other two were the Committee on Guild Affairs (*Komiteh-ye Omour-i Senfi*)and the Traders' Towhidi Guild. They were tied to diverse political groups. SMGTB was connected to the liberals, the Committee on Guild Affairs to the IRP, and the Traders' Towhidi Guild to the Mojahedin. In the course of the conflict between the IRP and Bani-Sadr/Mojahedin, a group of the bazaar activists and organizers were either executed or fled the country [123] In all likelihood, the presence of these diverse political tendencies within the bazaar hindered its capacity for collective action.

True, the merchants had considerable financial power. On the eve of the revolution, the bazaar controlled "a third of imports and two-thirds of retail trade."[124] The expulsion of international capital and the flight of industrialists and bankers provided an exceptional opportunity for the fast accumulation of wealth by the bazaaris. They effectively exploited the economic situation of the postrevolutionary period.

"Buy cheap and sell dear" is the golden rule of trade, and merchants were effectively applying this principle in their economic transactions. Under economic conditions where effective demand was outstripping supplies, hoarding and overcharging became the rule of business. When a commodity was imported, merchants made a profit several times over. The Iranian importer often requested the foreign commissioner selling the commodity to record in the invoice a higher price than he was to be paid. The merchant then purchased foreign currency equal to the amount specified in the invoice from the Iranian government at a rate much below the free market. The difference between this amount and the actual amount he paid the commissioner was deposited in the merchant's private account in a foreign bank.[125] Defrauding the government was, of course, one among many ways that merchants were able to reap windfall profits. After the commodity passed through customs, it began its complex journey through the hands of several merchants until it reached the wholesaler. At this point the commodity was transferred from this middleman to the next, from one commodity seller to the next hoarder. At each point the price of the commodity was increased. By the time the commodity reached the consumer, it cost as much as a hundred times its original price.[126]

Although the government had drawn up a price list for all commodities, it was not able to control hoarding and overcharging. Newspapers frequently reported the list of items being hoarded or overpriced. To control prices, the government set up special courts on guild affairs (*dadgah-i vizhah-i umur-i senfi*) in the summer of 1980 and launched an antiprofiteering campaign.[127] Within a year, about 7,000 complaints regarding overpricing had been filed in these courts. By the end of 1982, these courts had fined hoarders and overchargers a total of about R 12 billion.[128] On several occasions leaders of the Islamic Republic tried to persuade merchants to voluntarily reduce prices and expose the hoarders and overpricers in their ranks, and President Bani-Sadr threatened the bazaaris that overpricing would have grave consequence for the commercial sector.[129] Ayatollah Montazari pleaded that the "esteemed bazaaris and respected merchants should take care of the hoarders themselves because the bazaar's reputation was at stake."[130] Furthermore, Hojatuleslam Hashemi Rafsanjani (then the speaker of the parliament) complained that "the greedy and opportunist capitalists have imposed poverty on our society."[131] However, the fines issued by the courts and the ulama's preachings on the un-Islamic nature of hoarding and overpricing proved ineffective in controlling the rapid escalation of prices and the concentration of wealth by the commercial sector.

In regard to how much wealth the bazaaris actually accumulated in the short period following the breakdown of the Shah's regime, no accurate data are available. However, scattered statistics reported in the major newspapers, as well as those mentioned by government authorities, are indicative of the extent of concentration of economic resources. Of the total imports valued at $15 billion in 1980, $10.5 billion (70 percent) belonged to the private sector. These figures gain added significance when one realizes that in 1977, of the total $16 billion in imports, only $7.5 billion (47 percent) belonged to the private sector.[132] A government authority indicated that the profits of the commercial sector in 1980 and 1981 were unprecedented. In 1980 alone the profit accrued in foreign trade was R 1,200 billion.[133] In the same year, ten merchants held a monopoly on the importation of iron, with a total value of about R 200 billion. The profit of each major iron importer was estimated to be R 2 billion a year.[134] It was claimed that the income of the "swindlers" from the sale of illegal cigarettes was R 210 billion in 1980.[135] Forty major wholesalers with a capital of R 3 to R 4 billion reportedly managed to corner the market in fruits and vegetables in Tehran. With their huge capital, these wholesalers and contacts (all together numbering between four to five hundred people) purchased fruits and vegetables from producers at a low price and then were able to make R 40 billion in profits in 1980.[136]

Merchants could use their financial power to influence politics. By donating a small fraction of their profits to religious institutions and the ulama, merchants were able to expand their influence in the Islamic Republic. A cut in such donations could have considerably weakened any ayatollah, including Ayatollah Khomeini. Since the Islamic Republic was desperately in need of funds to finance its war effort with Iraq, the assistance of the bazaar was all the more vital. No exact data on bazaar donations are available, but scattered information indicates that the bazaar's contributions to the religious institutions and the war were indeed considerable. For example, Hashemi Rafsanjani once indicated that the bazaar of Qum (which has only limited financial power) was able to raise R 130 million toward financing the war in just a single day.[137]

Nevertheless, the merchants' greed backfired and was a major reason for the nationalization of foreign trade. Hojatuleslam Khatemi, Khomeini's representative in the Reconstruction Crusade in East Azarbayjan, indicated that "in the past three or four years some people have accumulated more wealth than they would have been able to accumulate under the previous regime in forty years. This is causing social inequality. Our objective is to narrow the gap between the rich and the poor, but we are doing just the opposite. The rich are becoming richer and the poor are becoming poorer."[138] In the same vein, Hojatuleslam Hashemi Rafsanjani exclaimed that "even in capitalist societies a businessman does not feel he has the right to sell a commodity for 5 to ten times the price he had bought it for under the pretext of commercial freedom, and then pays no taxes."[139] The profiteering of the merchants caused much outrage among the public as well as in the parliament.[140]

Therefore, the clue to understanding the landowners' and merchants' capacity to protect their own interests vis-à-vis the popular support for land reform and nationalization of foreign trade is to consider the ideological context in which class conflict was taking place. Merchants and landowners were successful because of the built-in bias of the Islamic discourse in favor of the property-owning classes. Furthermore, the "Islamization" of the country as set by the dynamics of Shi'i revolutionary discourse encouraged the reestablishment and revitalization of the traditional organizations of the bazaar, which had been undermined under the Pahlavis. There were ideological and historical precedents for the establishment of various bazaar-based organizations, while such precedents did not exist for the formation of workers' and peasants' unions.

The landowners did not have much difficulty invoking religious principles against land reform. From the very first moment that Isfahani announced the government's plan for land redistribution, the landowners' were strongly opposed to it. They caused disturbances in the countryside and attributed these to peasants provoked by Isfahani's announcement. The landowners accused Isfahani of being a Communist and labeled his land reform bill as part of a Communist conspiracy.[141] They also staged a sit-in at the office of the Revolutionary Council to express their opposition to the land reform bill.[142] The conservative ulama were also mobilized against the bill. In particular, Ayatollah Ruhani in Qum and Ayatollah Hasan Qumi in Mashhad voiced their opposition.[143] Ayatollah Ruhani argued that the bill was contrary to the law of Islam and questioned Isfahani's knowledge of Islam and his competence in interpreting Islamic laws.[144] Landowners also secured *fatva* from leading ulama against the land reform. Ayatollah Golpayegani issued a statement declaring the law to be in violation of Islamic tenets. Ayatollahs Ruhani, Mahallati, Qumi, and Shirazi also criticized the measure. The Society of Seminary Teachers at Qum, a group considered close to Khomeini, issued a declaration warning against bills "damaging to the interests of the oppressed . . . which appear in the dress of Islam" and added that the land reform measure would lead to "the ruin of the cultivated lands."[145]

The landowners also came up with their own "land reform" program, which was confined to the distribution of barren and unutilized lands among the peasants. The suggested program was then distributed to the bureaucrats in the Ministry of Agriculture. Although the measure proposed by the landowners could hardly be labeled a land reform, it did serve the conservative ulama for defending landed interests. No ayatollah could then be easily singled out by the social revolutionary forces as being anti–land reform. As a case in point, Ayatollah Ruhani, while consistently attacking Isfahani's land reform bill, argued that he was not against a land reform program per se.[146]

Given that the religious opposition was partly a reaction to the Shah's land reform program of the sixties, the landowners and the conservative ulama easily invoked past arguments against the reform, while no ideological precedent existed in Islam that favored land redistribution among the peasants. For example, in Hamadan, landlords circulated an older *fatva* by Khomeini, which had prohibited the usurpation of land. Even Ayatollah Taleqani, considered the most radical and socially conscious cleric, never questioned the legitimacy of private ownership of land in his book *Islam va Malikiyyat* (Islam and private property). The idea of Islamic socialism never attracted an interested audience among the ulama. Thus when the Council of Constitutional Guardians pronounced the land reform bill to be contrary to the law of Islam, there was not much the social revolutionary forces could do short of questioning the legitimacy of the council itself. However, for those pro–land reform activists who believed in the Islamic Republic, this option was not acceptable, and the land reform debate could not be taken out of the Islamic discourse. And those who were against the government did not have the right to speak.

Likewise, the merchants effectively used religion to question the legitimacy of the nationalization bill. When the Reja-ie government was engaged in drawing up a plan for nationalizing foreign trade, the merchants' opposition to the policy was reflected in their support of the liberal Qotbzadeh in November 1980.[147] In early January 1981, the merchants distributed leaflets threatening to "use all our forces to overthrow the existing government." Addressing Prime Minister Reja-ie, the leaflet continued: "Mr. Reja-ie, for the sake of Islam, we demand that you resign from the job; you are incapable of handling its responsibilities and should free the position for a devout Muslim. Otherwise, the Muslim people will have no choice but to force you out of office. But then you must answer for the problems you created as a result of your ignorance and incompetence."[148] The merchants also mobilized the conservative ulama, who objected to the nationalization of foreign trade on the grounds that it was contrary to the law of Islam. In March 1980, for example, Ayatollah Qumi of Mashhad condemned the arbitrary nationalization and expropriation of private property.[149]

In short, backed by the conservative ulama, the merchants advanced two sets of arguments against nationalization of foreign trade. The first was the standard right-wing argument, well-known in the West—that is, that the state was a bad manager. As early as late summer 1979, Ayatollah Azari-Qumi indicated that "we have supported the owners of capital and industry in order to prevent the decline of production and employment. The capitalists who fled the country are free to return and continue their work. As Bazargan has indicated, the government is not a good merchant."[150] It was further argued that the state-run factories were inefficient and sustained losses and that government employees were "inexperienced and lazy." They would be unable to handle the annual imports of 240,000 items of various commodities.[151] And despite the government's assurance that nationalization of foreign trade would not affect small businesses and retailers, merchants claimed that it would destroy small businesses and retail traders and consequently could cause five million people to lose their jobs,[152] despite the government's assurance that the nationalization would not affect small businesses and retailers. The second argument was based on religion and anti-Communism. It was argued that "the *Shari'ah* of Islam does not allow anyone to point a finger at the merchants. From the beginning of Islam, the bazaar has been operating in this manner, and anything else is *kufr* and Communism."[153]

The process of the "Islamization" of Iranian society generated a favorable ideological context for the bazaaris to reestablish and revitalize Islamic institutions in the bazaar. As early as 1979, a merchant of the bazaar, Khamoushi, formed the Committee on Guild Affairs, which soon became a highly influential organization defending the interests of the bazaar against government intervention in the distribution of commodities.[154] Khamoushi repeatedly insisted that the nationalized factories should be sold to the private sector.[155] Other organizations controlled by the merchants were the Organization of Islamic Economy (*Sazman-i Eqtesadi-ye Islami*) and the Interest Free Loan Fund (*Sandouq-ha-ye Qarzul Hasaneh*).[156] These organizations were in turn used by the merchants as a vehicle to mobilize support against the foreign trade nationalization bill.

The merchants' organizing efforts were also directly aided by some of the leading officials within the government and the IRP. Prominent among these officials was Habibullah Asgar-Owladi, a right-wing and influential member of the IRP who later became the minister of commerce. In a series of editorials published in *Jomhouri-ye Islami,* Asgar-

Owladi outlined the tasks of the "devout Muslim of the bazaar" by calling on the bazaaris "to form and strengthen the Islamic Societies of the Bazaar."[157] Asgar-Owladi charged that the counterrevolution and hypocrites were spreading rumors aimed at a total exclusion of the bazaar—and for that matter the whole private sector—from domestic and foreign trade, the exclusion of "distribution cooperatives," and nationalization of all the commercial transactions both domestic and foreign, wholesale and retail.[158] He encouraged the bazaaris to organize their own "distribution cooperatives" in the bazaar and warned them against any unauthorized governmental interference in foreign trade and the distribution of commodities.[159]

When Asgar-Owladi was appointed as the minister of commerce, the merchants virtually monopolized the ministry and related offices.[160] The Ministry of Commerce granted the merchants a monopoly over the distribution of imported and local goods, which they often sold at high prices in the free market. When the government expressed a favorable attitude toward the expansion and consolidation of cooperatives, the merchants were quick to establish the Distribution Cooperatives (*Ta'avoniha-ye Touzi'*), which really amounted to being unions for large capitalists. Exposing the merchants' trick, a government authority complained that

> a cooperative society does not mean that five, ten, or fifty large capitalists form a joint-stock company to undertake the distribution of several commodities and legitimize their plundering of the people under the cover of "cooperative." A cooperative venture for the distribution of a given commodity must include all the individuals who are involved in the distribution of that commodity, including the most minor retail traders.[161]

The merchants' action was further exposed by an *Ittila'at* headline: "A Distribution Cooperative or the Joint-Stock Company of the Merchants?"[162]

The merchants who had the closest ties to Ayatollah Khomeini gained considerable control over the financially strong Mostaz'afin Foundation (formerly the Pahlavi Foundation). The amount of the foundation's assets was not clear. According to one source, the foundation had "one thousand companies: land and sea transportation lines; 357 factories (of which one hundred were large operations); farms, hospitals, dairy farms; lands and various real estate (100,000 houses, apartments, and hotels); and, finally, a treasure of jewelry, antiques, carpets, and expensive paintings."[163] The first director of the Mostaz'afin Foundation was Mohandes Khamoushi, the brother of the same Khamoushi who organized and headed the Committee on Guild Affairs. During the period that he was director of the foundation, there were so many charges of misuse of the foundation's fund and of various questionable deals by the bazaaris that Ayatollah Khomeini once commented, "I have heard that the Mostaz'afin Foundation is turned into a *mostakbarin* foundation" (i.e., that a foundation for the needy had been turned into a foundation for the greedy). Although Khamoushi was fired, bazaar merchants continued to occupy key positions in the foundation. Among these were Haj Refiq-Doust, a wealthy bazaari from Tehran, who was the director of the agricultural and gardening section, and Haj Masha'allah Kashani (known as Masha'allah the butcher), who was the director of the foundation's animal husbandry department.[164]

The merchants and landowners were directly aided by the Hujjatiyyah, the ultra-right-wing religious organization. Formed in the early 1930s, the Hujjatiyyah had been inspired by the writings of Mirza Mehdi Isfahani, which stated that the Twelfth Imam was infallible and that his authority could not be encroached upon by any Muslim, who could at most be considered his deputy. As Islamic purists, Hujjatiyyah members advocated the complete purification of Iranian Muslim society, starting with the elimination of the (heretic) Baha'is and the (godless) Communists. This organization was recognized by SAVAK under the condition that it would remain solely a religious institution and not interfere in politics. Hujjatiyyah's main function was to harass the Baha'is, while attempting to convert them to Shi'i Islam. The organization had sympathizers among the ulama, including Ayatollah Golpayegani, and, most important, Ayatollah Kho-ei. The organization owned companies, schools, hospitals, and financial organizations. Before the Revolution, it had connections with the court. After the revolution, its main activities ranged from persistently lobbying against any radical economic measure adopted by the Islamic Republic to harassing or assassinating members of radical political organizations and the ulama who were in favor of radical economic change. It had members and sympathizers in the parliament, the government, and the Council of Constitutional Guardians. Noteworthy among Hujjatiyyah connections were Mohammad Gharzai (oil minister), Ahmad Tavakkoli (labor minister), Habibullah Asgar-Owladi (minister of commerce), and Ali Akbar Parvarish (minister of education), all of whom were members of the Musavi cabinet in 1981. The leader of the Hujjatiyyah, Hojatuleslam Abol-Qasim Khazali, was a member of the Council of Constitutional Guardians.[165]

It is interesting to note that the Left and the supporters of the social revolutionary measures were quite successful in exposing their enemy, effectively discrediting counter social revolutionary politicians and forcing them out of office. Bazargan, Bani-Sadr, and Qotbzadeh were ridiculed by the Left. The Feda'iyan eagerly published the documents against Ayatollah Shari'atmadari that were given to them by the followers of Ayatollah Khomeini. And, as previously noted, Mohandes Khamoushi, who was in charge of the Mostaz'afin Foundation, was fired; the staunch antilabor and anti-Communist labor minister, Tavakkoli, was forced out of office; and Asgar-Owladi, the bazaar's major spokesperson and activist, was forced to resign. What is more, the parliament passed all the social revolutionary measures. Nevertheless, when the Council of Constitutional Guardians declared that the social revolutionary measures were un-Islamic, the debate was by and large concluded. The dominant Shi'i discourse had managed to exclude the social revolutionary solutions to the economic problems of the postrevolutionary period.

In the second parliamentary election, held in 1984, the bazaaris were able to strengthen their position within the government by sending their representatives to the parliament. Indeed Ayatollah Khomeini, who by now had retreated from his original pledge to support and defend the impoverished masses, openly supported the bazaar, calling upon the bazaaris to nominate their own candidates for the parliament.[166] However, factional disputes within the government and the ulama prevented official Islamic groups from drawing up a common list of candidates; thus each group ended up presenting its own list. Nevertheless, a high percentage of the candidates in virtually all these lists were the same as in the list of the bazaar's candidates (see table 7.3). According to this table, between 67 and 81 percent of the candidates nominated by these Islamic organizations were identical to the bazaar's candidates in Tehran. The bazaaris' success in sending their own men to the parliament further enhanced their power in directing the policy of the Islamic Republic.[167] Yielding to the increasing pressures of the dominant classes and its economic difficulties, the government began to

TABLE 7.3

Percentage of Overlap Between Candidates of the Official and Semiofficial Political Groups and the Candidates of the Bazaar

Name of Organization	Percent of Overlap with Candidates on the Bazaar's List
Bazaar	100
Mojahedin of Islamic Revolution	81
Feda'iyan-i Islam	70
Islamic Republican party	70
Community of Fighting Clergy of Tehran (*Jame-eh-ye Rouhaniyat-i Mobariz-i Tehran*)	67
Organization of Fajr-i Islam	67

SOURCE: Organization of the Iranian People's Feda'iyan (majority), *Kar*, no. 4 (Khurdad 1363/1984), p. 2.

rebuild a relationship with the West, including the United States. The *New York Times* reported that "through October of this year [1983] more than $1 billion worth of goods has been formally traded between Iran and the United States. And Government and private economists familiar with Iran say the levels could be twice as high if indirect transactions through agents or other intermediaries are included."[168] Moreover, the Islamic Republic started to revive the prerevolutionary regional arrangements. The Regional Cooperation for Development (RCD), which was the economic basis of the Central Treaty Organization (CENTO), was revived under a new label—the Economic Cooperation Organization (ECO), consisting of the same three countries that had been involved in the RCD in prerevolutionary Iran: Turkey, Pakistan, and Iran.[169]

Finally, the shortage of skilled labor and technical experts was another factor that necessitated a more pragmatic approach toward the West. This shortage was mainly produced by the cultural revolution, which had led to the purge of "un-Islamic" elements from various institutions in the Islamic Republic. Further, on the eve of the revolution and during the initial radicalization period, many investors had fled the country, leaving the nationalized factories to be managed by the Islamic Republic The ulama did not have the expertise for this, and the result was a managerial crisis. Nabavi, the minister of heavy industries, admitted that most of the managers were revolutionaries but were inexperienced. The average employment period for managers in these industries was eleven to twelve months, after which they resigned.[170] The government's inability to run the nationalized factories lent credence to the right wing's claim that "the government was not a good capitalist." Thus, under pressure from private capital (which demanded a greater role in controlling the economy) and driven by its own need for more revenues to finance its war efforts, the Islamic Republic began to privatize the public sector.[171] Under these conditions, Khomeini announced his Eight Points Command, which marked the beginning of economic liberalization.[172]

Granted that the social revolutionary movement was effectively defeated, can one still argue that the bazaaris were also under pressure from the government and that the conflict had really been between the private and the public sectors? Ashraf has advanced such an argument:

> On the whole, however, the bazaaris have been threatened by such unprecedented radical governmental measures as nationalization of foreign trade and elimination of brokerage junction through the development of cooperative societies. Further, comparing the 1970s to the 1980s, one can observe a much more vigorous and ruthless antiprofiteering campaign launched by the revolutionary organizations against the bazaaris.[173]

The merchants' effective lobbying against the nationalization of foreign trade and the consolidation of their economic and political power needs no further elaboration. However, Ashraf's claim in regarding the "ruthlessness" of the antiprofiteering campaign of the Islamic Republic in comparison to the Shah's as an indication of state-bazaar conflict invites some comments. First, these campaigns should be evaluated within the context of the overall policies of the state. The economic policies of the Shah had been oriented toward protecting the interests of international capital and the dependent bourgeoisie, and his antiprofiteering campaign contributed to the mobilization of the bazaaris against him. However, the overall orientation of the Islamic Republic during the reversal period and thereafter was to protect the interests of the merchants (and the landowners) against the revolutionary attacks from below. Within this context, the antiprofiteering campaign of the Islamic Republic was, at best, nothing but an effort to punish the greediest bazaaris in return for protecting the whole class of merchants. Finally, in practice the campaign seems to have been directed against the retail traders. Although no exact data on differential sentencing of the hoarders and overchargers are available, statements by some authorities point to the fact that the retail traders were the ones who were most severely punished, not the merchants. According to Hojatuleslam Borhani, the under secretary for the Office of Islamic Revolutionary Attorney for the Committee on Guild Affairs:

> In our prosecution of the hoarders and overchargers, we are facing some obstacles. If a retail trader convicted of overcharging is sentenced, no one would stand up in his defense. Of course he should not be defended. But the problem is that the grand overchargers and hoarders are being protected by some people in the government. I know a merchant who was convicted of overcharging as much as R 23 million. But unfortunately he was later hired as a purchasing consultant by one of the ministries.[174]

In another interview, the same authority complained that:

> Three large capitalists were fined over R 420 million by the court for overcharging the prices of plastic materials and steel. One of the three was formerly a rope seller. After the Revolution, he obtained loans from Bank Melli and Bank Bazargani (the Branch of Bazaar-i Ahangaran), and began importing industrial machineries from Japan. He then established a factory which was worth over R 700 million. Interestingly enough, the fine of R 340 million was equal to 30 percent of the value of the plastic bags his factory was producing in a period of three months. . . . However, when we attempted to sentence these people, the Guards were unable to find them. Indeed whenever we catch one of these big capitalists, we see that he is being protected by some people in the government. . . . The only thing some authorities know about responsibility is to protect the capitalists. After four years of Islamic Revolution, in the name of Islam they are defending capitalism and imposing economic hardship on the deprived people.[175]

Again Asgar-Owladi stood up in defense of the bazaar by claiming that, "Contrary to those who attack the bazaar in their writings and sayings, I see the bazaar as the barricades of the ulama. . . . The bazaaris should not worry about their trade."[176] It is true that the merchants and landowners are continuing to pressure the government to privatize the economy. Such demands, however, should be viewed in terms of the collective power of the country's new dominant classes, rather than as a conflict between the public and the private sectors, as if the latter were an undifferentiated entity.

The Revolution Is Over

The revolutionary crisis began when Shi'i discourse took over the protest movement and transformed social discontent into revolutionary crisis. The power of Shi'i revolutionary discourse that motivated the people to take direct action against the Shah stemmed from the fact that it meant many things to many people. Various mechanisms were also noted through which the revolutionary ideology autonomously contributed to the making of the Iranian Revolution. In the postrevolutionary period, Shi'i discourse also contributed to the shaping of significant events. These events, in turn, channeled ideology in a manner to resonate with the dominant interests. When Khomeini and his followers brutally repressed the opposition and eliminated their rivals, when he agreed to the ceasefire with Iraq (that ran contrary to the dynamic of Shi'i discourse), and when merchants and landowners effectively blocked the movements of the dominated classes and removed social revolutionary issues from the agenda of the Islamic Republic, one may conclude that the revolution was over. Shi'i revolutionary discourse had become state ideology and at the same time was structured in favor of the merchants and the landowners.

What Kind of Revolution?

What fundamental changes were wrought by the Iranian Revolution? What were the distinguishing features of the postrevolutionary political order? Considering what has been said in this chapter, the Iranian Revolution does not conform to the existing historical categories known as bourgeois, socialist, and national liberation revolutions. True, one may argue that the Iranian case resembles a national liberation revolution. Earlier, the Shah had regained power with the direct assistance of the United States and Great Britain, and his economic policies favored the interests of international capital. The Shah was a pillar of U.S. policy in the Middle East. The indigenous classes were all excluded from positions of major economic and political decision-making and thus became united in their struggle against the Shah. Nevertheless, national liberation movements refer to the struggles of indigenous classes and groups against direct foreign domination (i.e., military occupation or colonialism). The Pahlavi state was not a system of *direct* foreign domination. The concept of "liberation" is even more problematic if one considers the intensification of political and social repressions under the Islamic Republic. The revolution overthrew the Shah's political dictatorship but installed a more intense political and social dictatorship in the Islamic Republic.

Ulyanovsky, a political theorist from the former Soviet Union, considers the Iranian case to be a democratic, anti-imperialist, bourgeois, and Islamic revolution:

> —Considering its moving force, the form of struggle and the general demands of the people for social justice, the Iranian Revolution was a people's revolution and hence it was democratic.
> —Considering its main direction, the revolution was anti-monarchical and anti-imperialist and strongly anti-U.S.
> —Considering its social content, it was a bourgeois revolution (for the anti-capitalist tendencies were not materialized); and considering the basic form of ideology and the role of the Shi'i leadership, it was an Islamic Revolution.[177]

The contention that the revolution was both "democratic" and "bourgeois" is problematic. First, the facts that the struggle against the Shah was conducted by a majority of the public and that the public overwhelmingly endorsed the formation of the Islamic Republic do not in themselves make the Iranian Revolution democratic. The revolution did not end arbitrary rule, nor did it expand the collective capacity of the dominated classes. Workers did not gain the right to strike and form unions, and the land reform movement failed. Even Khomeini and his followers rejected democracy on the grounds that it was a Western concept. Second, Ulyanovsky's argument regarding the bourgeois nature of the Revolution is based upon what did not occur in postrevolutionary Iran, by itself a questionable criterion. To be sure, the revolution overthrew the dominance of international capital and the dependent bourgeoisie, while expanding the economic and political power of the indigenous bourgeoisie. Yet prerevolutionary Iran was already a capitalist society, and, therefore, the concept of a bourgeoisie revolution does not apply to the changes produced by the revolution.

Finally, the dominant view in the literature is that the revolution was Islamic.[178] Therefore, it was unique. Islamic discourse shaped the revolutionary movement of 1977–79 and autonomously contributed to the causes and processes of the Iranian Revolution. Islam also conditioned political conflict and class struggle in the postrevolutionary period. The revolution also expanded the ulama's authority from the religious to the political arena and led to the formation of some sort of theocracy. Society was not to be governed by the general will of the people but by the law of Islam as it was interpreted by the jurisprudent. According to the Constitution of the Islamic Republic, the jurisprudent had veto power over all the decisions of the executive and legislative branches of the government.

Nevertheless, the concept of Islamic Revolution could be misleading because it does not capture the real content of the postrevolutionary changes. For one thing, the principle of governance by the jurisprudent worked so far as Khomeini was alive, and as Bazargan has aptly stated, the Islamic Republic "is a dress sewn to fit the Ayatollah."[179] Governance by the jurisprudent proved to be problematic. The most learned religious scholar (i.e., the *faqih*) may not necessarily be interested in politics or follow a political line consistent with the desires and wishes of the followers of Ayatollah Khomeini. Ayatollah Shari'atmadari, whose views contradicted Khomeini's, was dealt with harshly, and subsequently his title and clerical position were taken away. And Ayatollah Montazari, who was the official *faqih* and successor to Khomeini, later fell from grace and was expelled from the polity. For another, with the end of the revolution, Islamic discourse became the ideology of power. In contrast to the revolutionary situation of 1977–79, Islam was no longer the most important organizing principle of society.

Third World Fascism?

Under the Islamic Republic, many traditional social institutions were revived and the society was considerably desecularized. Nevertheless, the postrevolutionary outcomes do not represent the triumph of traditionalism over modernity. Nor is the present regime the restoration of a past rule. While the Islamic Republic is rather a new experience in Iranian history, it is not a unique historical category. This is because this new type of government displays intriguing similarities to reactionary "revolutions" of the fascist type. Such similarities may be established by focusing on some of the key observable features of the Islamic Republic and its underlying dynamics of class and political conflict. These features are: the salience of ideology, the autonomy of the state, and terror and the system of police control.

Ideology. One of the conspicuous features of both fascism and the Islamic Republic is ideology. To be sure, all states have a certain ideology, which justifies their practice and rule over the people. But common to the ideologies of both regimes, in Togliati's words, is "an amalgam of contradictory elements"[180] such as stress on heroism, violence and the glorification of death, antiliberalism, antimaterialism, and anti-Communism. For example, "Fascism," says Palmeiri,

> turns toward the individual and tells him: Thy life has no absolute, no eternal value whatsoever; thy life can assume worth only inasmuch as it is devoted and, if necessary, sacrificed to the triumph of an idea. Men live today, die tomorrow, but ideas live forever. And the one who will seek to save his own life shall truly lose it, because only by offering it in holocaust to an everlasting Idea does individual life partake of the character of immortality.[181]

It is, the same authority continues, fascist "ambition to place ideals above wants, sacrifice above desires, heroism, martyrdom and death above cowardice, safety and well-being."[182] Similarly, martyrdom (*Shahadat*) and heroism are the central concepts of the ideology of the Islamic Republic. According to Ayatollah Motahhari:

> From the Islamic point of view, only that person is regarded as having secured the status of *shahid* [martyred] who Islam recognizes as having acted according to its own standards. Only he who is killed in an effort to achieve the highest Islamic objectives and is really motivated by a desire to safeguard true human values attains this position, which is one of the highest to which one can aspire. . . .
>
> With respect to the proximity of the *shahid* to God, the noble Quran says: "Think not of those who were slain in the way of God as dead. Nay, they are alive, finding their sustenance with their Lord."
> . . . *Shahadat* is heroic and admirable, because it results from a voluntary, conscious and selfless action. It is the only type of death which is higher, greater and holier than life itself.[183]

As for the antimaterialist view of life propagated by both regimes, the leaders of the Islamic Republic often argued that the people did not make revolution for material well-being and that the issue was not "the availability of oranges and grapes." The revolution was rather for the spiritual revival and return to the fundamentals of Islam.[184] In the same vein, a fascist ideologue complained that "the values which modern man prizes and covets are not invisible, spiritual values, but material and tangible ones. Did not recently the head of a great nation announce as supreme blessing for his people the presence of an automobile in every garage and a chicken in every pot?"[185]

The Autonomy of the State. Another important characteristic of the fascist state is its relative autonomy from the dominant classes. The state's autonomy under fascism is believed to have originated from the internal contradictions of dominant classes and their contradictions with the dominated classes.[186] Similarly, the revolutionary movement under the ulama's leadership throughout its rise and conquest of power had been relatively autonomous from the indigenous dominant classes. True, historically the politics of the ulama had been conditioned by their underlying class bases—the merchants, the petty bourgeoisie, and the landowners. The relativity of this autonomy should be emphasized because while the merchants and the landowners were unable to dictate state policies directly, they were in a favorable position to effectively veto the social revolutionary measures.

Terror and the System of Police Control. Like most Fascist rulers, Khomeini and his followers came to power in a perfectly constitutional manner. While in power, they used various revolutionary committees, the IRP, the mosques, and the mass media inherited from the previous regime to mobilize support for their objectives. The ruling clerics used the bands of *Hezbullah* to harass and repress rival political groups. The role of the *Hezbullah* was to disrupt the rallies and meetings of other groups under the implicit (and often explicit) approval of the Revolutionary Guards. In turn, the government (under the pretext of maintaining order and security) would ban all political gatherings and rallies. Policing the everyday activities of the people was also conducted by groups such as *Gasht-i Sarullah* and *Jandullah,* which were in charge of enforcing the Islamic moral code as well as helping to mobilize volunteers for the war (often hunting down eligible young men and forcing them to perform their compulsory military service).

Covert actions and conspiracies were another significant means of repressing dissident political groups during the initial years of the Islamic Republic. However, with the consolidation of the Islamic Republic and the emergence of the reign of terror, open repression supplanted secrecy and the use of arbitrary power mocked the constitution. The murder of the leaders and members of the Central Organ of the Peasants' Council in Turkman-Sahra exemplifies this process: to destroy the peasants' movement in this area and eliminate the influence of the Feda'iyan, the Revolutionary Guards arrested the leaders of the peasants' council for questioning. Later on, their bodies were discovered in a remote area. At that time, the leaders of the Islamic Republic denied their involvement in the murder of these popular leaders of the Turkman. Ayatollah Sadiq Khalkhali, who was suspected of the act, announced, "I did not have anything to do with the killing of the four leaders of Turkman-Sahra. If anyone can provide evidence that they were executed under my order, I shall condemn myself to be executed."[187] In another interview, Khalkhali further claimed that he was not aware of their arrest, that he did not even know their names, and that he was in Tehran when he heard the news of their executions.[188] Over four years later, in the fall of 1984, Khalkhali confessed that it was he who had murdered these people: "In Gonabad I executed ninety-four people, including Tooma'j, Jorjani, Vahedi, and Makhtoom. I myself executed these people. I executed ninety-four people, not just one person. . . . I beat the people of the Turkman."[189] Khalkhali made these confessions to indicate his loyalty and service to the Islamic Republic, not to confess to a crime punishable by execution as he had announced four years earlier.

The above case, however, was for political control. In general, violence under the Islamic Republic had gone far beyond the suppression of opposition groups as a rational means of protecting the state. The regime's repressive measures included: sending young teenagers to the minefields in its war with Iraq; executing thousands of political prisoners; and torturing political prisoners, not simply to obtain information but also in order to get them to confess their "crimes" on television and radio and to testify to "the morality and rightfulness" of the Islamic Republic.[190] To use Arendt's terminology, terror is the essence of the Islamic Republic.

Moore has very intelligently uncovered the centrality of violence under fascism—a centrality in full accord with the repressive character of the Islamic Republic. "The stress on violence," says Moore,

goes far beyond any cold, rational appreciation of the factual importance of violence in politics to a mystical worship of "hardness" for
its own sake. Blood and death often acquire overtones of erotic attraction, though in its less exalted moment fascism was thoroughly
"healthy" and "normal," promising return to a cosy bourgeois, and
even prebourgeois peasant womb.[191]

However, the substantial identification of fascism with the Islamic
Republic is not simply based on abstracting certain formal features
common to both regimes. For in that case one could also come up with
enough differences between the two—namely, the centrality of the party under the Islamic Republic began to decline, and the IRP was later
dissolved; also, the government's initial target of attack was the dependent bourgeoisie and international capital rather than the working-
class movement; and the economic and political contexts from which
the Islamic Republic arose were quite different from those of fascism.

These differences, however, do not seem to be crucial enough to question the similarity in the underlying class and political dynamic that
characterizes both the fascist regime and the Islamic Republic. In both
cases, the major class basis of support had been the petty bourgeoisie,
who were drawn into revolutionary activities as a result of economic
pressure from the monopoly capital. This class was crucial in bringing
both regimes to power. The influence of the petty bourgeoisie in both
cases was largely expressed on political (their extensive participation in
the party and other organs of the government) and ideological (status
quo anticapitalism) levels. Moreover, the crisis of the Left was also an
important factor facilitating the consolidation of power in both regimes. However, neither regime could be defined as a dictatorship of the
petty bourgeoisie; indeed in both cases, with the consolidation of the
state's power, the influence of the petty bourgeoisie began to decline. As
the fascist Grand Council constituted the supreme body for decision-
making,[192] the Council of Constitutional Guardians became the center
of power that subordinated the party and the parliament to its decisions. As Poulantzas has noted, "By nationalizations and by expropri-
ating the old bourgeoisie, also by dominating the state apparatus, the
petty bourgeoisie upper ranks of this apparatus often manage to sub-
stitute themselves for the old bourgeoisie."[193] A similar process characterized the decline of the political power of the petty bourgeoisie in
postrevolutionary Iran. Finally, both regimes rested on a solid coalition

between two classes: in the case of fascism it was a coalition between the feudal landowners and the bourgeoisie, while under the Islamic Republic it was the landowners and the merchants. While the state under the late Shah functioned to disorganize and destroy all major associations in society, the Islamic Republic functioned to organize the merchants and landowners but disorganize the peasants and the working class.

The fascist state emerged under conditions of political crisis within the context of advanced capitalism. The Islamic Republic, on the other hand, emerged under difficult economic conditions within a third world context. Such a context, which is characterized by a low level of economic development and technology, limited the expansionist aims of the Islamic Republic. Thus, to emphasize its difference with first world fascism, the Iranian case is suggested as a third world variant of fascism.

The Iranian Revolution and the Idea of Progress

In Marx's view, revolutions, by resolving the contradiction between the forces and relations of production and eliminating the rule of the old social classes, pave the way for human progress and the development of history. In his commentary on the French Revolution, for example, Marx credited the gigantic broom of the French Revolution for sweeping away all the "medieval rubbish":

> The centralized State power, with its ubiquitous organs of standing army, police, bureaucracy, clergy, and judicature—organs wrought after the plan of a systematic and hierarchic division of labor—originates from the days of absolute monarchy, serving nascent middle-class society as a mighty weapon in its struggle against feudalism. Still, its development remained clogged by all manner of medieval rubbish, seignorial rights, local privileges, municipal and guild monopolies and provincial constitutions. The gigantic broom of the French Revolution of the eighteenth century swept away all these relics of bygone times, thus clearing simultaneously the social soil of its last hindrances to the superstructure of the modern State edifice raised under the First Empire, itself the offspring of the coalition wars of old semi-feudal Europe against modern France.[194]

The Iranian Revolution, however, does not conform to the Marxian model. First, in postrevolutionary Iran, one witnesses an expansion of what might be called "scientific underdevelopment." The cultural revolution launched in the spring of 1980 and the subsequent shutdown of all universities and colleges for nearly three years had devastating effects on academia. The leaders of the Islamic Republic canceled those college-level science courses that in one way or another contradicted their views of nature (the social sciences were subjected to even more restrictions). Courses dealing with evolution and certain portions of biology and geology courses were omitted from school curricula. In high schools, the use of laboratory experiments and scientific field trips were eliminated, while the performance of religious ceremonies increased considerably.[195] Close to four thousand university professors were purged. At Tehran University, the number of scientific personnel declined from 2,100 in 1978 to 1,500 in 1984.[196] And the Minister of Sciences, in his report to the parliament, confessed that the number of university professors had declined from 13,900 in 1978 to 6,500 in 1984.[197]

Second, Iran also experienced some degree of "social underdevelopment." The most vivid example is penal law under the Islamic Republic. If we accept the view that there is an evolutionary process in the development of penal laws and criminal sentencing from cruel measures based upon revenge and retaliation to a more humanitarian treatment of criminals (such as the use of correction institutions, probations, and similar measures), then the penal law of the Islamic Republic is a definite revival of the medieval philosophy of punishment—penalties mainly, if not solely, based on revenge. Iran's notorious law of retaliation [*Qanoun-i Qisas*] is a case in point. This law contains two parts: retaliation through execution [*Qisas-i Nafs*] and retaliation through the removal of the same organ that the offender has injured or damaged. The whole law consists of eighty articles. The following are a few examples:

> *Article 5:* If a Muslim man intentionally kills a Muslim woman, he is condemned to death, but the woman's guardian should pay half of the man's bloodmoney to the offender before he is executed.
> *Article 6:* If a Muslim woman intentionally kills a Muslim man, she is condemned to death and receives no bloodmoney.
> *Article 33:* (a) Intentional homicide will be proven with the witnessing of two honest men. (b) Unintentional homicide will be proven with the witnessing of two honest men or one honest man and two honest women.

It should be noted that both in penalties and as witnesses two women are needed to equal one man.

The specification of *Qisas-i Ozv* is a further indication of penal cruelty. According to Article 62, if the offender has caused the removal of the victim's right hand, then his/her right hand should be removed; in cases where the offender has no right hand, then his/her left hand should be removed; and in cases where the offender has no hand at all, then his/her leg should be removed. (Theft under certain conditions is also punishable by the removal of the offender's fingers). Extremely harsh punishments are also applied to cases such as drinking, homosexuality, and adultery.[198]

Third, there has been a revival of patriarchal relationships in family and society. The Islamic Republic officially sanctions the superiority of men over women in society, and husband over wife in the family. As mentioned above, the laws of the Islamic Republic imply that one man is worth two women, both in terms of witnessing and in terms of capital punishment. Furthermore, women's inheritance rights are half those of men. Women are also prohibited from becoming singers (on the grounds that women's voices are sexually stimulating) or athletes,[199] and are barred from studying in certain fields such as agriculture, technical engineering, geology, mining, and archaeology.[200] The Islamic Republic's view concerning women is described by Reja-ie, a woman representative in the parliament of the Islamic Republic: "A woman, like a child, is stubborn and inflexible and does not know her own good, and in order to train her, physical punishment and violence may become necessary."[201] Within the family, the Islamic Republic has revived and reinforced many patriarchal relationships. Polygamy is officially sanctioned, and men are allowed to have as many as four permanent wives (and an unspecified number of "temporary" wives). In many respects, a woman is expected to follow the order of her husband.[202]

Therefore, although the Iranian Revolution overthrew the monarchy and many hereditary privileges, thus far it has not led to the emergence of modern social institutions characteristic of other social revolutions. Marx may have been correct when he stated that the French Revolution was a gigantic broom that swept away all the medieval rubbish of the Middle Ages. However, in the present case, it was the gigantic broom of the Iranian Revolution that swept all the medieval rubbish back in.

Conclusion: Ideology and Revolution

The Iranian case provided a serious anomaly to many currently dominant theories of revolution. The revolution occurred without the breakdown of the state, without the presence of a serious economic or political crisis, and without even the participating groups and classes having the kind of organizational resources necessary to paralyze the formidable power of the state. More crucial was the role played by ideology in the emergence of revolutionary crisis and in sustaining the revolutionary movement against the state. Therefore, the chief problem encountered in this work was how to incorporate ideology into a coherent explanation of the causes and processes of the Iranian Revolution, and to suggest a model on revolution that could be applied to other cases. To this end, three major presuppositions in the existing theories of revolution were addressed. First, all these theories have either reduced the dynamic of ideology to its psychological functions for disoriented individuals under the situation of social strain, to a dynamic of political power or class interests; or they have over looked the role of ideology in revolution altogether. Second, they rest on the assumption that human action is either dictated by abstract values or rational interests. Finally, these theories have conceptualized revolution only in terms of its content—that is, as a set of fundamental changes transpiring in a short period of time. As an alternative, ideology in this book has been treated as an autonomous category, with a dynamic of its own, not reducible to its psychological function or to the dynamic of political or class interests. Revolutionary ideology is conceptualized as an episodic discourse, a set of general principles, concepts, symbols, and rituals that human actors use in addressing the problems of social life in a particular historical period. The second assumption is also dropped because, as Swidler aptly states, people do not act piece by piece according to their interests or values; rather, they develop strategies of action. Ideology contributes to the cause of human action by shaping these strategies. Finally, this book has argued that a theory of revolution should take the revolutionary phenomenon seriously. Revolution is not simply a content produced by the dynamic of contention for power and class conflict but also a mode of historical action that is shaped by the dynamic of revolutionary ideology.

Revolution As a Content

Political conflict and class struggle are permanent features of all societies; these may be sporadic or periodic, having different degrees of intensity and generality. Class struggle is often confined within civil society, and political conflict is usually directed toward the redistribution of power without aiming to overthrow the state. Revolution is a particular form of conflict that is directed toward the seizure and transformation of state power, and may culminate in a social transformation. Social scientists have suggested a variety of ways that sociopolitical conflicts culminate in political crisis and then revolution. For example, for Wolf peasant-based social revolution in the twentieth century has occurred as a result of the interaction between capitalist infiltration of agrarian society, the ensuing socioeconomic and political crises, and the capacity of the peasants to develop a response to the crises. For Paige, on the other hand, agrarian revolution occurs when the relationship between the cultivators (the exploited class) and the noncultivators (the surplus appropriating class) is organized in a particular fashion. Finally, for Skocpol, the breakdown of a state's repressive capacity is a precondition for the outbreak of a social revolution.

Likewise, the simultaneity of the struggle of diverse classes and groups contributed to the making of the Iranian Revolution. The overlapping of two sets of class conflict underlay the revolutionary movement of 1977–79. One was the struggle of the merchants and petty bourgeoisie against international capital and dependent bourgeoisie for control of the market. The process of dependent development deepened this conflict. The second set was the struggle between workers and capitalists, which intensified as a result of the economic difficulties of the 1970s. Some of the salient features of the postrevolutionary outcomes were also determined by class. Class struggle was manifested in the emergence of three significant issues: land reform, labor law, and the nationalization of foreign trade. The final resolution of the conflicts over these issues in favor of the merchants and landowners was attributed to their class capacity vis-à-vis workers and peasants.

Class conflict, however, was analyzed in conjunction with the generation of political power. The role of the postcoup bureaucratic-authoritarian state in systematically fragmenting and disorganizing the indigenous classes in society channeled the oppositional activities into the medium of religion. Moreover, its intervention in the economy in favor of international capital was an important factor in antagonizing all the indigenous classes. The state's ideology, which glorified pre-Islamic kingship and culture, shaped the ideology of the opposition. In the postrevolutionary period, the political processes at both the national and international level had also a decisive role in shaping the postrevolutionary outcomes. The outbreak of the Iran-Iraq war, while facilitating the consolidation of the Islamic Republic, undermined the social revolutionary movement. Finally, the Islamic Republic systematically disorganized workers and peasants, but organized merchants and landowners, hence contributing to the failure of the social revolutionary movement.

Revolution As a Mode

However, rational contentions for power and class conflict do not capture the specificity of the revolutionary phenomenon. The emergence of revolutionary action cannot be automatically deduced from the structural conditions preceding the outbreak of revolution or from the organization of the groups and classes involved. The state's repressive apparatus may break down, the dominant classes may be weakened, and social conflict may intensify; yet revolution may not necessarily follow—as was shown to be the case in Iran in 1941. Alternatively, the breakdown of the state, economic transformation, and the massive rebuilding of the state's bureaucratic and repressive structures into a new state regime may occur without a revolution. For example, the Syrian Baath party, after seizing power through a coup, made considerable changes in the state's structure and economy in a short period of time that were quite revolutionary in content. But a revolution is more than a set of rapid institutional changes in a relatively short period of time.

The central feature of the phenomenon of revolution is ideology. In fact, it is difficult to think of the Iranian Revolution without considering the role of Shi'i Islam in making and sustaining the revolutionary movement of 1977–79, and in contributing to the shaping of the postrevolutionary outcomes. The overthrow of the monarchy did not originate from the dynamic of the interests, opportunity, and solidarity structures of the diverse classes and groups involved in the Iranian Revolution. There was nothing inherent in the interests and organization of the bazaar and workers that necessitated the overthrow of the monarchy in a revolutionary manner. The interests of international capital and the state were not incompatible with those of the bazaaris, or even the workers. It was quite possible to incorporate the merchants of the bazaar into the alliance between the state and international capital. Likewise, some sort of accommodation was possible between the institution of monarchy and the Shi'i ecclesiastical establishment. When Sharif-Emami was appointed prime minister in August 1978, the leading ulama such as Ayatollah Shari'atmadari were willing to make a compromise with the Shah.

The revolutionary crisis began when the social discontent was expressed in terms of Shi'i revolutionary discourse. Dual sovereignty emerged because the state and the opposition were constituted by and through two mutually negating ideological universes. The themes of Shi'i revolutionary discourse (that Iran's problems were related to the West's cultural domination and the un-Islamic nature of the institution of monarchy, and that there was a religious solution to these problems) contradicted in essence the monarchy-centered nationalist discourse. Further, the discursive field generated by revolutionary Islam—that is, its symbolic structure, religious rituals, and theme of martyrdom— played a crucial role in providing an effective channel of communication among the various participants, in maintaining a continuity in the people's mobilization against the Shah, and in transcending the social differences in society in a communitarian direction. Shi'i revolutionary discourse transcended the class-divided and segmented Iranian society into an Islamic community (i.e., *ummat*) in conflict with a boundless tyrant (i.e., *taghut*). The dynamic of Shi'i revolutionary discourse also shaped the postrevolutionary events and structured the legitimacy of the arguments put forward by diverse political groups and social classes in advancing their interests.

The revolution was over when Shi'i revolutionary discourse was reduced to the ideology of the Islamic Republic, and at the same time was channeled to defend the interests of the merchants and landowners. The autonomy and the enhanced power of Shi'i revolutionary discourse lay in the fact that it represented different things to the diverse groups and classes involved in the revolution. However, when Shi'i revolutionary discourse, through its own dynamic, assisted the consolidation of power by Khomeini and his followers and expanded the capacity of the merchants and landowners to defend their interests vis-à-vis the peasants and workers, it was conforming to the dominant political and economic interests. Shi'i discourse became closely associated with the state and the newly constituted dominant classes. Its revolutionary role was over.

Social Structure and Ideology

The model on ideology and revolution advanced in this work does not contradict the explanatory logic of the structural theories of revolution. The constitution of the state and its opposition in terms of mutually negating ideological universes does not alone explain the *success* of revolution. The (de facto) coalition between the dominated classes, the availability of a favorable opportunity for collective action, and the breakdown of the state's repressive capacity are important, if not central, conditions for the success of revolution. In explaining the contrast between Iran and Egypt, it was argued that the coalition between the merchants and the petty bourgeoisie was an important factor for the bazaar's political dynamism and the power of religious opposition in Iran. Egypt's divided Islamic movement, on the other hand, paralleled the existence of diverse political orientations between the indigenous dominant classes and the petty bourgeoisie. Moreover, the success of the Syrian state in resisting the revolutionary challenge of the Islamic opposition was partly related to its strong basis in the rural areas and among workers, while in Iran, in contrast, the state failed to establish a solid alliance with the peasants or workers.

Nevertheless, as this work has demonstrated, class and state action must be analyzed within the context of the dominant discourse in society. For example, the merchant class has been one of the most important actors in Iran's contemporary history. Coalesced with the petty bourgeoisie, the merchants of the bazaar were the leaders of the tobacco movement of 1890–92 and the Constitutional Revolution of

1905–11, the supporters of Mosaddeq's oil nationalization movement of the early 1950s, and the prime beneficiaries of the postrevolutionary outcomes. However, their political actions in these different episodes were shaped by the dominant discourse in society. The merchants participated in the Constitutional Revolution under the banner of secularism, nationalism, and democracy. In the 1941–53 period, national-liberalism shaped the bazaaris' political actions in the Society of Merchants and Guilds. But in postrevolutionary Iran, the Committee on Guild Affairs turned out to be more effective in organizing the bazaaris and defending their interests than the Society of Merchants and Guilds of Tehran Bazaar. The latter failed partly because it was rooted in national-liberal ideology, while the former was shaped by Islamic revolutionary discourse.

Likewise, the state's actions in contemporary Iran were shaped by discourse. Reza Shah's success in implementing a modernization program that undermined the socioeconomic and political power of the ulama, glorified pre-Islamic kingship and culture, and changed the way people dressed (including prohibiting the veil) cannot be explained simply in terms of his leadership capability and military power. He was successful because his ideology and the dominant cultural trend within civil society belonged to the same ideological universe. But under his son the ideology of the opposition began to change. The postcoup social critics and ideologues began to resort to Islam in their attempt to address Iran's problems. The more the Shah insisted on his secular antireligious ideology, the less he was applauded by his critics—and the more his discourse widened the gap between the state and civil society.

Finally, the ulama's political behavior was also conditioned by the kind of discourse dominant in society. During the Constitutional Revolution when the themes of nationalism, secularism, and democracy informed politics, the leading ulama such as Sayyid Mohammad Tabataba-ie and Hosein Na'ini advanced an Islamic justification for constitutionalism. And the prominent Shaykh Fazlullah Nuri—who had developed a strong critique of the constitutional movement, defended an Islamic conception of government, and allied with the royalist forces—was eventually executed. In the national-liberal episode, when the ideology of national-liberalism was the dominant discourse, the prominent Burujirdi attempted to depoliticize religion and instructed the ulama not to participate in political parties. But when revolutionary Islam was the dominant discourse of the opposition, the ulama had every reason to interfere in politics. When Ayatollah Khomeini, among other things, categorically rejected the concept of democracy on the grounds it was a Western concept (by and large the same kind of argument that brought Nuri's execution), the majority of the public followed him. While the ulama's relationships with the state and social classes are important in determining their politics, such relationships must be analyzed within the context of the kind of discourse dominant in society in order to fully understand the diverse political behavior and varying success of such prominent ayatollahs as Nuri, Burujirdi, and Khomeini.

The Iranian case has implications for the sociological theories of revolution. The individualistic theories of revolution rest on the notion that there is a discontinuity between revolutionary and routine contentions for power. In contrast, the organizational theories of revolution reject such a notion by emphasizing that revolutionary action is a form of resource mobilization similar in logic to routine contentions for power. The foregoing analysis, however, modifies this claim. Since revolution is a mode, there is a serious difference between revolutionary and routine contentions for power. Revolutionary action is dictated by the dynamic of revolutionary ideology, while economic and political considerations play a secondary role. People behave differently in a revolutionary movement. The availability of resources in a revolutionary situation is quite important, but, as the Iranian case demonstrates, groups who are successful in realizing their objectives are often the ones whose action is consistent with the dynamic of ideology. It is not simply that ideology contributes to the resources of certain groups vis-à-vis others. It is rather that the resource itself is constituted by and through discourse.

The relative contribution of ideology to the making of revolution may vary from case to case. For future research, analyses of the rise of the revolutionary ideology should, first, proceed with an account of the nature of the broad episodic context in which it emerges. This includes changes in the economy and class relations, the nature of the international context (including not only the world economy and interstate system but also the nature of international ideological relations), and the nature of the relationships between the state and civil society. Second, since revolutionary ideology is produced within the context of the state-opposition dialectic, the ideology of the state provides an important clue for understanding the probable nature of the ideology of its opposition. Third, the probability of the emergence of revolutionary ideology is enhanced if the state's ideology and the dominant cultural trend within civil society belong to different ideological universes. Finally, considerations should be given to the basic themes, ritual performances, and symbolic structures of the revolutionary ideology. These are the basic parameters that determine the internal dynamics of ideology as they shape human actions and limit the number of options available to diverse actors.

Notes

Introduction: Theories of Revolution

1. These are: the Iranian Revolution following excessively rapid modernization; the collapse of the state without the occurrence of war or pressure from abroad; and the fact of the revolution's being deliberately "made" by a mass-based social movement. See Theda Skocpol, "Rentier State and Shi'a Islam in the Iranian Revolution," p. 267.

2. François Furet, *Interpreting the French Revolution*.

3. For example, according to Tilly, theories of collective action are based on four broad traditions in sociology: Marxist, Durkheimian, Mill and utilitarian, and Weberian (see Tilly, *From Mobilization to Revolution*, chapter 2). Skocpol specifies four clusters of theories of revolution: Marxist, political conflict theories, aggregate psychological, and systems/value consensus theories. She also makes a distinction between the structural theory of revolution which becomes explicit in her work and voluntaristic theories of revolution (see Skocpol, *States and Social Revolutions*, chapter 1).

4. Tilly, "Revolution and Collective Violence," p. 487.

5. Johnson, *Revolution and the Social System* and *Revolutionary Change*.

6. Arendt, *The Origin of Totalitarianism* and *On Revolution;* and Kornhauser, *The Politics of Mass Society.*

7. Davies, "Toward a Theory of Revolution" and "The J-Curve of Rising and Declining Satisfaction," pp. 761–809, and Gurr, *Why Men Rebel*.

8. Huntington, *Political Order in Changing Societies*.

9. The claim that marginal and disoriented individuals are the most likely participants of revolutionary movements has been questioned by investigators. For example, for an empirical critique of the mass society theory see Oberschall, *Social Conflicts and Social Movements,* pp. 104–13. For critiques of marginality theory see Paige, "Political Orientation and Riot Participation," pp. 810–20; and Portes, "Political Primitivism," pp. 820–35.

10. Cantril, *The Psychology of Social Movements*, p. 64; and Toch, *Social Psychology*, p. 12.

11. Kornhauser, *The Politics of Mass Society*, p. 112.

12. Johnson, *Revolutionary Change*, pp. 82–83.

13. Schwartz, "Theory of Revolutionary Behavior," pp. 109–32.

14. Toch, *Social Psychology*, p. 17.

15. Smelser, *Theory of Collective Behavior*, pp. 79–84.

16. Dion, "Political Ideology," p. 52; and Apter, *Ideology and Discontent*, p. 18.

17. Wuthnow, "State Structures and Ideological Outcomes," p. 816.

18. Johnson, *Revolutionary Change*, pp. 119–34.

19. Davies, "Toward a Theory of Revolution."

20. Kornhauser, *The Politics of Mass Society*.

21. Toch, *Social Psychology*, p. 30.

22. Cantril, *The Psychology of Social Movements*, pp. 210–70.

23. Watt, "Shi'ism Under the Umayyads," pp. 158–72.

24. Algar, *Religion and State*, p. 2.

25. Savory, "The Problem of Sovereignty," p. 10; see also Lambton, "The Persian Ulama," pp. 245–68.

26. Arjomand, *The Turban for the Crown*, pp. 4–5.

27. Ibid., p. 107.

28. Ibid., p. 236n12.

29. Kazemi, *Poverty and Revolution;* and Parsa, *Social Origins of the Iranian Revolution*.

30. Arjomand, *The Turban for the Crown*, pp. 15, 106.

31. Abrahamian, *Iran Between Two Revolutions*, p. 6.

32. Ibid., p. 435.

33. Oberschall, *Social Conflicts*, p. 28.

34. Ibid.

35. Ibid., p. 33.

36. Tilly, *From Mobilization to Revolution*, p. 98.

37. Ibid., p. 191.

38. Zaret, "Religion and the Rise of Liberal-Democratic Ideology," p. 164.

39. Tilly, *From Mobilization to Revolution*, p. 203.

40. Fulbrook, *Piety and Politics*, p. 16.

41. Zaret, *The Heavenly Contract*, p. 5.

42. Wuthnow, "State Structures and Ideological Outcomes."

43. Stepan, "State Power and the Strength of Civil Society," p. 338.

44. Neuhouser, "The Radicalization of the Brazilian Catholic Church," pp. 233–44.

45. Keddie, "The Roots of Ulama Power," p. 223.

46. Marx, "Preface to *A Contribution to the Critique of Political Economy*," p. 182.

47. Keddie, "The Iranian Revolution," p. 591.

48. Keddie, *Roots of Revolution*, p. 273.

49. Ibid., pp. 164–69.

50. Parsa, *Social Origins of the Iranian Revolution*, pp. 29–30.

51. Ibid., p. 124.

52. Ibid., p. 14.

53. Ibid., p. 23.

54. Swidler, "Culture in Action," p. 277.

55. Wuthnow, *Communities of Discourse*, p. 16.

56. Therborn, *The Ideology of Power*, p. 81.

57. Geertz, *The Interpretation of Culture*, p. 219; and Smelser, *Theory of Collective Behavior*, p. 207.

58. Turner, *The Forest of Symbols*, p. 30.

59. Alexander, "Correcting Misinterpretations of Turner's Theory," p. 27.

60. Langer, *Philosophy in a New Key*, p. 117.

61. The correspondence theory of ideology establishes a causal relationship between social structure and ideology. Different versions of this theory are suggested in Weber's theory of *elective affinity*, Marx's theory of *substructure-superstructure*, and Durkheim's theory of the *mimetic* character of ideology.

62. Furet, *Interpreting the French Revolution*.

63. Huntington, *Political Order in Changing Societies*, p. 266.

64. Sewell, Jr., "Ideologies and Social Revolutions," pp. 57–85.

65. Furet, *Interpreting the French Revolution*, p. 22.

66. Ibid., p. 23.

67. The concept of ideological universe is borrowed from Berger and Luchmann, "Sociology of religion and sociology of knowledge," pp. 70–71.

68. Wuthnow, *Communities of Discourse*, p. 13.

69. Alexander, "Correcting Misinterpretations," pp. 27–28.

70. Therborn, *The Ideology of Power*, p. 117.

71. The concept of historical-structural is borrowed from Cardoso and Faletto and is used here in a similar sense. They argue that "Social structures are the product of man's collective behavior. Therefore, although enduring, social structures can be, and in fact are, continuously transformed by social movements. Consequently, our approach is both structural and historical—it emphasizes not just the structural conditioning of social life but also the historical transformation of structures by conflict, social movements, and class struggles. Thus our methodology is historical-structural." See Cardoso and Faletto, *Dependency and Development in Latin America*, p. x.

72. The contradictions between the forces and relations of production is not always central in all revolutions. Godelier, for example, suggests that this contradiction attains centrality only during the latter period of capitalist development and that during the period of capitalist ascendancy, when other modes of production still persist, it is the contradiction between modes of production, not within the capitalist mode, that is central for understanding the generation of class struggles and revolutionary movements. The importance of various contradictions identified

within Marxist theory, in other words, is historically variable, rather than rigidly fixed. See Godelier, *Rationality and Irrationality in Economics,* pp. 77–82.

73. Larrain, *Marxism and Ideology,* p. 166.

74. Ibid.

75. Thompson, *The Making of the English Working Class,* p. 9.

76. The tendency toward structural reductionism and formalism is evident in the works of Poulantzas and Balibar, especially when these authors attempt to explain variations in different structures—types of mode of production as functions of diverse combinations of different instances (ideological, political, and economic). In particular, one may cite Balibar's definition of the determination of the economy in the last instance: "In different structures, the economy is determinant in that it determines which of the instances of the social structure occupies the determinant place." See Etienne Balibar, "On the Basic Concepts of Historical Materialism," p. 224, in Althusser and Balibar, *Reading Capital.*

Similarly, Poulantzas attempts to derive different forms of the capitalist state by virtue of its relations to socioeconomic relations, "by reference to the *degree* and the *specific forms*" of its autonomy from economic structure (see Poulantzas, *Political Power and Social Classes,* p. 148). Less attempt is made to pose the question of the state's diverse forms within the context of concrete historical conditions (i.e., diverse forms of the state arise by virtue of its relations to the metropolitan states, changes in world politics and military competition, the particular class coalition constituting the basis of the state, the state's sources of revenues and its role in the economy, etc.). For a critique of structural abstractionism and formalism, see Laclau, *Politics and Ideology in Marxist Theory,* pp. 69–79.

77. See Griffin, Wallace, and Rubin, "Capitalist Resistance," pp. 147–48; and Przeworski, "Proletariat into a Class," pp. 373–401.

78. Aminzade, *Class, Politics and Early Industrial Capitalism,* p. xiii.

79. Tilly, *From Mobilization to Revolution;* see also Griffin, Wallace, and Rubin, "Capitalist Resistance."

80. Poulantzas, *Political Power,* p. 14.

81. See Coward and Ellis, *Language and Materialism,* p. 8.

82. Todd and Fisher, *Gender and Discourse,* p. 8.

83. Lenin, "The State and Revolution," *Collected Works,* 25:393.

84. See Wallerstein, *The Modern World-System* and *The Capitalist World Economy.*

85. Pompermayer, for example, argues that the reorganization of the world economy brings about a reorganization of the dependent state structures (Pompermayer, "The State and Dependent Development," pp. 25–27). See also Immanuel Wallerstein, "Comments on 'The State and Dependent Development' by Pompermayer," *Kapitalistate* 1 (1973): 28–29.

86. Hein and Stenzel, "The Capitalist State and Underdevelopment in Latin America."

87. For a discussion on how colonial experience structures the postcolonial state, see Alavi, "The State in Post-Colonial Societies," pp. 59–81; and Leys, "The Overdeveloped Post-Colonial State," pp. 39–58.

88. See O'Donnell, "Corporatism and the Question of the State," p. 54, and "Reflections on the Pattern of Change," pp. 3–38. See also Fitzgerald et al., *The State and Economic Development in Latin America*, p. 48.

89. Proponents of this view advance the theory of state capitalism in the periphery. State capitalism develops as a consequence of anti-imperialist struggles and the search for a "nonsocialist alternative" to dependency. The successful establishment of this form of state is attributed to the intensification of interimperialist rivalries and the decline of the United States' hegemony. This international conjuncture provided favorable conditions for state capitalist regimes to emerge and also to impose demands on and gain significant concessions from foreign capital. See James Petras, *Critical Perspectives on Imperialism and Social Class in the Third World;* Farsoun, "State Capitalism in Algeria,"pp. 3–30; Fernandez and Ocampo, "The Andean Pact and State Capitalism in Colombia"; and Pfeifer, "State Capitalism and Development," pp. 3–11.

90. See Amin, *Accumulation on a World Scale;* and Petras and Morley, "Development and Revolution," p. 4.

91. Skocpol, "Cultural Idioms," p. 91.

1. Episode and Discourse: The Rise and Decline of Nationalist-Liberal Ideology

1. Brecht, as cited in Wolf, *Peasant Wars of the Twentieth Century,* p. 275.

2. Ahmad, *Islamic Modernism,* p. ix; and Adams, *Islam and Modernism in Egypt,* p. 13.

3. Turner, *Weber and Islam,* p. 147.

4. See Butterworth, "Prudence versus Legitimacy," pp. 84–114.

5. Turner, *Weber and Islam,* p. 147.

6. See Marsot, *Egypt's Liberal Experiment;* Vatikiotis, *The History of Egypt;* and Ansari, *Egypt: The Stalled Society.*

7. Adami'yat, *Idi'olozhi-ye.*

8. Ahmad, *Islamic Modernism,* pp. 37–38.

9. Amir Ali, *The Spirit of Islam,* and Iqbal, *The Reconstruction of Religious Thought in Islam* and *Speeches and Statements of Iqbal;* and Smith, *Modern Islam in India.*

10. Sayeed, "Religion and Nation Building in Pakistan," pp. 279–91.

11. See Rabinovich, *Syria Under the Ba'th: 1963–66;* Torrey, *Syrian Politics and the Military;* and Seale, *The Struggle for Syria.*

12. Butterworth, "Prudence versus Legitimacy," p. 87.

13. See Mitchell, *The Society of the Muslim Brothers;* and Marsot, *Egypt's Liberal Experiment,* pp. 231–37.

14. Batatu, "Syria's Muslim Brethren," p. 12; Seale, *The Struggle for Syria,* p. 79; and Hinnebusch, "The Islamic Movement in Syria," p. 150.

15. Rabinovich, *Syria Under the Ba'th,* pp. 109–26; Lawson, "Social Bases for the Hamah Revolt," pp. 24–28; and Batatu, "Syria's Muslim Brethren," pp. , 12–20, 34, 36.

16. For more information on Jamma'at-i Islami, see Bahadur, *The Jamma'at-i Islami of Pakistan*.

17. Keddie, *Roots of Revolution*, p. 82; and Abrahamian, *Iran Between Two Revolutions*, pp. 164–65.

18. Ivanov, *Tarikh-i*, pp. 106–14.

19. Ibid., pp. 114–15.

20. Halliday, *Iran: Dictatorship and Development*, pp. 199–200. See also Kambakhsh, *Nazari*, pp. 62–63.

21. Mehraban, *Gousheha-ee*, pp. 119–28.

22. Ivanov, *Tarikh-i*, pp. 122–23.

23. Ibid., pp. 126–29, 140.

24. Abrahamian, *Iran Between Two Revolutions*, p. 251.

25. Azimi, *Iran: The Crisis of Democracy*.

26. Ibid., pp. 123–25.

27. Kasravi, *Chihil Maqalah-i Kasravi*, pp. 3–6.

28. Kasravi, *Dar Piramoun-i Islam*, pp. 4–5.

29. Ibid., pp. 5–33.

30. Ibid., pp. 34–64.

31. Cited in Faghfoory, "The Role of the Ulama in Twentieth-Century Iran," p. 63. The ulama and the landlords were also instrumental in assisting Reza Khan to power. See Moaddel, "The Shi'i Ulama and the State in Iran," pp. 534-35.

32. Cited in Mehraban, *Gousheha-ee*, p. 146 (my translation).

33. The Front's campaign for democracy had been triggered by voting frauds in the fifteenth parliamentary election. In October 1949, Mosaddeq led a crowd of politicians, university students, and bazaar traders into the Shah's palace to protest the lack of free elections. Once inside, the demonstrators elected a committee of twenty, headed by Mosaddeq, which soon became the nucleus of the National Front.

34. Walden, "The International Petroleum Cartel in Iran," p. 65.

35. Ibid., pp. 65–66; and Nirumand, *Iran: The New Imperialism in Action*, p. 32.

36. UN Department of Economic Affairs, *Development in the Middle East*, pp. 28–29.

37. Walden, "The International Petroleum Cartel," p. 71; and Nirumand, *Iran*, p. 33.

38. Anthony Eden, *Full Circle*, p. 229.

39. Cited in Nirumand, *Iran*, p. 61.

40. Mosaddeq, *UN Security Council Official Records*, pp. 19–20.

41. Saleh, *UN Security Council Official Records*, p. 15.

42. Mosaddeq, *UN Security Council Official Records*, p. 4.

43. See N. Gordon Levin, Jr., *Woodrow Wilson and World Politics* (New York: Oxford University Press, 1970).

44. *Time*, January 2, 1950, p. 60.

45. *Time*, March 20, 1950, p. 84; see also *Time*, February 13, 1950, p. 78.

46. Ibid., p. 77.

47. *Time*, March 20, 1950, p. 84.

48. Ibid., p. 85.

49. *US News and World Report*, April 6, 1951, p. 22.

50. *US News and World Report*, June 8, 1951, p. 16.

51. Keddie, *Roots of Revolution*, pp. 133–34; and Mehraban, *Gousheha-ee* , pp. 299–302.

52. Cited in Dshawanshir, *Tajrebeh-ye*, p. 53 (my translation).

53. See Spann, "Who Controls Crude Reserves?" pp. 221–22, 234. See also Baku, "Oil Revenue and Socio-Economic Development in Iran, 1963–1978," pp. 6, 66–67; and U.S. Government, "The International Petroleum Cartel," *Staff Report*, pp. 253–54.

54. *World Oil*, August 15, 1953, p. 92.

55. Walden, "The International Petroleum Cartel," p. 90.

56. Nirumand, *Iran*, p. 64.

57. *Staff Report*, "The International Petroleum Cartel," p. 254.

58. *World Oil*, March 1954, p. 242; and Walden, "The International Petroleum Cartel," p. 94.

59. Walden, "The International Petroleum Cartel," pp. 94–95.

60. Eden, *Full Circle*, p. 219.

61. Ibid., p. 222.

62. Ibid., p. 224.

63. *New York Times*, May 19, 1951, p. 4; and Dshawanshir, *Tajrebeh-ye*, pp. 115–16.

64. See Levy, "Economic Review," p. 94.

65. Ibid.

66. Dshawanshir, *Tajrebeh-ye*, pp. 153–58.

67. *New York Times*, March 21, 1952, p. 3.

68. White House Press Release, July 9, 1953.

69. Walden, "The International Petroleum Cartel," p. 81.

70. *New York Times*, December 8, 1952, p. 6.

71. Walden, "The International Petroleum Cartel," pp. 82–83.

72. *New York Times*, August 29, 1952, p. 5.

73. Walden, "The International Petroleum Cartel," p. 84.

74. *New York Times*, September 19, 1952, p. 8.

75. Nirumand, *Iran*, p. 71.

76. Walden, "The International Petroleum Cartel," pp. 85–86.

77. *New York Times*, January 3, 1952, p. 58.

78. Walden, "The International Petroleum Cartel," p. 97.

79. *New York Times*, August 30, 1952, p. 2.

80. Dshawanshir, *Tajrebeh-ye*, p. 242.

81. Eden, *Full Circle*, p. 230.

82. Cited in Dshawanshir, *Tajrebeh-ye*, p. 159.

83. Ibid.

84. Nirumand, *Iran*, pp. 109–10.
85. Dshawanshir, *Tajrebeh-ye*, pp. 158–86.
86. Keddie, *Roots of Revolution*, p. 136; and Abrahamian, *Iran Between Two Revolutions*, p. 273. It should be noted that the Society of Merchants and Guilds did support Mosaddeq after the coup. But this fact alone is not enough to argue that the Iranian bourgeoisie as a whole supported Mosaddeq during the final weeks of his premiership.
87. Abrahamian, *Iran Between Two Revolutions*, pp. 273–79.
88. See Kermit Roosevelt, *Countercoup*. For an analysis of the role of the International Petroleum Cartel in dictating U. S. policy in the Middle East and in encouraging the United States to participate in the coup against Mosaddeq, see Moaddel, "State-Centered vs. Class-Centered Perspectives in International Politics,"pp. 1–21.
89. Cited in Dshawanshir, *Tajrebeh-ye*, pp. 282–83.

2. The State and the Problem of National Integration

1. Stepan, "State Power and the Strength of Civil Society," p. 338.
2. See Fox, "Has Brazil Moved Toward State Capitalism?" p. 79. For discussions on the bureaucratic-authoritarian states in Latin America see O'Donnell, "Corporatism and the Question of the State" and "Reflections on the Pattern of Change"; and Fitzgerald et al., *The State and Economic Development in Latin America*.
3. Cited in Mahdavi, "Patterns and Problems of Economic Development in Rentier States," p. 442.
4. Huntington, *Political Order in Changing Societies*, p.196.
5. In fact, O'Donnell overemphasizes the subjective aspects of the precoup period as perceived by the authoritarian regime: that there was a need for order and that there was a Communist threat. In the case of Iran, such arguments were simply an ideological cover-up of the underlying material interests governing the actions of the parties who engineered and executed the coup.
6. This is not to argue that the Iranian state perfectly fits in the bureaucratic-authoritarian model, although the concept captures the reality of Iranian politics better than such concepts as patrimonialism, rentier state, and oriental despotism. Moreover, the BA paradigm is overly structural—despite O'Donnell's structural-historical approach—because it disregards the role of ideological and broader cultural factors in the constitution of the state and its opposition.
7. Out of those arrested, 71 were sentenced to death and 192 to life imprisonment; 129 were given fifteen-year sentences and the rest from three to ten years. After the execution of twenty-six officers, the government bowed before world public opinion and stopped the executions. Kambakhsh, *Nazari beh*, p. 217.
8. Cottam, *Nationalism in Iran*, p. 323.
9. See Halliday, *Iran: Dictatorship and Development*, pp. 75–90. Ex-CIA director William Colby, in a speech at Utah State University, said that "the CIA cre-

ated SAVAK, the Iranian Police Force, and taught it proper methods of intelligence." *Herald Journal Logan* (Utah), November 10, 1978, p. 2, col. 2.

10. In 1974, *Newsweek* magazine reported that by some estimates as many as 60,000 Iranians were full-time SAVAK operatives. What is more, according to a Western diplomat in Tehran, one out of every eight adults in the country was at least an occasional SAVAK informer. SAVAK used all means necessary to hunt down dissidents. It has been said that Iran had 20,000 political prisoners in jail at this time. Amnesty International maintained that large numbers of Iranians had been secretly executed for political opposition to the Shah (*Newsweek*, October 14, 1974, p. 61).

11. Abrahamian, *Iran Between Two Revolutions,* p., 420.

12. The Army intervened when SAVAK failed to control antigovernment movements. The military was used in crushing the mass uprising of June 1963 in Tehran and several other cities, and during the revolutionary movement of 1977–79. From 1963 to 1978 the Army frequently occupied universities, remained garrisoned near towns, and was sent into tribal areas on a number of small-scale campaigns. Halliday, *Iran: Dictatorship and Development,* p. 76.

13. Reich, "The United States and Iran," p. 7; and Sampson, *The Arms Bazaar,* p. 242.

14. Packard, as cited in Sampson, *The Arms Bazaar,* pp. 242–43.

15. Ibid.

16. Reich, "The United States and Iran," pp. 7–8; and Moran, "Iranian Defense Expenditure and the Social Crisis," p. 178.

17. Sampson, *The Arms Bazaar,* p. 244.

18. *Washington Post,* August 7, 1976. For a more detailed discussion of how the arms industry's salesmen were manipulating both the American and Iranian governments through their agents, see Sampson, *The Arms Bazaar,* chapter 14.

19. Abrahamian, *Iran Between Two Revolutions,* p. 435.

20. Halliday, *Iran: Dictatorship and Development,* pp. 72–73.

21. Moran, "Iranian Defense Expenditure," p. 180.

22. Indications of rapid state expansion during this period are the increases in its shares of aggregate consumption, gross domestic capital formation, and its expenditures as a percent of GNP. For example, public consumption in 1959–60 was 13 percent of aggregate consumption, while in 1975–76 this value increased to 33 percent. Similarly, in 1959–60, public investment was 39 percent of gross domestic capital formation, while in 1975–76 this value increased to 59 percent. During the same periods, public expenditures constituted 18 and 38.8 percent of GNP, respectively. See Karim Pakravan, "Government Intervention in the Industry of Iran, 1964–78" (Stanford, Calif.: Hoover Institute on War, Revolution, and Peace, July 1981), Working Paper.

23. Abrahamian, *Iran Between Two Revolutions,* p. 434.

24. Ibid., p. 438.

25. See Baldwin, *Planning and Development in Iran.*

26. Graham, *Iran: The Illusion of Power,* p. 85.

27. Zonis, *The Political Elite of Iran,* p. 86.

28. *Salnamah-ye Amari-ye Keshvar* [Annual national statistics], 1976.

29. Zonis, *The Political Elite*, pp. 88–90.

30. See Weber, *Economy and Society.*

31. See Moaddel, "The Shi'i Ulama," pp. 522–24; and Arjomand, *The Shadow of God and the Hidden Imam.*

32. Adami'yat, *Idi'olozhi-ye*, p. 193.

33. See Faghfoory, "The Role of the Ulama," pp. 73–92; Akhavi, *Religion and Politics in Contemporary Iran;* and Gallagher, "Contemporary Islam."

34. Halliday, *Iran: Dictatorship and Development*, p.59.

35. Faghfoory, "The Role of the Ulama," p. 90. This statement should be qualified because the Pahlavis utilized religious cleavages for the attainment of their political goals. In particular, when the Shah was signing the infamous contract with the international oil consortium, he unleashed the reactionary ulama in an anti-Baha'i campaign to divert attention away from the oil issue. The Shah also approved the establishment of the anti-Baha'i and anti-Communist Hujjatiyyah. Hujjatiyyah functioned in harassing the Baha'i in order to convert them to Shi'i Islam, thus it channeled the attention of Muslim activities away from political issues.

36. See Kasravi, *Din va Siyasat;* and Abrahamian, *Iran Between Two Revolutions,* 118–54.

37. Pahlavi, *Mission for My Country,* pp. 125–27.

38. Halliday, *Iran: Dictatorship and Development*, p. 27.

39. Pahlavi, *The White Revolution*, p. 15.

40. Ibid., p. 12.

41. Zabih, *Iran's Revolutionary Upheaval*, p. 3.

42. Lenczowski, ed, *Iran Under the Pahlavis*, p. 477.

43. Cited in Halliday, *Iran: Dictatorship and Development*, p. 58. Resort to such arguments by authoritarian rulers was not confined to the Iranian regime. Henderson in his analysis of the Chilean state after the coup maintains that "one of the most characteristic elements in the military's justification for their intervention is that which relates the coup to the inability of the 'politicians' to control events." See Henderson, "The Chilean State After the Coup," p. 132.

44. Zabih, *Iran's Revolutionary Upheaval*, p. 6.

45. Ibid., p. 7.

46. Ibid., p. 9.

3. The State and the Patterning of Class Conflict

1. Evans, *Dependent Development.*

2. Looney, *Economic Origins of the Iranian Revolution*, p. 26.

3. Abrahamian, *Iran Between Two Revolutions*, pp. 432–34; Halliday, *Iran: Dictatorship and Development*, pp. 15, 151; *Rahe Tudeh*, February 3, 1984, p. 5; and International Labor Office, *Employment and Income Policies for Iran*, p. 55, table 8.

4. For discussions on dependent development and the "export enclave" econ-

omy, see Cardoso and Faletto, *Dependency and Development;* Devuall et al., "A Formal Model of 'Dependencia' Theory," pp. 312–50; de Janvry and Garramon, "Laws of Motion of Capital" pp. 29–38; and Jaffee, "Export Dependence and Economic Growth," pp. 102–18.

5. O'Donnell, "Reflections on the Pattern of Change," pp. 21–22. In O'Donnell's view, the inclusion of the national bourgeoisie in the alliance is a necessity for the survival of the BA regime: "Neither the BA nor any other modern state ceases to be a national state. That is why it does not seem possible for the BA long to remain as impervious to its own society as it does during the periods of economic orthodoxy and the duo" (p. 20); and "the domination of the BA lacks, both politically and ideologically, a crucial component—the national and private ingredient that only the local bourgeoisie can contribute" (p. 22).

6. David E. Lilienthal, *Journals* (1969), 4:2.

7. Ibid., p. 80

8. Richards, "Land Reform and Agribusiness in Iran," p. 12.

9. Lilienthal, *Journals* (1969), 4:4.

10. Cited in ibid., p. 9.

11. Ibid.

12. Ibid., p. 10.

13. Bharier, *Economic Development in Iran,* pp. 90–95; and Looney, *Economic Origins,* p. 12.

14. Griggs, "Oil and Water Rebuild an Ancient Land," p. 128.

15. Ibid. See also Richards, "Land Reform and Agribusiness," p. 13.

16. Lilienthal, *Journals* (1971) 5:453.

17. Abrahamian, *Iran Between Two Revolutions,* p. 149.

18. See Keddie, "The Iranian Village Before and After Land Reform," p. 165.

19. Following World War II, the U.S. government encouraged land reform in countries under its influence. The initial thinking on this was developed in relation to Japan, where a group of sociologists, including Talcott Parsons, saw the need for a stable state to have a contented peasantry. Subsequent to the reforms in Japan, U.S. advisers helped to supervise reforms in China (prior to 1949), Korea, Taiwan, the Philippines, Egypt, Bolivia, and Iran (see Halliday, *Iran: Dictatorship and Development,* pp. 134–35). It is noteworthy that the Shah frequently stated his disappointment with U.S. pressures for reforms. Addressing an American reporter, the Shah once complained that "your worst period was in 1961 and 1962. But even before that, there were your great American 'liberals' wanting to impose their way of 'democracy' on others, thinking their way is wonderful. I think that policy has changed now" (see *U.S. News & World Report,* January 27, 1969, p. 49).

20. Keddie, "The Iranian Village," p. 165.

21. Cited in ibid., pp. 165–66.

22. Ibid., pp. 157–70.

23. Cited in Zonis, *The Political Elite of Iran,* pp. 58–59.

24. Three kinds of agricultural units were initiated by the state: rural cooperatives, farm corporations, and agribusinesses. The farm cooperatives were initially

promoted by Arsanjani. After his dismissal, these cooperatives were organized into the Central Organization of Rural Cooperatives (CORC). The Shah then brought in an army general, Esmail Riahi, as Minister of Agriculture, and a colonel, A. A. Valian, as Deputy Minister. CORC was then changed into the Ministry of Land Reform and Rural Cooperation, and then into the Ministry of Cooperation and Rural Affairs. According to government statistics, there were 838 cooperatives in 1968, which increased to 8,361 in 1972, and then declined to 2,886 in 1976. The membership, however, increased consistently from 1,260,000 in 1968 to 2,868,000 in 1976. See *Salnamah-ye Amari-ye Keshvar* [Annual national statistics], tables 125 and 289.

In contrast with farm corporations and agribusinesses, farm cooperatives were somewhat popular among peasant farmers. Nevertheless, the flow of government funds to these cooperatives had been a trickle compared to its expenditures in other areas. For example, in the period 1967–70, credits granted through cooperatives as a percentage of total credit in the agricultural sector ranged from 27 to 34 percent. Considering that credit to the agricultural sector as a percentage of total credit over the 1967–70 period declined from 10.7 to 8.1 percent, in 1970 only 2.7 percent of all credit granted in the country flowed through the cooperatives. See Richards, "Land Reform and Agribusiness," pp. 9–10.

25. *Salnamah-ye Amari-ye Keshvar* (1976).

26. *Barrasy-ye Sherkatha-ye Sahamy-ye Zerai* [A survey of the farm corporations] (N.p.: Organization of the Iranian People's Fedai'yan Guerrilla, n.d.), p. 9.

27. Cited in Brun and Dumont, "Iran: Imperial Pretensions and Agricultural Dependence," p. 18.

28. Besides the formation of these unpopular farm corporations, the state went as far as planning to dislocate the peasants in order to create populated rural regions. On June 9, 1975, a bill was passed for the creation of what were called "poles of development." Priority was given to twenty poles covering a potential area of 4.5 million acres, while government support was deliberately withheld from farms in the marginal zones. To discourage villagers from living outside these poles, the agricultural minister, Mansoor Rowhani had said:

> The agricultural bank is not to grant credit in the area nor is the National Petroleum Company to sell fuel cheaply. The Minister of Agriculture is not to ensure the protection of crops in the region or to make available the rent or sale of farm machinery. . . . No schools or dispensaries will be built and there will be no provision of roads or electricity. Thus the population living outside will be encouraged to migrate to the poles. (Brun and Dumont, "Iran," p.18)

29. The resistance of landowners was paramount in Khuzistan, where its governor-general, with the backing of the landowners, opposed the pilot irrigation project (which was one of the conditions the World Bank had laid down in 1959 for giving loans to Iran). Land reform solved this problem, and D&R technicians were forced to deal directly with the peasants until the staff of the newly created

Khuzistan Water and Power Authority (KWPA) had received the necessary training. Richards, "Land Reform and Agribusiness," p. 13.

"A child conceived by us [as Lilienthal called it] KWPA was considered as the Iranian regional agency similar to TVA that would take over the functions and responsibilities D&R was carrying such as operating the dam on Dez, the sugar plantation and refinery, irrigation facilities, the obligation to collect water charges, the power system, and so on." Lilienthal, *Journals* (1971), 5:137.

30. Richards, "Land Reform and Agribusiness," p. 14.

31. Field, "Agro-business and Agricultural Planning in Iran," p. 69.

32. Aresvik, *The Agricultural Development of Iran*, p. 105.

33. Halliday, *Iran: Dictatorship and Development*, pp. 117–18.

34. Richards, "Land Reform and Agribusiness," pp. 17–18. However, it should be noted that the sugar cane plantation near Haft Tapeh was exceptionally successful. By 1971, Haft Tapeh's 26,000 acres were producing one of the world's highest unit yields—twelve tons per hectare—and providing around 60,000 tons or 10 percent of Iran's sugar consumption (ibid.· p. 13; and Griggs, "Oil and Water," p. 128).

35. Brun and Dumont, "Iran," pp. 15–16.

36. Prior to 1953, Iran experienced little industrial development. Foreign investment, apart from the Anglo-Iranian Oil Company, was practically nonexistent for a variety of reasons, such as the lack of sufficient infrastructures, political instability, the absence of assurances of favorable legal treatment and exchange facilities for transfer of earnings, and the unwillingness of foreign capitalists to invest. The few foreign ventures operating in Iran were intimately connected with the government, even where some private financing was present. Investment by private foreign investors reached its nadir in 1951, when the AIOC was nationalized and subsequently shut down.

37. Benedick, *Industrial Finance in Iran*, p. 57. Favorable laws concerning taxes and subsidies were also passed. A complete five-year tax exemption to new industries outside the area of Tehran, and a 50 percent tax cut to those who were inside the area, were granted. An incentive to joint stock companies was a provision exempting 10 percent of profits from taxation. Further subsidies in the form of import duty rebates, subsidization of water, electricity, and energy costs, etc., were offered to the industries selected for growth.

38. Issawi, *Economic History of Iran*, p. 346.

39. Oveisi, "Entrepreneurial Activities of the Public Sector in the Economic Development Process," p. 13.

40. Benedick, *Industrial Finance*, p. 119

41. Ibid., pp. 120–21, and 251. See also Safari, *Enhesarha-ye*, pp. 52–54.

42. Benedick, *Industrial Finance*, p. 124.

43. Safari, *Enhesarha-ye*, pp. 53–54.

44. Ibid., p. 58.

45. Ibid., pp. 58–59.

46. According to one source, Russo-Iran Bank belongs to the Iranian govern-

ment. See Mohammad Atiqpour, *Naqsh-i Bazaar va Bazaari-ha dar Enqilab-i Iran* [The role of the bazaar and bazaaris in the Iranian Revolution] (Tehran: Keyhan Printing Office, 1358/1979).

47. For the list of these companies and their fields of activities see Safari, *Enhesarha-ye,* pp. 59–61.

48. Ibid., p. 54.

49. These figures are drawn from Bank Markazi Iran (henceforth, BMI), *Annual Report and Balance Sheet* (various issues).

50. Karim Pakravan, "Government Intervention in the Industry of Iran, 1964–78" (Stanford, Calif.: Hoover Institute on War, Revolution, and Peace, July 1981), Working Paper, p. 25.

51. Ibid., p. 27.

52. BMI, *Annual Report* (various issues).

53. UN Conference on Trade and Development (henceforth, UNCTAD), *Examination of Recent Developments,* p. 21.

54. BMI, *Annual Report* (1970), p. 9.

55. Ibid.

56. Walton, "Economic Development and Revolutionary Upheavals in Iran," p. 284.

57. BMI, *Annual Report* (1975), p. 32.

58. Graham, *Iran: The Illusion of Power,* p. 87.

59. The rapid expansion of government spending created a number of infrastructural bottlenecks that impeded economic growth. One was overloading the already overburdened port facilities. The existing port equipment in the Persian Gulf was insufficient and poorly maintained. Ships were having to wait up to 160 days and more before entering the harbor. Such delays cost the government a substantial amount of money. The total cost was difficult to quantify. The only readily identifiable costs were demurrage charges for keeping ships waiting at anchor. In 1974–75 these charges cost Iran over $1 billion, almost 5 percent of Iran's total foreign exchange earnings. Other infrastructural bottlenecks included the lack of enough skilled workers, inadequate transportation facilities, and an insufficient supply of electricity (see Graham, *Iran,* pp. 87–88).

60. The traditional manufacturing section includes such branches as textiles, wearing apparel, carpets, tobacco, food processing, paper products, and wood industries. The "modern" manufacturing sections, in turn, may be divided into the oil-dependent and import-substitution activities. See Baku, "Oil Revenue and Socio-Economic Development in Iran," p. 122.

61. BMI, *Annual Report* (1975), p. 3.

62. Ibid., p. 4. For data on fluctuations of the index of the purchasing power of export, see UNCTAD, *Handbook of International Trade and Development Statistics,* p. 428.

63. BMI, *Annual Report* (1975), pp. 4–6.

64. Ibid., pp. 4–5.

65. BMI, *Annual Report* (1976), p. 2.

66. Ibid., p. 6.

67. Ibid., p. 14

68. BMI, *Annual Reports* (1959–77). See also Pesaran, "The System of Dependent Capitalism in Pre- and Post-Revolutionary Iran," p. 508.

69. This index is weighted on the basis of the share of each industrial country in the total imports of Iran. See BMI, *Annual Report* (1975), p. 73.

70. The rise in the prices of meat, poultry, and fish by 25.8 percent, in fresh fruit and vegetables by 25.9 percent, in rice by 51.6 percent, and in dairy products by 16.6 percent contributed to the increase in the price index of the food group. After the food group index, the housing group index (with a rise of 19.5 percent, compared to 17.6 percent in 1973) had the next highest share in the rate of growth of the consumer price index. See BMI, *Annual Report* (1975), p. 71.

71. BMI, *Annual Report* (1978), p. 54.

72. Ibid., p. 49; and BMI, *Annual Report* (1977), p. 43. It should be noted that some researchers have claimed that government statistics on inflation were underestimated. According to Graham, for example, official figures were produced for inflation—but they were doctored to produce publicly acceptable norms. Published prices tended to reflect what they ought to have been, rather than what they were. Graham's statement is based on comments by an expatriate economist who assisted in the preparation of a new price index in 1976 (see Graham, *Iran,* pp. 91–92). Many Iranian economists also expressed great suspicion about official figures. Julian Bharier further stresses the unreliability of government statistics.

73. BMI, *Annual Report* (1977), p. 43.

74. Ibid., p. 45.

75. BMI, *Annual Report* (1978), pp. 51–52.

76. International Monetary Fund (IMF), *Government Finance Statistics Yearbook* (1982), 6:344.

77. Graham, *Iran,* p. 91.

78. BMI, *Annual Report* (1975), p. 70. According to Looney, government subsidies for food products rose to $1,000 million annually from 1974 to 1976. See Looney, *Economic Origins,* p. 151.

79. See note 59.

80. Graham, *Iran,* p. 98.

81. Stempel, *Inside the Iranian Revolution,* p. 83.

82. Bornschier and Chase-Dunn, *Transnational Corporations and Underdevelopment.*

83. Galtung, "A Structural Theory of Imperialism," pp. 81–117.

84. UNCTAD, *Handbook.*

85. Sylvan et al., "The Peripheral Economies,," pp. 79–111.

86. Taylor and Jodice. *World Handbook of Political and Social Indicators,* p. 19.

87. Ibid., p. 21.

88. Ibid., p. 62.

89. Ibid., p. 29.

90. Ibid., pp. 19–37. The indicators are standardized per million population. They are aggregated for the period 1976–81 and logtransformed (based 10) to reduce the skew of the distribution.

91. Jackson et al., "Conflict and Coercion in Dependent States," pp. 627–57.

92. Sylvan et al., "The Peripheral Economies," p. 341.

93. Ibid.

94. For an extended analysis of the relationship between dependence, vulnerability, and political conflict for ninety-one countries, see Mansoor Moaddel and Scott Werker, "Vulnerability and Political Conflict in the World Economy: A Cross-National Analysis of Modernization and World-System Theory" (1991), Working Paper. This study shows that dependence has no significant direct effect on political conflict, but by increasing vulnerability to the destabilizing influence of the world economy, it indirectly contributes to the outbreak of political conflict.

4. The State and the Indigenous Classes

1. For an extensive discussion and literature review on the petty bourgeoisie and the middle class, see Burris, "The Discovery of the New Middle Class," pp. 317–49.

2. Poulantzas, Classes in Contemporary Capitalism, p. 204. See also Wright, Class, Crisis and the State, chapter 2.

3. For an extensive description of different types of handicraft production see Wulf, The Traditional Crafts of Persia.

4. Tabari, Foroupashi, p. 29.

5. Karl Marx, cited in Aminzade, Class, Politics, and Early Industrial Capitalism, pp. 2–3.

6. Afshari, "The Pishivaran and Merchants in Pre-Capitalist Iranian Society," p. 135.

7. Floor, "The Guilds in Iran," p. 100.

8. Lambton, Theory and Practice, p. 128. Floor, on the other hand, stresses the second factor by indicating that "guilds grew out of corporate bodies of craftsmen, created by the government for fiscal and administrative purposes" ("The Guilds in Iran," p. 102).

9. Floor, "The Guilds in Iran," p. 108.

10. Ibid., p. 107

11. Ibid., p. 105; and Lambton, Theory and Practice, p. 22.

12. Lambton, Theory and Practice, p. 19.

13. Ibid., p. 20.

14. Marx, as cited in Laclau, Politics and Ideology in Marxist Theory , p. 24.

15. Issawi, ed., The Economic History of Iran, 1800-1914, p. 71.

16. Ibid., p. 130.

17. Ibid., p. 17.

18. Lambton, Landlord and Peasant in Persia, p. 134.

19. Issawi, Economic History of Iran, p. 131.

20. See Olson, "Persian Gulf Trade."

21. Issawi, Economic History of Iran, p. 132.

22. Ibid., p. 17.

23. Floor, "The Merchants [*tujjar*] in Qajar Iran," p. 101.

24. Lambton, *Theory and Practice*, p. 130n1.

25. Ibid., p. 107.

26. Torrey, *Commercial-Theological Terms in the Koran*, pp. 2–3.

27. Ibid., pp. 3, 8.

28. Ibid., p. 4.

29. Ibid., p. 48.

30. Rodinson, *Islam and Capitalism*, pp. 16–17.

31. Ibid., p. 111; and Rodinson, *Marxism and the Muslim World*, p. 145. Islam's procommerce orientation is evidently a reflection of the dominant socioeconomic order within which the Islamic movement arose. By the seventh century, the city of Mecca had gained considerable commercial importance as a result of its proximity to the Red Sea and its location on the caravan trade route from Ethiopia and India through Yemen (as the go-between), and then to the Byzantine provinces of Syria, Palestine, and Egypt (see Petrushevsky, *Islam in Iran*, p. 4). Therefore, Muhammad's use of commercial concepts to convey his message—above and beyond being a reflection of his own former experience as a merchant—was particularly necessary because these were easy to understand for the Meccans, a tribe of merchants, and for the men of Medina who were familiar with trading activity. See Rodinson, *Islam and Capitalism*, p. 81; and Thompson, *An Economic and Social History of the Middle Ages*.

32. Lambton, *Theory and Practice*, p. 122.

33. Floor, "The Merchants," p. 102.

34. Issawi, *Economic History of Iran*, p. 24.

35. Floor, "The Merchants," p. 102.

36. Fasa'ie, Hasan Hosein, *Farsnamah-ye Nasiri* (Tehran: Amir Kabir 1367/1988), pp. 918–19, 951–52, 956–58.

37. Lambton, *Theory and Practice*, p. 10.

38. Floor, "The Merchants," pp., 104–107.

39. Bonine, "Shops and Shopkeepers," p. 233.

40. Thaiss, "The Bazaar as a Case Study of Religion and Social Change," pp. 193–94.

41. The concept of "exploitation through trade" is used by Marxists, including Marx himself. For example, Dobb, in his analysis of the development of capitalism in Europe, indicates that "the class of merchants, as soon as it assumed any corporate forms, was quick to acquire powers of monopoly, which fenced its ranks from competitions and served to turn the terms of exchange to its own advantage in its dealings with producer and consumer. . . . [This] may be termed a sort of 'exploitation through trade,' by dint of which a surplus accrued to merchant capital at the expense both of urban craftsmen and of the peasant producer of the countryside, and even at the expense of the more powerful aristocratic consumer, from whom a part of feudal revenue or feudal accumulation passed into bourgeois hands." See Dobb, *Studies in the Development of Capitalism*, p. 88.

Marx refers to commercial profits as "profit upon alienation." In many cases, "the principal gains were not made by the exportation of the products of home industries, but by the promotion of the exchange of products of commercially and otherwise economically undeveloped societies and by the exploitation of both spheres of production. . . . To buy cheap in order to sell dear is rule of trade. It is not supposed to be an exchange of equivalents. The quantitative ratio in which products are exchanged is at first quite arbitrary." Cited in ibid., p. 89; see also Karl Marx, *Capital* 3:387, 388.

42. Dobb, *Studies,* p. 84.

43. Ibid., p. 88.

44. See Aminzade, *Class, Politics, and Early Industrial Capitalism.*

45. For a detailed analysis of the development of capitalism see Dobb, *Studies,* particularly chapters 3 through 7.

46. Foreign economic interventions were facilitated by treaties with Britain in 1801, the Gulistan and Turkmanchai treaties with Russia in 1813 and 1828, and the Anglo-Persian Commercial Treaty of 1841. These agreements imposed low and uniform duties on imports and exports and banned the use of monopolies or prohibitions in foreign trade (see Issawi, *Economic History of Iran,* p. 17).

47. Floor, "The Merchants," pp. 124–25

48. Cited in Floor, "The Merchants," p. 129.

49. Ibid.

50. Issawi, *Economic History of Iran,* p. 76.

51. Ibid.

52. Ibid.

53. Cited in Issawi, *Economic History of Iran,* p. 258.

54. Ibid., p. 259.

55. Ibid., pp. 103–4.

56. Ibid., p. 77.

57. Ibid., pp. 80–81.

58. Ibid., p. 81.

59. Abrahamian, *Iran Between Two Revolutions,* p. 55.

60. Cited in ibid. See Curzon, *Persia and the Persian Question,* 1:480.

61. Abrahamian, *Iran Between Two Revolutions,* p. 56.

62. Ibid., pp. 56–87. See also Sheikholeslami, "The Sale of Offices in Qajar Iran," pp. 104–18.

63. Floor, "The Merchants," p. 133. See also Curzon, *Persia,* 2:573; and Issawi, *Economic History of Iran,* pp. 71–72.

64. Floor, "The Merchants," 130. See also Issawi, *Economic History of Iran,* p. 259; and Ashraf, "Historical Obstacles to the Development of a Bourgeoisie in Iran," pp. 322–26.

65. Cited in Abrahamian, *Iran Between Two Revolutions,* p. 59.

66. Keddie, *Roots of Revolution,* p. 28.

67. Abrahamian, *Iran Between Two Revolutions,* p. 60.

68. Floor, "The Merchants," 133. See also Mostowfi, *Tarikh-i Edjtemai,* 1:493–96.

69. Floor, "The Merchants," p. 133.

70. See *Correspondence,* pp. 210–11 (*Sessional Papers* 79).

71. Adami'yat, *Shourish,* p. 13.

72. Cited in ibid., p. 15.

73. Adami'yat, *Shourish,* p. 19; and Karbala'i, *Qarardad-i,* p. 31.

74. Adami'yat, *Shourish,* p. 21.

75. Ibid., pp. 31–32; and *Correspondence,* May 6, 1891.

76. Adami'yat, *Shourish,* pp. 49–53.

77. *Correspondence,* October 6, 1891.

78. Karbala'i, *Qarardad-i,* pp. 67–68.

79. Cited in Karbala'i, *Qarardad-i,* pp. 68–69.

80. Adami'yat, *Shourish,* p. 75.

81. Abrahamian, *Iran Between Two Revolutions,* p. 62.

82. Cited in Nikki Keddie, *Sayyid Jamal al-Din "al-Afghani,"* p. 193.

83. See Adami'yat, *Idi'olozhi-ye,* pp. 195–223. For an important proponent of the absolutist ideology, see Tabataba-ei, *Hoquq-i Doval va Milal;* and for an informative discussion on the connection between the state and religious establishment, see Arjomand, *The Shadow of God.*

84. Floor, "The Merchants," p. 134.

85. Zahra Shaji'ie, *Namayandigan-i Shura-ye Melli* (University of Tehran, 1965), table 2, p. 176, and table 3, p. 179.

86. Floor, "The Guilds in Iran," p. 109.

87. Ibid., pp. 151–52.

88. Lambton, *Theory and Practice,* p. 30.

89. Abrahamian, *Iran Between Two Revolutions,* pp. 152–53.

90. Lambton, *Theory and Practice,* p. 24.

91. Ashraf, "Bazaar-Mosque Alliance," pp. 548–49.

92. See Iranian Government, *A'in-Nameh-ye Tashkil-i Itihadiyeh-ye Sinfi va Tanzim-i Umur-i Asnaf va Pishevaran* (Tehran: Mehr, 1336/1957).

93. Binder, *Iran: Political Development in a Changing Society,* pp. 186–87.

94. These data, extracted from Dahnavi, *Qiyam-i Khounin-i,* were originally reported in terms of the occupations of the individuals involved in the incident, some of whom were simply arrested during or after the demonstration. However, some people were shot and wounded or killed while participating, and these were taken to local hospitals. These 579 cases represent those whose occupations were reported. The total number of cases actually came to around 700. The missing cases are either those whose occupations were not reported, or those who were considered unidentified (*majhoul ul-hovi-yeh*).

95. Jazani also makes a similar observation that industrial workers did not significantly participate in the 1963 demonstrations. See *Tarh-i,* p. 168.

96. As table 4.1 indicates, the students were quite considerably involved in this event. But like ulama, students do not constitute a class. Nevertheless, the family backgrounds of these students could be an important explanatory variable on the kind of students most likely to oppose the Shah at that time. If the analysis ad-

vanced in this chapter is correct, then a high proportion of these students should have family backgrounds from the merchant or petty bourgeois class.

97. These data are based on a survey of 1,189 families that was conducted in Tehran in 1977. Bayat reports only the percentage distribution of both fathers' and sons' class backgrounds. The data on the fathers (rather than the sons) are used for comparison because they are more contemporaneous with the data on the class backgrounds of the participants in the June 1963 demonstration. If the data on the sons' class backgrounds are included, the difference between the two columns would be even greater. In order to make the two sets of data comparable, only sums of the class cases in table 4.1 were used as a base for computing the percentage distribution—that is, nonclass cases such as the students, the ulama, housewives, and the unemployed were not included. Finally, in order to match the categories in table 4.1 with those reported by Bayat regarding the internal composition of the working class and what he terms as traditional middle class, apprentices were included in the working-class category, and peasants and farmers were included among the traditional petty bourgeoisie. Consequently, the test becomes more conservative than would be the case if the proportion of the traditional petty bourgeoisie in the survey (24.1 percent) was compared with its proportion among the participants in the demonstration (53.5 percent).

98. Pahlavi, *Answer to History,* p. 156.

99. Keddie, *Roots of Revolution,* p. 171.

100. International Labor Office, *Employment and Income Policies for Iran,* pp. 50–81.

101. Jazani, *The Socio-economic Analysis of a Dependent Capitalist State,* pp. 27–28. The crushing of traditional industry was not simply the consequence of the growth of modern commercial establishments. It was also, in some cases, the result of the conscious policy of the state. In 1972, for instance, the state decided to modernize Tehran's bakeries, not only by mechanizing traditional bread-making but by replacing local bread with French baguettes and English-processed bread. Iranian consumers' tastes were ignored in this decision. In addition, it was envisaged that closure of the existing small bakeries would mean the loss of 12,000 bakery workers' jobs, which, as each Iranian worker had an average of four dependents, could affect up to 50,000 people. However, only about half of these jobs were actually lost, because many Iranians chose to eat the bread they were used to and refused to purchase the new bread. See Wilson, "Technology Transfer Threatens Traditional Industries," p. 3.

Bonine, however, indicates that not all the traditional occupations have declined. For example, while blacksmiths, coppersmiths, giveh-makers and sellers, tailors, and leather workers have decreased in number and have been replaced by retailing shops, the carpet sellers and the cloth-sellers have increased (see "Shops and Shopkeepers," p. 254). Furthermore, "one of the few traditional crafts that has grown in Yazd during the last few decades is goldsmith" (p. 256).

102. Halliday, *Iran: Dictatorship and Development,* pp. 14–15.

103. Wilson, "Industry Feels the Squeeze from High-wage Labour," p. 10

104. Graham, *Iran: The Illusion of Power*, p. 221.

105. Fischer, *Iran: From Religious Dispute to Revolution*, pp. 121, 191; Ashraf, "Bazaar-Mosque Alliance," p. 557; and Agayev, "Revolutionary Movements and Reforms in Iran," p. 241.

106. Jazani, *Tarh-i*, p. 165.

107. Kambakhsh, *Nazari*, p. 14.

108. Ibid., p. 47.

109. International Labor Office, *Employment and Income Policies*, p. 24.

110. Ibid., p. 55, table 8.

111. Cited in Kazemi, *Poverty and Revolution*, p. 47.

112. Halliday, *Iran: Dictatorship and Development*, p. 202.

113. Schmitter, "Still Century of Corporatism?" pp. 99–100. For further analyses of corporatism, see Malloy, ed., *Authoritarianism and Corporatism in Latin America*, particularly the articles by Collier and Collier, "Who Does What, to Whom, and How," and O'Donnell, "Corporatism and the Question of the State."

114. Safari, "Siasat-i Kargari-ye Regime," p. 29.

115. Cited in ibid., p. 100.

116. Cited in ibid.

117. Ibid., p. 99.

118. Halliday, *Iran: Dictatorship and Development*, p. 203.

119. Manouchehr Azmoun, the labor minister, in an interview stated that profit-sharing was directly related to productivity. If the workers' productivity in certain units had not reached the level to produce considerable profits for the company, then management was not obligated to share this with the workers. See *Navid* (the official publication of the Tudeh party), no. 6 (Isfand 1355/1976), p. 8.

120. Halliday, *Iran: Dictatorship and Development*, p. 206. See also N. Nahid, "Dar Bareh-ye Gostaresh-i Etesabat-i Kargari dar Iran" [On the expansion of workers' strikes in Iran], *Donya*, no. 9 (1355/1976); and M. Keyhan, "Jonbesh-i Etesabi-ye Kargaran" [Strike movement of workers in Iran], *Donya*, no. 8 (1357/1978).

5. *The Rise of Revolutionary Islam*

1. See Issawi, *Economic History of Iran*, p. 17; and Lambton, *Landlord and Peasant in Persia*, p. 134.

2. Arjomand, *The Shadow of God*, p. 225.

3. Keddie, *Religion and Rebellion in Iran*, p. 65.

4. Nateq, "Sar Aghaz," p. 52.

5. Adami'yat, *Shourish*, pp. 31–32.

6. *Correspondence*, May 6, 1891.

7. *Correspondence*, July 27, 1891.

8. *Correspondence*, October 6, 1891.

9. Cited in Adami'yat, *Shourish*, p. 62.

10. Adami'yat, *Idi'olozhi-ye*, p. 193

11. Hairi, *Shi'ism and Constitutionalism in Iran*, p. 194.

12. Abrahamian, *Iran Between Two Revolutions*, pp. 90–94.

13. Hairi, *Shi'ism and Constitutionalism*, pp. 193–99.

14. Adami'yat, *Idi'olozhi-ye*, p. 226 (my translation).

15. Cited in Hairi, *Shi'ism and Constitutionalism*, p. 194.

16. Nateq, "Sar Aghaz," p. 48.

17. Akhavi, *Religion and Politics in Contemporary Iran*, p. 29; and Mehraban, *Gousheha-ie*, pp. 17–18.

18. On Reza Shah's educational, judicial, and related policies, see Akhavi, *Religion and Politics*, chapter 2; and Faghfoory, "The Role of the Ulama," p. 63.

19. Mehraban, *Gousheha-ie*, p. 22.

20. Akhavi, *Religion and Politics*, pp. 23–59.

21. Mehraban, *Gousheha-ie*, p. 218.

22. Cited in ibid., p. 223 (my translation).

23. Mehraban, *Gousheha-ie*, p. 221.

24. Mehran, *Gousheha-ie*, p. 213; and Akhavi, *Religion and Politics*, p. 63.

25. Akhavi, *Religion and Politics*, p. 64.

26. Ibid., p. 65.

27. Ibid., p. 67.

28. Mehraban, *Gousheha-ie*, p. 176; *Dad*, no. 1074 (Mehr 1326/1947); and Jazani, *Tarh-i*, pp. 63–65.

29. Jazani, *Tarh-i*, pp. 163–64 (my translation); see also Nirumand, *Iran: The New Imperialism in Action*, pp. 79–80.

30. Lambton, *The Persian Land Reform*, pp. 56, 108, 112.

31. According to one source, "the Land Reform Organization suggests that some 15 per cent of cultivated land is 'private endowment, public endowment or a combination of these', whilst other sources put the total as much as one quarter of the total cultivated land. Scarcia . . . puts the figure for vaqf as low as 1 to 2 per cent. It is clear whichever way one regards the situation, that awqaf land still represents a large element in the Iranian landholding system, especially in Khurasan." See Fisher, *The Cambridge History of Iran*, 1:688.

32. Bazargan, *Inqilab-i*, p. 17.

33. Jazani, *Tarh-i*, p. 91–92. See also Bazargan, *Inqilab-i*, p. 17.

34. Jazani, *Tarh-i*, pp. 129–58.

35. Ale-Ahmad, *Dar Khedmat*, p. 336; and Grouhe Ettihadi-ye-he Komonisti, *Che Nabayad Kard?* [What is not to be done?] (N.p., 1356/1978).

36. Ale-Ahmad, *Dar Khedmat*, p. 355.

37. See Jazani, *Tarh-i*; and Mas'oud Ahmadzadeh, *Mobarezeh-ye Mosallahaneh, Ham Strategy Ham Taktik* [Armed struggle both as strategy and tactic] (No place: Organization of the Iranian People's Feda'iyan Guerrilla, n.d.).

38. See the letter of the leaders of the Second National Front to Mosaddeq in *Che Nabayad Kard?* (appendix).

39. Bazargan, *Defa'at*, pp. 27–28.

40. Abrahamian, *Iran Between Two Revolutions,* p. 458.

41. See Jazani, *Tarh-i,* pp. 62, 88; and Abrahamian, *Iran Between Two Revolutions,* pp. 457–58.

42. Khomeini, *Islam and Revolution,* pp. 49–50.

43. Ibid., pp. 50–51.

44. Yann Richard, "Contemporary Shi'i Thought," in Keddie, *Roots of Revolution,* p. 207.

45. Khomeini, *Islam and Revolution,* p. 44.

46. Rose, "*Velayat-i Faqih* and the Recovery of Islamic Identity," p. 180.

47. Ibid., p. 177.

48. Khomeini's criticism of the government and antireligious intellectuals such as Kasravi began as early as 1943. Although in his earlier writings he equated anti-ulama activities with betraying the country, he accepted the idea of constitutional monarchy. See Ruhollah Khomeini, *Kashf-ul Asrar* [Revealing the secrets] (n.p., 1323/1944). It was in the post-1963 period that he began developing the idea of an Islamic government in which religious jurists play the central role. See Ruholla Khomeini, *Hokumat-i Islami* [Islamic government] (Tehran: Amir Kabir Publications, 1360/1981).

49. Rose, "*Velayat-i Faqih* and the Recovery of Islamic Identity," p. 188.

50. Ale-Ahamd, *Plagued by the West,* p. 6.

51. Ibid., p. 9.

52. Ibid., pp. 32–33.

53. Ale-Ahmad, *Dar Khedmat,* p. 355.

54. Ibid., p. 15.

55. Ibid., pp. 49–50.

56. Ibid., pp. 261–72.

57. Ibid., p. 432 (my translation).

58. Adami'yat, "Ashoftegy dar Fekr-i Tarikhi," pp. 538–50.

59. Shari'ati, *Islamshenasi,* p. 23.

60. Ibid. (my translation).

61. Shari'ati, *What Is to Be Done,* p. 19.

62. Shari'ati, *Marxism and Other Western Fallacies,* p.92.

63. Mostafa Shoa'ie'yan, "Jihad-i Emruz ya Tez-i Bara-ye Basij" [Today's jihad or a thesis for mobilization], in *Chand Neveshteh* [A few essays] (No place: N.p., 1964), p. 24.

64. The Tudeh Party, *Asnad va Didgahah: Hizb-i Tudeh-ye Iran az Aghaz Peydayesh-ta Inqilab-i Bahman 1357* [Documents and viewpoints: The Tudeh party from the beginning until the Revolution of Bahman 1357] (Tehran: Tudeh Publications, 1360/1981), pp. 461–69.

65. Bazargan, *Inqilab-i,* pp. 24–27; and Ashraf and Banuazizi, "The State, Classes, and Modes of Mobilization," pp. 3–40.

66. Pahlavi, *Answer to History,* pp. 155–56.

67. *Navid,* no. 6 (Isfand 1355/1976), p. 8; and *Keyhan International,* October 26, 1976.

68. *Navid,* no. 16 (5 Bahman 1356/1977), p. 6.

69. Ashraf, "Dihqanan, Zamin va Inqilab," pp. 18–19.

70. Bill, *The Eagle and the Lion,* p. 236.

71. Rose, "*Velayat-i Faqih* and the Recovery of Islamic Identity," p. 188.

72. Khomeini, *Hokumat-i Islami,* p. 44.

73. Ashraf and Banuazizi "The State, Classes, and Modes of Mobilization," pp. 26–28.

74. "Iran va Isti'mar-i Surkh va Siah" [Iran and red and black colonialism], *Ittila'at* (17 Dey 1356/January 7, 1978), p. 7.

75. *Navid,* no. 6 (Aban 1356/1977), p. 7, and no. 12 (19 Azar 1356/1976), pp. 6–8; and Bazargan, *Inqilab-i,* p. 17.

76. Davani, *Nahzat-i,* 7:20–67; and *Navid,* no. 15 (21 Dey 1356/1978), pp. 1–2, and no. 16 (5 Bahman 1356/1978), pp. 3–4.

77. See Tabari and Yeganeh, *In the Shadow of Islam;* and Nashat, *Women and Revolution in Iran.*

78. Ashraf and Banuazizi, "The State, Classes, and Modes of Mobilization," p. 8; Fischer, *Iran: From Religous Dispute to Revolution,* pp. 195–96; Bazargan *Inqilabi,* pp. 28–29.

79. Bazargan, *Inqilab-i,* pp. 33–34.

80. Ibid., p. 31.

81. Davani, *Nahzat-i,* 9:6–46.

82. Ibid.,9:72–75.

6. *Contrasting Cases: Islam and Politics in Egypt and Syria*

1. Gismondi, "Transformation in the Holy," p. 14.

2. Tilly, *Big Structures, Large Processes, Huge Comparisons,* p. 82.

3. Issawi, *Egypt in Revolution,* p. 18.

4. Comments by Afaf Lutfi al-Sayyid Marsot to author (hereafter, Marsot's comments).

5. Figures for 1813 and 1877 are from Issawi, *Egypt: An Economic and Social Analysis,* p. 14; and for 1911 from Hussein, *Class Conflict in Egypt,* p. 55.

6. Crouchley, "The Development of Commerce in the Reign of Mohammad Ali," p. 305.

7. Ibid., pp. 311–12.

8. It should be noted that in 1837 there was a sudden fall in the value of cotton owing to a great drop in price. This fall was, to a certain extent, compensated for by an increase in cereals, the sales of which progressed year by year from 1838. Thus, throughout this period, cotton and cereals maintained a seesaw movement, the one rising as the other fell, according to the movements of prices year by year (Crouchley, "The Development of Commerce," p. 313).

9. Marsot's comments. Issawi, on the other hand, claims that Egypt stood up to the shock thanks to cotton. See Issawi, *Egypt: An Economic and Social Analysis,* p. 15.

10. Hussein, *Class Conflict in Egypt,* pp. 44–46.

11. Issawi, *Egypt in Revolution,* p. 32; and Hussein, *Class Conflict in Egypt,* pp. 56–57.

12. Marsot, *Egypt's Liberal Experiment,* pp. 13–14.

13. Vatikiotis, *History of Egypt,* p. 30.

14. Ibid., p. 50.

15. Ibid., p. 51; and Crecelius, "Nonideological Responses of the Egyptian Ulama to Modernization," p. 176.

16. Crecelius, "Nonideological Responses," p. 18.

17. Lawson, "Social Origins of Aggressive Foreign Policy."

18. Vatikiotis, *History of Egypt,* p. 66.

19. Marsot, *Egypt's Liberal Experiment,* p. 43.

20. Issawi, *Egypt: An Economic and Social Analysis,* p. 8.

21. Lawson, "Social Origins," pp. 78–79.

22. See Gran, *Islamic Roots of Capitalism,* pp. 21–26; and Baer, *Egyptian Guilds in Modern Times.*

23. Marsot, *Egypt in the Reign of Muhammad Ali,* p. 6.

24. Ibid., pp. 5–6.

25. Marsot's comments.

26. Lawson, "Social Origins," p. 109.

27. Ibid., p. 112; Gran, *Islamic Roots of Capitalism,* p. 47.

28. Lawson, "Social Origins," p. 113.

29. Crecelius, "Nonideological Responses," p. 167.

30. Gran, *Islamic Roots of Capitalism,* p. 47.

31. Marsot, "The Role of the Ulama in Egypt," p. 271.

32. Marsot, *Egypt in the Reign of Muhammad Ali,* p. 43.

33. Ibid., p. 49.

34. Marsot, "The Role of the Ulama in Egypt," p. 274.

35. Lawson, "Social Origins," p. 122.

36. Hunter, *Egypt Under the Khedives,* p. 17.

37. Lawson, "Social Origins," p. 122.

38. Marsot, *Egypt in the Reign of Muhammad Ali,* pp. 132–35.

39. Marsot, *Egypt's Liberal Experiment,* p. 11.

40. Ibid., p. 12.

41. Marsot, *Egypt in the Reign of Muhammad Ali,* p. 67.

42. Crecelius, "Nonideological Responses," 181.

43. Lawson, "Social Origins," pp. 123–24.

44. Marsot, *Egypt in the Reign of Muhammad Ali,* pp. 185, 190; Lawson, "Social Origins," p. 211; Walz, *Trade Between Egypt and Bild al-Sudan,* pp. 238–39, and "Asyut in the 1260's (1844–53)," p. 118; Gran, *Islamic Roots of Capitalism,* pp. 116, 232n5; and Hourani, "The Syrian in Egypt in the Eighteenth and Nineteenth Centuries."

45. These were Greeks, Armenians, and Jews from various countries.

46. Issawi, *Egypt: An Economic and Social Analysis,* pp. 17–18.

47. Hussein, *Class Conflict in Egypt,* p. 22. Marsot, on the other hand, states that these foreign merchants never became "Egyptianized" and always remained alien in order to benefit from the capitulatory rights and greater tax advantages awarded with the treaty of Balta-Lima. Only Muslim merchants of Syrian, Moroccan, or Ottoman origin were "Egyptianized"; the rest were either foreign and Christian or Jewish.

48. Cuno, "The Origin of Private Ownership of Land in Egypt," p. 245.

49. Mustafa, "The Breakdown of the Monopoly System in Egypt," pp. 291–307.

50. Ansari, *Egypt: The Stalled Society,* p. 63.

51. Marsot, *Egypt's Liberal Experiment,* p. 12.

52. Ansari, *Egypt: The Stalled Society,* p. 74.

53. Marsot, *Egypt's Liberal Experiment,* p. 12.

54. Ibid., p. 205.

55. Ibid., p. 14.

56. Ansari, *Egypt: The Stalled Society,* p. 63.

57. Hussein, *Class Conflict in Egypt,* p. 68.

58. Adams, *Islam and Modernism in Egypt,* p. 1.

59. Ibid., pp. 226–27.

60. Marsot, *Egypt's Liberal Experiment,* p. 36; Vatikiotis, *History of Egypt,* p. 60; and Baer, *Egyptian Guilds,* pp.130–45.

61. Hussein, *Class Conflict in Egypt,* p. 51.

62. Issawi, *Egypt: An Economic and Social Analysis,* p. 151.

63. Hussein, *Class Conflict in Egypt,* p. 56, table 9.

64. Ibid., p. 57, table 10.

65. Marsot, *Protest Movements and Religious Undercurrents in Egypt: Past and Present,* p. 5.

66. Ibid.

67. Mitchell, *The Society of the Muslim Brothers,* p. 17.

68. Ibid., p. 330.

69. Marsot, *Egypt's Liberal Experiment,* p. 234.

70. Mitchell, *The Society of the Muslim Brothers,* p. 39.

71. Ibid., pp. 26–27, 33, 309–10.

72. Grant, *The Syrian Desert,* pp. 45–78.

73. Petran, *Syria,* p. 41.

74. Ibid., pp. 42–43.

75. Nyrop, *Syria: A Country Study,* pp. 97–98.

76. Drysdale, "The Asad Regime and Its Troubles," p. 5.

77. Nyrop, *Syria: A Country Study,* p. 135.

78. Ibid., p. 18; and Torrey, *Syrian Politics and the Military,* p. 5.

79. Nyrop, *Syria: A Country Study,* pp. 19–22.

80. Torrey, *Syrian Politics,* p. 54.

81. Ibid., p. 53; and Seale, *The Struggle for Syria,* p. 24.

82. Nyrop, *Syria: A Country Study,* pp. 27–28.

83. Keilany, "Socialism and Economic Change in Syria," p. 63; and Drysdale, "The Asad Regime," p. 3.

84. Holmström, "Syria," p. 11.

85. Rabinovich, *Syria Under the Ba'th,* pp. 9–10.

86. Ibid., pp. 86–87.

87. Hinnebusch, "The Islamic Movement in Syria," p. 159.

88. Petran, *Syria,* pp. 70–71.

89. Garzouzi, "Land Reform in Syria," p. 83.

90. Petran, *Syria,* p. 85.

91. Torrey, *Syrian Politics,* pp. 22–24; and Nyrop, *Syria: A Country Study,* p. 61.

92. Torrey, *Syrian Politics,* pp. 51–53.

93. Winder, "Syrian Deputies," p. 38.

94. Petran, *Syria,* pp. 70–71.

95. Seale, *The Struggle for Syria,* p. 37.

96. Galvani, "Syria and the Baath Party," p. 5.

97. Nyrop, *Syria: A Country Study,* p. 30.

98. Hinnebusch, "The Islamic Movement in Syria," pp. 140–41.

99. Batatu, "Syria's Muslim Brethren," p. 12.100. See Marx Alexander (pseud. for Walter Z. Lacqueur), "Communist Strategy in the Middle East," p. 396; and Torrey, *Syrian Politics,* p. 61.

101. Batatu, "Syria's Muslim Brothers," p. 18.

102. Ajami, *The Arab Predicament,* p. 40.

103. Hinnebusch, "The Islamic Movement in Syria," pp. 157–59.

104. Batatu, "Syria's Muslim Brothers," pp. 13–15.

105. Hinnebusch, "The Islamic Movement in Syria," p. 164.

106. Galvani, "Syria and the Baath Party," p. 10.

107. Seale, *"The Struggle for Syria,* pp. 38–41.

108. Galvani, "Syria and the Baath Party," p. 11.

109. Keilany, "Socialism and Economic Change in Syria," pp. 64–65; and Lawson, "Social Bases for the Hamah Revolt," p. 26.

110. Hinnebusch, "The Islamic Movement in Syria," pp. 157–58.

111. Batatu, "Syria's Muslim Brothers," p. 18.

112. Hinnebusch, "The Islamic Movement in Syria," p. 166.

113. Van Dam, *The Struggle for Power in Syria,* p. 15.

114. Hinnebusch, "The Islamic Movement in Syria," p. 139.

115. Van Dam, *The Struggle for Power in Syria,* p. 22.

116. Ibid., pp. 33–35.

117. Drysdale, "The Asad Regime," p. 10.

118. Hinnebusch, "The Islamic Movement in Syria," p. 161.

119. Batatu, "Syria's Muslim Brothers,"p. 16; and Devlin, *Syria: Modern State in an Ancient Land,* pp. 75–96.

7. Islamic Discourse and Postrevolutionary Conflicts

1. See Skocpol, *States and Social Revolutions,* p. 172.

2. Halliday, "Iran's Revolution: The First Year," pp. 3–4.

3. For a list of the members of Bazargan's cabinet see *Jomhouri-ye Islami,* 16 Aban 1358/1979, p. 2.

4. It should be noted that Bani-Sadr sounded more like a radical in the 1977–79 period, when he advocated such economic measures as nationalization of foreign trade and banks as well as a radical redistribution of wealth. He adopted a liberal program in 1980–81, when he was elected the country's first president.

5. Keddie, *Roots of Revolution,* p. 237.

6. Ervand Abrahamian, "The Guerrilla Movement in Iran, 1963–1977," *MERIP Reports,* nos. 75–76 (March–April 1980), pp. 9–10.

7. Another secular Muslim organization was *Jonbesh-i Mosalmanan-i Mobariz* (the Movement of Muslim Fighters), which emerged in the postrevolutionary period. Led by Dr. Payman—a Muslim socialist—this organization displayed a strong pro-workers and pro-peasants tendency. Its members were active in the seven-member committees in charge of land reform and the Reconstruction Crusade. Their views were reflected in the weekly *Ummat.* For background on their social and political views, see *Ummat* (5 Ordibihisht 1358/1979), special issue, pp. 1–4. With the political consolidation of the right-wing elements within the Islamic Republic, this movement lost its influence and after about two years of activity was dissolved by its leadership.

8. Abrahamian, *Iran Between Two Revolutions,* pp. 451–89.

9. See *Jomhouri-ye Islami* (16 Aban 1358/1979), p. 2.

10. See *Ittila'at* (3 Ordibihisht 1358/1979), p. 7.

11. See *Ittila'at* (19 Mehr 1358/1979), p. 2 (my translation). In contrast, Ayatollah Montazari argued that "If everyone in society votes for a president but the *faqih* disapproves him, the people's vote has no value for me" (*Ittila'at,* 22 Mehr 1358/1979, p. 1).

12. In response to the criticism that the size of the Assembly of Experts was too small, Khomeini argued that: "They say there should be a constituent assembly of the Western type, with 600 or 700 members. First, it takes several months to determine memberships and, second, several years to pass the constitution. These rotten roots wanted this delay perhaps to organize themselves and design a conspiracy." See *Jomhouri-ye Islami* (28 Khurdad 1358/1979), p. 2 (my translation).

13. Bazargan, *Inqilab-i,* p. 95n1.

14. This interpretation is reinforced considering a statement made by one of the students who participated in the seizure of the U.S. embassy: "Our concern was that if we do not seize the embassy today or tomorrow, it is probable that the Mojahedin or Fida'iyan would take the initiative and do just that." See *Majara-ye Posht-i Pardeh-ye Gerougangiri* [The untold story behind the seizure of the U.S. embassy], (N.p.: Kanoun-i Towhidi Asnaf, 1359/1981), p. 24.

15. Davani, *Nahazat-i,* 11:395.

16. Bazargan, *Inqilab-i*, pp. 89–95.

17. *Jomhouri-ye Islami* (29 Azar 1358/1979), p. 1.

18. These documents were published in *Kar*, the weekly paper of the Organization of the Iranian People's Fida'iyan Guerrilla (special issues, dated 12, 14, and 19 of Dey 1358/1959).

19. *Jomhouri-ye Islami* (30 Azar 1358/1979), p. 1.

20. See *The Constitution of the Islamic Republic of Iran* [Qanoun-i Asasi-ye Jomhouri-ye Islami-ye Iran] (Tehran: Nashr-i Vahdat, n.d.).

21. *Jomhouri-ye Islami* (20 Dey 1358/1979), p. 1.

22. *Jomhouri-ye Islami* (23 Dey 1358/1979), p. 1.

23. *Jomhouri-ye Islami* (25 Dey 1358/1979), p. 1.

24. *Jomhouri-ye Islami* (30 Farvardin 1359/1980), p. 1.

25. *Jomhouri-ye Islami* (31 Farvardin 1359.1980), p. 1.

26. *Jomhouri-ye Islami* (1 Ordibihisht 1359/1980), p. 9.

27. *Aksariyat*, Organization of the Iranian People's Fida'iyan (OIPF), no. 33 (November 19, 1984), p. 6.

28. *Aksariyat*, no. 25 (September 24, 1984), p. 4.

29. For a list of the groups who participated in the coalition see *Jomhouri-ye Islami* (22 Isfand 1358/1980), p. 1.

30. Cited in *Kar* (8 Mehr 1359/1980), p. 8 (my translation). See also *Jomhouri-ye Islami* (2 and 19 Shahrivar 1359/1980).

31. Cited in *Kar* (6 Azar 1359/1980), p. 15 (my translation). See also *Inqilab-i Islami* (19 Aban 1359).

32. Cited in *Kar* (6 Azar 1359/1980), p. 15.

33. See Mojahedin, *Varshekasteqi-ye*, p. 3.

34. Ibid., p. 1 (my translation).

35. Ibid., pp. 17–74 (my translations).

36. Ibid., p. 38 (my translation).

37. *Jomhouri-ye Islami* (22 Ordibihisht 1360/1981), p. 1; and (15 Ordibihisht 1360/1981), pp. 1, 5.

38. Geertz, *The Interpretation of Culture*, p. 211.

39. *Jomhouri-ye Islami* (10 Tir 1360/1981), p. 1.

40. For the list of over 10,000 people who were executed by the government of the Islamic Republic during this period, see *Mojahed*, no. 261 (special issue, 15 Shahrivar 1364/1985).

41. *Mardom*, the organ of the Central Committee of the Tudeh Party of Iran (21 Aban 1358/1979), p. 6 (my translation).

42. Skocpol, *States and Social Revolutions*, p. 186.

43. See Tilly, "War Making and State Making as Organized Crime," p. 170.

44. For background on the Iran-Iraq conflict, see Desouki, ed., *The Iraq-Iran War;* Jiman Taqavi, "The Iran-Iraq War," pp. 63–82; Hunseler, "The Historical Antecedent of the Shatt-al-Arab Dispute," pp. 8–19; Hiro, *Iran Under the Ayatullahs*, pp. 104–70; Abdulghani, *Iraq and Iran: The Years of Crisis;* and Firzli, ed., *The Iraq-Iran Conflict*.

45. See *MERIP Reports* (November 1980); and Abdulghani, *Iraq and Iran*, pp. 193–200.

46. Cited in Hiro, *Iran Under the Ayatullahs*, p. 106.

47. According to the *Nation* (October 25, 1980), the Iraqi government was training a "liberation army" and had set up radio stations to broadcast counterrevolutionary messages to Iran. The same issue reported that the Iraqi aim was probably to seize Khuzistan quickly, perhaps later withdrawing in favor of the exile forces or possibly installing an indigenous puppet regime in the name of Arab autonomy. Such a circumstance might have been expected to produce an Iranian civil war, the collapse of the Islamic Republic, the permanent partition of Iran, or some combination of those. And the *Militant* (October 10, 1980) reported that Hussein had given refuge and sites for training camps to former secret police agents and army officers of the Shah. Headed by General Gholam Ali Oveissi, one of the Shah's most brutal commanders, these people were being organized for an invasion of Iran. Oveissi shuttled between the borders area, Baghdad, and Washington. Shahpour Bakhtiyar, the Shah's last prime minister, was also a frequent visitor in Baghdad. He forged an alliance with Oveissi and announced plans to form a provisional government.

48. Hickman, *Ravaged and Reborn: The Iranian Army*, p. 22.

49. Ibid., p. 22.

50. Cited in Ibid., p. 24.

51. Ibid.

52. Ibid., p. 22.

53. Bazargan, *Inqilab-i*, pp. 154–55.

54. Rose, "The Post-Revolutionary Purge of Iran's Armed Forces," p. 187.

55. The ulama's mistrust of the army is best summarized in Ayatollah Montazari's assertion that "we can only defend the country with a force we trust." Cited in Hichman, *Ravaged and Reborn*, p. 23.

56. See MERI (Middle East Research Institute), University of Pennsylvania, *Report: Iran* (Dover, N.H.: Croom Helm, 1985), p. 33.

57. Ibid., p. 20. One indication of the increase in people's mobilization in defense of the country and the Islamic Republic is that "the initial resistance by the Iranians in the Khorramshahr and Abadan areas was mustered by an unprepared conglomeration of Pasdars, police, paramilitary groups, and volunteers." See O'Ballance, "The Iraqi-Iranian War," p. 57.

58. Hickman, *Ravaged and Reborn*, p. 30.

59. O'Ballance, "The Iraqi-Iranian War," p. 16.

60. Bazargan, *Inqilab-i*, pp. 156–58.8

61. It is not clear whether the leaders and members of the IRP also came from the same family backgrounds. However, data on the occupational positions of the fathers of thirty-two leaders of the IRP killed in the explosion of the party's headquarters in Tehran indicate that seven (22 percent) were farmers, ten (31 percent) had petty-bourgeois-type occupations (*Kassib*), twelve (38 percent) were ulama, two (6 percent) were teachers, and one (3 percent) was a medical doctor. These IRP members thus seem to have come from family backgrounds similar to the members

of the parliament. However, due to the size of the sample and its nonrandom selection, these findings cannot be generalized to the whole IRP membership. See the Public Relations of the Parliament of the Islamic Republic, *Negarish Be Avvalin Majlis-i Shura-i Eslami* [A glance at the first Islamic parliament] (Tehran, 1364/1985), pp. 314–29.

62. See Nik-A'een, *Dar Bareh-ye Mas'aleh-ye Arzi*, pp. 96–117; Ashraf, "Dihqanan, Zamin va Inqilab," p. 26; and *Rahe Tudeh*, no. 78 (February 3, 1984), p. 15.

63. Bakhash, *The Reign of the Ayatullahs*, p. 197; and *Ummat* (19 Dey 1358/1979), pp. 1, 5.

64. Ashraf, "Dihqanan, Zamin va Inqilab," p. 27.

65. These figures were reported to a seminar organized by the ministry of agriculture concerning the problems of agriculture in Iran in mid-November 1979. See Nik-A'een, *Dar Bareh-ye Mas'aleh-ye Arzi*, p. 105.

66. Azar, "Mobarizat-i Dihqani dar Iran," pp. 74–76.

67. See *Ummat* (10 Bahman 1358/1980), p. 5; and (11 Tir 1359/1980), p. 4.

68. *Ittila'at* (13 Mehr 1358/1979).

69. Cited in *Inqilab-i Islami* (19 Mehr 1358/1979), p. 5. See also *Mardom* (26 Mehr 1358/1979); and Eizadi's interview with *Jomhouri-ye Islami* (19 Mehr 1358/1979), pp. 5, 8.

70. *Ittila'at* (16 Isfand 1358/1980), p. 1.

71. *Jomhouri-ye Islami* (9 Aban 1358/1979), pp. 1–2 (my translation).

72. *Jomhouri-ye Islami* (11 Khurdad 1359/1980), pp. 1, 4 (my translation).

73. Cited in *Mardom* (17 Aban 1358/1979), p. 6.

74. See *Kayhan* (6 Shahrivar 1362/1983).

75. Ashraf, "Dihqanan, Zamin va Inqilab," pp. 33–34.

76. *Ittila'at* (10 Azar 1358/1979); and Ashraf, "Dihqanan, Zamin va Inqilab," p. 31.

77. *Ittila'at* (19 Aban 1359/1980), p. 5 (my translation).

78. *Jomhuri-ye Islami* reported the rallies of tens of thousands of people in favor of an Islamic land reform (5 Dey 1358/1980).

79. *Ittila'at* (19 Aban 1359/1981), p. 5.

80. Bakhash, *The Reign of the Ayatullahs*, p. 202.

81. Ashraf, "Dihqanan, Zamin va Inqilab," p. 33.

82. Cited in *Kargaran Pishtaz-i Jonbesh-i Tudeh-i,* OIPF (majority), (Bahman 1363/1984), p. 4 (my translation).

83. Cited in ibid., p. 48.

84. Azad, "Workers' and Peasants' Councils in Iran," p. 17.

85. Ibid., p. 21.

86. Goodey, "Workers Councils in Iranian Factories," p. 5.

87. Bakhash, *The Reign of the Ayatullahs*, pp. 179–80. For the list of the names of the fifty-one individuals whose properties were nationalized see *Inqilab-i Islami* (14 Tir 1358/1979), p. 12.

88. *Rahe Tudeh*, (January 13, 1984), p. 9. See also the interview with the minister of heavy industry of Iran in *Ittila'at* (May 17, 1361/1982).

89. Azad, "Workers' and Peasants' Councils," p. 20.

90. Ibid., p. 22.

91. *Ummat* (15 Isfand 1358/1979), p. 5.

92. *Ittila'at* (7 Farvardin 1359/1980), p. 9.

93. To gain background on the seriousness of the problem of hoarding and for a partial list of the items that were hoarded, see *Kayhan* (8 Farvardin; 26 and 27 Ordibihisht; 3 Khurdad; and 24 Shahrivar 1360/1981); and *Ittila'at* (26 and 28 Farvardin 1361/1982).

94. For example, see *Ittila'at* (4 Dey 1361), pp. 5–6.

95. See *Kar* (16 Dey 1360/1981), no. 142, OIPF (majority, Keshtgar faction), p. 25.

96. *Ittila'at* (23 Ordibihisht 1361/1982), p. 7.

97. *Ittila'at* (23 Farvardin 1362/1983), p. 5; and (21 Farvardin 1362), p. 5.

98. *Ittila'at* (31 Farvardin 1362/1983), p. 6.

99. *Ittila'at* (12 Khurdad 1362/1983), p. 14.

100. *Ittila'at* (18 Dey 1359/1980).

101. *Ummat* (24 Dey 1359/1980), p. 11.

102. According to Hojjat-ul Islam Harandi, "In the new plan . . . the principal objective is the omission of the seven-member committees and their central organs" (*Ittila'at*, 13 Aban 1363/1984). Sharif, a member of the central organ of these committees, indicated that "based on our sources, we have come to the conclusion that the existance of these committees . . . is endangered" (ibid). See also *Nameh Mardom*, no. 29 (December 20, 1984), p. 5.

103. In late 1983 and early 1984, the parliament passed a law concerning the barren lands (*Tarh-i Qanoun-i Arazi-ye Mouqoufeh*). According to this law, all the endowed lands that were sold without legal grounds or somehow came under the ownership of peasants have no validity and should be returned to their previous status. Cited in *Aksariyat*, no. 2 (April 13, 1984), p. 3. This law provided the legal grounds for the intensification of the landlords' attacks and pressure on the peasants to return the land they had obtained during the initial revolutionary phase.

104. Cited in Azad, "Workers' and Peasants' Councils," p. 19.

105. Cited in OIPF (majority), *Tahlili az Hoqouq-i Senfi va Shura-i-ye Kargaran va Zahmatkashan dar Jomhouri-ye Islami-ye Iran* [An analysis of the occupational and organizational rights of workers and toilers under the Islamic Republic of Iran] (N.p.: Kaveh Publications, 1361/1982), p. 10.

106. *Jomhouri-ye Islami* (6 Isfand 1359/1981), p. 5.

107. The allegations of Kianouri, the first secretary of the Tudeh party, were not without substance. In Tavakkoli's draft bill the word "work-taker" (*karpazir*) was substituted for the word "worker" (*kargar*), and "worker-giver" (*kardeh*) was substituted for the word "manager" (*karfarma*). Kianouri charged that these terminologies were borrowed from Nazi labor theories, for the words "work-taker" and "work-giver" are literal translations of the German words *Arbeitnehmer* and *Arbeitgeber*, respectively. Furthermore, when Tavakkoli and his assistance Motamid Reza-ie argued that there was a unity between labor and capital, Kianouri re-

sponded that such an assertion was also derived from Nazi labor theory. Under the pretext of advancing a labor front (*Arbeitsfront*), the Nazis had destroyed working-class organizations. See Nuroddin Kianouri, *Questions and Answers*, Tehran: Tudeh Party of Iran (29 Aban 1361/1982), pp. 21–34.

108. Cited in *Rahe Tudeh*, no. 79 (February 10, 1984), p. 16. See also *Ittila'at* (14 Mehr 1362/1983).

109. For the Guardians' reasons for rejecting the nationalization bill, see *Ittila'at* (6 Azar 1361/1982), pp. 15–16. See also "Iran Foreign Trade—The Guardians' View," *Middle East Economic Digest* 28, no. 35 (August 31, 1984), p. 12.

110. *Ittila'at* (31 Farvardin 1362/1983), p. 6.

111. *Ittila'at* (22 Farvardin 1362/1983), p. 5.

112. *Ittila'at* (5 Aban 1360/1981), p. 5.

113. Markaz-i Amar-i Iran, *Amar-i Kargah-ha-yi Kuchak-i Shah-ri* (Tehran: 1359/1981), pp. 10–11, tables 1–2.

114. Markaz-i Amar-i Iran, *Amar-i Kargah'ha-yi Bozorg-i San'ati-ye Sal-i 1360* (Tehran: Isfand 1361/1983), pp. 13, 7, and table 13.

115. Ibid., p. 13.

116. Halliday, *Iran: Dictatorship and Development*, pp. 108–09; and Kazemi and Abrahamian, "The Non-Revolutionary Peasantry of Modern Iran," pp., 259–304.

117. For a discussion of *boneh* and its transformation see Saifynijad, *Boneh*, especially pp. 180–83.

118. Ashraf, "Dihqanan, Zamin va Inqilab," p. 26; Bakhash, *The Reign of the Ayatullahs*, p. 198; and Momeni, *Masa'leh-ye Arzi*, pp. 338–39.

119. See the section on terror under the Islamic Republic in the latter part of this chapter.

120. Ashraf, "Dihqanan, Zamin va Inqilab," p. 23.

121. *Rahe Tudeh*, (February 3, 1984), p. 15. On the concentration of land ownership see Abrahamian, "Structural Causes of the Iranian Revolution," p. 23, table iv.

122. *Ummat* (26 Aban 1359/1980), pp. 1, 4, and (11 Isfand 1359/1981), pp. 1, 4.

123. Parsa, *Social Origins of the Iranian Revolution*, p. 282.

124. Halliday, *Iran: Dictatorship and Development*, p. 15.

125. *Ittila'at* (10 Aban 1360/1981), p. 5.

126. *Ittila'at* (6 Aban 1360/1981), pp. 5, 11.

127. *Ittila'at* (4 Tir 1359/1980).

128. *Ittila'at* (31 Farvardin 1362/1983), p. 6.

129. *Ittila'at* (24 Farvardin 1359/1980), p. 2.

130. *Ittila'at* (14 Khurdad 1359), p. 12.

131. *Ittila'at* (21 Dey 1361/1982), p. 5.

132. *Ittila'at* (10 Aban 1360/1981), p. 5.

133. *Ittila'at* (7 Aban 1360/1981), p. 5, and (2 Dey 1360/1981), pp. 3, 21.

134. *Ittila'at* (10 Aban 1360/1981), p. 5.

135. *Ittila'at* (11 Aban 1360/1981), p. 6.

136. *Ittila'at* (4 Mordad 1360/1981), p. 5, and (4 Tir 1360/1991).

137. Cited in *Rahe Tudeh* (January 27, 1984), p. 14.

138. *Ittila'at* (31 Farvardin 1362/1983), p. 5.

139. *Ittila'at* (20 Farvardin 1362/1983), p. 1.

140. For example A'bedizadeh, the representative of Khoy in the parliament, complained that millionaires had become billionaires (*Ittila'at*, 13 Ordibihisht 1362/1983). Ayatollah Malakouti said that "After the revolution, the profits of some people were even higher than under the Shah. For example, I know someone who has made 36 million tomans within a period of four months" (*Kayhan*, 4 Aban 1361/1982). And Ayatollah Sedouqi complained that "one of these carpet sellers told a friend that the profit they made in this year was equal to twenty years of carpet selling [under the Shah]" (*Jomhouri-ye Islami*, 13 Tir 1362/1983).

141. *Ittila'at* (20 Farvardin 1359/1980); and *Ummat* (19 Dey 1358/1979), p. 5.

142. *Ittila'at* (19 Aban 1359/1980).

143. *Ittila'at* (20 Farvardin 1359/1980).

144. *Ittila'at* (2 Ordibihisht 1359/1980), p. 4.

145. Bakhash, *The Reign of the Ayatullahs*, p. 204; and *Ummat* (11 Isfand 1359/1980), pp. 1, 4.

146. *Ittila'at* (2 Ordibihisht 1359/1980), p. 4.

147. *Ittila'at* (25 Aban 1359/1980), p. 4; *Mizan* (19 Aban 1359/1980), p. 1, and (25 Aban 1359/1980), p. 2; and *Jomhouri-ye Islami* (25 Aban 1359/1980), p. 2.

148. Cited in *Ummat* (22 Dey 1359/1981), p. 3.

149. Bakhash, *The Reign of the Ayatullahs*, p. 194.

150. *Ittila'at* (Shahrivar 1358/1979), and (30 Dey 1358/1980), p. 4.

151. *Ittila'at* (20 Farvardin 1360/1981), p. 14.

152. *Ittila'at* (4 Khurdad 1360/1981), p. 5.

153. *Ittila'at* (6 Aban 1360/1981), p. 5.

154. *Ittila'at* (2 Dey 1360/1981), p. 3, and (16 Azar 1360/1981), p. 5.

155. *Ittila'at* (28 Mordad 1360/1981), p. 5.

156. *Rahe Tudeh*, no. 77 (January 27, 1984), p. 9.

157. *Jomhouri-ye Islami* (7 Ordibihisht 1360), pp. 1, 3.

158. *Jomhouri-ye Islami* (15 Ordibihisht 1360/1981), p. 1.

159. *Jomhouri-ye Islami* (22 Ordibihisht 1360/1981), pp. 1, 5.

160. *Rahe Tudeh*, no. 77 (January 27, 1984), p. 8. Noteworthy is Khamoushi's statement in this respect: "The Ministry of Commerce initially had little interest in cooperating with us. But recently, particularly after the appointment of our esteemed brother, Mr. Asgar-Owladi, the ministry has become more cooperative. The minister of commerce has even appointed a person in the Committee on Guild Affairs to be the active liaison between us and the ministry of commerce" (*Ittila'at*, 16 Azar 1360/1981, p. 5).

161. *Ittila'at* (16 Farvardin 1361/1982), pp. 5, 14 (my translation).

162. *Ittila'at* (17 Azar 1360/1981), p. 5.

163. *Rahe Tudeh* (January 27, 1984), p. 9 (my translation). See also Taba'taba'ei, "Report on Six-Month Activities and Current Programs of the Mostaz'afan Foundation," *Ittila'at* (5 Khurdad 1362/1983), p. 14.

164. *Rahe Tudeh*, no. 77 (January 27, 1984), p. 9.

165. See Hiro, *Iran Under the Ayatullas*, p. 243; and *Mahiyyat-i Zed-i Enqilabi-ye Anjomani Hujjatiyyah ra Beshenasim* [The counter-revolutionary essence of the Hujjatiyyah Organization exposed], 3 vols. (N.p., n.d.). These contain some reliable documents on the history, activities, resources, and social bases of the Hujjatiyyah. For example, in the city of Isfahan alone, the Hujjatiyyah had nineteen capitalists and large landowners among its members and leaders (see ibid., 3:23–24), in addition to connections with Ayatollahs Khademi, Golpayegani, Kho-ei, Shams-Abadi, and other less influential ulama (ibid., 3:19–21), and also owned and controlled twelve financial organizations, foundations, hospitals, and high schools.

166. Indeed contrary to his previous pledges to defend the impoverished masses, Khomeini advised officials of the government and the ulama to: "involve the bazaar in the affairs [of the government]. . . . In my view this is a very important issue. I have repeatedly said this. . . . This is among the issues which are of utmost importance" (cited in *Aksariyat*, no. 23, September 7, 1984, p. 2). In another speech (January 2, 1984), Khomeini repeated his support for the bazaar: "We must not feel disheartened and must try to have the Bazaar nominate its own people for the elections. You must not feel obligated to anyone, to do as they [*sic*] decide. The Bazaar should have its own will. You must awaken the people in the Bazaar so that in Tehran and other cities they nominate good people to the parliament, so that the next parliament is better than the present one" (cited in *Kar International*, no. 12, March–April 1984, p. 16).

167. See *Kar*, OIPF (majority), no 40 (Khurdad 1984).

168. *New York Times*, December 26, 1983, p. 1 (business section). One report claims that many companies dealing with Iran in Turkey are indeed subsidiaries of U.S.-based and French-based corporations. See *Nameh Mardom*, no. 36 (February 7, 1985),p. 3.

169. The RCD treaty, made up of Iran, Turkey, and Pakistan, was initiated by the United States and Britain in 1964. This treaty was considered an economic basis and supplement of CENTO, a military pact between Iran, Turkey, and Pakistan. See *Kar International*, no. 13 (May–June 1984), p. 6.

170. *Ittila'at* (9 Tir 1361).

171. For example, Taba'taba'ei, the new director of the Mostaz'afan Foundation, indicated that the government had decided to sell lands, real estate, and small industrial establishments to private citizens. Furthermore, in his response to a a reporter's comment that "some workers of the [nationalized] factories have expressed their dismay with the government's decision to return these factories to the original owners," Taba'taba'ei indicated that "our objectives are the implementation of the law of Islam not the satisfaction [of people]. See *Ittila'at* (5 Khurdad 1362/1983), p. 14. See also *Middle East Economic Digest* (November 25, 1983), pp. 11–12.

172. The Eight Point Commands of Ayatollah Khomeini, which were issued in late 1982, are perhaps the official beginning of the Islamic Republic's economic liberalization in postrevolutionary Iran. Theoretically, these commands are measures to ensure conformity to the law and to prevent arbitrary decisions by different ulama and government authorities. In practice, however, it became a legal weapon that was used by the landowners and capitalists to intensify their attacks on workers and peasants. Take, for example, command Number Five (which sanctioned the principle of private property and the right of an individual over his/her properties): theoretically, it could be considered a positive step to protect individual rights and property; in practice, this point could easily be used by the landowners and capitalists to gain control over properties that had either been seized by the peasants or nationalized by the government. For details of these Eight Commands see *Kayhan* (25 Azar 1361/1982). That the Eight Commands of Ayatollah Khomeini enhanced the power of the dominant classes could be observed from Khamoushi's subsequent statement: "Now no governor, if he is a follower of the commands, dare to discredit any members of the merchants' guilds by accusing him of being pro-Shah because he happened to appear in a photograph with the Shah ten years ago" (cited in *Rahe Tudeh*, January 27, 1984, pp. 9, 14).

173. Ashraf, "Bazaar-Mosque Alliance," p. 563.

174. *Ittila'at* (4 Dey 1361/1982), p. 5 (my translation).

175. *Ittila'at* (10 Bahman 1361/1982), p. 2 (my translation). Sediq Taqva-ie, an attorny for the Committee on Guild Affairs in Tehran, also points to the connection between the Ministry of Commerce and large capitalists. See *Ittila'at* (23 Dey 1361/1982), p. 2.

176. *Ittila'at* (8 Isfand 1361/1982), p. 2 (my translation).

177. Ulyanovsky, "The Iranian Revolution and Its Outcomes," pp. 110–11 (in Russian).

178. See Algar, *The Islamic Revolution;* Arjomand, *The Turban for the Crown;* and Cottam, "Nationalism and Islamic Revolution in Iran," pp. 263–77.

179. Bazargan, *Inqilab-i*, p. 198.

180. Cited in Poulantzas, *Fascism and Dictatorship*, p. 253.

181. Palmeiri, *The Philosophy of Fascism*, p. 33. See also Marcuse, "The Struggle Against Liberalism in the Totalitarian View of the State," pp. 3–42.

182. Palmeiri, *The Philosophy of Fascism*, p. 39.

183. Mutahhari, "Shahid," pp. 125–26, 128.

184. *Jomhouri-ye Islami* (19 Shahrivar 1359/1980).

185. Palmeiri, *The Philosophy of Fascism*, p. 44.

186. Poulantzas, *Fascism and Dictatorship*, pp. 85–86.

187. *Ittila'at* (6 Isfand 1358/1980), p. 4; and *Jomhouri-ye Islami* (7 Isfand 1358/1980), p. 6.

188. *Jomhouri-ye Islami* (9 Isfand 1358/1980), p. 4.

189. Cited in *Aksariyat*, no. 44 (February 11, 1985).

190. For the list of people killed by the Islamic Republic during the reign of terror, see *Mojahid*, no. 261 (Special Issue, 15 Shahrivar 1364/1985).

191. Moore, *Social Origins of Dictatorship and Democracy,* p. 447.

192. Poulantzas, *Fascism and Dictatorship,* p. 352.

193. Ibid., p. 257.

194. Marx, "Civil War in France," p. 289.

195. *Aksariyat,* no. 25 (September 24, 1984), p. 4.

196. *Aksariyat,* no. 30 (October 29, 1984), p. 9.

197. Cited in *Aksariyat,* no. 43 (February 4, 1985), p. 3.

198. See the Islamic Republic of Iran, *Layehe-ye Qisas va Qavanin-i A'n* [The retaliation bill and its laws].

199. See Roghayyeh-i Daneshgari, *Az Ranj va Razm-i Zanan-i Iran* [On the suffering and struggle of Iranian women] (N.p.: OIPF-Majority, 1984), p. 22.

200. Ibid., p. 23. Women are also banned from becoming judges, and many women judges were fired from their jobs by the authorities of the Islamic Republic. According to Moqtada-ei, a member of the Supreme Court of the Islamic Republic, "Sixty women judges were fired from their occupations, and of this group those who were qualified were rehired to perform non-judiciary duties in the court." See also *Ittila'at* (19 Mehr 1361/1982).

201. Cited in Daneshgari, *Az Rang,* p. 24. See also *Sobh-i Azadigan* (10 Mehre 1962/1983).

202. Daneshgari, *Az Rang,* pp. 24–28.

Bibliography

Abdulghani, Jasim M. *Iraq and Iran: The Years of Crisis*. Baltimore, Md.: Johns Hopkins University Press, 1984.

Abrahamian, Ervand. "The Causes of the Constitutional Revolution in Iran." *International Journal of Middle East Studies* 10 (1979): 381–414.

—— *Iran Between Two Revolutions*. Princeton: Princeton University Press, 1982.

—— "Structural Causes of the Iranian Revolution." *MERIP Reports* 87 (May 1980): 21–26.

Adami'yat, Fereydoun. "Ashoftegy dar Fekr-i Tarikhi" [Confusion in historical thinking]. In Ali Dahbashi, ed., *Yadnamey-ye Jalal-i Ale-Ahmad* [For Jalal Ale-Ahmad], pp. 538–50. Tehran: Pasargad, 1364/1985.

—— *Idi'olozhi-ye Nahzat-i Mashrutiyat-i Iran* [The ideology of the Constitutional Movement in Iran]. Tehran: Payam, 1976.

—— *Shourish bar Imtiyaz'nameye Rizhi* [Rebellion against the Regie concession]. Tehran: Payam, 1360/1981.

Adams, Charles C. *Islam and Modernism in Egypt*. New York: Russell and Russell, 1968.

Afshari, Mohammad Reza. "The Pishivaran and Merchants in Pre-Capitalist Iranian Society: An Essay on the Background and Causes of the Constitutional Revolution." *International Journal of Middle East Studies* 15 (1983): 133–55.

Agayev, S. L. "Revolutionary Movements and Reforms in Iran." In Rostilavo Ulyanovski, ed., *The Revolutionary Process in the East: Past and Present,* pp. 226–53. Moscow: Progress Publishers, 1985.

Ahmad, Aziz. *Islamic Modernism in India and Pakistan: 1857–1964*. London: Oxford University Press, 1967.

Ajami, Fouad. *The Arab Predicament: Arab Political Thought and Practice Since 1967*. Cambridge: Cambridge University Press, 1967.

Akhavi, Shahrough. *Religion and Politics in Contemporary Iran*. Albany: State University of New York Press, 1980.

Alavi, Hamza. "The State in Post-Colonial Societies: Pakistan and Bangladesh." *New Left Review* 74 (1972): 59–81.

Ale-Ahmad, Jalal. *Dar Khedmat va Khianat-i Roushanfikran* [Concerning the service and betrayal of the intellectuals]. Tehran: Ravaq Publications, n.d.

—— *Plagued by the West* [Gharbzadegi]. Translated by Paul Sprachman. New York: Columbia University Press, 1982.

Alexander, Bobby C. "Correcting Misinterpretations of Turner's Theory: An African-American Pentecostal Illustration." *Journal for the Scientific Study of Religion* 30, no. 1 (1991): 26–44.

Alexander, Marx (pseud. for Walter Z. Lacqueur). "Communist Strategy in the Middle East." *Twentieth Century* (November 1951).

Algar, Hamid. *The Islamic Revolution in Iran.* London: Open Press, 1983.

—— "The Oppositional Role of the Ulama in Twentieth-Century Iran." In Nikkie R. Keddie, ed., *Scholars, Saints, and Sufis,* pp. 231–55. Berkeley and Los Angeles: University of California Press, 1972.

—— *Religion and State in Modern Iran.* Berkeley: University of California Press, 1969.

—— *The Roots of Islamic Revolution.* London: Open Press, 1983.

Ali, Amir. *The Spirit of Islam.* London, 1922.

Althusser, Louis. *For Marx.* London: Verso, 1979.

—— "Ideology and Ideological State Apparatuses." In *Lenin and Philosphy,* pp. 121–73. London: New Left Books, 1971.

Althusser, Louis, and Etienne Balibar. *Reading Capital.* London: Verso, 1979.

Amin, Samir. *Accumulation on a World Scale.* New York: Monthly Review Press, 1974.

Aminzade, Ronald. *Class, Politics, and Early Industrial Capitalism.* Albany: State University of New York Press, 1981.

Ansari, Hamied. *Egypt: The Stalled Society.* Albany: State University of New York Press, 1986.

Apter, David, ed. *Choice and Politics of Allocation: A Developmental Approach.* New Haven: Yale University Pres, 1977.

—— *Ideology and Discontent.* New York: Free Press, 1964.

Arendt, Hannah. *The Origin of Totalitarianism.* Cleveland: Meridian Books, 1958.

—— *On Revolution.* New York: Viking, 1965.

Aresvik, Oddvar. *The Agricultural Development of Iran.* New York: Praeger, 1976.

Arjomand, Said A. *The Shadow of God and the Hidden Imam.* Chicago: University of Chicago Press, 1979.

—— *The Turban for the Crown: The Islamic Revolution in Iran.* New York: Oxford University Press, 1988.

Arjomand, Said A., ed. *From Nationalism to Revolutionary Islam.* Albany: State University of New York Press, 1984.

Ashraf, Ahmad. "Bazaar-Mosque Alliance: The Social Basis of Revolts and Revolutions." *Politics, Culture, and Society* 1, no. 4 (Summer 1988): 538–67.

—— "Dihqanan, Zamin va Inqilab" [Peasants, land, and revolution]. In *Masael-i*

Arzi va Dihqani [The agrarian and peasant problems], pp. 6–49. Tehran: Agah, 1361/1982.

——— "Historical Obstacles to the Development of a Bourgeoisie in Iran." In M. A. Cook, ed., *Studies in the Economic History of the Middle East.* London: Oxford University Press, 1970.

Ashraf, Ahmad, and Ali Banuazizi. "The State, Classes, and Modes of Mobilization in the Iranian Revolution." *State, Culture and Society* 1, no. 3 (Spring 1985): 3–40.

Azad, Shahrzad. "Workers' and Peasants' Councils in Iran." *Monthly Review* 32, no. 5 (October 1980): 14–29.

Azar, Gil. "Mobarizat-i Dehqani dar Iran" [Peasant struggles in Iran]. *Donya* 7 (Mehr 1359/1980): 74–77.

Azimi, Fakhreddin. *Iran: The Crisis of Democracy.* London: I. B. Tauris, 1989.

Baer, Gabriel. *Egyptian Guilds in Modern Times.* Jerusalem: Israel Oriental Society, 1964.

Bahadur, Kalim. *The Jamma'at-i Islami of Pakistan.* New Delhi: Chetana, 1977.

Bakhash, Shaul. *The Reign of the Ayatullahs: Iran and the Islamic Revolution.* New York: Basic Books, 1984.

Baku, Esmail. "Oil Revenue and Socio-Economic Development in Iran, 1963–1978." Ph.D. diss., University of Wisconsin–Madison, 1980.

Baldwin, George B. *Planning and Development in Iran.* Baltimore: John Hopkins University Press, 1967.

Banani, Amin. *The Modernization of Iran.* Stanford, Calif.: Stanford University Press, 1961.

Bank Markazi Iran. *Annual Report and Balance Sheet* (various issues).

Bartsch, William H. "The Impact of the Oil Industry on the Economy of Iran." In Raymond F. Mikesell, ed., *Foreign Investment in Petroleum and Mineral Industries,* pp. 237–63. Baltimore, Md.: John Hopkins University Press, 1971.

Batatu, Hann. "Syria's Muslim Brethren." *MERIP Reports* (November–December 1982): 12–34, 36.

Bazargan, Mehdi. *Defa'at* [Defenses]. Tehran: Modarres Publications, 1350/1971.

——— *Inqilab-i Iran dar Du Harakat* [The Iranian Revolution in two stages]. Tehran: Mehdi Bazargan, 1363/1984.

Benedick, Richard E. *Industrial Finance in Iran.* Boston: Division of Research, Harvard Business School, 1964.

Berger, Peter L., and Thomas Luckmann. "Sociology of Religion and Sociology of Knowledge." In Roland Robertson, ed., *Sociology of Religion,* pp. 61–73. Baltimore, Md.: Penguin Books, 1969.

Bharier, Julian. *Economic Development in Iran, 1900–1970.* London: Oxford University Press, 1971.

Bill, James A. *The Eagle and the Lion.* New Haven: Yale University Press, 1988.

Binder, Leonard. *Iran: Political Development in a Changing Society.* Berkeley: University of California Press, 1962.

Bonine, Michael E. "Shops and Shopkeepers: Dynamics of an Iranian Provincial Bazaar." In Bonine and Nikki R. Keddie, eds., *Modern Iran: The Dialectics of Continuity and Change.* Albany: State University of New York Press, 1981.

Bornschier, Volker, and Christopher Chase-Dunn. *Transnational Corporations and Underdevelopment.* New York: Praeger, 1985.

Bottomore, Tom, ed. *A Dictionary of Marxist Thought.* Cambridge: Harvard University Press, 1983.

Braudel, Fernand. *On History.* Translated by Sarah Matthews. Chicago: University of Chicago Press, 1980.

Brenner, Robert. "Agrarian Class Structure and Economic Development in Preindustrial Europe." *Past and Present* 70 (1976): 30–113.

Brun, Thiery, and Rene Dumont. "Iran: Imperial Pretensions and Agricultural Dependence." *MERIP Reports* 8, no. 8 (October 1978): 15–20.

Burawoy, Michael. "The Politics of Production and Production of Politics: A Comparative Analysis of Piecework Machine Shops in the United States and Hungary." In Maurice Zeitlin, *Political Power and Social Theory,* pp. 261–99. Greenwich, Conn.: JAI Press, 1980.

Burris, Val. "The Discovery of the New Middle Class." *Theory and Society* 15 (1986): 317–49.

Butterworth, Charles E. "Prudence versus Legitimacy: The Persistent Theme in Islamic Political Thought." In Ali E. Hillal Dessouki, *Islamic Resurgence in the Arab World,* pp. 84–114. New York: Praeger, 1982.

Cantril, Hadely. *The Psychology of Social Movements.* New York: John Wiley, 1941.

Cardoso, Fernando Henrique, and Enzo Faletto. *Dependency and Development in Latin America.* Berkeley: University of California Press, 1979.

Collier, David, and Ruth B. Collier. "Who Does What, to Whom, and How: Toward a Comparative Analysis of Latin American Corporatism." In James M. Malloy, ed., *Authoritarianism and Corporatism in Latin America,* pp. 489–512. Pittsburgh: University of Pittsburgh Press, 1977.

Correspondence. "Correspondence Respecting the Persian Tobacco Concession." Great Britain. *Sessional Papers* 79 (1892).

—— May 6, 1891. "Acting Consul-General Paton to Mr. R. J. Kennedy."

—— June 2, 1891. "Mr. R. J. Kennedy to the Marquis of Salisbury."

—— July 27, 1891. "Mr. R. J. Kennedy to the Marquis of Salisbury."

—— August 15, 1891. "Acting Consul-General Paton to Mr. R. J. Kennedy."

—— September 9, 1891. "Mr. R. J. Kennedy to the Marquis of Salisbury."

—— September 10, 1891. "Acting Consul-General Paton to Mr. R. J. Kennedy."

—— October 6, 1891. "Mr. R. J. Kennedy to the Marquis of Salisbury."

—— November 20, 1891. "Consul Preece to Sir F. Lascelles."

—— January 18, 1892. "Sir F. Lascelles to the Marquis of Salisbury."

Cottam, Richard W. *Nationalism in Iran.* Pittsburgh: University of Pittsburgh Press, 1979.

—— "Nationalism and Islamic Revolution in Iran." *Canadian Review of Studies in Nationalism* 9 (Fall 1982): 263–77.

Coward, Rosalind, and John Ellis. *Language and Materialism*. London: Routledge and Kegan Paul, 1977.

Crecelius, Daniel. "Nonideological Responses of the Egyptian Ulama to Modernization." In Nikki R. Keddie, ed., *Scholars, Saints, and Sufis*, pp. 167–210. Berkeley: University of California Press, 1972.

Crouchley, A. E. "The Development of Commerce in the Reign of Mohammad Ali." *L'Egypte Contemporaine*, nos. 158–69 (March–February 1937): 305–18.

Cuno, Kenneth M. "The Origin of Private Ownership of Land in Egypt: A Reappraisal." *International Journal of Middle East Studies* 12 (1980): 245–75.

Curzon, George. *Persia and the Persian Question*. London: Longmans Green, 1982.

—— "Memorandum on the Agreement." In *Document on British Foreign Policy, 1919–1939*, Vol. 6.

Dahnavi [no first name]. *Qiyam-i Khounin-i Panzdah-i Khordad bi Ravayat-i Asnad* [The bloody uprising of the fifteenth of Khurdad according to the documents]. Tehran: Rasa Institute of Cultural Services, 1981.

Davani, Ali. *Nahzat-i Rohaniyun-i Iran* [The Movement of the Clergy in Iran]. 11 vols. Tehran: Imam Reza Cultural Foundation, 1981.

Davies, James C. "The J-Curve of Rising and Declining Satisfaction as a Cause of Some Great Revolutions and a Contained Rebellion." In Hugh D. Graham and Ted R. Gurr, eds., *Violence in America*, pp. 671–709. New York: Signet, 1969.

—— "Toward a Theory of Revolution." *American Sociological Review* 27 (1962): 5–18.

De Janvry, Alain, and Carlos Garramon. "Laws of Motion of Capital in the Center-Periphery Structure." *Review of Radical Political Economy* 9, no.2 (1977): 29–38.

De Jong, F. *Turuq and Turuq-Linked Institutions in Nineteenth Century Egypt*. Leiden: E. J. Brill, 1978.

Desouki, Ali E. Hillah, ed. *The Iraq-Iran War*. Princeton: Princeton University Press, 1984.

Deutsch, Karl W. "Social Mobilization and Political Development." *American Political Science Review* 55 (1961): 493–514.

Devlin, John F. *Syria: Modern State in an Ancient Land*. Boulder, Colo.: Westview, 1983.

Devuall, Raymond, Steven Jackson, Bruce M. Russett, Duncan Snidal, and David Sylvan. " A Formal Model of 'Dependencia' Theory: Structure and Measurement." In Merritt and Russett, *From National Development to Global Community*, pp. 312–50. London: Allen and Unwin, 1981.

Dion, Leon. "Polical Ideology as a Tool of Functional Analysis in Socio-political Dynamics: An Hypothesis." *Canadian Journal of Economics and Political Science* 35 (February–November 1959): 47–59.

Dobb, Maurice. *Studies in the Development of Capitalism.* New York: International Publishers, 1978.

Drysdale, Alasdair. "The Asad Regime and Its Troubles." *MERIP Reports* (November–December 1982): 3–11, 36.

Dshawanshir, Farajullah M. *Tajrebeh-ye Bist-to Hasht-i Mordad* [The experience of twenty-eight of Mordad]. Tehran: Tudeh, 1980.

Eden, Anthony. *Full Circle.* Boston: Houghton Mifflin, 1960.

Esping-Andersen, Gosta, Roger Friedland, and Erik Olin Wright. "Modes of Class Struggle and the Capitalist State." *Kapitalistate,* nos. 4–5 (1976): 186–218.

Evans, Peter. *Dependent Development: The Alliance of Multinational, State, and Local Capital in Brazil.* Princeton: Princeton University Press, 1979.

Evans, Peter, Dietrich Rueschemeyer, and Theda Skocpol. *Bringing the State Back In.* New York: Cambridge University Press, 1985.

Faghfoory, Mohammad H. "The Role of the Ulama in Twentieth-Century Iran with Particular Reference to Ayatollah Haj Sayyid Abul-Qasim Kashani." Ph.D. diss., University of Wisconsin–Madison,1977.

Fanon, Frantz. *The Wretched of the Earth.* New York: Grove, 1963.

Farsoun, Karen. "State Capitalism in Algeria." *MERIP Reports* 35 (February 1975): 3–30.

Fernandez, Raul A., and Jose F. Ocampo. "The Andean Pact and State Capitalism in Colombia." *Latin American Perspectives* 2, no. 6 (Fall 1975): 3.

Field, Michael. "Agro-business and Agricultural Planning in Iran." *World Crops* (March–April 1972): 68–72.

Firzli, Nicola, ed. *The Iraq-Iran Conflict.* Paris: Editions du Monde Arabe, 1981.

Fischer, Michael J. *Iran: From Religious Dispute to Revolution.* Cambridge: Harvard University Press, 1980.

Fisher, W. B. *The Cambridge History of Iran.* Cambridge: Cambridge University Press, 1968.

Fitzgerald, Edmund, Valpy Knox, Edgardo Floto, and David Lehmann, eds. *The State and Economic Development in Latin America.* Cambridge: Center of Latin American Studies, Cambridge University, 1977.

Floor, Willem M. "Change and Development in the Judicial System of Qajar Iran (1800–1925)." In Edmund Bosworth and Carole Hillenbrand, eds., *Qajar Iran,* pp. 113–47. Edinburgh: Edinburgh University Press, 1983.

—— "The Guilds in Iran—An Overview from the Earliest Beginnings till 1972." *Zeitschrift der Deutschen Morgenlandisschen Geselschaft* 125 (1975): 99–116.

—— "The Merchants [*tujjar*] in Qajar Iran." *Zeitschrift der Deutschen Morgenlandischen Gesellschaft* 126 (1976): 101–35.

—— "The Revolutionary Character of the Ulama: Wishful Thinking or Reality?" In Nikki R. Keddie, ed., *Religion and Politics in Iran,* pp. 73–79. New Haven: Yale University Press, 1983.

Fox, Jonathan. "Has Brazil Moved Toward State Capitalism?" *Latin American Perspectives* 7, no. 1 (1980): 64–86.

Fulbrook, Mary. *Piety and Politics: Religion and the Rise of Absolutism in En-*

gland, Wurttemberg and Prussia. Cambridge: Cambridge University Press, 1983.

Furet, François. *Interpreting the French Revolution.* New York: Cambridge University Press, 1981.

Gallagher, Charles F. "Contemporary Islam: The Plateau of Particularism, Problems of Religion and Nationalism in Iran." *American Universities Field Staff* 15, no. 2 (July 1966): 1–25.

Galtung, Johan. "A Structural Theory of Imperialism." *Journal of Peace Research* 8, no. 2 (1971): 81–117.

Galvani, John. "Syria and the Baath Party." *MERIP Reports* 25 (February 1974): 3–16.

Garzouzi, Eva. "Land Reform in Syria." *Middle East Journal* 17, nos. 1–2 (Winter–Spring 1963): 83–90.

Gasiorowski, Mark J. "The 1953 Coup d'Etat in Iran." *International Journal of Middle East Studies* 19, no. 3 (August 1987): 261–86.

Geertz, Clifford. *The Interpretation of Culture.* New York: Basic Books, 1973.

Giddens, Anthony. *A Contemporary Critique of Historical Materialism.* Berkeley: University of California Press, 1983.

—— *Nation-States and Violence.* Berkeley: University of California Press, 1985.

Gismondi, Michael A. "Transformation in the Holy: Religious Resistance and Hegemonic Struggles in the Nicaraguan Revolution." *Latin American Perspectives* 13, no. 3 (Summer 1986): 13–36.

Godelier, Maurice. *Rationality and Irrationality in Economics.* London: New Left Books, 1972.

Gold, David A., Y. H. Lo, and Erik O. Wright. "Recent Developments in Marxist Theories of the Capitalist State." *Monthly Review* (October 1975), part 1, pp. 29–41; and (November 1975), part 2, pp. 36–51.

Goodey, Chris. "Workers Councils in Iranian Factories." *MERIP Reports* 88 (June 1980): 5–9.

Grady, Henry F. "What Went Wrong in Iran?" *Saturday Evening Post,* January 5, 1952, pp. 56–58.

Graham, Robert. *Iran: The Illusion of Power.* New York: St. Martin's, 1979.

Gran, Peter. *Islamic Roots of Capitalism.* Austin: University of Texas Press, 1979.

Grant, Christian P. *The Syrian Desert.* New York: Macmillan, 1968.

Griffin, Larry J., Michael E. Wallace, and Beth A. Rubin. "Capitalist Resistance to the Organization of Labor Force Before the New Deal: Why? How? Success?" *American Sociological Review* 51 (April 1986): 147–67.

Griggs, Lee. "Oil and Water Rebuild an Ancient Land." *Fortune,* November 1970, pp. 89–90, 128.

Gurr, Tedd R. *Why Men Rebel.* Princeton: Princeton University Press, 1970.

Hairi, Hadi. *Shi'ism and Constitutionalism in Iran.* Leiden, Nethelands: E. J. Brill, 1977.

Halliday, Fred. *Iran: Dictatorship and Development.* New York: Penguin Books, 1979.

—— "Iran's Revolution: The First Year." *MERIP Reports* 88 (June 1980):3–5.

Hamilton, Nora. *The Limits of State Autonomy: Post Revolutionary Mexico.* Princeton: Pinceton University Press, 1982.

Hein, Wolfgang, and Konrad Stenzel. "The Capitalist State and Underdevelopment in Latin America–The Case of Venezuela." *Kapitalistate* 2 (1973).

Hendersen, Barrie. "The Chilean State After the Coup." *Socialist Registers* (1977): 121–41.

Hickman, William F. *Ravaged and Reborn: The Iranian Army.* Washington, D.C.: Brookings Institution, 1982.

Hinnebusch, Raymond A. "The Islamic Movement in Syria: Sectarian Conflict and Urban Rebellion in an Authoritarian Populist Regime." In Ali E. Hillal Dessouki, ed., *Islamic Resurgence in the Arab World*, pp. 138–69. New York: Praeger, 1982.

Hiro, Dilip. *Iran Under the Ayatullahs.* London: Routledge and Kegan Paul, 1985.

Holloway, John, and Sol Picciotto, eds. *State and Capital: A Marxist Debate.* London: Edward Arnold, 1978.

Holmström, David. "Syria—Unity, Liberty and Socialism." *Middle East International* 22 (London, April 1973): 11–13.

Holt, Peter M., ed. *Political and Social Change in Modern Egypt.* London: Oxford University Press, 1968.

Hoselitz, Bert F., and Wilbert E. Moore. *Industrialization and Society.* The Hague: Mouton, 1963.

Hourani, Albert. "The Syrian in Egypt in the Eighteenth and Nineteenth Centuries." In *Colloque International sur l'Histoire du Caire*, pp. 221–33. Cairo: General Egyptian Book Organization, 1969.

Howard, Harry N. "The Development of United States Policy in the Near East, South Asia, and Africa During 1954: Part I." *Department of State Bulletin* (February 14, 1955): 256–67.

Hunseler, Peter. "The Historical Antecedent of the Shatt-al-Arab Dispute." In M. S. El Azhary, *The Iran-Iraq War*, pp. 8–19. London: Croom Helm, 1984.

Hunter, Robert F. *Egypt Under the Khedives, 1805–1879: From Household Government to Modern Bureaucracy.* Pittsburgh: University of Pittsburgh Press, 1984.

Huntington, Samuel. *Political Order in Changing Societies.* New Haven: Yale University Press, 1968.

Hussein, Mahmoud. *Class Conflict in Egypt, 1945–1970.* New York: Monthly Review Press, 1973.

International Labor Office. *Employment and Income Policies for Iran.* Geneva: ILO, 1973.

International Monetary Fund. *Government Finance Statistics Yearbook: 1982.* Washington, D.C.: IMF, 1983.

Iqbal, Allama Muhammad. *The Reconstruction of Religious Thought in Islam.* London: Oxford University Press, 1934.

—— *Speeches and Statements of Iqbal.* Compiled by A. R. Tariq. Lahore: Sh. Ghulam Ali, 1973.

Issawi, Charles. *Egypt: An Economic and Social Analysis.* London: Oxford University Press, 1947.

—— *Egypt in Revolution: An Economic Analysis.* London: Oxford University Press, 1963.

—— "Social Structure and Ideology in Iraq, Lebanon, Syria, and the UAR." *Journal of International Affairs* 19, no. 1 (1965): 39–46.

Issawi, Charles, ed. *The Economic History of Iran, 1800–1914.* Chicago: University of Chicago Press, 1971.

Ivanov, Mikhail S. *Tarikh-i Novin-i Iran* [The history of modern Iran]. Stokholm: Tudeh, 1977.

Jackson, Steven, Bruce Russett, Duncan Snidal, and David Sylvan. "Conflict and Coercion in Dependent States." *Journal of Conflict Resolution* 22 (1978): 627–57.

Jaffee, David. "Export Dependence and Economic Growth: A Reformation and Respecification." *Social Forces* 64, no. 1, (1985): 102–18.

Jazani, Bijan. *The Socio-economic Analysis of a Dependent Capitalist State.* London: Iran Committee, 1973.

—— *Tarh-i Jame-eh Shenasi va Estratejik-i Inqelabi-ye Iran* [A sociological and strategic scheme for the revolutionary movement in Iran]. N.p.: Organization of the Iranian People's Feda'iyan Guerillas, 1978.

Jessop, Bob. "Recent Theories of the Capitalist State." *Cambridge Journal of Economics* 1 (1977): 353–73.

Johnson, Chalmers. *Revolution and the Social System.* Stanford: Hoover Institution, Stanford University, 1964.

—— *Revolutionary Change.* Boston: Little Brown, 1966.

Kambakhsh, Abdolsamad. *Nazari beh Jonbesh-i Komonisti va Kargari dar Iran* [A short survey of the workers' and Communist movement in Iran]. Stokholm: Tudeh, 1972.

Karbala'i, Shaykh Hasan. *Qarardad-i Rizhi-ye 1890 M.* [The Regie contract of 1890]. Tehran: Mobarizan, 1361/1982.

Kasravi, Ahmad. *Chihil Magalah-i Kasravi* [Forty essays by Kasravi]. Edited by Yahya Zoka-ie. Tehran: Kitab-Khaneh-i Tohuri, 1335/1956.

—— *Dar Piramoun-i Islam* [On Islam]. Tehran: Paydar Bookstore, 1348/1969.

—— *Din va Siyasat* [Religion and politics]. 2d ed. Tehran: 1348/1960.

Kazemi, Farhad. *Poverty and Revolution in Iran.* New York: New York University Press, 1980.

Kazemi, Farhad, and Ervand Abrahamian. "The Non-Revolutionary Peasantry of Modern Iran." *Iranian Studies* 11 (1978): 259–304.

Keddie, Nikki R. "The Iranian Revolution in Comparative Perspective." *American Historical Review* 88, no. 3 (June 1983): 579–98.

—— "The Iranian Village Before and After Land Reform." In Henry Bernstein, ed., *Underdevelopment and Development,* pp. 142–74. Baltimore, Md.: Penguin Books, 1973.

—— *Religion and Rebellion in Iran: The Tobacco Protest of 1891–92.* London: Cass, 1966.

—— *Roots of Revolution: An Interpretive History of Modern Iran.* New Haven: Yale University Press, 1981.

—— "The Roots of Ulama Power in Modern Iran." In Keddie, ed., *Scholars, Saints and Sufis,* pp. 211–29. Los Angeles: University of California Press, 1972.

—— *Sayyid Jamal al-Din "al-Afghani."* Berkeley and Los Angeles: University of California Press, 1972.

Keilany, Ziad. "Socialism and Economic Change in Syria." *Middle Eastern Studies* 9 (January 1973): 61–72.

Khomeini, Ruhollah. *Islam and Revolution: The Writings and Declarations of Imam Khomeini.* Translated and annotated by Hamid Algar. Berkeley: Mizan Press, 1981.

Kornhauser, William. *The Politics of Mass Society.* Glencoe, Ill.: Free Press, 1959.

Krasin, Yu. "Ideology and Policy in the Revolutionary Movement." *The Contemporary Revolutionary Process Theoretical Essay,* pp. 140-53. Moscow: Progress Publishers, 1985.

Laclau, Ernesto. *Politics and Ideology in Marxist Theory.* London: Verso, 1979.

Lambton, Ann K. S. *Landlord and Peasant in Persia: A Study of Land Tenure and Land Revenue Administration.* Oxford: Oxford University Press, 1953.

—— *The Persian Land Reform, 1962–66.* Oxford: Clarendon Press, 1969.

—— "The Persian Ulama and Constitutional Reform." In T. Fahd, ed., *Le Shi'isme Imamite,* pp. 245–68. Paris: Presses Universitaires de France, 1970.

—— *Theory and Practice in Medieval Persian Government.* London: Variorum Reprints, 1980.

Langer, Susanne K. *Philosophy in a New Key.* Cambridge: Harvard University Press, 1951.

Larrain, Jorge. *Marxism and Ideology.* London: Macmillan, 1983.

Lawson, Fred H. "Social Bases for the Hamah Revolt." *MERIP Reports* (November–December 1982): 24–28.

—— "Social Origins of Aggressive Foreign Policy: The Case of Muhammad 'Ali of Egypt, 1800–1830." Ph.D. diss., University of California, Los Angeles, 1982.

Lenczowski, George, ed. *Iran Under the Pahlavis.* Stanford, Calif.: Hoover Institute Press, 1978.

Lenin, V. I. "The Collapse of the Second International." *Collected Works,* 21:205–59. Moscow: Progress, 1980.

—— "Development of Capitalism in Russia." *Collected Works,* vol. 3. Moscow: Progress, 1980.

—— "Imperialism, the Highest Stage of Capitalism." *Collected Works,* 22:185–304. Moscow: Progress, 1980.

—— "May Day Action by the Revolutionary Proletariat." *Collected Works,* 19:218–27. Moscow: Progress, 1980.

—— "The State and Revolution." *Collected Works,* 25:381–492. Moscow: Progress, 1980.

—— "What Is to Be Done?" *Collected Works,* 5:347–529. Moscow: Progress, 1980.

Levy, Walter. "Economic Review: Economic Problems Facing a Settlement of the Iranian Oil Controversy." *Middle East Journal* 8, no. 1 (1954): 91–95.

Leys, Colin. "The Overdeveloped Post-Colonial State: A Re-evaluation." *Review of African Political Economy* 5 (January–April 1976): 39–48.

Lilienthal, David E. *Journals.* 5 vols. New York: Harper and Row.

Looney, Robert E. *Economic Origins of the Iranian Revolution.* New York: Pergamon, 1982.

MacDonald, William. "Persia and British Honor." *The Nation,* September 13, 1919: 371–72.

Mahdavi, Hosein. "Patterns and Problems of Economic Development in Rentier States: The Case of Iran." In M. A. Cook, ed., *Studies in the Economic History of the Middle East.* London: Oxford University Press, 1970.

Malloy, James M. *Authoritarianism and Corporatism in Latin America.* Pittsburgh: University of Pittsburgh Press, 1977.

Mannheim, Karl. *Ideology and Utopia.* New York: Harvest, 1986.

Marcuse, Herbert. *An Essay on Liberation.* Boston: Beacon Press, 1969.

—— "The Struggle Against Liberalism in the Totalitarian View of the State." In *Negations: Essays in Critical Theory,* pp. 3–42. Middlesex, England: Penguin Books, 1968.

Marsot, Afaf Lutfi al-Sayyid. *Egypt in the Reign of Muhammed Ali.* Cambridge: Cambridge University Press, 1984.

—— *Egypt's Liberal Experiment 1922–1936.* Berkeley and Los Angeles: University of California Press, 1977.

—— *Protest Movements and Religious Undercurrents in Egypt: Past and Present.* Washington, D.C.: Center for Contemporary Arab Studies, Georgetown University, 1984.

—— "The Role of the Ulama in Egypt During the Early 19th Century." In Peter M. Holt, ed., *Political and Social Change in Modern Egypt,* pp. 264–80. London: Oxford University Press, 1968.

Marx, Karl. "Civil War in France." In Karl Marx and Frederick Engels, *Selected Works,* pp. 274–313. New York: International Publishers, 1977.

—— "The German Ideology." *Collected Works,* 5:19-116. New York: International Publishers, 1977.

—— "The Holy Family." *Collected Works* 4:1–211. New York: International Publishers, 1975.

—— "The Eighteenth Brumaire of Louis Bonaparte." In Marx and Engels, *Selected Works,* pp. 97–180. New York: International Publishers, 1977.

—— "Preface to *A Contribution to the Critique of Political Economy.*" In Marx and Engels, *Selected Works,* pp. 181–85. New York: International Publishers, 1977.

Mehraban, Rasoul. *Gousheha-ie az Tarikhi Moaser-i Iran* [Aspects of the contemporary history of Iran]. Tehran: Otared, 1361/1982.

Miller, Arthur S. "The Corporation as a Private Government in the World Community." *Virginia Law Review* 46, no. 8 (December 1960): 1539–72.

Mitchell, Richard P. *The Society of the Muslim Brothers*. London: Oxford University Press, 1969.

Moaddel, Mansoor. "The Shi'i Ulama and the State in Iran." *Theory and Society* 15 (1986): 519–56.

—— "State-Centered vs. Class-Centered Perspectives in International Politics: The Case of U.S. and British Participation in the 1953 Coup Against Premier Mosaddeq in Iran." *Studies in Comparative International Development* (Summer 1989): 3–22.

Mojahedin. *Varshekasteqi-ye Tarikhi-ye Dark-i Khorden Bourgeoi-ei Az Islam* [The historical bankruptcy of the petty bourgeois' understanding of Islam] (N.p.: Organization of the People's Mojahedin of Iran, 1983).

Momeni, Baqir. *Masa'leh-ye Arzi va Janq-i Tabaqa'ati dar Iran* [The agrarian problem and class struggle in Iran]. Tehran: Payvand Publications, 1359/1980.

Moore, Barrington, Jr. *Social Origins of Dictatorship and Democracy: Lord and Peasant in the Making of the Modern World*. Boston: Beacon Press, 1966.

Moran, Theodore H. "Iranian Defense Expenditure and the Social Crisis." *International Security* 3, no. 3 (Winter 1978–79): 178–92.

Mosaddegh, Mohammad [Mosaddeq, Mohammed]. *UN Security Council Official Records*. 6th year, 560 meeting, S/PV. 560, 1951.

Mostowfi, Abdullah. *Tarikh-i Edjtemai va Edari-ye Doureh-ye Qajarieh* [The social and administrative history of the Qajar period]. Tehran: Zovvar Bookstore, 1942.

Mustafa, Abdel-Rahim. "The Breakdown of the Monopoly System in Egypt after the 1840s." In Peter M. Holt, ed., *Political and Social Change in Modern Egypt*, pp. 291–307. London: Oxford University Press, 1968.

Mutahhari, Ayatullah Murtada. "Shahid." In Mehdi Abedi and Gary Legenhausen, eds., *Jihad and Shahadat*, pp. 125–28. Houston: Institute for Research and Islamic Studies, 1986.

Nashat, Guity. *Women and Revolution in Iran*. Boulder, Colo.: Westview, 1983.

Nateq, Homa. "Sar Aghaz-i Eqtedar-i Eqtesadi va Siasi-ye Mollayan" [The rise of the political and economic dominance of the clergy]. *Alefba* 2 (Summer 1983): 48–65.

Neuhouser, Kevin. "The Radicalization of the Brazilian Catholic Church in Comparative Perspective." *American Sociological Review* 54 (April 1989): 233–44.

Nik-A'een, Amir. *Dar Bareh-ye Mas'aleh-ye Arzi va Jonbesh-i Dehghani dar Iran* [Concerning the problem of land and the peasant movement in Iran]. Tehran: Organization of Democratic Youth and Students of Iran, 1359/1980.

Nirumand, Bahman. *Iran: The New Imperialism in Action*. New York: Monthly Review Press, 1967.

Nyrop, Richard F. *Syria: A Country Study*. Washington, D.C.: American University, 1972.

O'Ballance, Edgar. "The Iraqi-Iranian War: The First Round." *Parameters: Journal of the U.S. Army War College* 11, no. 1 (March 1981): 54–59.

Oberschall, Anthony, R. "Rising Expectations and Political Turmoil." *Journal of Development Studies* 6, no. 1 (October 1969): 5–22.

—— Social Conflicts and Social Movements. Englewood Cliffs, N.J.: Prentice-Hall, 1973.

O'Brien, Philip J. "The Emperor Has No Clothes: Class and State in Latin America." In Fitzgerald, Knox, Floto, and Lehman, eds., The State and Economic Development in Latin America, pp. 34–64. Cambridge: Center of Latin American Studies, Cambridge University, 1977.

O'Donnell, Guillermo. "Corporatism and the Question of the State." In James Malloy, ed., Authoritarianism and Corporatism in Latin America, pp. 47–88. Pittsburgh: University of Pittsburgh Press, 1977.

—— "Reflections on the Pattern of Change in the Bureaucratic-Authoritarian State." Latin American Research Review 13, no. 1 (1978): 3–38.

Orum, Anthony M. Introduction to Political Sociology. Englewood Cliffs, N.J.: Prentice-Hall, 1978.

Oveisi, Hadi F. "Entrepreneurial Activities of the Public Sector in the Economic Development Process: A Comparative Study of Mexico and Iran." Ph.D. diss., University of Texas–Austin, 1979.

Owen, Edward Roger John. Cotton and the Egyptian Economy, 1820–1914: A Study in Trade and Development. Oxford: Clarendon, 1969.

Pahlavi, Mohammad Reza. Answer to History. Translated by Michael Joseph. New York: Stein and Day, 1980.

—— Mission for My Country. New York: McGraw-Hill, 1961.

—— The White Revolution. 2d ed. Tehran: 1967.

Paige, Jeffery M. Agrarian Revolution: Social Movements and Export Agriculture in the Underdeveloped World. New York: Free Press, 1975.

—— "Political Orientation and Riot Participation." American Sociological Review 36 (October 1971): 810–20.

Palmeiri, Mario. The Philosophy of Fascism. Chicago: Dante Alighieri Society, 1936.

Parsa, Misagh. Social Origins of the Iranian Revolution. New Brunswick, N.J.: Rutgers University Press, 1989.

Pesaran, M. H. "The System of Dependent Capitalism in Pre- and Post-Revolutionary Iran." International Journal of Middle East Studies 14 (1982): 501–22

Petran, Tabitha. Syria. New York: Praeger, 1972.

Petras, James F. Critical Perspectives on Imperialism and Social Class in the Third World. New York: Monthly Review Press, 1978.

Petras, James F., and Morris H. Morley. "Development and Revolution: Contradictions in the Advanced Third World Countries–Brazil, South Africa, and Iran." Studies in Comparative International Development 4 (Spring 1981): 3–43.

Petrushevsky, Ilya Pavlovich. Islam in Iran. Albany, N.Y.: Dumy Press, 1985.

Pfeifer, Karen. "State Capitalism and Development." Middle East Research and Information Project Reports 9, no. 5 (June 1979): 3–11.

Pompermayer, Malori J. "The State and Dependent Development." Kapitalistate 1 (1973): 25–27.

Portes, Alejandro. "Political Primitivism, Differential Socialization, and Lower-Class Leftist Radicalism." *American Sociological Review* 36 (October 1971): 820–35.

Poulantzas, Nicos. *Classes in Contemporary Capitalism.* London: Verso, 1978.

—— *Fascism and Dictatorship: The Third International and the Problem of Fascism.* London: New Left Books,1974.

—— *Political Power and Social Classes.* London: Verso, 1978.

Przeworski, Adam. "Material Bases of Consent: Economic and Politics in a Hegemonic System." In Maurice Zeitlin, ed., *Political Power and Socia Theory,* pp. 21–66. Greenwich, Conn.: JAI Press, 1980.

—— "Proletariat into a Class: The Process of Class Formation from Karl Kautsky's 'The Class Struggle' to Recent Controversies." *Politics and Society* 7 (1977): 373–401.

Rabinovich, Itmar. *Syria Under the Ba'th: 1963–66.* Jerusalem: Israel University Press, 1972.

Reich, Bernard. "The United States and Iran: An Overview." In *Economic Consequences of the Iranian Revolution in Iran.* Washington: Joint Economic Committee of the U.S. Congress, 1979.

Rezazadeh, Farhad. "Agricultural Development in Iran: Evaluation of State Planning and Policies in Relation to Agriculture." Ph.D. diss., Iowa State University, 1979).

Richards, Helmut. "Land Reform and Agribusiness in Iran." *MERIP Reports* 43 (December 1975): 3–24.

Rodinson, Maxime. *Islam and Capitalism.* London: Penquin Books, 1974.

—— *Marxism and the Muslim World.* New York: Monthly Review Press. 1985.

Roosevelt, Kermit. *Countercoup: The Struggle for the Control of Iran.* New York: McGraw-Hill, 1979.

Rose, Gregory F. "The Post-Revolutionary Purge of Iran's Armed Forces: A Revisionist Assessment." *Iranian Studies* 17, nos. 2–3 (Spring–Summer 1984): 153–94.

—— "*Velayat-i Faqih* and the Recovery of Islamic Identity in the Thought of Ayatullah Khomeini." In Nikki R. Keddie, ed., *Religion and Politics in Iran: Shi'ism from Quietism to Revolution,* pp. 166-88. New Haven: Yale University Press, 1983.

Rotblat, Howard J. "Social Organization and Development in an Iranian Provincial Bazaar." *Economic Development and Cultural Change* 23 (1975): 292–305.

Safari, Hamid. *Enhesarha-ye Bein-ul-malali dar Iran* [International monopolies in Iran]. Tehran: Tudeh, 1980.

—— "Siasat-i Kargari-ye Regime va Tabaqeh-ye Kargar-i Iran" [The labor policy of the [Shah's] regime and the Iranian working class]. *Donya* 2 (1351/1972): 29–31.

Saifynijad, Javad. *Boneh: Qabl va Ba'ad az Islahat-i Arzi* [Boneh: Before and after the land reform]. Tehran: Toos, 1353/1974.

Saleh, Allahyar. *UN Security Council Official Records*. Sixth year, 563d meeting, S/PV. 563, 1951.

Sampson, Anthony. *The Arms Bazaar: From Lebanon to Lockheed*. New York: Viking, 1977.

Savory, Roger M. "The Problem of Sovereignty in an Ithna Ashari ('Twelver') Shi'i State." *Middle East Review* (Summer 1979): 5–11.

Sayeed, Khalid Bin. "Religion and Nation Building in Pakistan." *Middle East Journal* 17, no. 3 (Summer 1963): 279–91.

Schmitter, Phillippe C. "Still Century of Corporatism?" *Review of Politics* (1974): 85–131.

Schwartz, David C. "A Theory of Revolutionary Behavior." In James C. Davies, ed., *When Men Revolt and Why*, pp. 109–32. New York: Free Press, 1971.

Seale, Patrick. *The Struggle for Syria: A Study of Post-War Arab Politics: 1945–58*, London: Oxford University Press, 1965.

Sewell, William Jr. "Ideologies and Social Revolutions: Reflections on the French Case." *Journal of Modern History* 57, no. 11 (March 1985): 57–85.

Shari'ati, Ali. *Islamshenasi* [*Islamology*]. Mashhad: Tous, 1347/1969.

—— *Marxism and Other Western Fallacies: An Islamic Critique*. Translated by R. Campbell. Berkeley: Mizan Press, 1980.

—— *What Is to Be Done*. Translated by A. Alidust and F. Rajaee. Houston: Institute for Research on Islamic Studies, 1986.

Sheikholeslami, A. Reza. "The Sale of Offices in Qajar Iran, 1858–1896." *Iranian Studies* 4 (Spring–Summer 1971): 104–18.

Skocpol, Theda. "Cultural Idioms and Political Ideologies in the Revolutionary Reconstruction of State Power: A Rejoinder to Sewell." *Journal of Modern History* 51 (March 1984): 86–96.

—— "Rentier State and Shi'a Islam in the Iranian Revolution." *Theory and Society* 11, no. 3 (May 1982): 265–83.

—— *States and Social Revolutions: A Comparative Analysis of France, Russia, and China*. Cambridge: Cambridge University Press, 1979.

Skocpol, Theda, ed. *Vision and Method in Historical Sociology*. New York: Cambridge University Press, 1984.

Smelser, Neil J. *Theory of Collective Behavior*. New York: Free Press of Glencoe, 1963.

Smith, Michel F. *Marketing in Iran*. U.S. Department of Commerce, December 1977.

Smith, Wilfred Cantwell. *Modern Islam in India*. Lahore: Sh. Mohammad Ashraf, 1963.

Soboul, Albert. "Classes and Class Struggle During the French Revolution." *Science and Society* 17, no. 5 (Summer 1953): 238–57.

Spann, Robert E. "Danger Signs Abroad." *World Oil* (June 1952): 291, 296.

—— "Who Controls Crude Reserves Outside of the United States?" *World Oil* 140, no. 1 (January 1955): 221–22, 234.

Stempel, John D. *Inside the Iranian Revolution*. Bloomington: Indiana University Press, 1981.

Stepan, Alfred. "State Power and the Strength of Civil Society in the Southern Cone of Latin America." In Evans et al., *Bringing the State Back In*, pp. 317–43. New York: Cambridge University Press, 1985.

Swidler, Ann. "Culture in Action: Symbols and Strategies." *American Sociological Review* 51 (April 1986): 273–86.

Sylvan, David, Duncan Snidal, Bruce M. Russett, Steven Jackson, and Raymond Duvall, "The Peripheral Economies: Penetration and Economic Distortion, 1970–1975." In William R. Thompson, ed., *Approaches to World System Analysis*. pp. 79–111. Beverly Hills, Calif.: Sage, 1983.

Tabari, Ehsan. *Foroupashi-ye Nizam-i Sunnati va Zayeshi Sarmayedari* [The decline of traditional order and the emergence of capitalism in Iran]. N.p.: Tudeh, 1976.

—— *Jame'eh-i Iran dar Douran-i Reza Shah* [Iranian society under Reza Shah]. Tehran: Tudeh, 1977.

Tabari, Azar, and Nahid Yeganeh. *In the Shadow of Islam: The Women's Movement in Iran*. London: Zed Press, 1982.

Tabataba-ei, Mohammad Rafi'a. *Hoquq-i Doval va Milal* [The rights of states and nations]. Tabriz: 1312/1934.

Taqavi, Jiman. "The Iran-Iraq War: The First Three Years." In Barry M. Rosen, ed., *Iran Since the Revolution: Internal Dynamic, Regional Conflict, and the Superpowers*, pp. 63–82. New York: Columbia University Press, 1985.

Taylor, Charles, and David A. Jodice. *World Handbook of Political and Social Indicators*. 3d ed. New Haven: Yale University Press, 1983.

Thaiss, Gustav. "The Bazaar as a Case Study of Religion and Social Change." In Ehsan Yarshater, ed., *Iran Faces the Seventies*, pp. 189–216. New York: Praeger, 1971.

—— "Religious Symbolism and Social Change: The Drama of Husain." In Nikki R. Keddie, ed., *Scholars, Saints, and Sufis*, pp. 349–66. Berkeley and Los Angeles: University of California Press, 1972.

Therborn, Goran. *The Ideology of Power and the Power of Ideology*. London: Verso, 1980.

—— *Science, Class and Society*. London: Verso, 1980.

—— *What Does the Ruling Class Do When It Rules?* London: New Left Books, 1978.

Thompson, Edward P. *The Making of the English Working Class*. London: Victor Gollancz, 1964.

Thompson, James Westfall. *An Economic and Social History of the Middle Ages*. Vol.1. New York: Ungar, 1959.

Thompson, William R. *Approaches to World System Analysis*. Beverly Hills, Calif.: Sage, 1983.

Tilly, Charles. *Big Structures, Large Processes, Huge Comparisons*. New York: Russell Sage Foundation, 1984.

—— *From Mobilization to Revolution*. Reading, Mass.: Addison-Wesley, 1978.

—— "Revolution and Collective Violence." In Fred I. Greenstein and Nelson W. Polsby, eds., *Handbook of Political Science*, pp. 483–556. Reading, Mass.: Addison-Wesley, 1975.

—— "War Making and State Making as Organized Crime." In Peter B. Evans, Dietrich Rueschemeyer, and Theda Skocpol, eds., *Bringing the State Back In*, pp. 169–91. New York: Cambridge University Press, 1985.

Toch, Hans. *The Social Psychology of Social Movements*. New York: Bobbs-Merrill, 1965.

Todd, Alexander Dundas, and Sue Fisher, eds. *Gender and Discourse: The Power of Talk*. Norwood, N.J.: Ablex Publishing, 1989.

Torrey, Charles C. *The Commercial-Theological Terms in the Koran*. Leyden, Netherlands: E. J. Brill, 1892.

Torrey, Gordon H. *Syrian Politics and the Military 1945–1958*. Columbus: Ohio State University Press, 1964.

Turner, Bryan S. *Weber and Islam*. Boston: Routledge and Kegan Paul, 1974.

Turner, Victor. *The Forest of Symbols: Aspects of Ndembu Ritual*. Ithaca: Cornell University Press, 1967.

Ulyanovsky, Rostilove. "The Iranian Revolution and Its Outcomes." *Kommunist* 10 (July 1982). (Theoretical and political journal of the Central Committee of the Communist Party of the Soviet Union, published in Russian).

—— *National Liberation*. Moscow: Progress Publishers, 1978.

UN Conference on Trade and Development. *Examination of Recent Developments and Long-term Trends in World Trade and Development in Accordance with the Aims and Functions of UNCTAD*. TD/138, March 21, 1972.

—— *Handbook of International Trade and Development Statistics*. Geneva: UNCTAD, 1980 (Supplement).

UN Department of Economic Affairs. *Development in the Middle East*. New York: 1958–59.

U.S. Congress. *Hearings Before the Antitrust Subcommittee on the Judiciary on Current Antitrust Problems*. 84th Cong., 1st sess., ser. 3, May 1955.

U.S. Department of Commerce. *Iran: A Survey of Business Opportunities*. Washington, D.C.: GPO, October 1977.

U.S. Government. "The International Petroleum Cartel," *Staff Report*. Washington, D.C.: GPO, 1952.

Van Dam, Nikolaos. *The Struggle for Power in Syria: Sectarianism, Regionalism and Tribalism in Politics, 1961–1978*. New York: St. Martin's, 1979.

Vatikiotis, Panayiotis J. *The History of Egypt*. 2d ed. Baltimore, Md.: Johns Hopkins University Press, 1980.

Walden, Jerrold L. "The International Petroleum Cartel in Iran—Private Power and the Public Interest." *Journal of Public Law* 11, no. 1 (Spring 1962): 64–121.

Wallerstein, Immanuel. *The Capitalist World Economy*. Cambridge: Cambridge University Press, 1979.

—— *The Modern World-System: Capitalist Agriculture and the Origin of the Eu-*

ropean World Economy in the Sixteenth Century. New York: Academic Press, 1974.

—— "The World-Economy and the State Structures in Peripheral and Dependent Countries (the so-called Third World)." Paper prepared for UNITAR International Conference on Alternative Development Strategies and the Future of Asia, New Delhi, March 11–17, 1980.

Walton, Thomas. "Economic Development and Revolutionary Upheavals in Iran." *Cambridge Journal of Economics* 4 (1980): 271–92.

Walz, Terence. "Asyut in the 1260's (1844–53)." *Journal of the American Research Center in Egypt* 15 (1978): 113–26.

—— *Trade Between Egypt and Bilad al-Sudan: 1700–1820.* Institut Français d'Archeologie Orientale du Caire, 1978.

Watt, Montgomery. "Shi'ism Under the Umayyads" (parts 3 and 4). *Journal of the Royal Asiatic Society* (1960): 158–72.

Weber, Max. *Economy and Society.* Edited by Guenther Roth and Clau Withich. Berkeley and Los Angeles: University of California Press, 1978.

Williams, Raymond. *Marxism and Literature.* Oxford: Oxford University Press, 1977.

Wilson, Rodney. "Industry Feels the Squeeze from High-wage Labour." *Middle East Economic Digest* (June 30, 1978): 3–4.

—— "Technology Transfer Threatens Traditional Industries." *Middle East Economic Digest* (November 1987): 3–4.

Winder, R. Bayly. "Syrian Deputies and Cabinet Ministers, 1919–1959" (part 2). *Middle East Journal* 17, nos. 1–2 (Winter–Spring 1963): 35–54.

Woddis, Jack. *New Theories of Revolution.* New York: International Publishers, 1972.

Wolf, Eric R. *Peasant Wars of the Twentieth Century.* New York: Harper and Row, 1969.

Wright, Erik O. *Class, Crisis, and the State.* London: Verso, 1979.

—— *Classes.* London: Verso, 1985.

Wulf, Hans E. *The Traditional Crafts of Persia: Their Development, Technology, and Influence on Eastern and Western Civilizations.* Cambridge: MIT Press, 1956.

Wuthnow, Robert. *Communities of Discourse: Ideology and Social Structure in the Reformation, the Enlightenment, and European Socialism.* Cambridge: Harvard University Press, 1989.

—— "Rethinking Weber's View of Ideology." *Theory and Society* 16 (1987): 123–37.

—— "State Structures and Ideological Outcomes." *American Sociological Review* 50 (December 1985): 799–821.

Zabih, Sepehr. *Iran's Revolutionary Upheaval: An Interpretive Essay.* San Francisco: Alchemy Books, 1979.

Zaret, David. *The Heavenly Contract: Ideology and Organization in Pre-Revolutionary Puritanism.* Chicago: University of Chicago Press, 1985.

——— "Religion and the Rise of Liberal-Democratic Ideology in Seventeenth-Century England." *American Sociological Review* 54 (April 1989): 163–79.

Zonis, Marvin. *The Political Elite of Iran*. Princeton: Princeton University Press, 1971.

Index